WEBSTER'S
FAMILY
ENCYCLOPEDIA

WEBSTER'S FAMILY ENCYCLOPEDIA

VOLUME 2

1995 Edition

Exclusively distributed by
Archer Worldwide, Inc.
Great Neck, New York, USA

Abbreviations Used in Webster's Family Encyclopedia

AD	After Christ	ht	height	N.M.	New Mexico
Adm.	Admiral	i.e.	that is	NNE	north-northeast
Ala.	Alabama	in	inches	NNW	north-northwest
Apr	April	Ind.	Indiana	Nov	November
AR	Autonomous Republic	Ill.	Illinois	NW	northwest
		Jan	January	N.Y.	New York
at no	atomic number	K	Kelvin	OAS	Organization of American States
at wt	atomic weight	Kans.	Kansas		
Aug	August	kg	kilograms	Oct	October
b.	born	km	kilometers	Okla.	Oklahoma
BC	Before Christ	kph	kilometers per hour	OPEC	Organization of Petroleum Exporting Countries
bp	boiling point				
C	Celsius, Centigrade	kW	kilowatts		
		lb	pounds	Pa.	Pennsylvania
c.	circa	Lt.	Lieutenant	PLO	Palestine Liberation Organization
Calif.	California	Lt. Gen.	Lieutenant General		
Capt.	Captain			Pres.	President
CIS	Commonwealth of Independent States	m	meters	R.I.	Rhode Island
		M. Sgt.	Master Sergeant	S	south, southern
		Mar	March	S.C.	South Carolina
cm	centimeters	Mass.	Massachusetts	SE	southeast
Co.	Company	Md.	Maryland	Sen.	Senator
Col.	Colonel	mi	miles	Sept	September
Conn.	Connecticut	Mich.	Michigan	Sgt.	Sergeant
d.	died	Minn.	Minnesota	sq mi	square miles
Dec	December	Miss.	Mississippi	SSE	south-southeast
Del.	Delaware	mm	millimeters	SSW	south-southwest
E	east, eastern	Mo.	Missouri	SW	southwest
EC	European Community	MP	Member of Parliament	Tenn.	Tennessee
				Tex.	Texas
e.g.	for example	mp	melting point	UN	United Nations
est	estimated	mph	miles per hour	US	United States
F	Fahrenheit	N	north, northern	USSR	Union of Soviet Socialist Republics
Feb	February	NATO	North Atlantic Treaty Organization		
Fl. Lt.	Flight Lieutenant			Va.	Virginia
Fla.	Florida	NE	northeast	Vt.	Vermont
ft	feet	Neb.	Nebraska	W	west, western
Ga.	Georgia	N.H.	New Hampshire	wt	weight
Gen.	General	N.J.	New Jersey		
Gov.	Governor				

Beijing (also: Peking) 39 55N 116 25E The capital of the People's Republic of China, an administratively autonomous city situated in the NE of the country in Hobei province. The city has expanded considerably since 1949, and there has been rapid development of industries, including iron and steel, machinery, and textiles. A symmetrically laid-out city, its architecture preserves many reminders of its past. It consists basically of two walled cities, the N inner city and the S outer city; the old Imperial City lies within the inner city and at its center the moated "Forbidden City" contains the Imperial Palaces (now museums). There are three universities, the oldest being Peking University (1898). *History*: the site has a long history of human habitation. As Ta-tu, it first became the capital (of N China) under the Yuan dynasty in 1272. Later, when the capital was moved to Nanjing, it became known as Pei-p'ing (*or* Beibing), a name still used by the Republic of China. As Peking (1420), it once more became the capital under the third Ming emperor. In 1928 the Nationalist (Guomindang) government moved the capital to Nanjing and from 1937 until 1945 Peking was occupied by the Japanese. It became the capital of the People's Republic of China in 1949. Pro-democracy demonstrations in the city in 1989 were violently suppressed by military forces. Population (1989 est): 6,800,000.

BEIJING *Commuters stopping on their way to work in order to read the latest wall posters. Worldwide attention was attracted in 1979 by the appearance on "Democracy Wall" of posters critical of the Chinese regime.*

Beira 19 49S 34 52E A port in E Mozambique, on the Mozambique Channel. Founded in 1891 by the Portuguese, it became a major port serving central S Africa. It was the main export outlet of Rhodesia (now Zimbabwe) until Mozambique's independence (1975). Exports include ores, cotton, and food products. Population (1985 est): 270,000.

Beirut 33 52N 35 30E The capital of the Lebanon, situated on the E Mediterranean Sea. After centuries of Turkish domination, it was held by the French from World War I until 1941, when it became the capital of the newly independent Lebanon. Much was badly damaged in the civil war (1975–76), in 1982 when Israeli forces besieged the city and forced the Palestine Liberation Organization to leave, and in subsequent fighting. It has four universities. Population (1985 est): 1,910,000.

Béjart, Maurice (Maurice-Jean de Berger; 1928–   ) French ballet dancer and choreographer. His works are characterized by such diverse influences as jazz and Indian mysticism. In 1954 he founded his own company, which was renamed Le Ballet du XXme Siècle when it became based in Brussels in 1960.

bel. *See* decibel.

Belarus, Republic of (Belorussia *or* White Russia) Independent nation in E Europe, formerly the Belorussian SSR, a constituent republic in the W central Soviet Union. The majority of its inhabitants are Belorussians, an Eastern *Slav people. Belarus has an important engineering industry and the largest petrochemical complex in Europe. Cereals are the basis of agriculture, and dairy farming and pig breeding are expanding. Formed in 1919 as Belorussia, it was badly devastated in World War II. Although it was a part of the USSR, it had a separate seat in the UN from 1945. When Communism collapsed in the USSR in 1991, Belorussia declared independence as Belarus. It joined the Commonwealth of Independent States (CIS) in 1991 and the UN as an independent nation in 1992. Area: 80,134 sq mi (207,600 sq km). Population (1987 est): 10,080,000. Capital: Minsk.

Belasco, David (1853–1931) US theater manager and dramatist. Most of his plays were adaptations and collaborations. He is best remembered for his spectacular productions involving experimental scenic and lighting effects, and for his promotion of young actors.

Belau (formerly Palau) A group of islands in the W Pacific Ocean, within the UN Trust Territory of the *Pacific Islands. Self-government was achieved in 1981, and the islands became the Republic of Belau. Area: 184 sq mi (476 sq km). Population (1988 est): 14,000.

bel canto (Italian: fine singing) A delicate and lyrical style of singing that was developed in Italian opera during the 17th and 18th centuries. Notable singers included Farinelli (1705–82) and Jenny *Lind. During the 19th century, the enlargement of orchestras resulted in the development of a more declamatory style of singing.

Belém 1 27S 48 29W A port in N Brazil, the capital of Pará State on the Rio do Pará. It exports products from the Amazon basin including nuts, jute, and rubber. Its university was founded in 1957. Population (1980 est): 758,117.

belemnite The fossilized shell of an extinct *cuttlefish, sometimes called a thunderbolt. Cylindrical and pointed at one end, they are most commonly found in deposits of the Jurassic and Cretaceous periods (150–65 million years ago).

Belfast 54 40N 5 50W The capital of Northern Ireland, a seaport situated where the Lagan River enters Belfast Low on the border between Co Antrim and Co Down. It is the province's commercial and administrative center and its industries include shipbuilding, electronics, and engineering. The principal buildings, including the City Hall (1906) and Parliament Buildings (1932) at Stormont, were built in the late 19th and early 20th centuries. Queen's University received a royal charter in 1909. *History*: large-scale growth of Belfast came with the expansion of the linen-making and ship-building industries in the 19th century; it became a city in 1888. The Parliament of Northern Ireland sat in the city from 1921 to 1972. Its recent history has been marked by the conflict between Protestant and Roman Catholic communities; each has become increasingly concentrated in ghettoes. This has led to an exacerbation of the housing problem, which is now one of the worst in Europe. The British army has maintained a presence on the streets of Belfast since August, 1969. Population (1985): 300,000.

Belfort 44 17N 1 32E A city in E France, the capital of the Territoire de Belfort. Strategically situated between the Vosges and Jura mountains, it has been besieged many times. Industries include wine. Population (1980): 52,000.

Belgae The Germanic tribes occupying NE *Gaul in ancient Roman times. Julius Caesar named them and considered them the most warlike of the Gauls.

He defeated them in 57 BC but they continued their opposition to the Romans from SE Britain, to which area they had been migrating from about 100 BC.

Belgaum 15 54N 74 36E A city in India, in Karnataka. Manufactures include cotton, furniture, and leather. Population (1981 est): 300,000.

Belgian Congo. *See* Zaïre, Republic of.

Belgium, Kingdom of (French name: Belgique, Flemish name: België) A country in NW Europe, on the North Sea. It is generally low lying except for the Ardennes in the SE. The main rivers are the Scheldt and the Meuse and these and others are linked by canals to form an extensive network of inland waterways. The population is divided between the French and the Flemish, with small minorities of Germans and others. *Economy*: highly industrialized, with coal and iron resources supporting considerable heavy industry. Food processing and textiles are also important. Agriculture is highly intensive, the main cash crop being sugar beet. Belgium is an important center for trade and has been since the middle ages. It still has one of the highest proportions of export revenue to total income in the world. In 1921 a customs union was formed with Luxembourg and in 1948 both joined with the Netherlands to form the *Benelux Economic Union. Belgium is also a member of the EEC and almost two-thirds of its trade is with other members. Main exports include iron and steel, chemicals, machinery, and motor vehicles. *History*: the name Belgium comes from the *Belgae, a Celtic tribe named by Caesar, and the area was part of the Roman Empire until about the end of the 2nd century AD, when it was invaded by Germanic tribes. In medieval times it was divided into several counties, duchies, and the bishopric of Liège, during which time the cities of Ghent, Bruges, and Ypres rose to virtual independence and economic prosperity through the wool industry. Particularly in view of its strategic position, Belgium had considerable importance in the balance of power in Europe over the centuries and from the Middle Ages onward—it was ruled by several European nations in turn, including Austria, Spain, and France. After being occupied by France during the Napoleonic Wars, it was joined to the Netherlands in 1815. Following an uprising, it became independent in 1830, and the National Congress elected Prince Leopold of Saxe-Coburg as King of the Belgians (*see* Leopold I) in 1831. The country was eventually recognized by all of Europe in 1839. In spite of efforts to remain neutral it was attacked and occupied by Germany in both World Wars. When the Germans invaded in 1940, King *Leopold III surrendered immediately but the government struggled on in exile in London. In 1950, after a political crisis, the king was persuaded to abdicate in favor of his son, *Baudouin. The main political problem since World War II has been tension between the French-speaking Walloons in the S and the Flemish-speaking community in the N. Efforts are being made to create a federal structure of government under which the Flemish, French-speaking, and bilingual Brussels regions would obtain a large measure of regional autonomy. The loss in 1960 of the Belgian Congo, now Zaïre, had an adverse effect on Belgium's economy. Dr. Wilfried Martens, who led a series of coalition governments from 1979, resigned in March, 1981, and was succeeded by Mark Eyskens. Dr. Martens was reappointed as prime minister of a fresh coalition government in December, 1981, and remained in that post until 1992, when he was defeated by Flemish Christian Democrat, Jean-Luc Dehaene. Dehaene included both French-speaking and Flemish-speaking factions in his coalition government. Baudouin died in 1993 and was succeeded by his brother Albert. Official languages: French, Flemish, Dutch, and German. Official currency: Belgian franc of 100 centimes. Area: 11,778 sq mi (30,513 sq km). Population (1990): 9,895,000. Capital: Brussels. Main port: Antwerp.

Belgorod-Dnestrovski (Romanian name: Cetatea Alba) 46 10N 30 19E A port in the SW Ukraine on the Dnestr estuary. A commercial center, it has fishing, fish-processing, and winemaking industries. *History*: founded by Greek colonists in the 6th century BC, it subsequently passed to the Romans and then the Byzantines. Turkish from 1484, it was acquired by Russia in the 19th century. It was under Romanian rule from 1918 to 1940. Population (1981 est): 255,000.

Belgrade (Serbo-Croat name: Beograd) 44 50N 20 30E The capital of Yugoslavia and of Serbia, situated in the NE at the confluence of the Danube and Sava Rivers. A settlement and route center from very early times, it became the Serbian capital in the early 15th century. It later suffered Turkish and Austrian occupations but again became capital of Serbia in the late 19th century and of Yugoslavia after World War I. It was occupied by the Germans in World War II and has expanded considerably in the years since then. The University of Belgrade was founded in 1863 and the Arts University in 1973. Population (1981): 1,470,000.

Belinsky, Vissarion (1811–48) Russian literary critic, an influential advocate of social realism and naturalism. He championed *Pushkin, *Lermontov, and *Gogol, whom he later denounced as a betrayer of naturalism.

Belisarius (c. 505–65 AD) Byzantine general of *Justinian I's reign. After successfully checking Persian invasions on the empire's eastern frontier and overthrowing the African Vandal kingdom (534), Belisarius began his conquest of the Ostrogoths of Italy, and captured Rome, Naples, and Ravenna (540) before being recalled to Constantinople. In 546 he returned to Italy to quell the resurgent Ostrogoths but was again recalled, his command being given to *Narses.

Belitung (*or* Billiton) An Indonesian island in the Java Sea. Its tin mines, now government owned, have attracted a large Chinese community. Area: 1866 sq mi (4833 sq km). Chief town: Tanjungpandan.

Belize (name until 1973: British Honduras) A country in Central America, on the Caribbean Sea between Mexico and Guatemala. The country is generally low lying, rising to the Maya Mountains in the SW. It is subject to hurricanes, one of which severely damaged the former capital, Belize City, in 1961. The population is of African, Spanish-American, and Mayan Indian descent, with small minorities of E Indians, Syrians, and Chinese. *Economy*: mainly agricultural; although almost half the country is forested, the combined value of sugar and citrus exports have exceeded that of timber since the early 1960s. *History*: archeological evidence suggests that the area was once an important Mayan settlement. The coast was discovered by Columbus in 1502 but the first European occupation was an independent settlement of British woodcutters, which held out against the Spanish throughout the 17th century. From the late 18th century more control was exercised by the British government and in 1862 it became a colony under Jamaica. It became an independent colony in 1884 and attained internal self-government in 1964. Claims, based on early Spanish treaties, were made to it by Guatemala but despite disputes Belize achieved full independence in 1981, becoming the last Commonwealth country on the American mainland to obtain self-government. An ongoing border dispute with Guatemala had delayed Belize's complete independence, and it was not resolved until 1991. Despite its small size geographically and its lack of political strength, Belize has been able to maintain a relatively steady economic and social equilibrium in comparison with its Latin American neighbors. Belize joined the Organization of American States (OAS) in 1991. Prime minister: George C. Price. Official language: English; Spanish is also widely spoken. Official currency: Belize dollar of 100 cents. Area: 8867 sq mi (22,963 sq km). Population (1990 est): 180,400. Capital: Belmopan.

Belize City 17 29N 88 10W The chief port of Belize, on the Caribbean coast. It was formerly capital of Belize but following a severe hurricane (1961), Belmopan, which became capital in 1970, was constructed inland. The main exports are timber, coconuts, and corn. Population (1988 est): 49,000.

Bell, Alexander Graham (1847–1922) Scottish-born US scientist and inventor. He went to Canada in 1870 and to the US in 1873, where he became professor of vocal physiology at Boston University. Bell's work in telegraphy and telephony led to the invention of the telephone, which he patented in 1876. He demonstrated at American exhibitions and had formed the Bell Telephone Co. by 1877. He also performed basic work in sound recording, electro-optical communication, and aerodynamics.

ALEXANDER GRAHAM BELL *Inaugurating the New York–Chicago telephone line in 1892.*

belladonna. *See* deadly nightshade.

belladonna lily. *See* Amaryllis.

Bellarmine, St Robert (1542–1621) Italian Jesuit theologian, cardinal (from 1549), and archbishop of Capua (1602–05): canonized in 1930. An influential counter-Reformation theologian, he held Galileo in high esteem and privately advised him to regard the Copernican system as hypothetical, although he formally pronounced the system "false and erroneous." His writings include *Disputationes de controversiis Christianae fidei* (1586–93), a statement of Catholic doctrine, and he played an important part in the revised edition of the Vulgate published in 1592. Stoneware wine jugs with a bearded face made in the Rhineland between about 1550 and 1700 became known as Bellarmines, on the grounds that they were Protestant caricatures of the cardinal.

Bellay, Joachim de (1522–60) French poet. In 1549 he published *Défense et illustration de la langue française*, the manifesto of the *Pléiade, and *Olive*, the first book of love sonnets in French. While accompanying his cousin Cardinal Jean du Bellay on a mission to Rome, he wrote *Antiquités de Rome* (1558) and *Regrets* (1558).

Belle Fourche River A river rising in NE Wyoming and flowing E to South Dakota where it joins the Cheyenne River. The Belle Fourche Reservoir is formed by a dam just over the South Dakota border and is connected to the river by a canal. Length: 350 mi (564 km).

Belle-Isle, Charles Fouquet de, Duc de (1684–1761) French marshal, who rose to prominence during the Wars of the Spanish (1701–14) and Polish (1733) Successions. His influence at court led to France's opposition to Maria Theresa in the War of Austrian Succession (1740–48). As minister of war (1758–60), he implemented a series of army reforms.

Bellerophon In Greek mythology, the grandson of Sisyphus and son of Glaucus, King of Corinth. Sent by Iobates, King of Lycia, to kill the *Chimera, he was able to carry out his task by flying above the dragon on Pegasus, a winged horse he had previously captured and tamed with the aid of Athena.

Bellingshausen, Fabian Gottlieb, Baron von (1778–1852) Russian explorer. In 1819 he led an expedition to the Antarctic, surveying the South Georgia and South Sandwich Islands and discovering the islands Peter I and Alexander I. The Bellingshausen Sea was named for him.

Bellingshausen Sea A section of the S Pacific Ocean bordering on Antarctica, extending between the Antarctic Peninsula and Ellsworth Land. It always contains pack ice.

Bellini, Jacopo (c. 1400–c. 1470) Venetian painter, who was a pupil of *Gentile da Fabriano. In the early 1420s he probably visited Florence, where he became familiar with the artistic developments of the Renaissance. Although his few surviving paintings retain the decorative conventions of Byzantine and Gothic art, his two sketchbooks (British Museum and Louvre) reveal a remarkable understanding of perspective. They influenced his son-in-law Andrea *Mantegna and his two sons, who both trained under him. The eldest, **Gentile Bellini** (c. 1429–1507), is best known for his portraits and procession scenes. *The Procession in St Mark's Square* (Accademia, Venice) depicts his native city with a realism that anticipates Canaletto. In 1479 he accompanied the Doge to Constantinople, where he painted Sultan Mehmed II (National Gallery, London). Gentile's brother **Giovanni Bellini** (c. 1430–1516) was an important influence on Venetian art, especially through his pupils *Titian and *Giorgione. His early work is indebted to Mantegna. From about 1475 his use of the Flemish technique of oil painting, introduced to him by *Antonello da Messina, led to his richer use of color and softer treatment of form. His paintings included several altarpieces, such as *Madonna and Saints* (S Zaccaria, Venice) in which he gave great importance to the landscape, and portraits, such as *Doge Loredano* (National Gallery, London).

Bellini, Vincenzo (1801–35) Italian opera composer. Of his 11 operas, *La somnambula* and *Norma* (both 1831) and *I Puritani* (1835) remain popular, although they require singers of outstanding ability to meet the demands of the *coloratura style.

Bello, Andrés (1781–1865) Venezuelan scholar and poet. He accompanied Simón Bolívar on a revolutionary mission to London in 1810 and stayed there until 1829. The pastoral poems of *Silvas americanas* (1826–27) are influenced by Virgil. He founded the University of Chile (1843), drafted the country's legal code, and wrote books on many subjects, including a definitive Spanish grammar (1847).

Belloc, (Joseph-Pierre) Hilaire (1870–1953) British poet and essayist. Born in France, he was educated at Oxford and served as a Liberal in Parliament from 1906 to 1910. His works include essays, historical biographies, and satirical novels, often illustrated by his friend G. K. *Chesterton. A devout Roman Catholic, he vigorously opposed the socialism of G. B. *Shaw and H. G. *Wells. His most popular works are light verse, such as *Cautionary Tales* (1907).

Bellow, Saul (1915–   ) Canadian-born US novelist, the son of poor Russian Jewish immigrants. His first novel, *Dangling Man* (1944), influenced by *existentialism, was followed by *The Adventures of Augie March* (1953) and *Henderson the Rain King* (1959). His later novels, such as *Mr Sammler's Planet* (1970), *Humboldt's Gift* (1975), *The Dean's December* (1982), *Him With His Foot in His Mouth* (1984), and *More Die of Heartbreak* (1987), are more ironic and reflective studies of harassed Jewish intellectuals in a bewildering urban chaos. He won the Nobel Prize in 1976.

Bellows, George (Wesley) (1882–1925) US painter. One of the eight members of the *Ashcan School, he painted realistic scenes, primarily of New York City and environs. His well-known works include *Stag at Sharkey's* (1907), *Up the Hudson* (1908), *Men of the Docks* (1912), *The Cliff Dwellers* (1913), and *Dempsey Through the Ropes* (1924).

Belmonte y García, Juan (1892–1962) Spanish matador, who was active from 1913 until 1934 and was regarded as one of the greatest of all time. His technique of working very close to bulls, using his cape to induce them to move around him, revolutionized bullfighting.

Belmopan 17 12N 88 00W The capital of Belize, on the Belize River about 50 mi (80 km) inland from Belize City, which it succeeded as capital in 1970 after the latter was damaged by a hurricane in 1961. Population (1985 est): 3500.

Belo Horizonte 19 54S 43 54W A city in SE Brazil, in Minas Gerais state. Founded in 1897, it was Brazil's first planned city. Distinctive architecture includes Oscar Niemayer's Chapel of São Francisco. The chief industries include cotton textiles, meat processing, and iron and steel. It is the site of two universities. Population (1985 est): 3,050,000.

Belorussian Soviet Socialist Republic (Belorussia *or* White Russia). *See* Belarus.

Belshazzar In the Old Testament, the son of *Nebuchadnezzar and the last King of Babylon. At a feast given by him, the prophet Daniel interpreted the supernatural handwriting that appeared on the wall—*Mene, Mene, Tekel, Upharsin*—as foretelling the destruction of Babylon and Belshazzar's downfall (Daniel 5.25).

beluga 1. A giant *sturgeon, *Huso huso*, up to 28 ft (8.4 m) long, that occurs in the Caspian and Black Seas and the Volga River of E Europe. It is a highly prolific egg producer and the source of the best caviar. 2. *See* white whale.

Belyi, Andrei (Boris Nikolaevich Bugaev; 1880–1934) Russian symbolist poet and critic. He studied mathematics and philosophy at Moscow University, but his interest in mysticism led him into symbolism. In 1901 he published *Simfoniya*, an attempted synthesis of all the arts around a prose poem, and several volumes of poetry and criticism. Disillusioned with the aftermath of the Revolution, he lived abroad from 1921 to 1923.

Bemba A Central *Bantu people of NE Zambia and neighboring areas of Zaïre and Rhodesia whose language has become widely spoken in Zambia. They were traditionally ruled by members of the matrilineal royal clan from which the supreme chief, or Chitimukulu, came.

Bembo, Pietro (1470–1547) Italian scholar. He was secretary to Pope Leo X from 1513 to 1521 and was made cardinal in 1539. His most important work, *Prose della volgar lingua* (1525), set out to develop Italian into a literary language equal to Latin. *Rime* (1530) is a collection of his Italian poetry.

Benares. *See* Varanasi.

Ben Bella, Ahmed (1919–   ) Algerian statesman; president (1963–65). A leading figure in the struggle for the independence of Algeria, after service in the French army during World War II he helped to form the *Front de Libération Nationale (FLN) in 1954. Imprisoned by the French for six years, he was released at independence in 1962 and elected prime minister (1962–63) and then president. He was overthrown in 1965 by *Boumédienne, imprisoned until 1980, went into exile, and returned to Algeria in 1990.

Benchley, Robert Charles (1889–1945) US humorist. He edited *Vanity Fair* and worked as drama critic for *Life* and the *New Yorker*. He published 15 volumes of his collected humorous essays, including *My Ten Years in a Quandary* (1936). Other works include *Of All Things* (1921), *The Treasurer's Report* (1930), *Inside Benchley* (1941), and *Benchley Beside Himself* (1943). He acted in several films and himself made 46 short comic films. His grandson **Peter Benchley** (1940–   ) is also a popular novelist. He is the author of *Jaws* (1974), *The Deep* (1976), *The Island* (1979), and *The Girl of the Sea of Cortez* (1982).

Benda, Julien (1867–1956) French novelist and philosopher. An advocate of the classical ideals of reason and order, he wrote several books attacking the philosophy of *Bergson. His most famous work, *La Trahison des clercs* (1927), demanded that the intellectual's commitment to truth should not be compromised by political or emotional involvements.

Bendigo 36 48S 144 21E A city in Australia, in central Victoria. It grew rapidly following a gold discovery in 1851 and is now a commercial center with the third largest livestock market in Australia. Population (1991): 53,944.

bends. *See* decompression sickness.

Benedict XV (Giacomo della Chiesa; 1854–1922) Pope (1914–22). A papal diplomat, he was elected shortly after the outbreak of World War I, in which he maintained a strict neutrality while attempting to negotiate peace and to curb atrocities. Thereafter he reformed papal administration and diplomacy and was a notable supporter of missionary activity.

Benedictines The monks and nuns belonging to the Roman Catholic Order of St Benedict (OSB), a union of independent abbeys all of which follow the Rule of St *Benedict of Nursia. They have always acted as scholars and educators and were responsible for preserving the learning of antiquity after the fall of the Roman Empire. They have also exercised a great influence in maintaining high standards for the sacred art and music used in the liturgy. The liqueur Bénédictine is named for the order and is made at Fécamp, France.

Benedict of Nursia, St (c. 480–c. 550) Italian saint, the father of western monasticism. Educated in Rome, he withdrew from society about 500 and lived for a time as a hermit near Rome. He eventually established 12 monasteries with 12 monks each. About 525 he and a few monks established themselves at Monte Cassino, where he drew up his monastic rule, which provided for government by an elected abbot, residence in one place, obedience, observance of prayers at fixed hours (the Divine Office), common ownership of property, and a life of work, prayer, and study. The Rule was originally intended for laymen, and Benedict himself was apparently not ordained. He was buried at Monte Cassino. Feast day: Mar 21. Emblems: a broken cup and a raven.

benefit of clergy The development in England of the 12th-century canon law that criminous clerks (criminal clerics) should not be tried by both ecclesiastical and secular courts. Henry II's acceptance of this principle gave all clerics the right to be tried solely in ecclesiastical courts. These could not inflict capital punishment, from which clergy were thus immune. Much abused in the later Middle Ages, the privilege was increasingly limited during and after the Reformation although it was not finally abolished until the early 19th century.

Bene Israel (Hebrew: Children of Israel) Indian Jewish community of uncertain origin, now concentrated mainly in Bombay.

Benelux The customs union formed by *Bel*gium, the *Net*herlands, and *Lux*emborg in 1948. It was the first free-trade market in Europe. The three countries standardized prices, welfare benefits, wages, and taxes and allowed free immigration and movement of labor and capital between them. All three countries are now members of the *EEC, which has similar aims.

Beneš, Edvard (1884–1948) Czechoslovak statesman. In 1918 Beneš helped Tomáš *Masaryk to found Czechoslovakia and became foreign minister, playing an important role in the League of Nations. In 1935 he became president but went into exile when he was forced to cede the *Sudetenland to Germany (1938). He spent World War II as president of a provisional government in London, returning to Czechoslovakia in 1945. He resigned the presidency in 1948, when Czechoslovakia became a communist state.

Benét, Stephen Vincent (1898–1943) US poet and novelist. Son of an army officer, he wrote chiefly on themes of American history and myth. His best-known works are the epic poems *John Brown's Body* (1928), about the Civil War, which won a Pulitzer Prize (1929), and *Western Star*, which was awarded the same prize in 1944. He also wrote the short story *The Devil and Daniel Webster* (1937).

Benevento 41 08N 14 46E A town in S Italy, in Campania. It has Roman remains and a 9th-century cathedral. Its manufactures include leather goods, agricultural machinery, confectionery, and Strega liqueur. Population: 59,016.

Bengal A region of the Indian subcontinent, in the NE on the Bay of Bengal around the vast Ganges and Brahmaputra deltas. Divided between India and Bangladesh, it has a flourishing culture. *History*: on the fringe of early Indian civilization, Bengal became the center of Buddhist (8th–12th centuries), Hindu (11th–13th centuries), and finally Islamic dynasties. The base for British expansion through India, it was partitioned between India and Pakistan at independence (1947). *See also* West Bengal.

Bengal, Bay of The shallow NE limb of the Indian Ocean, between the Indian subcontinent on the W and Burma and the Andaman and Nicobar Islands on the E. Shipping and coastal life are dominated by the NE winter monsoon and the SW summer monsoon.

Bengali An Indo-Aryan language spoken by 80 million people in Bangladesh and West Bengal (India). The literary form of the language uses many *Sanskrit words. It was the first Indian language to imitate western literary modes in fiction, drama, and poetry. There is a distinct colloquial form.

Benghazi (*or* Banghazi; Italian name: Bengasi) 32 07N 20 05E The second largest city in Libya, on the Gulf of Sidra. Severely damaged during World War II, it has experienced recent growth with the development of local oilfields; other industries include light engineering. Population (1988 est): 446,000.

Benguela (*or* Benguella) 12 34S 13 24E A town in W Angola, on the Atlantic Ocean. It is overshadowed as a port by Lobito; industries include fish drying and soap production. Population (1983 est): 155,000.

Ben-Gurion, David (1886–1973) Israeli statesman, known as the Father of the Nation. He was Israel's first prime minister (1948–53, 1955–63). Born David Gruen in Poland, he adopted the Hebrew name Ben-Gurion after arriving in Palestine in 1906. In 1917 he joined the British Army's Jewish Legion to free Palestine from Ottoman control (achieved in 1918) and after the establishment of British rule worked to establish a Jewish home in Palestine, promised in the *Balfour Declaration. In 1920 he founded the General Federation of Labor (the Histadrut) and in 1930, the Israeli Workers' Party (Mapai). Becoming chairman of the Zionist Executive in 1935, he led the Zionist effort to establish a Jewish state, finally achieved in 1948. As prime minister he formed an Israeli army from the various guerrilla groups and adopted a tough line against Arab attack. After resigning the prime ministership in 1963, he was leader of the opposition party, the Rafi, until his retirement in 1970.

Beni, Río A river in Bolivia. Rising near La Paz, it flows generally NE to join the Río Mamoré. Length: over 1000 mi (1600 km).

Benin, People's Republic of (name until 1975: Dahomey) A country in West Africa, on the Gulf of Guinea. Flat forests and swamps in the S rise to plateaus in the center and to mountains in the N. The population is mainly Fon and Yoruba in the N and Somba and Bariba in the S. *Economy*: chiefly agricultural, the main crops being corn, cassava, rice, and vegetables. Cotton has been introduced in the N and coffee in the S, and these provide the main exports. Forests produce palm oil and kernels, and there is some freshwater fishing. Offshore oil has been found and hydroelectric schemes are being planned in conjunction with Togo. Most industry has been nationalized. *History*: the powerful Aja kingdom of Dahomey was a center of the slave trade in the 17th century but was conquered by the French in 1893 and became part of French West Africa. Dahomey attained self-government in 1958 and became an independent republic within the French Community in 1960. Until 1972, the country was shaken by a series of military coups. In 1972, Lt. Col. Ahmed (Malthieu) Kerékou seized power. In 1974 he established a Marxist-Leninist state. In 1983 the expulsion from Nigeria of 2,000,000 illegal aliens, mostly from Ghana, brought a mass exodus of homeless people through Benin as they made their way back to their native countries. Causing a crisis situation in Benin, the refugee problem led to long-term serious disruptions since many of the stranded remained in that country. In 1989, Kerékou cleared the way for democracy by abandoning Marxist-Leninism and providing for multiparty elections. He was defeated by Nicephore Soglo in the 1991 presidential elections. Official language: French. Official currency: CFA (Communauté financière africaine) franc of 100 centimes. Area: 43,464 sq mi (112,600 sq km). Population (1990 est): 4,840,000. Capital: Porto Novo. Main port: Cotonou.

Benin City 6 19N 5 41E A city in Nigeria. It is an important center for the rubber industry and also exports palm oil. Population (1990 est): 198,000.

Benjamin In the Old Testament, the youngest son of Jacob by Rachel, who died during childbirth. He was named Ben-oni (son of ill luck) by Rachel before she died but called Benjamin (son of good luck) by Jacob. He became his father's favorite after Joseph was sold into slavery in Egypt. Figuratively he represents the especially loved younger son. His descendants formed one of the 12 *tribes of Israel and later, with the tribe of Judah, formed the southern kingdom of Judah.

DAVID BEN-GURION *The father of the Israeli nation, noted for his informality, had a magnetic personality that caused him to be revered throughout the world.*

Benjamin, Judah Philip (1811–84) US statesman and lawyer. A lawyer by profession, he served in the Louisiana legislature and the US Senate (1852–61) before becoming attorney general (1861) of the Confederacy at the beginning of the Civil War. He then served as secretary of war (1861–62) and secretary of state (1862–65) until the collapse of the Confederacy, at which time he went to England and practiced law.

Benn, Gottfried (1886–1956) German poet. He worked as a doctor in Berlin and, during both World Wars, in the army. His early expressionist style, evident in *Morgue* (1912) and *Fleisch* (1917), gave way to the more precise intellectual style evident in *Statische Gedichte* (1948). His theories of poetry, contained in *Probleme der Lyrik* (1951), attracted T. S. *Eliot.

Bennett, (Enoch) Arnold (1837–1931) British novelist. A magazine editor in London, he published his first novel, *A Man from the North*, in 1898 and lived in Paris from 1902 to 1912. His best-known novels are about life in Staffordshire, where he grew up. They include *Anna of the Five Towns* (1902), *The Old Wives' Tale* (1908), and *Clayhanger* (1910).

Bennett, James Gordon (1795–1872) US newspaper editor, born in Scotland. After writing for several newspapers, he distinguished himself as Washington correspondent for the *New York Enquirer*. In 1835, he founded the *New York Herald* (1835), in which he pioneered many of the techniques of modern journalism, including the use of the telegraph to speed news gathering. His son **James Gordon Bennett** (1841–1918) became editor of the *Herald* in 1867. He financed several explorers, including Stanley in his quest for Livingstone, an Arctic expedition, and the quest for the Northwest Passage.

Bennett, Richard Bedford, Viscount (1870–1947) Canadian statesman; Conservative prime minister (1930–35). A lawyer and businessman, he was a champion of protective tariffs. In 1932 he presided over the Imperial Economic Conference in Ottawa, which established bilateral trade agreements between countries in the British Commonwealth.

Ben Nevis 56 48N 5 00W The highest mountain in the British Isles, in the Highland Region of Scotland, in the Grampians. Height: 4406 ft (1343 m).

Bennington, Battle of (1777) A Revolutionary War battle in which colonial troops were victorious over the British at Bennington, Vt. British and Loyalist troops, commanded by a German colonel, Friedrich Baume, planned to raid Bennington's supply stores, but they were stopped by American troops. This battle marked the beginning of the decline of Gen. John *Burgoyne's N campaign in America.

Benny, Jack (Benjamin Kubelsky; 1894–1974) US entertainer. A comedian in vaudeville from an early age, he began making motion pictures in 1929. His act was centered around comic playing of the violin, delayed doubletake, stinginess, and, from 1933, always being 39 years old. He had his own radio (1932–55) and television shows (1950–65).

Benoni 26 12S 28 18E A city in South Africa, in the S Transvaal on the Witwatersrand. Founded in 1903 as a gold-mining center, it is an important industrial city, especially for engineering. Population (1985): 95,000.

Bent, William (1809–69) US pioneer and fur trader. Colorado's first white settler, he established Bent's Fort (1832), a trading post.

Bentham, Jeremy (1748–1832) British philosopher, pioneer of *utilitarianism. From a wealthy middle-class background, he began his law studies at 15. He preferred legal theory to practice and in 1776 published *A Fragment on Goverment*. In 1789 *Principles of Morals and Legislation* presented utilitarianism to the world. He retired to the country in 1814, a hero to republicans across Europe, and wrote copiously on politics and ethics until his death. He founded the *Westminster Review* (1823) to promote philosophical radicalism.

Bentivoglio An aristocratic family that ruled Bologna (Italy) from 1447 until 1506. **Sante Bentivoglio** (1424–63) established his family's supremacy in Bologna. He and his son **Giovanni Bentivoglio** (1443–1508) were notable patrons of the arts. Increasingly autocratic, and unpopular, Giovanni and his family were expelled from Bologna in 1506 with the support of Pope *Julius II. Subsequent members of the family, notably **Guido Bentivoglio** (1579–1644), were famous diplomats and authors, but the family never regained its former political power.

Benton, Thomas Hart (1889–1975) US painter of rural life. As the leader and spokesman of the American Regionalist painters of the 1930s, Benton advocated the need to free US painting from the overwhelming influence of French abstract art and to create an indigenous artistic tradition. He is also known for his murals for such public institutions as the New School of Social Research, New York, and the Missouri State Capitol in Jefferson City.

Bentsen, Lloyd (Millard, Jr.) (1921–   ) US politician. A Democratic senator (1971–93) from Texas, he was the unsuccessful vice-presidential nominee on the ticket with presidential candidate Michael *Dukakis in 1988. Bentsen became secretary of the treasury under President Clinton in 1993.

bentwood furniture Furniture constructed by a mass-production process invented by a Viennese designer Michael Thonet (1796–1871). It involved steaming beechwood rods and laminated board until they could be bent into the desired shapes. The shaped sections were transported unassembled and screwed together at the destination. Typical chairs, coat stands, etc., are curved in rococo style. The technique has been exploited by modern designers, such as Marcel *Breuer and many Scandinavian designers.

Benxi (*or* Pen-ki) 41 21N 123 45E A city in NE China, in Liaoning province. It is a center of iron and steel production. Population (1986 est): 700,000.

Benz, Karl (Friedrich) (1844–1929) German engineer and □automobile manufacturer. In 1885 he built the first automobile to be driven by an internal-combustion engine. The Benz Company merged with Daimler in 1926 to form Daimler-Benz, the makers of Mercedes-Benz automobiles.

Benzedrine. *See* amphetamine.

benzene (*or* benzol; C_6H_6) A colorless highly flammable liquid. It is the simplest □aromatic compound, its molecules consisting of a ring of six carbon atoms each with a hydrogen atom attached. Benzene is obtained from *oil and from *coal tar. It is widely used in the chemical industry, for example in making *detergents, *nylon, and *insecticides.

benzodiazepines A class of tranquilizing drugs that act by depressing specific areas of the brain. Despite this, overdosage of these drugs is rarely dangerous. Benzodiazepines, such as diazepam (Valium) and chlordiazepoxide (Librium), are used as *sedatives. Diazepam is also used to control epileptic seizures and chlordiazepoxide is helpful in the treatment of alcohol-withdrawal symptoms. Nitrazepam (Mogadon) is used as a sleeping pill (*see* hypnotics). Both nitrazepam and diazepam are habit forming.

benzoic acid (C_6H_5COOH) A white crystalline powder, the simplest of the carboxylic acids (*see* fatty acids). It occurs naturally in many plants and is used in preserving food.

benzoin 1. ($C_6H_5CHOHCOC_6H_5$) A white or yellowish crystalline substance used to make other organic compounds. **2.** (*or* gum benjamin) A fragrant gum resin obtained from the trunk of a SE Asian tree, *Styrax benzoin*. It is used in medicine (as a constituent of friar's balsam), in cosmetics, and in perfumery.

Ben-Zvi, Itzhak (1884–1963) Israeli statesman; president (1952–63). Born in Russia, where he was an active Zionist, he went to Palestine in 1907. With David *Ben-Gurion, Ben-Zvi helped to found the state of Israel (1947). He was also a noted archeologist.

Beowulf An Anglo-Saxon epic poem preserved in a late 10th-century manuscript. Probably composed or at least reworked in the 8th century by a Christian poet sympathetic to pagan ideals of honor and courage, it alludes to historical events of early 6th-century Scandinavia. In the first part the hero, Beowulf, kills the marauding monster, Grendel, and when Grendel's mother attempts vengeance he tracks her to her underwater cave and kills her. In the second part, Beowulf, now king of the Swedish tribe of Geats, slays a dragon and seizes its hoard of treasure, but is mortally wounded.

Bérain the Elder, Jean (1637–1711) French designer, engraver, and painter; royal designer to Louis XIV of France. He designed festival decorations, furniture, tapestries, and opera costumes for the court, often decorated with immense detail, which influenced the later rococo style. He used many Chinese motifs in his designs to satisfy the king's fondness for oriental art.

Beranger, Pierre Jean de (1780–1857) French poet and songwriter. His satirical verse and republican sentiments led to his imprisonment under the Bourbon monarchy.

Berbera 10 30N 45 25E A port in N Somalia, on the Gulf of Aden. It has a deepwater harbor and exports sheep, leather, ghee, frankincense, and myrrh. Population (1980 est): 65,000.

Berberis A genus of deciduous or evergreen spiny shrubs (over 400 species), commonly known as barberry, mostly native to Central and E Asia and South America but also occurring in parts of Europe, Africa, and North America. The small yellow or orange flowers usually grow in clusters and the fruits are bright-red berries. Several species are widely grown as ornamentals for their flowers, fruits, or attractive autumn foliage. Berberis is implicated in a rust disease of wheat and is therefore outlawed in some areas. Family: *Berberidaceae*.

Berbers A Muslim people occupying parts of N Africa (Morocco, Algeria, Tunisia, and adjacent regions) and speaking a non-Semitic language. Prior to the Arab conquests of the 7th century AD and the establishment of Arabic speech, Berber languages were spoken over the whole of the area from Egypt to the Atlantic. Though Arabic has long been the dominant language it has not entirely ousted Berber, which is spoken by an estimated ten million people, and Morocco is still predominantly Berber in population. The Berbers played an important role in the Islamic conquest of the Iberian peninsula in the 8th century and in the subsequent occupation of Spain. The Berbers are largely agriculturalists, although some still follow a nomadic way of life.

Berchtesgaden 47 38N 13 00E A resort in SE Germany, in the Bavarian Alps. It is the site of Hitler's fortified mountain retreat, the Berghof. Salt has been mined here since the 12th century. Population (1989 est): 7,750.

Berdyaev, Nikolai (1874–1948) Russian mystical philosopher. He was expelled from Russia (1922) for teaching religion and until World War II his academy near Paris and his journal *The Path* spread his ideas in Europe. He saw communism as an ungodly manifestation of Russia's messianic destiny. *Dreams and Reality* (1950) summarizes his ideas.

Berdyansk (name from 1939 until 1958: Osipenko) 46 45N 36 47E A port in the Ukraine on the Sea of Azov. It is a seaside resort and its most important economic activities relate to fishing. Flour milling and oil refining are also carried out. Population (1985): 130,000.

Berenson, Bernard (1865–1959) US art historian, whose works set new standards of criticism. Inspired by the beauty of Italy, where he spent most of his life, he wrote the definitive *Italian Painters of the Renaissance* (1894–1907). His aesthetic delight is captured in *Drawings of the Florentine Painters* (1903).

Berezniki 59 26N 56 49E A port in E European Russia, on the Kama River. Founded in 1883, it is a large center for the chemical industry in Russia. Population (1987): 200,000.

Berg, Alban (1885–1935) Austrian composer. A friend and pupil of *Schoenberg, he adopted *atonality and used *serialism, though in a highly personal and original fashion. His greatest works are the operas *Wozzeck* (1915–21) from the play by *Büchner and *Lulu* (1928–35) from plays by *Wedekind, the intensely personal *Lyric Suite* (for string quartet; 1925–26), and a violin concerto (1935).

Bergamo 45 42N 9 40E A city in Italy, in Lombardy in the foothills of the Alps. It has a 12th-century romanesque cathedral. Machinery, textiles, and cement are manufactured. Population (1988): 119,000.

bergamot A tree, *Citrus bergamia*, closely related to the orange. An essence (oil of bergamot) extracted from the rind of its fruit is used in perfumery, for which the tree is cultivated in S Italy and Sicily. *See* Citrus.

The name is also given to two plants of the mint family (*Labiatae*): *Mentha citrata*, which yields an extract similar to oil of bergamot, and *Monarda citriodora* (lemon bergamot) sometimes used in a tealike beverage.

Bergen 60 23N 5 20E A seaport and second largest city in Norway, situated in the SW. Founded about 1070 AD, it became the chief commercial city and the country's capital (12th–13th centuries). It had important connections with Hanseatic merchants (14th–18th centuries). It was rebuilt after damage by fire in 1702, 1855, and 1916 and by bombing during World War II. It is a cultural center with a university (1948), several museums, and art galleries. Other notable buildings include the 12th-century Mariakirke (a stone-built church) and the 13th-century Håkonshall (a royal palace). Its industries include ship building and oil refining. It exports fish products and base metals. Population (1988): 210,000.

Bergen, Candice (1946–   ) US film and television actress, noted for her title role as a television journalist in the television series *Murphy Brown*. The daughter of ventriloquist Edgar Bergen, she worked as a model and photographer before turning to acting full time in such films as *Starting Over*. From its inception in 1988, *Murphy Brown* showcased her comedic talents and droll humor.

Bergenia A genus of herbaceous perennial plants (6 species), native to central and E Asia but often cultivated as ornamentals for their attractive foliage and early-blooming pink or white flowers. Family: *Saxifragaceae*.

Bergius, Friedrich (1884–1949) German chemist, who shared the 1931 Nobel Prize with C. Bosch for research in high-pressure chemical techniques. He manufactured light motor fuels from either coal or heavy petroleum residues by treating them with hydrogen under high pressure and temperature (1913). This process was used extensively by Germany in World War II. After Germany's defeat he emigrated to Spain and then to Argentina.

Bergman, Ingmar (1918–   ) Swedish film and stage director. His films, which express his austere human vision with great intensity, include *The Seventh Seal* (1956), *Wild Strawberries* (1957), *Persona* (1966), *Scenes from a Marriage* (1974), *Autumn Sonata* (1978), and *Fanny and Alexander* (1983). He was director of the Royal Dramatic Theater, Stockholm, from 1963 to 1966.

Bergman, Ingrid (1915–82) Swedish actress. She went to Hollywood in 1939 and became an international film star, appearing in such films as *Casablanca* (1942), *For Whom the Bell Tolls* (1943), *Notorious* (1946), and numerous other major films, her last being *Autumn Sonata* (1978). She also played in several notable stage productions. She received Academy Awards as best actress for *Gaslight* (1944) and *Anastasia* (1956).

Bergson, Henri (1859–1941) French philosopher and psychologist, one of the greatest thinkers of his time. To reconcile free will and *determinism, Bergson distinguishes between consciousness, an indivisible flow of cumulative states in which (free) will operates, and the external physical world where causality reigns and objects and events are fixed and discrete. He championed creative against analytic thinking in stylish and penetrating works that include *Matière et mémoire* (1896) and *L'Évolution créatrice* (1907). He won the Nobel Prize for Literature in 1927.

Beria, Lavrenti Pavlovich (1899–1953) Soviet politician. Head of the Soviet secret police from 1938, Beria became a member of the politburo (now the presidium) in 1946. After Stalin's death in March 1953, he was involved in a power struggle with Malenkov and Khrushchev. He was accused of conspiracy in July, tried secretly, and executed in December.

beriberi A disease caused by deficiency of *vitamin B_1 (thiamine), common in areas where the staple diet is polished rice (thiamine occurs mainly in the rice husks). Dry beriberi affects the peripheral nerves, causing muscular weakness and pain. Wet beriberi is probably the result of combined protein malnutrition and thiamine deficiency: it causes accumulation of fluid and swelling of the limbs, leading eventually to heart failure. Treatment consists of providing a diet with adequate thiamine and vitamin supplements.

Bering, Vitus Jonassen (*or* V. J. Behring; 1681–1741) Danish navigator. In 1724 he was commissioned by the Russians to explore the area between Siberia and America. He made several voyages from Kamchatka on the last of which (1741) he sighted Alaska from the strait named for him. On his way back, suffering from scurvy, he was wrecked off Bering Island, where he died. The Bering Sea is also named for him.

Bering Sea A section of the N Pacific Ocean between Siberia, Alaska, and the Aleutian Islands. Navigation is difficult, with storms and a partial ice covering in winter. The NE continental shelf contains oil and gas.

Bering Strait A narrow shallow channel between Asia and North America, connecting the Bering Sea with the Arctic Ocean. During the Ice Age it bridged the continents when the sea level fell.

Berkeley 37 53N 122 17W A city in California on San Francisco Bay. It is the headquarters of the University of California, where *berkelium was discovered. Its manufactures include soap, paint, and chemicals. Population (1990): 102,724.

Berkeley, Busby (William Berkeley Enos; 1895–1976) US dance director. He is best known for his elaborate choreography for Hollywood film musicals in the 1930s and 1940s. These include *42nd Street* (1933), the *Gold Diggers* series (1933–37), and *Babes in Arms* (1939).

Berkeley, George (1685–1753) Irish bishop and idealist philosopher. In *A New Theory of Vision* (1709), *Principles of Human Knowledge* (1710), and *Three Dialogues between Hylas and Philonous* (1713), he argued that the material world exists only in being perceived by the mind, a view that influenced *Hume and, indirectly, *Kant. Berkeley's later works, such as *Siris* (1744) are interesting but increasingly eccentric.

Berkeley, Sir William (1606–77) English colonist; governor of Virginia (1641–49, 1660–77). His attempts to foster trade relations with the Indians were thwarted by Nathaniel Bacon (1647–76), who led a force against the Indians that was defeated by Berkeley's troops (Bacon's Rebellion). Berkeley is also noted as the author of a play, *The Lost Lady* (1638).

berkelium (Bk) A synthetic transuranic element synthesized by Seaborg and others in 1949 by bombarding americium with helium ions. The longest-lived isotope (^{249}Bk) has a half-life of 314 days; visible amounts of the chloride ($BkCl_3$) have been produced. At no 97; at wt 247.

Berkshire A county of S England. Under local government reorganization in 1974 it lost a substantial part of the NW to Oxfordshire, while gaining part of SW Buckinghamshire, including Slough. It consists mainly of lowlands rising to the Berkshire Downs in the N. It is bordered by the River Thames in the NE and crossed by the River Kennet. It is predominantly agricultural; chief products are barley, dairy produce, pigs, and poultry. Industries include paints, plastics, and pharmaceutical goods at Slough and light engineering and horticulture at Reading; the Atomic Research Establishment is at Aldermaston. Area: 485 sq mi (1256 sq km). Population (1987): 741,000. Administrative center: Reading.

Berle, Adolf Augustus, Jr. (1895–1971) US lawyer and statesman. A member of Pres. Franklin D. *Roosevelt's "Brain Trust," he was a planner for both the federal government and New York State from 1934 until 1937. He was US assistant secretary of state for Latin American affairs (1938–44), ambassador to Brazil (1945–46), and special adviser on Latin America during Pres. John F. Kennedy's administration.

Berlichingen, Götz von (1480–1562) German knight and mercenary. A professional adventurer, he was already famous for his exploits, in which he lost his right hand, when he became a rebel leader in the *Peasants' War (1525). After a period of imprisonment he continued his career, serving Emperor Charles V against the Turks in the 1540s. His exploits inspired Goethe's *Götz von Berlichingen* (1773).

Berlin 52 31N 13 20E The largest city in Germany, in the N, on the Spree River, divided from 1948 until 1989 into East Berlin, long capital of the German Democratic Republic (East Germany), and West Berlin, part of the Federal Republic of Germany (West Germany). Designated as the capital of reunited Germany in 1990. *History*: founded in the 13th century, it was an important strategic and commercial center and a member of the Hanseatic League. Its independence was reduced by the *Hohenzollern Electors of Brandenburg from the 15th century, but it became their capital and grew in importance with their increasing power, becoming the capital of Prussia in the 18th century and of the German Empire in 1871. Badly damaged in World War II, it was occupied by the four major powers after the defeat of Germany. In 1948 Berlin became two separate administrative units: Soviet-controlled East Berlin and West Berlin, formed from the US, UK, and French zones. The Soviet Union blockaded the city for almost a year but it failed to extend its influence to West Berlin (*see* Berlin airlift). In 1961 a dividing wall was built to curb the flow of refugees from E to W. The wall was destroyed by jubilant Berliners in late 1989. Population (1990): 3,102,500.

East Berlin Former capital of East Germany, 1948–89. Postwar recovery was slower than in West Berlin. Industrial products include electrical goods, chemicals, machinery, and clothing. This part of the city is the site of Humboldt University, formerly Frederick William University (1810), where famous scholars such as Humboldt, Fichte, Hegel, and Ranke worked. Area: 156 sq mi (403 sq km).

West Berlin The largest city and a *Land* of West Germany when Berlin was divided, 1948–89. It formed an enclave within East Germany. Despite difficulties in communications it was an active industrial and commercial center, subsidized by West Germany. Its numerous industries include the manufacture of electrical equipment, clothing, and chemicals as well as publishing and printing. A major landmark is the Kaiser Wilhelm Church, the ruins of which have been preserved as a reminder of the World Wars. The Free University of Berlin was established in 1948. Area: 188 sq mi (480 sq km).

Berlin, Congress of (1878) A meeting of European powers, which revised the Treaty of *San Stefano that had ended the 1877–78 Russo-Turkish War. The

BERLIN *King Edward VII and Queen Alexandra of Great Britain entering Berlin through the Brandenburg Gate on a state visit to the Emperor William II in 1906.*

Congress, which was dominated by the German chancellor, *Bismarck, limited
Russian naval expansion, permitted Austria-Hungary to occupy Bosnia-Herze-
govina, and gained Turkish recognition of the independence of Serbia, Romania,
and Montenegro and of Bulgarian autonomy under Turkish suzerainty.

Berlin, Irving (Israel Baline; 1888–1989) US composer of musical comedies
and film scores, born in Russia. He emigrated with his family to the US in 1893.
He wrote "Alexander's Ragtime Band" while working as a singing waiter and
subsequently composed the music for many musicals, including *Annie Get Your
Gun* (1946), *Call Me Madam* (1950), and *Mr President* (1962). His songs include "God Bless America," "White Christmas," and "Blue Skies."

Berlin, Sir Isaiah (1909–   ) British philosopher and historian. Although
based mostly in Oxford, he was also a diplomat in Washington and Moscow. His
works include *The Inevitability of History* (1954), *The Age of Enlightenment*
(1956), and *Two Concepts of Liberty* (1959).

Berlin airlift (1948–49) An operation by the Allies after World War II to supply isolated West Berlin with the necessities of life. In 1948 the Soviet Union
cut off all rail, road, and water links with the city in an attempt to force the Allies to abandon their rights there. The airlift continued until the blockade was
lifted as a result of an embargo on exports from the E European states.

Berliner Ensemble A theater company founded by Bertolt *Brecht in East
Berlin in 1949. It became fully independent after its move to the Theater am
Schiffbauerdamm in 1945 and was directed after Brecht's death in 1956 by his
widow, Helene Weigel (1900–71). The company devoted itself exclusively to
works written or adapted by Brecht, and its several European tours won international acclaim for his work.

Berlin West Africa Conference (1884–85) A series of meetings held at
Berlin under the chairmanship of *Bismarck to settle the dispute over possession of the Congo Basin (Central Africa). Among the powers that attended were
France, Germany, the UK, Belgium, and Portugal. The Conference declared that
the Congo Basin should be neutral with free trade and shipping and that an independent Congo Free State be established; it forbade slave trading.

Berlioz, (Louis) Hector (1803–69) French Romantic composer and conductor. Against family opposition he abandoned medicine for music. His first successful work, the *Symphonie Fantastique* (1830–31), was influenced by his love
for an Irish actress, Harriet Smithson (1800–54). As winner of the Prix de Rome
he went to Italy to study; on his return in 1833 he married Harriet. His dramatic
symphony *Harold in Italy* (1834) and choral symphony *Romeo and Juliet*
(1839) were popular successes, but the cantata *The Damnation of Faust* (1846)
and the opera *Benvenuto Cellini* (1834–38) failed. The oratorio *The Childhood
of Christ* (1850–54) was his last major success, for his two-part opera *The Tro-
jans* (1856–59) was not performed complete in his lifetime. Other orchestral
works include the overture *Le Corsair* (1851–52) and *Le Carnaval romain*
(1844). He was the author of a famous treatise on orchestration and a volume of
memoirs.

Bermejo, Río A river of S central South America. Rising in S Bolivia, it flows
SE into Argentina to join the Paraguay River. Length: 650 mi (1046 km).

Bermuda A British crown colony, comprising some 300 coral islands (of
which 20 are inhabited), in the W Atlantic Ocean. The largest island is Bermuda
(*or* Great Bermuda), while smaller ones include Somerset, Ireland, and St
George. *Economy*: the subtropical climate with its mild winters has contributed
to tourism, which forms the basis of the islands' economy. Agricultural products
include vegetables and bananas; onions, potatoes, and lily bulbs are exported to

the US. *History*: visited by the Spanish navigator Juan de Bermudez, they were first settled in 1609. They became self-governing in 1968 but demands for independence have grown; the governor was assassinated in 1973 and there was serious rioting in December 1977. The island's governor, Sir Richard Posnett, resigned in 1983 after accusations of irregularities in his expense account. Governor: Viscount Dunrossil. Official language: English. Official currency: Bermuda dollar of 100 cents. Area: 20 sq mi (53 sq km). Population (1992 est): 60,000. Capital: Hamilton.

Bermuda Triangle The most notorious of several geographic regions, all lying roughly between 30° and 40° of latitude, in which numerous ships and aircraft have vanished without trace. The Triangle covers about 1,500,000 sq mi (3,900,000 sq km) between Bermuda, Florida, and Puerto Rico. No generally satisfactory explanation of these disappearances has been advanced, but the great depth of the sea and powerful currents may explain the lack of wreckage.

Bern (French name: Berne) 46 57N 95 58W The capital of Switzerland, on the Aare River. Founded as a military post in the 12th century, it joined the Swiss Confederation in 1353 and became the capital in 1848. Its many notable buildings include the gothic cathedral (15th century). Since the 16th century it has had a bear pit, now maintained as a tourist attraction. The university was founded in 1834. It has considerable industry and contains the headquarters of several international organizations. Population (1991 est): 135,000.

Bernadette of Lourdes, St (1844–79) French peasant girl, who in 1858 claimed to have had 18 visions of the Virgin Mary at a grotto near Lourdes. At 20 she became a nun. She was canonized in 1933. The shrine built at the spot is a place of international pilgrimage where miraculous cures are claimed to have occurred. Feast day: Feb 18 or Apr 16.

Bernadotte, Folke, Count (1895–1948) The nephew of Gustavus V of Sweden (1858–1950; reigned 1907–50). He became president of the Swedish Red Cross in 1946. In 1948 he was appointed mediator in Palestine but was assassinated by Jewish terrorists.

Bernadotte, Jean Baptiste Jules (c. 1763–1844) French marshal, who was King of Sweden (1818–44) as Charles XIV John, founding the present Swedish royal house. Rising from the ranks, he became famous under Napoleon with whose support in 1810 Bernadotte was adopted as heir by the dying Charles XIII of Sweden. Turning against Napoleon, Bernadotte contributed to his defeat at Leipzig (1813). In 1814 he forced Denmark to cede Norway to the Swedish monarchy.

Bernanos, Georges (1888–1948) French novelist and Catholic polemicist. His constant theme was the war between good and evil, characteristically portrayed in his best-known book, *The Diary of a Country Priest* (1936). Disturbed by European political trends, he lived in exile in Brazil from 1938 to 1945.

Bernard, Claude (1813–78) French physiologist, who helped establish the experimental principles used in modern research. A student of François *Magendie, Bernard discovered that a secretion of the pancreas breaks down fat into its constituents and that the liver is able to synthesize glucose from glycogen. He also showed how blood flow through capillaries is regulated by contraction of their walls, controlled by vasoconstrictor nerves. Bernard developed the concept of the internal environment (*milieu intérieur*) of the body, the regulation of which is a basic physiological function.

Bernardin de Saint-Pierre, Jacques Henri (1737–1814) French naturalist and writer. He was a disciple of Rousseau, whose ideas influenced the didactic

romance for which he is chiefly remembered, *Paul et Virginie* (1787), which is
set on the island of Mauritius.

Bernard of Chartres (died c. 1130) French scholastic philosopher, who
taught at Chartres (1114–24). A Platonist, he held a realist theory of universals
(*see* realism) but tried to reconcile Platonic and Aristotelian metaphysics. His
only extant work is a treatise on Neoplatonism.

Bernard of Clairvaux, St (1090–1153) French theologian and Doctor of the
Church. A Cistercian, he established in 1115 a monastery at Clairvaux that became a model of reform and influenced other monasteries in France and elsewhere. He was chosen by Pope Eugenius III to preach the second Crusade in
1146. His faith was based on an exalted mysticism, which is the subject of many
of his Latin writings. Feast day: Aug 20. Emblem: a beehive.

Bernard of Menthon, St (923–1008) Italian churchman and vicar general of
the diocese of Aosta. A native of Savoy, he established hospices on two Alpine
passes, which are named for him, as are the dogs that were kept by the monks
and trained to aid travelers. Feast day: May 28.

Berne Convention An international *copyright agreement of 1866. Its main
provision guarantees copyright in all signatory countries of any work copy-
righted in any one of them. The US is still not a signatory.

Bernese Oberland (*or* Bernese Alps) A section of the Alps in SW Switzerland, 65 mi (105 km) long, between the Rhône and Aare Rivers. Its mountain
peaks include the Eiger and the Finsteraarhorn and it is a popular area for mountain climbing.

Bernhard of Saxe-Weimar, Duke (1604–39) German general, who fought
for the Protestants in the *Thirty Years' War. He took command of the forces of
Gustavus Adolphus on Gustavus's death in 1632 and campaigned successfully
in S Germany. After losing at Nördlingen (1634) he held command for the
French in SW Germany.

Bernhardt, Sarah (Sarah Henriette Rosine Bernard; 1844–1923) French actress. Her voice and emotional power were especially suited to tragic roles.
Plays in which she gave notable performances include *Phèdre* (1879), *La Dame
aux camélias*, and *L'Aiglon* by Edmond Rostand. Her worldwide tours gained
her international acclaim. She was also manager of several theaters in Paris and
opened the old Théâtre des Nations as the Théâtre Sarah Bernhardt.

Bernina, Piz 46 23N 9 54E A mountain in SE Switzerland, in the Alps near St
Moritz. Height: 13,284 ft (4049 m).

Bernini, Gian Lorenzo (1598–1680) Italian *baroque sculptor and architect,
born in Naples, the son of a sculptor. Precociously talented, he worked chiefly in
□Rome under papal patronage. His first major sculptures were for Cardinal Scipione Borghese and included *Apollo and Daphne* (1622–24; Borghese Gallery,
Rome). Encouraged by Urban VIII, he extended his talents into the fields of
painting and, more successfully, architecture, major works being the baldachin
over the tomb of St Peter (1624–33) and the piazza and colonnade (1656–67) of
St Peter's, Rome. Later sculptures included fountains for Roman piazzas, *The
Ecstasy of St Teresa* (1645–52, Cornaro Chapel, Sta Maria della Vittoria, Rome),
and such portrait busts as *Louis XIV* (1665; Versailles).

Bernoulli A family of notable Swiss mathematicians and physicists, who, as
Flemish Protestants, were driven out of the Netherlands in the 1580s. The most
famous was **Daniel Bernoulli** (1700–82), who made important contributions to
fluid dynamics, especially his discovery in 1738 of *Bernoulli's principle concerning the speed and pressure of fluid flow. He also attempted to explain the

properties of gases at varying temperatures and pressures by regarding the gas as consisting of many tiny particles. His father **Jean Bernoulli** (1667–1748) and uncle **Jacques Bernoulli** (1654–1705) were both eminent mathematicians, who often worked together and jointly developed the calculus of variations. Jean also made discoveries in *probability theory and Jacques in *complex numbers. Daniel's brother **Nicolas Bernoulli** (1695–1726) also contributed to the theory of probability.

SARAH BERNHARDT *In the role of Hamlet at a London theater (1889).*

Bernoulli's principle The principle of conservation of energy applied to fluid flow. If the effects of friction are neglected the total energy of the flow at any point in a pipe is equal to the sum of the kinetic energy due to the flow velocity, the gravitational potential energy due to height, and the energy of pressure in the fluid itself. Bernoulli's theorem states that the sum of these three components is constant throughout a flow system. Named for Daniel *Bernoulli.

Bernstein, Eduard (1850–1932) German politician. A journalist, Bernstein joined the Socialist Democratic Party in 1872. In 1878 he was exiled from Germany on account of his political beliefs. He returned to Berlin in 1901, becoming the leader of the revisionist movement. He was elected to the Reichstag in 1902. As a protest against his party's support of World War I, he joined the Independent Social Democrats. His most important book, *Evolutionary Socialism* (1898), contains his criticisms of Marxist theory.

Bernstein, Leonard (1918–90) US conductor, composer, and pianist. From 1958 to 1969 he was musical director and conductor of the New York Philharmonic Orchestra and became famous for his concerts and recordings. He composed symphonies, choral works, and songs, often containing jazz and folk elements, including *Jeremiah* (1944), *Fancy Free* (1944), and *Chichester Psalms* (1965). His musicals, such as *On the Town* (1944) and *West Side Story* (1957), were widely popular. □Stern, Isaac.

Berre, Étang de A saltwater lagoon in S France, in the Bouches-du-Rhône department. Connected by canal to the Mediterranean Sea (through the Rove tunnel) and the Gulf of Fos, it has important oil refineries and saltworks situated around its shores. Area: 60 sq mi (155 sq km).

Berruguete, Pedro (c. 1450–c. 1504) Castilian Renaissance painter. In the 1470s he worked in Italy at the court of Urbino, where he painted *Federigo da Montefeltro and his Son* (Urbino). On returning to Spain (1482), he painted frescoes for Toledo cathedral and altarpieces for the Dominican order in Avila.

His son **Alonso Berruguete** (c. 1489–1561) was a mannerist painter and sculptor, who worked in Italy (c. 1504–c. 1517) and became court painter to Emperor Charles V (1518). He combined his talents in his masterpiece, the San Benito altarpiece, (now dismantled) in Valladolid.

berry Loosely, any small succulent *fruit. Botanically, a berry is a simple fruit with a thin skin and pulpy flesh containing many loose seeds: the tomato and grape are examples. Blackberries and raspberries are not strictly berries, but collections of small *drupes.

Berry A French province that was sold to the crown by the Viscount of Bourges in 1101 and was absorbed by the departments of Cher and Indre in 1790.

Berry, Chuck (Charles Edward B., 1926–) US singer and songwriter, who was one of the first musicians to popularize rock and roll. His songs, such as "Maybellene," "Johnny B. Goode," and "Roll Over, Beethoven" influenced the Beatles, the Rolling Stones, and others.

Berry, Jean de France, Duc de (1340–1416) The third son of John II of France, who was appointed (1358) governor of Auvergne, Languedoc, Périgord, and Poitou, where his repressive policies caused a peasants' revolt (1381–84). He was coregent during the minority (1380–88) of his nephew Charles VI.

Berry, Marie-Caroline de Bourbon-Sicile, Duchesse de (1798–1870) The wife of Charles, Duc de Berry (1778–1820), the son of Charles X of France. After Charles X's death, she conspired to obtain the French throne for her son Henri, Comte de Chambord (1820–83), instigating an unsuccessful revolt in the Vendée (1832).

Berryman, John (1914–72) US poet. On the University of Minnesota faculty from 1955, his poetry is collected in *Poems* (1942), *The Dispossessed* (1948), *Homage to Mistress Bradstreet* (1956), *Berryman's Sonnets* (1967), *Love and Fame* (1971), and *Delusions* (1972; posthumously). *The Dream Songs* (1969) includes *77 Dream Songs* (1964; Pulitzer Prize) and *His Toy, His Dream, His Rest* (1968). He also wrote a critical biography, *Stephen Crane* (1950); a novel, *Recovery* (1973), was published after his suicide in 1972.

berserkers (Old Norse: bear-shirts) In Scandinavian mythology, savage warriors whose frenzy in battle transformed them from men into wolves or bears and made them immune from being harmed by the sword or fire. In the frenzy of battle they would howl and foam at the mouth—hence the phrase "to go berserk." They were devotees of *Odin and, in early Scandinavian history, warriors called berserkers were often employed as bodyguards to nobles.

Berthelot, (Pierre Eugène) Marcelin (1827–1907) French chemist and politician, who became professor at the Collège de France (1865). A pioneer of organic chemical synthesis, he demolished the theory that organic compounds contained a "vital force." As a student of chemical thermodynamics he distinguished between endothermic and exothermic reactions, but wrongly concluded that the heat of a reaction was its driving force. He became a senator in 1881 and foreign secretary in 1895.

Berthollet, Claude Louis, Comte (1748–1822) French chemist and physician. He discovered potassium chlorate and introduced bleaching by chlorine; he also showed that ammonia consists of hydrogen and nitrogen. Berthollet helped to clarify the concept of chemical affinity and, working with *Lavoisier, developed a new chemical nomenclature. He traveled to Egypt as scientific adviser to Napoleon, who made him a senator and a count.

Bertillon, Alphonse (1853–1914) French criminal investigator, who developed a system for identifying criminals based on the description and measurement of physical characteristics. The system, also known as anthropometry, was eventually superseded by fingerprinting techniques. His brother **Jacques Bertillon** (1851–1922) was a statistician. As head of the Paris bureau of social statistics, he developed new systems of data analysis. He was particularly interested in the high incidence of alcoholism in France and the decline of the French population in comparison with rates in other countries.

Bertolucci, Bernardo (1940–   ) Italian film director. Many of his films are strongly influenced by Marxist ideology, notably *Before the Revolution* (1965) and the epic *1900* (1977). He achieved his greatest commercial success with the controversial *Last Tango in Paris* (1972). Other works include *The Last Emperor* (1987), for which he won an Academy Award, and *The Sheltering Sky* (1990).

Bertrand, Henri Gratien, Comte (1773–1844) French marshal, who in 1804 became an aide de camp to Napoleon, whose complete trust he won. He accompanied Napoleon into exile, both to Elba and St Helena, where he kept a diary that is an important historical source.

Bertran de Born (?1140–1215?) French knight and troubador poet. He composed lyrics glorifying love, ambition, and especially war. His castle at Hautefort was besieged and captured by Richard Lionheart, whose loyal officer he became.

Berwick, James Fitzjames, Duke of (1670–1734) Marshal of France, who was the illegitimate son of James II of England. He was educated in France and gained military experience in Europe. On the deposition of James (1688), Berwick supported his attempts to regain the throne and played a prominent part in the battle of the *Boyne. His victory in the employ of France at Almansa (1707) established Philip V on the Spanish throne. He was killed besieging Philippsburg in the War of the Polish Succession.

beryl A mineral consisting of beryllium alumino-silicate, found principally in granites and granite pegmatites. It occurs as crystals up to one meter in length and is white, pale blue, or green. It is the chief source of beryllium. *Aquamarine and *emerald are gem varieties.

beryllium (Be) A light (relative density 2.34) alkaline-earth metal that was discovered in 1828 by F. Wöhler and A. Bussy (1794–1882) independently. Its salts are highly toxic and require careful handling. It occurs in nature in such minerals as *beryl and phenacite (Be_2SiO_4). It is transparent to X-rays and is used as windows on X-ray tubes. Alloys with copper are extensively used and the oxide (BeO), having a high melting point (4590°F [2530°C]), is used as a ceramic. At no 4; at wt 9.0122; mp 741°F (1278°C); bp 1392°F (2450°C).

Berzelius, Jöns Jakob, Baron (1779–1848) Swedish chemist, whose main work was the discovery of atomic compositions of chemical compounds. He discovered the elements selenium (1817), silicon (1824), and thorium (1828) and determined the atomic and molecular weights of more than 2000 elements and compounds. He introduced the current notation for chemical formulae and the use of oxygen as a reference standard for atomic weights. Following the invention of electric cells, Berzelius experimented on electrolysis and developed a theory of electrostatic bonding in compounds. He published a standard textbook of chemistry in 1830.

Bes The Egyptian god of recreation, also associated with children and childbirth. Images of the god, represented as a grotesque dwarf with a tail, were kept in homes as protection against evil.

Besançon 47 14N 6 02E A city in E France, the capital of the Doubs department on the Doubs River. It has a cathedral (11th–13th centuries) and a university (1691). Victor Hugo was born here. It is the French watchmaking center and produces automobiles and textiles. Population (1982): 112,000.

Bessarabia A region largely in Moldova and Ukraine, until 1991 part of the Soviet Union, with a predominantly Moldavian population. Bessarabia is very fertile, the main crops being wine grapes, fruit, wheat, and tobacco; cattle and sheep are raised. The chief industry is agricultural processing. *History*: the region was colonized by the Greeks and later fell successively to the Romans, Huns, Magyars, Mongols, and Turks, passing to Russia in 1812. In 1918 Bessarabia declared its independence, later voting for union with Romania. In 1940 Romania ceded Bessarabia to the Soviet Union. Area: about 17,100 sq mi (44,300 sq km).

Bessarion, John (c. 1400–72) Greek scholar and cardinal. As Archbishop of Nicaea, he attempted to unite the Byzantine and Western Churches, eventually joining the latter and settling in Italy, where he became a cardinal in 1439. He was an outstanding scholar and exercised an important influence in introducing the study of Greek in the Renaissance. His large library of Greek manuscripts is preserved in Venice.

Bessemer, Sir Henry (1813–98) British engineer and inventor, who patented (1855) a process for manufacturing cheap steel (*see* Bessemer process). His Sheffield steelworks, built in 1859, are still producing steel. Bessemer was a prolific inventor, patenting some 114 inventions.

Bessemer process A steel-making process invented by Sir Henry *Bessemer in 1855. A long cylindrical vessel (Bessemer converter) is charged with molten pig iron; air, introduced through holes in the bottom of the converter, is blown through the iron to oxidize the carbon, silicon, and manganese impurities. Phosphorus is removed by reaction with the converter's basic refractory lining. Carbon, in the form of spiegel, is then added to give steel of the required carbon content. In the modern VLN (very low nitrogen) process, a mixture of oxygen and steam is blown through the iron instead of air, to avoid absorption of nitrogen by the steel.

Best, Charles Herbert (1899–1978) US physiologist, who, as an undergraduate research assistant to *Banting, helped discover the technique for isolating the hormone insulin from pancreatic tissue in 1921. Best also discovered choline, a B vitamin. The Banting and Best department of medical research was created at Toronto University in 1923.

bestiary A medieval treatise containing short accounts of different species of animal, both real and imaginary. Based on ancient Greek and Latin sources, bestiaries were very popular and were often fancifully illustrated. They were generally wildly inaccurate in their natural history, as their compilers were more interested in the morals to be drawn from each beast's real or supposed attributes than in scientific fact.

Bestuzhev-Riumin, Aleksei Petrovich, Count (1693–1766) Russian statesman. Bestuzhev served as a diplomat abroad until 1740. In the reign of the empress *Elizabeth he directed foreign policy and was Russia's chancellor from 1744 to 1758. He allied Russia with Austria and Britain against France and Prussia, a policy made obsolete by the realignment of European alliances on the eve of the *Seven Years' War. He was dismissed in 1758 and banished to his estate.

Beta Centauri A remote yet conspicuous blue giant, apparent magnitude 0.63 and about 425 light years distant, that is the second brightest star in the constellation Centaurus.

beta decay A radioactive process in which a neutron within a nucleus decays by the *weak interaction into a proton, an electron (beta particle), and an antineutrino; alternatively, a proton may decay into a neutron, a positron, and a neutrino. Since the nuclear charge changes by one in both cases, the nucleus is converted into the nucleus of another element.

betatron A type of particle *accelerator used for producing very high energy electrons. The electrons are accelerated around a circular path in an evacuated torus-shaped chamber, by means of a large pulsed magnetic field. Electron energies up to 300 MeV have been produced.

betel A mixture of the boiled dried seeds (**betel nuts**) of the areca, or betel palm (*Areca catechu*), and the leaves of the betel pepper (*Piper betle*), which produces copious salivation when chewed with lime—a practice common among the population of S Asia and the East Indies. Betel nuts contain an alkaloid of some value in expelling intestinal worms, and the mild stimulation resulting from chewing the mixture has led to its use in some religious ceremonies.

Betelgeuse An immense remote yet conspicuous red supergiant, over 500 light years distant, that is the second brightest star in the constellation *Orion. It is a *variable star with its magnitude ranging, usually, from 0.3 to 0.9 over a period of about 5.8 years.

Bethany (present-day name: Al-'Ayzariyah) 31 46N 35 15E A village on the *West Bank of the Jordan River, near Jerusalem. It is now named for Lazarus, whom Christ resurrected here (John 11.1–44).

Bethe, Hans Albrecht (1906–   ) US physicist, born in Germany. After studying under *Rutherford he returned to Germany but left when Hitler came to power. After two years in England he finally settled in the US, working on the atom bomb during World War II. His earlier researches in quantum electrodynamics proved valuable in working out the details of the nuclear fusion process that occurs in stars. For this work he received the 1967 Nobel Prize.

Bethlehem 31 42N 35 12E A city on the *West Bank of the Jordan River, near Jerusalem. The Church of the Nativity was built in 326 over the grotto that is the presumed birthplace of Jesus Christ. A university was founded here in 1973. Population: 30,000.

Bethlehem 40 36N 75 22W A city in the US, in Pennsylvania. A major steel center, it also has cement, textile, and electrical-equipment industries. Population (1980): 70,419.

Bethlen, Gábor (1580–1629) Prince of Transylvania (1613–29) a Protestant, who opposed Emperor Ferdinand II during the Thirty Years' War. Bethlen, after seizing northern Hungary, was elected King in 1620 but renounced the crown (1621) in exchange for Ferdinand's agreement to allow Hungarian Protestants to worship freely. Bethlen again took up arms against Ferdinand in 1623 and 1626 but then withdrew from the war.

Bethmann-Hollweg, Theobald von (1856–1921) German statesman. As minister of the interior, secretary of state, and chancellor (1909–17) successively, he instituted a number of electoral and legal reforms. In 1914, attempting to justify aggressive German foreign policy, he described the treaty guaranteeing Belgian neutrality as a "scrap of paper." In 1917 his efforts to secure a negotiated peace led to his overthrow by *Ludendorff and *Hindenburg.

Bethune, Mary McLeod (1875–1955) US educator and public official. Born in South Carolina of former slaves, she founded the Daytona Normal and Industrial Institute for Girls (Bethune-Cookman College since 1923) in Florida in 1904 and was the college's president (1923–42). She was also founder of the National Council of Negro Women in 1935 and was active in government affairs for minority groups.

Betjeman, Sir John (1906–84) British poet. He published his first book of poetry in 1933. His verse autobiography, *Summoned by Bells* (1960), reflected the nostalgia and gentle social satire characteristic of his other poems. He also revived and fostered interest in Victorian and Edwardian architecture. He became England's poet laureate in 1972 and served until his death.

betony A perennial herb, *Stachys officinalis* (or *Betonica officinalis*), up to 12 in (30 cm) high. It has round-toothed leaves and a dense head of reddish-purple tubular flowers arising from a square stem. Betony is found on open grassland, heaths, and hedgerows from Eurasia to N Africa. The leaves may be used for tea and for herbal tobacco. Family: *Labiatae*.

Bettelheim, Bruno (1903–90) US psychologist; born in Austria. After spending a year in German concentration camps, he came to the US (1939). From 1944, he taught educational psychology at the University of Chicago. His article "Individual and Mass Behavior in Extreme Situations" (1943) examined the human mind and stresses in the concentration camps. His theories about and work with disturbed children are documented in *Love is Not Enough* (1950) and *Truants From Life* (1954). Other works include *Dynamics of Prejudice* (1950), *The Empty Fortress* (1967), and *The Uses of Enchantment* (1976).

Betti, Ugo (1892–1953) Italian dramatist. He studied law and became a magistrate and, after 1944, librarian at the Ministry of Justice. The themes of many of his 26 plays, notably *Corruption in the Palace of Justice* (1944) and *The Fugitive* (1953), concern justice and social responsibility.

Beust, Friedrich Ferdinand, Count von (1809–86) German statesman; the chief opponent of *Bismarck. As prime minister of Saxony (1853–66) he allied Saxony with Austria in the Austro-Prussian War of 1866. He became chancellor of the Austrian Empire in 1867 and negotiated the *Augsleich* that established the Dual Monarchy of *Austria-Hungary. In domestic policy he was a liberal constitutionalist.

Bevan, Aneurin (1897–1960) British politician. A brilliant orator, Bevan clashed with the Labour Party in 1939 over its ambivalence toward Hitler. As minister of health (1945–51), he was the architect of the *National Health Service.

bevatron A type of *synchrotron used for accelerating protons at Berkeley, Ca. It can produce protons with energies up to 6 GeV.

Beverly Hills A city in California. A residential suburb of Los Angeles, it is the home of many film and television celebrities. Population (1990): 31,976.

Bevin, Ernest (1881–1951) British politician and labor leader. Bevin formed, and was general secretary (1921–40) of, the Transport and General Workers' Union and in 1937 became chairman of the TUC. In 1940 he became minister of labor, serving in Churchill's war cabinet. He was foreign secretary (1945–51) in the postwar Labour government, when he contributed to the formation of NATO.

Beza, Theodore (1519–1605) French Calvinist theologian. Trained as a lawyer, he went to Geneva in 1548, having formally renounced the Roman Catholic faith. He became professor of Greek at Lausanne University and first rector of the Geneva Academy (1559), which Calvin had just founded for the education of Protestant theologians. He is remembered both as a Bible translator and a defender of Protestantism. After Calvin's death (1564) Beza succeeded to his leadership of the Swiss Calvinists.

Béziers 43 21N 3 13E A city in S France, in the Hérault department. In 1209 many of the inhabitants were massacred by Simon de Montfort during the crusade against the Albigenses. It is a commercial center for wines and spirits and its manufactures include chemicals and textiles. Population: 85,677.

bezique A card game, usually for two players, that became popular in France about 1860. Two packs of 32 cards are used (standard packs with the cards from two to six removed). Each player is dealt eight cards; the next card indicates the trump suit and the rest form the stockpile. The object is to score points by collecting melds (certain combinations of cards) and to take tricks containing brisques (aces and tens). Play continues until one player's score reaches 1000 or 1500.

Bhagalpur 25 14N 86 59E A city in India, in Bihar. An agricultural trading center, its manufactures include textiles (especially silk). Its university was established in 1960. Population (1991): 254,993.

Bhagavadgita (Sanskrit: Song of the Lord) Hindu poem probably composed about 300 BC, forming part of the epic *Mahabharata*. It blends and reconciles a number of Hindu philosophies. Arjuna, one of the five Pandava brothers, is compelled to battle with his kinsmen, the Kauravas; he is persuaded by *Krishna, acting as his charioteer, of the virtue of selflessly performing the duties of caste. Krishna enumerates the ways by which one can attain liberation from the limitations of matter: by virtuous actions, by devotion to God, by philosophical speculation, by asceticism, or by meditation.

Bhamo 24 15N 97 15E A town in Myanmar, on the Irrawaddy River near the border with China. Principally a trading center, it has a government sugar factory.

Bharhut A Buddhist stupa (shrine) complex in Nagod state (N India), excavated in 1874. It provided evidence for the earliest phases of Buddhist architecture; carvings on the stone railings are the earliest representational reliefs from India (2nd century BC). Nothing now remains at the site.

Bhatpara 22 51N 88 31E A city in India, in West Bengal. It is an ancient seat of Sanskrit learning. Jute processing is the principal industry. Population (1991): 304,298.

Bhavachakra (Sanskrit: wheel of becoming) In Buddhism, an image of the cyclical nature of earthly existence, in the form of a wheel held by the demon of impermanence. Its segments represent the six possible states into which beings are reborn: the realms of gods, titans, hungry ghosts, humans, animals, and demons. At the center, turning the wheel, are greed, hatred, and delusion, depicted as a cockerel, snake, and pig, biting each other's tails. Around the rim, the 12 stages in the cycle of life are symbolically expressed.

Bhavnagar 21 59N 72 19E A port in India, in Gujarat on the Gulf of Cambay. An important industrial and commerical center, its manufactures include textiles, bricks, and tiles. Population (1991): 400,636.

Bhopal 23 17N 77 28E A city in India, the capital of Madhya Pradesh. Notable buildings include the unfinished Taj-ul-Masjid, the largest mosque in India. Its university was established in 1970. Bhopal's varied manufactures include vehicle parts and cotton textiles. In 1984 over 2000 people died after poisonous isocyanate gas escaped from the American-owned Union Carbide factory in the city. Population (1991): 1,063,662.

Bhutan, Kingdom of (Bhutanese name: Druk-yul) A small country in the E Himalayas, strategically positioned between India and Tibet. It is entirely mountainous, rising over 21,900 ft (7300 m) in the N. Over half the population are of Tibetan origin, known as Bhutias, with minorities of Nepalese in the S and Indians in the E. *Economy*: mainly agricultural; forests cover almost 70% of the land and there are plans for further planting. As well as traditional industries, such as bamboo and lacquer woodwork, other small industries are being encouraged and hydroelectricity is being developed. A new postal system was inaugurated in 1972 and since then postage stamps have been a valuable source of foreign currency, together with tourism, which has only recently been developed. *History*: although the early history of Bhutan is obscure it does appear to have existed as a political entity for many centuries. In 1865 part of S Bhutan was annexed by the British, following various border disputes, and a treaty was concluded in which Britain agreed to pay an annual subsidy. By a further treaty in 1910 Britain agreed not to interfere in Bhutan's internal affairs and in 1949 this was replaced by a similar treaty concluded with India. In 1910 Sir Ugyen Wangchuk was elected the first hereditary maharaja (now referred to as king). In 1969 the absolute monarchy was replaced by a "democratic monarchy" and power is now divided between the king, the Council of Ministers, the National Assembly, and the monastic head of Bhutan's lamas. Bhutan joined the UN in 1971 and the Nonaligned Movement in 1973; in 1983, it was one of the founders of South Asia Regional Cooperation (SARC). Head of state: King Jigme Singye Wangchuk. Official language: Dzongkha Bhutanese. Official currency: ngultrum of 100 chetrums. Area: 18,000 sq mi (46,600 sq km). Population (1990 est): 1,566,000. Capital: Thimphu.

Bhutto, Benazir (1947–   ) Pakistani political leader and prime minister (1988–90, 1993–   ). The daughter of executed prime minister Zulifikar Ali *Bhutto, she became active in the Pakistan People's Party (PPP) and led it to an election victory in 1988. The country's first woman prime minister, she had an ineffective ministry and was removed from office in 1990 on corruption charges. She again led the PPP to victory in the 1993 elections.

Bhutto, Zulfikar Ali (1928–79) Pakistani statesman; president (1971–73) and then prime minister (1973–77). He formed the Pakistan People's Party in 1967 and became president after the secession of East Pakistan (Bangladesh). Ousted by a military coup, he was defeated in the subsequent election and sentenced to death (1978) for conspiring to murder a political opponent. He was executed a year later in spite of worldwide pleas to General *Zia for clemency.

Biafra The Ibo secessionist eastern region of the Federal Republic of Nigeria (1967–70). In an attempt to protect the interests of the *Ibo people against the dominant *Hausa, a unilateral declaration of independence was made under the leadership of Lt. Col. Odumegwu Ojukwu. The federal government under General *Gowon refused to recognize the new state and took up arms against it. The decimated Ibo surrendered on Jan 15, 1970.

Biafra, Bight of. *See* Bonny, Bight of.

Bialik, Chaim Nachman (1873–1934) Jewish poet and translator, born in the Ukraine. The success of his major poem *The Talmud Student* (1894) established his reputation as the leading Hebrew poet of his time. His poetry is often lyrical and visionary but also condemns Jewish passivity in the face of oppression. He left the Soviet Union in 1921 and settled in Palestine in 1924.

Bialystok 53 09N 23 10E A city in NE Poland. It grew mainly under the Branicki family in the 18th century. In World War II the Germans killed half the population and destroyed the industry but cloth manufacture has been revived. Population (1985): 245,000.

Biarritz 43 29N 1 33W A city in SW France, in the Pyrénées-Atlantiques department on the Bay of Biscay. It became a fashionable resort under the patronage of the Empress Eugénie in the mid-19th century. Population: 27,653.

biathlon An athletic event consisting of combined shooting and cross-country *skiing, first included in the Winter Olympic Games in 1960; competitors ski 12.5 mi (20 km) with rifles and ammunition and at each of four points along the course take five shots at 164 yd (150 m).

Bible (Greek *biblia*, books) The collected books of the *Old Testament, the *New Testament, and the *Apocrypha. *Canon*: the canon of the Hebrew Old Testament was definitively established by the rabbinical council of Jamnia (90–100 AD), although most of the books had acquired authority much earlier. The council rejected a number of books that formed part of the Greek version of the Old Testament, the *Septuagint, and these constitute most of the Apocrypha, accepted in varying degrees as sacred scripture by some Christian Churches and rejected by others. The New Testament canon was also established gradually but had essentially its present form by the 3rd century AD. To Christians it represented the complete fulfillment of the prophecies of the Old Testament. *Divine inspiration and biblical criticism*: both Jews and Christians originally regarded their scriptures as divinely inspired, hence correct in every particular. Although Roman Catholics and Protestants differed as to whether the Bible was the sole source of revealed truth, all Christians agreed, until relatively recently, on the literal truth of the contents, a belief slowly eroded by the development of science from the 17th century onward. Despite the attempts to condemn scientific findings when these appeared to conflict with scripture, as in the case of *Galileo, scientific method was soon applied to the study of the Bible itself and the procedures of historical scholarship, textual criticism, archeology, etc., were brought to bear on all aspects of the text. *Texts*: the oldest extant complete manuscript of the Old Testament dates from the 11th century AD, but there are much earlier versions of parts of the text, for example the Pentateuch (*see also* Dead Sea Scrolls). The fact that there is almost no variation among the many manuscripts of the Old Testament attests to the care with which the Jewish scribes, known as the Masoretes, preserved the text from the 6th century AD onward. The earliest fragments of the New Testament date from the 2nd century AD; thereafter there are an extremely large number of manuscripts of quite early date.

Bible Societies Various Protestant organizations formed to promote and distribute Bibles to all peoples. One of the first societies, the Society for Promoting

Christian Knowledge, was founded in England in 1698. The American Bible Society distributes several million Bibles annually. In 1946 some 20 international societies combined to form the United Bible Societies.

Bibliothèque Nationale The national *library of France in Paris, containing around seven million volumes. It is based on the royal libraries of Charles the Wise (1364–80) and his successors, notably those of Louis XI, Charles VIII, and Francis I. From 1537 it received a copy of every book published in France. It was given its present name in 1795.

bicycles Light two-wheeled vehicles, the wheels of which are moved by cranks attached to pedals operated by the rider. Bicycles developed in the 19th century from a two-wheeled hobby-horse type of conveyance known as the dandy-horse or celeripede. Around 1840 a Scotsman, Kirkpatrick Macmillan, applied the dandy-horse principle to models with pedals. The first true bicycles, with rotary cranks on their front wheels, went into production in Paris in 1865. Known as velocipedes, these heavy-framed wooden-wheeled devices were nicknamed "boneshakers," but nevertheless popularized cycling as a pastime. To increase efficiency the front wheel was gradually made larger, resulting in the 20-year vogue of the ordinary (or pennyfarthing) bicycle. This was superseded by the so-called safety bicycle, which had a chain and sprocket drive to the rear wheel and was essentially the same as the modern bicycle. Invented by 1876, it went into production in 1885. Pneumatic rubber tires (1889), a freewheeling mechanism (1894), and variable gears (1899) were later refinements.

An inexpensive means of transport and recreation, bicycles have enjoyed a revival in developed countries since the fuel crises of the 1970s. Cycling is also a form of competitive sport. Racing first became popular in France, where the earliest race was held (1868) and now has a wide following throughout Europe (see Tour de France). Road races take place on public roads, sometimes through normal traffic, using lightweight bicycles with sophisticated gears. Track races are run on special steeply banked tracks and cyclo-cross races are held across country.

Bidault, Georges (1899–1983) French statesman; prime minister (1946, 1949–50). A leader of the French resistance during World War II, Bidault served as president of the Resistance Council in 1944 and foreign minister and president in de Gaulle's first (provisional) government. He broke with the Guallists over their policy toward Algerian independence, becoming head of the Organisation de l'Armée secrète, and from 1962 to 1968 lived in exile.

Biddle, John (1615–62) English religious leader, founder of Unitarianism (see Unitarians). While a schoolmaster he wrote his *Twelve Arguments* against the deity of the Holy Ghost, for which he was imprisoned in 1645. Although his adherents began to meet openly from 1652, he was arrested and banished under Cromwell and finally died in prison in London.

Biddle, Nicholas (1786–1844) US banker and financier. After serving in several government embassies abroad and in the Pennsylvania legislature, he became the president of the Second Bank of the United States in 1823. He advocated a strong national bank and ran it well. In 1832, when Biddle attempted to have the charter renewed, Pres. Andrew Jackson and his Democratic Party objected to the strong national influence of the bank, and by 1836 it had become a state bank of Pennsylvania. Biddle served as president of the bank until 1839.

Biedermeier style A style of furniture and painting that flourished under bourgeois patronage in Austria, Germany, and Scandinavia from about 1816 to about 1848. It was satirically named for the fictional character Gottlieb Biedermeier, who was created by the poet Ludwig Eichrocht (1827–92) to characterize bourgeois bad taste. Biedermeier furniture, which was the first to be mass produced, utilized French *Empire style design for modern functional purposes. Biedermeier paintings aimed at extreme naturalism in outdoor scenes and intimacy in interiors and portraits.

Biel (French name: Bienne) 47 09N 7 16E A city in NW Switzerland, on Lake Biel. It is the only official bilingual Swiss town (French and German). A watchmaking center, it also manufactures machinery. Population (1987): 83,000.

Biela's comet A comet, period 6.6 years, that was discovered in 1826 and was observed on its 1846 return to split in two. Although seen in 1852 the portions subsequently disintegrated. The resulting stream of meteoroids (*see* meteor) produced spectacular meteor storms in November 1872 and 1885. It was named for the Austrian astronomer Wilhelm von Biela (1782–1856).

Bielefeld 52 02N 8 32E A city in Germany, in North Rhine-Westphalia. Its linen mills were the first in Germany to be mechanized (1851). Silks, clothing, and machinery are also manufactured here. Population (1988): 299,000.

Bielsko-Biala 49 50N 19 00E A city in S Poland. It was formed in 1951 from two separate towns on the Biala River. It has an important textile industry. Population (1979 est): 160,000.

Bien Hoa 10 58N 106 50E An ancient city in S Vietnam, on the Dong Nai River. Known for its pottery, it also has paper, steel, and chemical industries, supplied by hydroelectric power. Population (1989 est): 190,000.

Bienne. *See* Biel.

Bierce, Ambrose Gwinnett (1842–?1914) US writer. After service in the Civil War, he became a journalist in California and London (1872–75). His story collections, *In the mid of Life* (1891), *Can Such Things Be?* (1893), and *The Devil's Dictionary* (1906), reflect his preoccupation with death and its aftermath. Not inappropriately, he disappeared in Mexico during *Villa's revolt.

bigamy The criminal offense of willfully and knowingly marrying a person while being married to another. Defenses to a charge of bigamy include an honest and reasonable belief in the death of the original marriage partner, especially if absent for seven years or more, and an honest and reasonable belief that the first marriage was invalid or has been dissolved. Although a person would not be guilty of bigamy if he can prove these defenses, the second marriage will still be invalid in such cases.

big-bang theory A cosmological theory (*see* cosmology), first proposed in the 1920s, that all the matter and radiation in the universe originated in an immense explosion that began the expansion of the universe, which still continues. The explosion occurred about 10 to 20 thousand million years ago. As the initially high temperature of the early constituents decreased, hydrogen and helium were able to form: the observed cosmic abundance of helium agrees very well with the predicted value. This matter eventually interacted to form galaxies. The theory also predicts that the radiation formed shortly after the explosion should by now have cooled to about three kelvin. This is indeed the temperature of the isotropic microwave background radiation, detected in 1965 and now considered strong evidence for the big-bang theory.

Big Bend National Park A national park in SW Texas, along the large bend of the Rio Grande on the Mexican border. Within the park are the Chisos Mountains, as well as desertland and numerous canyons. Established as a national park in 1944, Big Bend contains Indian fossils and ruins and many species of wildlife. Area: c. 1000 sq mi (c. 2600 sq km).

Bighorn Mountains A chain of mountains in N Wyoming arcing NW into S Montana, part of the Rocky Mountains. The highest point is Cloud Peak at 13,165 ft (4013 m). Bighorn Basin, to the W, is important for its oil fields.

bighorn A mountain sheep, *Ovis canadensis*, of North America. There is considerable variation within the species, ranging from the small Nelson's bighorn to the largest Rocky Mountain bighorns, which stand 40 in (100 cm) at the shoulder. Bighorns have transversely ribbed horns that grow in a spiral up to 40 in (100 cm) long.

Bihar A state in N India, bordering on Nepal. The densely populated rural Ganges plain in the N produces rice, other grains, sugar cane, pulses, and vegetables. The S Chota Nagpur plateau yields minerals, including much of the world's mica, and supports iron and steel and engineering works. *History*: the center of N Indian civilization from 1500 BC, Bihar was part of numerous empires and witnessed the early development of Buddhism and Jainism. It was a center of 19th-century Indian nationalism. Area: 67,116 sq mi (173,876 sq km). Population (1991): 86,338,853. Capital: Patna.

Bihari An Indo-Aryan language spoken in Bihar (India) and in Nepal by about 40 million people. It is related to *Bengali and less closely to *Hindi. There are three main dialects; only one, Maithili, has any significant literature.

Bijapur 16 52N 75 47E A city in India, the Karnataka. The ancient capital of a powerful Islamic kingdom (1489–1686), it has many fine Islamic buildings. Population (1991): 186,846.

Bikaner 28 01N 73 22E A city in India, in Rajasthan. The former center of a princely state, its fort (1571–1611) houses a fine collection of Sanskrit and Persian manuscripts. Bikaner is famous for the manufacture of carpets, shawls, and blankets. Population (1991): 415,355.

Bikini Atoll 11 35N 165 20E An atoll in the central Pacific Ocean in the *Marshall Islands. It was the site of US atomic and hydrogen bomb tests (some underwater) from 1946 to 1958.

Bilbao 43 15N 2 56W A port in N Spain, the largest city in the Basque Provinces of the Nervión River. One of Spain's chief ports, its exports include iron ore, lead, and wine. Metallurgical industries are especially important; others include chemicals, fishing, and ship building. Its university was founded in 1968. Population (1991): 368,710.

bilberry A deciduous shrub, *Vaccinium myrtillus*, 12–24 in (30–60 cm) high, also known as blaeberry, huckleberry, and whortleberry. It is found on acid moors and mountains in N Europe and N Asia. The green angular stems bear small pointed leaves that turn red in autumn. The globular pink flowers, which droop like tiny bells, develop into blue berries. These may be eaten raw or cooked, used in preserves, or used to make wine and spirits. Family: *Ericaceae* (heath family).

Bilbo, Theodore Gilmore (1877–1947) US politician, senator from Mississippi (1935–47). After graduation from Vanderbilt University law school in 1907, he served in Mississippi in the state senate (1908–12), as lieutenant governor (1912–16), and as governor (1916–20; 1928–32) before being elected to the US Senate as a Democrat. He was in favor of states' rights and advocated white supremacy.

Bilderdijk, Willem (1756–1831) Dutch poet and dramatist. He was a precursor of Romanticism in Dutch literature. Of his many poetic works, the most memorable is an unfinished epic poem on biblical themes entitled *De ondergang der eerste wareld* (*The Destruction of the First World*; 1810).

bile A yellow, green, or brown alkaline fluid secreted by the liver and stored in the *gall bladder. Contraction of the gall bladder, which is triggered by a hormone that is released from the duodenum in the presence of food, causes the bile to be expelled through the common bile duct into the intestine. Bile is composed of a mixture of bile salts (which emulsifies fatty foods for digestion) and bilirubin (a breakdown product of the blood pigment *hemoglobin).

bilharziasis. *See* schistosomiasis.

bill, parliamentary. *See* parliament.

billiards A game for two players or pairs of players, using cues and balls on a table. There are various forms but the table usually measures 10 × 5 ft (3 × 1.5 m) and a carom table has no pockets (holes around the edges of the table). Points are scored using three balls 2 in (5.2 cm) in diameter, which are white, white with a spot, and red. The white and the white-with-a-spot balls are cue balls, one for each player. The cue ball must strike both the other balls to score a carom. A player continues to shoot until he fails to make a carom. In three-cushion billiards the cue ball must hit the cushion (the interior ridge of the table) three times before striking the second object ball. *See also* pool; snooker.

Billiton. *See* Belitung.

bill of exchange (*or* bank draft) A written order signed by one person (drawer) requiring a second person (drawee) to pay on demand or at a stated date an amount of money to, or to the order of, a specified person or the bearer (payee). A check is a bill of exchange payable on demand and drawn on a banker. Bills of exchange are used in foreign trade and can be discounted (sold for cash before their maturity date at less than their face value).

Bill of Rights 1. (1791) The first ten amendments to the US Constitution, adopted as a whole in 1791 and described by Jefferson as "what the people are entitled to against every government on earth." They are (1) freedom of press, speech, and religion; (2) the right to bear arms; (3) prohibition of quartering of troops; (4) protection against unlawful search and seizure; (5) the right of due process of law; (6) the right to a fair and public trial; (7) the right to a trial by jury; (8) prohibition of cruel punishments; (9) protection of nonenumerated rights; and (10) reservation of powers, i.e. powers not reserved for the federal government reside in the states. **2.** (1689) The document that set out the conditions on which the British throne had been offered to William and Mary in 1688 (*see* Glorious Revolution). It incorporated the Declaration of Rights and declared that the monarch must rule according to the law and with parliamentary consent. MPs were to be freely elected and guaranteed freedom of speech. The Roman Catholic Stuart claim to the throne was terminated.

Billroth, Christian Albert Theodor (1829–94) Prussian-born surgeon. Billroth joined Vienna University in 1867 and—with the aid of antiseptic techniques—pioneered several important surgical operations on the stomach and intestine.

Billy the Kid (William H. Bonney/Henry McCarty; 1859–81) US outlaw. Born in New York City, he was raised in the west and is said to have killed his first man at the age of 12. He took part in the New Mexico cattle war of 1878, in which he killed a sheriff. By 1881, when he was gunned down by Sheriff Patrick Garrett, 21 deaths had been attributed to him.

bimetalism A monetary system in which currency was convertible into either of two metals (usually gold and silver) in a fixed ratio. When adopted by many countries at the beginning of the 19th century it proved unstable, as one metal was always undervalued and one overvalued. *Compare* gold standard.

binary star Two stars moving around each other under mutual gravitational attraction. The components of a **visual binary** can be distinguished by telescope whereas a **spectroscopic binary** can only be detected by spectroscope measurements, the components usually being very close. In an **eclipsing binary** the orbital plane is so oriented that one component passes alternately in front of and then behind the other, causing the combined brightness to fluctuate.

binary system A number system that uses only two digits 0 and 1. Numbers are expressed in powers of 2 instead of powers of 10, as in the decimal system. In binary notation, 2 is written as 10, 3 as 11, 4 as 100, 5 as 101, and so on. *Computers calculate in binary notation, the two digits corresponding to two switching positions (e.g. on or off) in the individual electronic devices in the logic circuits.

binding energy The energy released when protons and neutrons bind together to form an atomic nucleus. The mass of a nucleus is always less than the sum of the masses of the constituent protons and neutrons. The missing mass is converted into the binding energy according to *Einstein's law $E = mc^2$.

bindweed A widely distributed climbing plant of the temperate and subtropical genera *Convolvulus* and *Calystegia*. Bindweeds twine their stems around other plants for support and can be persistent weeds. The leaves are large and arrow-shaped and the conspicuous white, pink, or yellow flowers are funnel-shaped. Family: *Convolvulaceae*.

Black bindweed and copse bindweed (genus *Bilderdykia*; 3 species) lack the conspicuous flowers of the other bindweeds. Family: *Polygonaceae* (dock family).

Binet, Alfred (1857–1911) French psychologist, who pioneered the principles used in intelligence tests. Binet observed how his two young daughters responded to his tests using simple objects and pictures to assess their character and intelligence (*Experimental Study of Intelligence*, 1903). He later applied his techniques to measure the educational achievements of schoolchildren.

Bing, Sir Rudolf (1902–   ) British opera administrator, born in Austria. He was a founder (1933) and general manager of the Glyndebourne Festival Opera for more than a decade. He helped found the Edinburgh Festival and was its artistic manager (1947–49). He managed the Metropolitan Opera, New York, from 1950 until 1972.

Bingen 49 58N 7 55E A city in western Germany, in Rhineland-Palatinate at the confluence of the Rhine and Nahe Rivers. According to legend Archbishop Hatto II was devoured (c. 970) by mice on a nearby rock in the Rhine for maltreating his subjects. It is a center of the wine and tourist trades. Population (1989 est): 23,100.

Bingham, George Caleb (1811–79) US genre painter. With little formal training, he painted scenes of life along the Mississippi and Missouri Rivers and portraits in Washington, D.C. (1840–44). From 1844 his works were mostly river scenes and political events, an interest acquired from his time as a state legislator. Well-known works include *Fur Traders Descending the Missouri* (1845), *Shooting for the Beef* (1850), *The Trapper's Return* (1851), *Canvassing for a Vote* (1851), and *Stump Speaking* (1854).

Bingham, Hiram (1875–1956) US archeologist, explorer, educator, and politician. A teacher at Yale, he led expeditions to South America (1906–15), where he uncovered Vitcos and Machu Picchu, ancient Inca cities. He was a lieutenant governor of Connecticut (1923–24) and a US senator (1925–33). His works include *Inca Land* (1922) and *Lost City of the Incas* (1948).

bingo (former names: tombola; housy-housy) A gambling game that developed in the 1880s from the children's game of lotto. Each player buys a card containing lines of random numbers from 1 to 75, usually. The five vertical columns of numbers on the card are headed by the letters B-I-N-G-O. Balls, or slips or disks of cardboard or plastic, each with a letter and a number, are drawn and as they are called out, the players cover corresponding squares on their cards with counters; the first person to complete a line either vertically, horizontally, or diagonally, on the card wins.

binoculars A portable optical instrument used for magnifying distant objects. It consists of two telescopes fixed side by side, one for each eye, inside which there are a number of lenses for magnifying and focusing the image and usually prisms for altering the direction of the light and thus increasing the effective length of the telescope.

binomial nomenclature A system devised by *Linnaeus in the 18th century for the scientific naming of plants and animals, each species being identifed by two internationally recognized Latin names—the name of the genus (written with an initial capital letter) followed by the name of the species. The names are usually written in italics and the specific name may be followed by the author's name, usually abbreviated. Thus the wolf is *Canis lupus* L (for Linnaeus).

binomial theorem The theorem, discovered by *Newton in 1676, that the quantity $(a + n)^n$, where n is an integer, can be expanded in a series: $(a + b)^n = a^n + na^{n-1}b + [n(n-1) a^{n-2}b^2] / 2! + [n(n-1)(n-2) a^{n-3}b^3] / 3! + \ldots + b^n$ where, for example, 3! (called factorial three) is $3 \times 2 \times 1$.

binturong A mammal, *Arctictis binturong*, of SE Asia, closely related to the *palm civets. It has a dark-gray shaggy coat, tufted ears, shorts legs, and a bushy prehensile tail (24 in [60 cm] long): the animal measures up to 5 ft (1.5 m) long from head to tail. Binturongs live in trees and feed mainly on fruit and other vegetation; they are more vocal than civets, often growling or hissing.

bioassay A test of the strength or quantity of a biologically active substance by a comparison of its effect upon animals, isolated tissues, or microorganisms with that of a standard preparation.

Bío-Bío River A river in Chile. Rising in the Andes, it flows generally NW to enter the Pacific Ocean and forms the S boundary of middle Chile. Length: about 240 mi (390 km).

biochemistry The scientific study of the chemical composition and reactions of living organisms. Development of the appropriate analytical technique has enabled great advances in modern biochemistry, which dates from the 1900s. Central to biochemistry is *metabolism and the determination of the complex sequence of reactions involved in the digestion of food, the utilization of energy, the manufacture of new tissues, the breakdown of old tissues, and the formation of excretory products. Biochemists are also concerned with the role of *genes, *hormones, and *enzymes in initiating and controlling metabolic reactions. This understanding is necessary to determine the requirements of a balanced diet as well as the causes and possible treatment of many diseases.

biodegradable substances Materials that can be broken down by biological processes—such as decomposition by fungi and bacteria—and can therefore be reused by living organisms (*see* recycling). Substances that are **nonbiodegradable**, such as plastics, can persist in the environment, causing pollution.

bioengineering (*or* biomechanics) The application of biological and engineering principles to the design and manufacture of equipment for use in conjunction with biological systems. Examples include artificial limbs, heart pacemakers, heart-lung machines, and life-support systems for astronauts and deepsea divers, etc.

BINTURONG *This Asian mammal can be tamed and reputedly makes an affectionate pet.*

biofeedback Type of alternative medicine in which the patient attempts to treat chronic problems such as pain and headaches by focusing on the desired goal. Through watching the data output by sensors connected to the body, the patient learns to alter such functions as heart rate and muscle tension to lessen discomfort.

biogenetic law (*or* recapitulation theory) A theory postulated by Ernst *Haeckel in 1866 stating that the development of an animal in its lifetime (*see* ontogeny) tends to recapitulate the evolutionary development of its ancestors (*see* phylogeny).

biological control The control of pests by the use of living organisms. The controlling agent is usually a predator, parasite, or disease of the pest organism. For example, the virus disease myxomatosis was introduced to Australia and Britain to control the rabbit population. Recent methods of controlling insect pests include the release of sterile males to mate among the population, so reducing the number of eggs laid. Biological control avoids the indiscriminate action and environmental pollution of chemical pesticides.

biological sciences The scientific disciplines concerned with the study of life. The earliest recorded biological observations come from ancient Egypt but it was Greek and Roman scholars, such as *Aristotle, *Hippocrates, and *Galen, who made the first detailed anatomical descriptions of living things. Not until the 16th the 17th centuries were further advances made by such anatomists as *Vesalius and William *Harvey. The introduction of the microscope in the 17th century enabled microorganisms, tissues, and individual cells (*see* cytology) to be observed for the first time.

By the 18th century a wealth of descriptions of individual organisms had been produced and attempts were made to arrange them into related groups (*see* taxonomy), notably by *Linnaeus, whose system is still in use today, and Georges *Cuvier, whose studies of fossilized animal remains founded the science of paleontology. Various theories of *evolution culminated in the publication of Charles *Darwin's theory of the origin of species in 1858. Six years later, Gregor *Mendel reported his findings on the principles of inheritance, which are fundamental to *genetics, although it was not until 1953 that James *Watson and Francis *Crick determined the molecular structure of *DNA—the genetic material.

During the 20th century progress in *biochemistry, *physiology, *cell biology, and *biophysics has been made possible by innovations in microscopical and analytical techniques, such as electron microscopy, chromatography, and the use of *radioactive tracers. Biological discoveries have revolutionized both medicine and agriculture. *See also* botany; ecology; ethology; zoology.

biological warfare The use of disease-causing microorganisms as weapons. In World War I, the Germans infected Allied cavalry horses with bacteria causing *glanders. Although biological warfare is now officially banned by the major powers, research continues in developing new strains of such organisms as the plague bacterium (*Pasteurella pestis*) and the smallpox virus. The organisms are required to be highly virulent (but not necessarily lethal) and would be deployed probably in an aerosol package dropped by bombers or delivered in the warhead of a missile. Alternatively, they could be added to water or food supplies in a covert operation.

bioluminescence The production of light by living organisms, including certain bacteria, fungi, and various animals (e.g. fireflies and glowworms, protozoans, and bony fishes). In some the *luminescence is due to symbiotic light-producing bacteria. The light is emitted by the compound luciferin when it is oxidized: the reaction is catalyzed by an enzyme, luciferase. The emission of light may be continuous, as in bacteria, or intermittent, as in the flash of fireflies. The significance of bioluminescence is unknown in most species, but in some it serves to attract mates or lure prey.

biomass The total weight (mass) of all living organisms (or of all members of a particular species) found in a given area. Biomass is expressed as mass per unit area.

biomass energy. *See* alternative energy.

biome A geographical region that is characterized by a predominant type of vegetation and associated fauna. Examples include grassland, desert, tropical forest, etc.

bionics The study of living systems in order to design artificial systems based on similar principles. It assumes that most living creatures have adapted in the best possible way to their environments. The applications of bionics include the design of a ship's propeller modeled on a fish's tail and the use of knowledge of nerve physiology in data-processing systems.

bionomics. *See* ecology.

biophysics The scientific discipline concerned with the explanation of biological phenomena in terms of the laws of physics. Biophysics emerged in the 1940s with the work of such scientists as Max *Perutz and John *Kendrew, who applied the phenomenon of *X-ray diffraction to determine the structure of biological molecules; this was followed by Maurice *Wilkins' work on DNA. More recent topics include the nature of the nervous impulse, the properties of biological membranes, the mechanism of muscle contraction, and the operation of sense organs, showing how aspects of chemistry, physiology, and other biological disciplines are necessarily involved in biophysics.

biopsy The removal of a sample of living tissue from the body for microscopic examination. Biopsies are used to assist in the diagnosis of diseases, including cancer (from biopsies of tumors in the breast, lymphatic system, etc.), jaundice (from a liver biopsy), and anemia (from a bone-marrow biopsy).

biosphere The zone of the earth and its atmosphere that is occupied by living organisms. The most heavily populated regions of the biosphere are the surfaces of land and sea.

Biosphere 2 Controversial scientific experiment on human self-sufficiency, in which eight volunteers were sealed into a three-acre closed ecosystem in Arizona for two years (1991–93). The project's backers hoped to gather data that would help future space colonies and that would educate people about the earth's ecosystem. Although some external help was needed, the Biosphere team was generally successful in recycling water, air, and waste and in raising its own food. Some observers criticized the usefulness of the experiment's results.

biotin. *see* vitamin B complex.

birch A deciduous tree or shrub of the genus *Betula* (40 species), of the N hemisphere. Birches grow to a height of up to 80 ft (25 m) and have thin smooth bark, pale gray or yellowish-brown, that peels off in strips. The glossy leaves are usually triangular, with toothed edges. The flowers are male and female catkins producing tiny winged nuts. Birch wood, especially that of the Eurasian silver birch (*B. pendula*), is used for furniture. Birch bark is used for tanning and roofing, and the bark of the paper birch (*B. papyrifera*) was used by Indians to make birch-bark canoes. Family: *Betulaceae*.

bird A warm-blooded animal belonging to the class *Aves* (about 8600 species), adapted for flight by having forelimbs modified as wings and a body covering of *feathers. Other adaptations include a light skeleton with hollow bones and a large keel-shaped breastbone providing attachment for the powerful flight muscles. The jaws are elongated into a horny bill (teeth are absent or reduced). Birds have good eyesight and color vision and most are active by day, feeding on a wide variety of plant and animal material. Through flight, they have managed to colonize almost every available terrestrial, freshwater, and marine habitat.

Social behavior plays an important part in the life of birds, which show complex patterns of behavior in territorial and courtship displays, *nest building, egg incubation, and care of the young. Many communicate by means of song (*see* songbird) and some undergo long seasonal *migrations.

Birds are of great economic importance to man. The eggs and flesh of many provide food, several species being domesticated and bred for this purpose (*see* poultry). Wildfowl and game birds are hunted for sport, and the feathers of some birds provide ornamental plumes, pillow and duvet stuffings, etc. Other species are pests, for example by damaging crops (particularly cereals) or by fouling buildings in cities. Certain diseases, notably psittacosis, are transmitted to man by birds. Modern birds include both flying and flightless species (*see* ratite); they are grouped into 28 orders, the largest of which is the *Passeriformes* (*see* passerine bird). *See also* ornithology.

bird cherry A small tree, *Prunus padus*, of upland Europe, up to 50 ft (15 m) high with dark bark and pale-green oval leaves, finely serrated around the margins. The sweet-scented white flowers are grouped in loose clusters. The small black bitter-tasting fruits are fermented to make alcoholic drinks. Family: *Rosaceae. See also* cherry.

bird of paradise A bird, 12–25 in (30–65 cm) long, belonging to a family (*Paradisaeidae*; 40 species) occurring in New Guinea and neighboring islands. The male is usually brightly colored, with long tail feathers and ornamental plumes, and performs an acrobatic display to attract the dull-colored female. Their feathers are much prized and were formerly exported for use in ladies' hats.

bird-of-paradise flower A herbaceous perennial plant, *Strelitzia reginae*, native to South Africa and cultivated under glass in temperate regions and as a bedding plant in the tropics. The flower cluster, 8 in (20 cm) long, is orange, scarlet, and blue and resembles a bird's head. The oblong leaves rise to a height of 35 in (90 cm) from the rootstock. Family: *Musaceae* (banana family).

bird of prey A bird that hunts other animals for food, also called raptor. Birds of prey are divided into the noctural hunters, comprising the owls (order *Strigiformes*), and those that hunt by day, comprising the eagles, falcons, hawks, secretary bird, and the vultures (order *Falconiformes*). Live prey is normally taken but the vultures specialize in feeding on carrion. Birds of prey are characterized by their strong hooked bills for tearing flesh, clawed talons, and powerful flight with a high-speed dive onto prey.

Birdseye, Clarence (1886–1956) US inventor and industrialist. He worked on a method of fast-freezing food and packaging it and, by 1924, had founded a company that eventually became General Foods. Continuing to work on better methods of freezing, he accumulated over 300 patents and greatly reduced the amount of time needed for freezing.

bird's nest fern An Old World tropical *fern, *Asplenium nidus*, that has a dense rosette of upward-pointing leaves, 24–48 in (60–120 cm) long, with a central hollow forming a nest in which humus collects. The roots branch into this to obtain water and nutrients. The plant is grown for ornament. Family: *Aspleniaceae*.

bird's nest orchid A widely distributed saprophytic *orchid, *Neottia nidusavis*, most commonly growing in beech woodlands. Named from the dense round cluster of roots at the stem base, it reaches a height of 10–16 in (25–40 cm) and produces spikes of brown flowers in early summer.

bird spider Any of the large *tarantula spiders that may catch and eat small birds.

Birendra Bir Bikram Shah Dev (1945–   ) King of Nepal (1972–   ), following the death of his father Mahendra, whose policies he undertook to follow. He married (1970) Aishwarya Rajya Laxmi Devi Rana.

Birkenhead 53 24N 3 02W A port in NW England, in Merseyside on the Wirral Peninsula, linked with Liverpool across the River Mersey by road and rail tunnels and ferry. An important industrial center, it has ship building, engineering, and flour-milling industries. Population (1981): 123,907.

Birkhoff, George David (1864–1944) US mathematician, who gave the Maxwell-Boltzmann theory of gases a rigorous mathematical basis. He also produced a mathematical theory of aesthetics and a theory of gravitation. *See also* statistical mechanics.

Birmingham 52 30N 1 50W A city in central England, in the West Midlands. Britain's second largest city, it is a center of the motor-vehicles industry and besides general engineering and metal working also produces bicycles, firearms, chemicals, plastics, tires, chocolate, and jewelry. A cultural center, it possesses two universities, Aston University (1966) and Birmingham University (1900). Originally an Anglo-Saxon settlement, its development dates largely from the industrial revolution although its metalworking tradition is much older. It was severely damaged by bombing during World War II. Population (1981): 1,007,000.

Birmingham 33 30N 86 55W A city in Alabama. Settled in 1813, it is the state's largest city and the main industrial center of the South. It has an important iron and steel industry, which uses local iron ore deposits; other industries include chemicals, cement, and cotton. Population (1990): 265,968.

Biró, Laszlo (1900–85) Hungarian inventor, who in 1938 patented the ballpoint pen containing quick-drying ink.

Birobidzhan. *See* Jewish autonomous region.

birthmark A blemish that is present on the skin at birth. Known medically as a nevus, it is usually harmless and may disappear with age. Birthmarks are caused by a defect in the skin cells or by an abnormality of the underlying blood vessels.

birthstone In *astrology, a gemstone associated with a particular date of birth. The wearing of one's birthstone as a lucky charm originated in the ancient belief that certain gems had supernatural powers. The modern list of birthstones is usually as follows: January—garnet; February—amethyst; March—bloodstone; April—diamond; May—emerald; June—pearl; July—ruby; August—sardonyx; September—sapphire; October—opal; November—topaz; December—turquoise.

Biscay, Bay of (French name: Golfe de Gascogne; Spanish name: Golfo de Vizcaya) An inlet of the Atlantic Ocean, off the coast of W France and N Spain. It is comparatively deep and subject to gales and rough seas. The fish caught here include anchovies, cod, sardines, and tuna. Width: about 199 mi (320 km).

Biscayne Bay An inlet of the Atlantic Ocean in SE Florida. Miami is on its N shores and part of the Florida Keys form a buffer between the bay and ocean on the S end. Length: 40 mi (65 km); width: 2–10 mi (3.5–16 km).

bisexuality. *See* homosexuality.

Bishkek (former name: Frunze; name until 1925: Pishpek) 42 53N 74 46E The capital city of Kyrgyzstan, on the Chu River. Industries developed rapidly after World War II and include the manufacture of agricultural machinery, textiles, food, and tobacco products. Population (1987): 632,000.

Bishops' Wars (1639, 1640) The wars fought between the Scots and Charles I of Great Britain following his attempts to enforce the Anglican Prayer Book and government of the Church by bishops on the Presbyterian Scots.

Biskra 34 50N 5 45E An oasis city in N Algeria, on the N edge of the Sahara. It is an important center for the date trade. Population (1987): 128,300.

Bismarck 46 50N 100 48W The capital of North Dakota on the Missouri River. Named for Otto von Bismarck (1873) to entice German investment, it is an agricultural market center. Population (1990): 49,256.

Bismarck, Otto Eduard Leopold, Prince von (1815–98) Prussian statesman; first chancellor of the German Empire (1871–90). A conservative, known as the Iron Chancellor, Bismarck came to prominence after the collapse of the *Revolution of 1848. As Prussian foreign minister (1862–71) he was determined to establish Prussian hegemony in Germany and to undermine Austrian dominance there. He embroiled Austria in war over Schleswig-Holstein and following its defeat in the Austro-Prussian War of 1866 *William I of Prussia became president of the North German Confederation. After victory in the

*Franco-Prussian War (1870–71) William accepted the imperial crown and Bismarck became chancellor of the new German Empire. Bismarck's domestic policy in succeeding years was concerned chiefly with keeping liberalism at bay. He also came into conflict with the Roman Catholic Church (*see* Kulturkampf) and, abroad, presided over the Congress of *Berlin (1878) and formed the *Triple Alliance with Austria and Italy. Losing the support of William II, Bismarck resigned in 1890 over the abolition of antisocialist laws.

DROPPING THE PILOT.

BISMARCK *An English cartoon in Punch (1890) satirizes his resignation following disagreements with the emperor.*

Bismarck Archipelago A group of volcanic islands in the SW Pacific Ocean, in Papua New Guinea. It includes New Britain, New Ireland, and the Admiralty Islands. Area: 19,173 sq mi (49,658 sq km).

bismuth (Bi) A dense white brittle metal, similar in properties to tin and lead. It was first distinguished by C. Geoffroy in 1753. It is obtained as a by-product of lead, copper, tin, silver, and gold refining and also occurs naturally as the pure metal, the sulfide (Bi_2S_3), and the oxide (Bi_2O_3). It has unusual properties for a metal, having low thermal and electrical conductivity, and decreasing in volume on melting. With tin and cadmium it is used to make low-melting alloys in *fire prevention systems. At no 83; at wt 208.9808; mp 521°F (271.3°C); bp 2843°F (1560°C).

bison A massive hoofed ☐mammal belonging to the genus *Bison* (2 species). The North American bison (*B. bison*) was once abundant on the plains but is now found only on reserves. Over 60 in (150 cm) at the shoulder and weighing up to 2200 lb (1000 kg), it has a shaggy mane and low-slung head with incurved horns. The smaller European bison (*B. bonasus*), also called wisent, is now found only in zoos. Family: **Bovidae*.

Bissau 11 50N 15 37N The capital and chief port of Guinea-Bissau, on the Geba estuary. Founded by the Portuguese in 1687, it became capital of Portuguese Guinea in 1941. In 1974 Madina do Boe was chosen as the site of a planned new capital. Population (1988 est): 138,000.

bistort A perennial herb, *Polygonum bistorta*, of temperate Europe, also called snake-root or Easter-ledges. The upper leaves are triangular, with sheathing bases, and there is a dense terminal spike of tiny pink flowers. Family: *Polygonaceae* (dock family).

bit A *bi*nary digi*t*. The basic unit of information in information theory and computer memory stores. It is the amount of information needed to specify one of two alternatives, i.e. to distinguish between 1 and 0 in the *binary notation.

Bithynia An ancient region of Asia Minor, S of the Black Sea. Of Thracian origin, the Bithynians long remained independent, resisting the aggression of the Achaemenians, Alexander the Great, and the Seleucids. By the 3rd century BC it had become a kingdom and expanded territorially and commercially. Conflict with Pergamum and later Pontus brought Roman involvement. Bequeathed by Nicomedes IV (reigned 91–74 BC) to Rome, Bithynia became an increasingly important province as Rome's fronters expanded E.

Bitola (Turkish name: Monastir) 41 01N 21 21E A city in Macedonia. After five centuries of Turkish rule, it was taken by the Serbs in 1912. Its products include sugar, carpets, and textiles. Population (1981): 137,800.

bittern A bird belonging to the subfamily *Botaurinae*, occurring throughout the world in swamps and reedbeds. The European bittern (*Botaurus stellaris*) is a solitary bird, about 28 in (70 cm) long, with a yellow-brown dark-streaked plumage that provides excellent camouflage. The male produces a "booming" call. The little bittern (*Ixobrychus minutus*) is only 14 in (34 cm) long with buffish-white wing patches. Family: *Ardeidae* (herons, etc.).

Bitterroot Range A mountain chain in W Montana and E Idaho, part of the Rocky Mountains. It forms most of the border between the two states and includes the Beaverhead Mountains. The highest point is Scott Peak (11,393 ft; 3473 m); the Continental Divide runs through the S portion of the range.

bittersweet A perennial plant, the woody *nightshade.

bitumen The tarry residue left after *distillation of oil, lignite, or coal, consisting almost entirely of a mixture of carbon with large *hydrocarbon molecules. Its principal uses are in roadmaking, waterproofing buildings, and binding cement. Bitumen sometimes occurs naturally in asphalt lakes.

bivalve A *mollusk belonging to the class *Bivalvia* (also called *Lamellibranchia* and *Pelecypoda*; about 10,000 species). Bivalves are characterized by having two hinged shell plates (valves) and include *clams, *mussels, *oysters, and *scallops. Bivalves inhabit both salt and fresh water: some are free swimming; others burrow in sand, mud, or rock. They draw water between the shell valves using their ciliated gills and inner surfaces (mantle) to extract oxygen and food particles from it. Most bivalves are of separate sexes but some are hermaphrodite. Some hermaphrodite bivalves, including *Ostrea* oysters, incubate the fertilized eggs.

Bizerte (*or* Bizerta) 37 18N 9 52E A port in N Tunisia, on the Mediterranean Sea. It dates back to Phoenician times as a port and was known as Hippo Zarytus or Diarrhytus. Retained by the French as a naval base following Tunisian independence (1956), fighting broke out before France surrendered the base in 1963. Population: 62,000.

Bizet, Georges (Alexandre César Léopold B.; 1838–75) French composer. He studied under *Gounod and *Halévy and in 1855 produced his first major work, the symphony in C major. He won the Prix de Rome in 1857. Among his best-known works are the incidental music to *Daudet's play *L'Arlésienne* (1872) and the opera *Carmen* (1873–74), which was at first disliked by the public and attacked by the critics. This censure hastened Bizet's death, three months after the premiere; it is now one of the world's most popular operas.

Bjerknes, Vilhelm Friman Koren (1862–1951) Norwegian meteorologist and physicist. A pioneer of weather forecasting, his 1897 mathematical models of atmospheric and oceanic motions led to his full-scale meteorological predictions (1904). His son **Jakob Bjerknes,** also a meteorologist, initiated the use of high-altitude photography in weather surveys and forecasting (1952).

Björling, Jussi (Johann Jonaton B.; 1911–60) Swedish tenor. Trained at the Royal Opera School, Stockholm, he made his debut there in 1930. He sang in all the world's major opera houses.

Bjørnson, Bjørnstjerne (Martinius) (1832–1910) Norwegian novelist, poet, and playwright, who was also active in politics and worked as a theater director and newspaper editor. His works, based on the sagas and his knowledge of rural life, include the novel *På Guds veje* (*In God's Way*; 1889) and the plays *En fallit* (*The Bankrupt*; 1875) and *Det ny system* (*The New System*; 1879). He is also remembered as the author of the Norwegian national anthem. He was awarded the Nobel Prize in 1903.

Black, Hugo (LaFayette) (1886–1971) US jurist, politician, associate justice of the Supreme Court (1937–71). After holding several government jobs in Alabama, he served in the US Senate as a Democrat (1927–37) where he supported the establishment of the Tennessee Valley Authority and the Wages and Hours bill of 1937. Appointed to the Supreme Court by Pres. Franklin D. Roosevelt in 1937, he was generally known as a liberal and advocated a broad interpretation of the Constitution, especially of the rights guaranteed in the First Amendment.

Black, Joseph (1728–99) Scottish physician and chemist, born in Bordeaux, who became professor at Glasgow University and later at Edinburgh University. He independently discovered carbon dioxide, deduced its presence in air, and discovered the bicarbonate compounds. His work on heat led him to introduce the concepts caloric, heat of fusion, latent heat, specific heat, and thermal capacity. He was also the first to distinguish between heat and temperature.

Black and Tans The soldiers recruited by the British Government to fight the IRA in Ireland in 1920–21. Their name derives from their uniform, khaki with black caps and belts. They acted with great severity and were hated by the Irish.

black bear The native bear of North American forests, *Ursus* (or *Euarctos*) *americanus*. American black bears grow to a weight of 330 lb (150 kg); they climb well and eat berries, pine cones, and grass as well as small animals.

The name is also used for the Himalayan black, or moon, bear, *Selenarctos thibetanus*, which inhabits forests of central and E Asia and has a white V-shaped mark on its chest.

Blackbeard. *See* Teach, Edward.

black beetle. *See* cockroach.

blackberry (*or* bramble) A prickly scrambling shrub, *Rubus fruticosus* (an aggregate species), occurring worldwide. The stems, up to 16 ft (5 m) long, root wherever they touch the ground. The dark-green leaves usually consist of five oval toothed leaflets and the pinkish-white flowers are borne in terminal clusters. The fruits, each of which consists of an aggregate of several small berries, are eaten raw or made into pies, jellies, preserves, etc. Family: *Rosaceae*.

blackbird A songbird, *Turdus merula*, that is one of the commonest European birds, particularly in urban areas. The male, about 10 in (25 cm) long, is black with a bright-yellow bill and eye ring; the larger female is dark brown with a dark bill. Blackbirds feed chiefly on worms and other invertebrates but will also eat scraps. Family: *Turdidae* (thrushes).

blackbirding The kidnapping of Polynesians to provide slave labor for the sugar and cotton plantations of Australia and the South Pacific islands. Legislation against it was passed in Australia (1868) but was not effective, and it was not until the beginning of the 20th century that the practice died out.

black body A theoretical body that absorbs all the electromagnetic radiation falling upon it. When heated it emits radiation (black-body radiation) having a continuous distribution of wavelengths with a maximum at a particular wavelength, which depends only on the temperature of the body.

blackbuck A common antelope, *Antilope cervicapra*, of Indian grasslands. Blackbucks are about 31 in (80 cm) high; females are yellowish brown and males darker, both with white underparts. Males have ridged spiral horns up to 26 in (65 cm) long. They live in herds of 10–30 animals, grazing at dawn and dusk.

Blackburn 53 45N 2 29W A city in NW England, in Lancashire on the Leeds-Liverpool Canal. Traditionally a cotton-weaving town, its chief industry now is engineering (including carpet machinery); textiles, electronics, paper, and paint are also important. Population (1981): 88,236.

blackcap A European *warbler, *Sylvia atricapillus*. About 6 in (14 cm) long, it has an olive-brown plumage with paler underparts and a darker cap (black in the male and reddish-brown in the female). Blackcaps feed chiefly on insects but—before migrating—they eat fruit to build up energy reserves.

Black Codes (1865–66) Laws enacted by southern states regarding the rights of the free blacks. Interracial marriages were prohibited, public facilities were segregated, and work and court rights were restricted. The Civil Rights Act (1866) and the Fourteenth Amendment to the Constitution (1868) forced the states to repeal these laws.

Black Consciousness The recognition by minority black communities throughout the world of their identity, history, and culture, as distinct from that of whites. Political and social movements contributing to the development of black consciousness in the US have included the Universal Negro Improvement Association in the 1920s, the National Association for the Advancement of Colored People, the National Urban League (1911), the activities of civil rights leaders such as Martin Luther *King and Jesse *Jackson and the *Black Muslims.

blackcurrant A shrub, *Ribes nigrum*, native to most of Europe and N Asia and widely cultivated. The stems and three-lobed leaves emit a characteristic smell. The drooping clusters of greenish bell-shaped flowers develop into edible black berries, used in preserves, wine, beverages, and a source of vitamin C. Family: *Grossulariaceae* (gooseberry family).

Black Death The worst outbreak of *plague, principally bubonic but also pneumonic and septicemic, of the medieval period. Originating in the Far East, it spread through Europe and England in May 1348. Estimates of mortality rates vary from 20% to more than 50%. The outbreak had a profound effect not only on demographic trends but also upon rural society and the economy as a whole. Further outbreaks followed in the 1350s and 1370s.

black earth. *See* chernozem.

Blackett, Patrick Maynard Stuart, Baron (1897–1974) British physicist. He made the first cloud-chamber photographs showing nuclear disintegrations as a result of bombardment (1925) and identified the disintegration products. He improved the Wilson cloud-chamber detector and used it in the study of cosmic radiation, for which work he received the Nobel Prize (1948).

black-eyed Susan A North American perennial herb of the genus *Rudbeckia* (19 species) with showy flower heads, the rays generally yellow, darker at the base and disk flowers blackish and prominent. The plants grow to a height of 24 in (60 cm) and have rough narrow leaves. Also called coneflowers, many species (e.g. *R. fulgida* var *speciosa*) are cultivated in gardens. Family: *Compositae*.

blackfly Any black *aphid, especially the bean aphid (*Aphis fabae*). Bean aphids occur in masses on beans, spinach, dock, etc., in summer months. They overwinter as fertilized eggs in *Euonymus, Viburnum*, and *Philadelphus* trees.

black fly A small humpbacked fly, also called buffalo gnat and turkey gnat, belonging to a family (*Simuliidae*; about 300 species) of worldwide distribution. The bloodsucking females attack man and domestic animals and some are vectors of disease. In Africa, for example, *Simulium damnosum* and *S. neavei* transmit a filarial worm that causes "river blindness."

Blackfoot A North American Indian people inhabiting areas of Saskatchewan and Alberta in Canada and Montana in the US. The Blackfoot nation is actually a confederacy of three main sub-groups: the Siksikas, the Piegans (Pikuni), and the Bloods (Kainah). The language of all three groups is *Algonkian. In the 19th century, the Blackfoot were known as nomadic buffalo hunters and skilled horsemen who resisted the encroachment of settlers into their territory. The total Blackfoot population today is approximately 10,000.

Black Forest (German name: Schwarzwald) An extensively forested mountainous area in SW Germany, in Baden-Württemberg E of the Rhine Valley. Covered chiefly with coniferous forests, the timber industry is important with associated cuckoo-clock making and woodcrafts; it is also a popular tourist area.

black grouse A Eurasian *grouse, *Lyrurus tetrix*, of moorlands. The male (also called blackcock), 20 in (50 cm) long, has a glossy black plumage and a lyre-shaped tail; the female is reddish brown. Both have conspicuous red wattles above the eyes. In the breeding season the males perform an elaborate courtship display (lek) on a communal display ground.

Black Hand A Serbian secret society pledged to the liberation of Serbs from Habsburg and Ottoman rule. On June 28, 1914, they were responsible for the assassination of the Austrian archduke, Francis Ferdinand, an event contributing to the outbreak of World War I.

Black Hawk War (1832) A conflict between the US and the Sauk and Fox Indians. The Indian chief Black Hawk (1767–1838) resisted attempts to force his people W of the Mississippi River and near La Crosse, Wis., nearly a thousand Indians were massacred by the US army despite a flag of surrender.

Black Hills Mountains in SW South Dakota and NE Wyoming between the Belle Fourche River on the N and the Cheyenne River on the S. The highest point is Harney Peak (7242 ft; 2208 m). Its features include the Black Hills National Forest, Wind Cave National Park, Mount Rushmore National Memorial, and Devil's Tower National Monument.

black hole A celestial "object" that has undergone such total *gravitational collapse that no light can escape from it: its *escape velocity exceeds the speed of light (*see* velocity of light). Once a collapsing object's radius has shrunk below a critical value (the Schwarzschild radius) it becomes a black hole; for a star, this radius is about 6 mi (10 km) or less. The surface having this radius is called the event horizon of the black hole. The object will continue to contract until compressed to an infinite density at a single central point—a singularity. A black hole is thus a region of greatly distorted space (and time) the size of which increases with the mass of the contracting material.

No black hole has as yet been unambiguously detected. The collapsed core remaining from the *supernova explosions of massive stars are, however, promising candidates, especially if they are components of a *binary star and thus more easy to detect. The X-ray binary Cygnus X-1 has a probable black-hole component. It has been suggested that blackholes of immense size and mass (10^6 to 10^9 solar masses) may exist at the centers of certain galaxies and be powerful sources of energy.

Black Hole of Calcutta A small cell 18 ft $\times$ 12 ft (5.5 m $\times$ 4.5 m) in which over one hundred British soldiers were allegedly confined overnight in 1756. According to their commander John Holwell fewer than 25 men survived. The outrage was perpetrated by the Nawab of Bengal, who, objecting to the fortification of Calcutta by the East India Company, attacked and defeated the British garrison.

blackmail In law, the criminal offense of making any unreasonable demand with a view to gain, backed up by a threat of violence or injury to the person involved or to his property or by a threat of exposing his immorality or misconduct.

black mass An obscene and blasphemous parody of the Roman Catholic mass, celebrated by satanists in honor of the devil. A naked woman is usually present at or on the altar and participants take hallucinatory drugs or other potions. *See* satanism.

Blackmore, R(ichard) D(oddridge) (1825–1900) British historical novelist, famous chiefly for *Lorna Doone* (1869), a romance set on Exmoor during the Restoration.

Blackmun, Harry Andrew (1908–) US jurist, lawyer, and teacher; Supreme Court associate justice (1970–). After graduation from Harvard Law School (1932), he entered private practice in Minneapolis (1934), taught law at the University of Minnesota (1945–47), and was judge of the US 8th circuit court of appeals. He was appointed to the Supreme Court in 1970 by President *Nixon. He was conservative in his opinions on criminal matters, but was a moderate liberal regarding civil rights, maintaining in *Roe* v. *Wade* (1973) that abortion is the private choice of a woman.

Black Muslims Members of the Nation of Islam movement founded in Detroit in 1930 by W. D. Fard, known also as Walli Farrad and Wallace Fard Muhammad, and believed by Black Muslims to be the Mahdi or Savior. After the disappearance of Fard in 1933, the movement was led by Elijah Muhammad (1897–1975) and won support among blacks in northern industrial cities. One of the movement's most well-known leaders, Malcolm X (1925–65) was assassinated. Restricted to blacks, it aims to establish a new Islamic state and follows many Muslim practices, although some of its beliefs are unorthodox. After his father's death, Wallace Muhammad assumed leadership, bringing the sect closer to orthodox Islam.

Blackpool 53 50N 3 03W A resort in NW England, on the Lancashire coast. It is an entertainment center famous for its Tower (modeled on the Eiffel Tower), Pleasure Beach, and illuminations; it is also a conference center. Population (1981): 147,854.

Black Prince, Edward the. *See* Edward, the Black Prince.

Black Sea An inland sea bounded by Bulgaria, Romania, Moldova, Ukraine, Russia, Georgia, and Turkey; it is connected to the Mediterranean Sea via the Bosporus in the SW and to the sea of Azov in the N. The principal towns on its coast are Burgas and Varna in Bulgaria, Constanţa in Romania, Odessa and Sevastopol in Ukraine, and Trabzon in Turkey. Its salinity is kept low principally by the influx of fresh water from the Danube and Dnepr Rivers.

Blackshirts The colloquial name for the Fasci de Combattimento, founded by Mussolini in 1919 and forming the backbone of Italian *fascism. They wore distinctive black shirts; their name is also used in reference to the *SS.

black snake A small-headed venomous snake, *Pseudeschis porphyriacus*, of Australian wetlands. About 5 ft (1.5 m) long, it is blue-black with a red belly. Family: *Elapidae* (cobras, mambas, coral snakes). In North America the name is given to a nonvenomous snake, *Zamenis constrictor*.

Blackstone, Sir William (1723–80) British jurist. His fame rests largely on his *Commentaries on the Laws of England* (1765–69), a series of lectures delivered at Oxford. Highly influential in legal education, they presented the first comprehensive account of English law. Blackstone became a member of Parliament in 1791 and a judge in 1770.

black swan The only Australian *swan, *Cygnus atratus*. Almost 40 in (1 m) in length, both sexes have a pure black plumage, red bill, and a trumpeting call.

blackthorn (*or* sloe) A thorny shrub, *Prunus spinos*, forming dense thickets, up to 13 ft (4 m) high, in many parts of Europe and Asia. The clusters of white flowers usually appear before the leaves, which are oval and toothed. The bitter-tasting blue-black stone fruits are used to flavor sloe gin; the hard wood is used for walking sticks and tool handles. Family: *Rosaceae*.

blackwater fever A serious complication of malaria in which the malarial parasite causes widespread destruction of red blood cells, leading to the excretion of blood pigments in the urine (which becomes dark brown—hence the name). The patient has a high fever and jaundice and requires careful nursing, with blood transfusions if necessary.

Blackwell, Elizabeth (1821–1910) US physician, first woman doctor in the US. Born in England, she came to the US (1932) with her family and studied at Geneva Medical School (1847–49) in New York, the only school to admit her, and at various schools abroad. She opened her own hospital (1853; known as New York Infirmary from 1857), staffed it with women, and established training for nurses. The Women's Medical College of the New York Infirmary was founded in 1868. She returned to England in 1869 where she founded and taught at the London School of Medicine for Women.

black widow A venomous *spider, also called button or redback spider, that belongs to a genus (*Latrodectus*; about 6 species) found in tropical and subtropical regions. The female of *L. mactans*, the most common North American species, has a shiny black body, 1 in (25 mm) long, with red markings on the abdomen. (The male is about 0.24 in [6 mm] long and usually killed and eaten by the female after mating). The bite of this spider—although serious—is rarely fatal. Family: *Theridiidae*.

bladder In anatomy, any hollow organ containing fluid, especially the urinary bladder situated in the pelvis, into which urine drains from the *kidneys (via the ureters). Urine is stored in the bladder and released at intervals by relaxation of a circular (sphincter) muscle at its opening into the urethra (which leads to the exterior). Bladder emptying is normally under voluntary control. *See also* enuresis.

bladderwort A plant of the widely distributed genus *Utricularia* (about 200 species, many tropical). Most bladderworts are submerged aquatic plants with finely divided leaves bearing small bladders, which trap tiny aquatic animals by a trapdoor mechanism triggered by sensitive hairs. The two-lipped tubular flowers protrude above the water. Some bladderworts are troublesome weeds of ricefields. Family: *Lentibulariaceae*.

Blaine, James Gillespie (1830–93) US politician and statesman. A Republican, he served in the US House of Representatives (1863–76) and was speaker (1869–75). He became a US senator in 1876 and was appointed secretary of state by Pres. James A. Garfield in 1880. Blaine was the Republican candidate for president in 1884 and again served as secretary of state (1889–92) under Pres. Benjamin Harrison. He was outspoken in advocating the abolition of slavery; later, he was instrumental in securing American interests in the Panama Canal.

Blake, William (1757–1827) British visionary poet, painter, and engraver. His books of poems, the texts of which he engraved and illustrated, include *Songs of Innocence* (1789), *Songs of Experience* (1794), various "Prophetic Books," *Milton* (1808), and *Jerusalem* (1820). All were influenced by his unorthodox Christian and political beliefs and by such mystics as *Böhme. As an artist his imaginative watercolors for *The Book of Job* (1826) and Dante's *Divine Comedy* (1827) were inspired by his visions, gothic sculpture, and engravings after Michelangelo. Although largely unrecognized by his generation, he was a precursor of Romanticism.

Blanc, Louis (1811–82) French socialist. A utopian and revolutionary, from 1839 Blanc propagated his doctrines of economic equality in his journal *Revue du progrès*; the axiom "from each according to his ability, to each according to his needs" formed the basis of his thought. Although a member of the provisional government in the *Revolution of 1848, he found little support for his views among his colleagues and fled to England. Returning to Paris in 1870, he remained active in left-wing causes until his death. His books include *Organisation du travail* (1840).

Blanche of Castile (c. 1188–1252) The daughter of Alfonso VIII of Castile, she married (1200) *Louis VIII of France. As regent of France for her husband (1223–26) and her son *Louis IX (1226–36, 1248–52), she ruled firmly, suppressing a revolt of the nobility and effecting peace with England.

Bland-Allison Act (1878) US law that regulated the federal purchase and coinage of silver. Congressman Richard P. Bland (1835–99) campaigned for unlimited coinage of silver, which was unacceptable to Congress. When modified by Senator William R. Allison (1829–1908), the bill, which put limits on but provided for consistent coinage, passed.

blank verse Unrhymed iambic pentameter lines, the distinctive form of English narrative and dramatic verse since its introduction from Italy in the early 16th century by Henry Howard, Earl of *Surrey. It was used in the plays of *Marlowe and *Shakespeare. The form allows considerable variation and has been used by most major English poets to suit their different ends: in *Milton's

Paradise Lost (1667) it is formal and grand, in *Wordsworth's *Prelude* (1805) it is intimate and casual.

WILLIAM BLAKE *An engraving from The Book of Job. These biblical illustrations, of which Blake produced 22, were commissioned in 1821 and engraved 1823–25.*

Blanqui, Louis Auguste (1805–81) French revolutionary. Interested in the practice of revolution rather than in abstract ideas, Blanqui introduced the notion, later taken up by Marx, that revolutions must begin with the temporary dictatorship of a revolutionary elite devoted to the socialist cause. From 1830 he built up a network of secret societies committed to violent insurrection. In 1871, although in prison, he was elected president of the *Commune of Paris. His followers, the Blanquists, joined with the Marxists in 1881.

Blantyre (*or* Blantyre-Limbe) 15 46S 35 00E The largest city in Malawi, in the Shire Highlands. In 1956 it was linked with the nearby town of Limbe, a major railroad center, and is Malawi's chief commercial and industrial center. Industries include distilling, textiles, and cigarette production. Population (1987 est): 333,000.

Blarney 51 56N 8 34W A village in the Republic of Ireland, in Co Cork. Blarney Castle contains the famous Blarney Stone, which is kissed in order to receive the gift of "blarney" or smooth talk.

Blasco Ibáñez, Vicente (1867–1928) Spanish novelist. He wrote many novels set in Valencia but is best known for his World War I novels, especially *The Four Horsemen of the Apocalypse* (1916), three times filmed. He was frequently penalized for his political activities and in 1923 exiled himself to France.

blast furnace A furnace heated by solid fuel, usually coke, through which a blast of air is blown to aid combustion. Blast furnaces are used in the *smelting of ore. In steel making, iron ore, coke, and limestone are poured in at the top of a vertical furnace and hot air is blown in at the bottom to burn the coke. Molten iron is drawn off at the bottom. A glassy waste, called slag, is also produced.

blastula A hollow sphere of cells (blastomeres) produced by repeated *cleavage of a fertilized egg cell (zygote). It is an early stage in embryonic development, before differentiation into tissues and organs has begun. A blastula consists of an outer layer (the blastoderm) surrounding a cavity (the blastocoel).

Blaue Reiter, Der. *See* Blue Rider, The.

Blavatsky, Helen Petrovna (1831–91) Russian theosophist, who founded the Theosophical Society in New York in 1875. She later established a following in India, but her claims to supernatural powers were discredited by scientific investigations during the 1880s and 1890s. Her best-known book is *Isis Unveiled* (1877). *See also* theosophy.

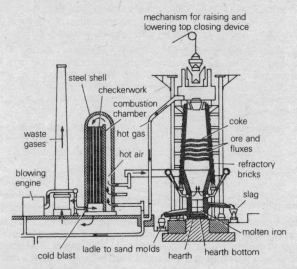

BLAST FURNACE

bleaching The whitening, lightening, or removing of color by chemical treatment, exposure to sunlight, air, or moisture. Most bleaching agents are oxidizing agents, which convert a pigment into an oxidized colorless form. Examples are hydrogen peroxide, *bleaching powder, and hypochlorites. In some processes reducing agents, such as sulfur dioxide, are used. Bleaching is an important part of textile and paper manufacture.

bleaching powder (or chloride of lime) A whitish powder containing calcium hypochlorite (Ca(OCl)$_2$), calcium chloride (CaCl$_2$), calcium hydroxide (Ca(OH)$_2$), and water. It reacts with dilute acids to produce chlorine, which acts as a bleaching agent.

bleak A fish, *Alburnus alburnus*, related to the *carp, with a slender silvery-green body, about 8 in (20 cm) long. It lives in schools near the surface of fresh waters in N Europe and feeds on invertebrates. The scales are used in the manufacture of artificial pearls.

bleeding. See hemorrhage.

bleeding heart An ornamental plant of the genus *Dicentra*, especially *D. spectabilis* from Siberia and Japan and *D. eximia* from North America. They are perennials with arching stems, up to 35 in (90 cm) long, bearing strings of large rose-red heart-shaped flowers with whitish tips, which glisten when the blooms are fresh. Some species have attractive fernlike foliage. Family: *Fumariaceae*.

Bleeding Kansas (1854–56) Name given to Kansas during conflicts between pro-slavery and abolitionist settlers. Bloody skirmishes among the territory's settlers were common before President Pierce established a fragile peace in 1856.

Blenheim, Battle of (August 13, 1704) The battle won by the Duke of *Marlborough and *Eugene of Savoy against the French army in the War of the *Spanish Succession. It was fought at Blenheim (now Blindheim) on the Danube River. Blenheim Palace was built for Marlborough by a grateful government.

Blenkinsop, John (1783–1831) British engineer, who built the first practical steam locomotive (1812), a twin-cylinder engine driving cogs that engaged with rack rails. It was used for transporting coal from Middleton to Leeds.

blenny A small fish belonging to a family (*Bleniidae*; about 300 species) found among rocks in shallow waters of tropical and temperate seas. Blennies have an elongated scaleless body with a blunt nose, a long dorsal fin, and one- to three-rayed pelvic fins located in front of the larger pectoral fins. Many have small tentacles on their heads. The name is also used for several other fish of the order *Perciformes*.

Blériot, Louis (1872–1936) French aviator. Beginning his career as a motor-car engineer, he was the first to fly the English Channel (1909), from Calais to Dover, in a monoplane. He later became a manufacturer of aircraft.

blesbok A small fast-running South African antelope, *Damaliscus dorcas*. About 44 in (110 cm) high at the shoulder, blesboks are red with a white muzzle, rump, and shanks and have lyre-shaped ridged horns. Bonteboks (*D. dorcas dorcas*) are a subspecies with a larger rump patch and more white on the legs.

blewits An edible *mushroom, *Tricholoma* (or *Lepista*) *saevum*, occurring mainly in open pastures. It has a bluish-gray stalk and a flat clay-colored cap, 2–5 in (6–12 cm) in diameter, producing pale-pink spores. The wood blewits (*T. nudum*) has a lilac or purple cap and is usually found beneath trees. It also is edible. Family: *Tricholomataceae*.

Bligh, William (1754–1817) British admiral. He accompanied *Cook on his second voyage around the world and in 1787 was sent to Tahiti on the *Bounty* to collect specimens of the breadfruit tree. Setting sail for home, his crew mutinied and deserted, leaving Bligh and 18 officers aboard a small boat without maps.

He eventually reached safety. He was made governor of New South Wales (1805–08) where another mutiny took place. (*See* Rum Rebellion.)

blight A severe disease of plants caused by pests, fungi, or other agents or by a mineral deficiency. Symptoms commonly include spotting followed by wilting, and the plant eventually withers and dies. The notorious potato blight that devastated Ireland in the mid-19th century was caused by the fungus *Phytophthora infestans*. Control measures against blights vary according to the cause of the disease.

blindness Partial or complete loss of sight (degrees of visual impairment less severe than total loss of sight are classified as blindness for administrative purposes). Sudden blindness may be caused by direct injury to the eye or to the part of the brain that receives the visual signals. Blindness that develops gradually is caused by a wide variety of diseases, including *trachoma, *glaucoma, *cataracts, diabetes mellitus, and tumors (especially of the pituitary gland), that compress the optic nerve. There are various aids available for the visually handicapped, including books in *Braille or on tape or records and specially trained *guide dogs. In many countries the blind are entitled to special education and financial benefits. *See also* color blindness.

blindworm. *See* slowworm.

blister An accumulation of fluid (usually colorless serum) within the skin. Blisters can be caused by continuous friction, sensitivity to chemicals, and *burns. They may also develop in certain diseases, including chickenpox. Blisters usually heal spontaneously, but some (especially severe burns or those on the feet, in contact with shoes) require dressings. They should not be burst intentionally as this provides an entrance for infection.

blister beetle A brightly colored beetle, about 0.4–0.6 in (10–15 mm) long, belonging to a widely distributed family (*Meloidae*; about 2000 species), which also includes the *oil beetles. The larvae are parasitic upon other insects, while the adults generally feed on plants—often causing severe damage. Their secretion of cantharidin, a powerful blistering agent, has led to the medicinal use of various European and Asian species, especially *Spanish fly.

Blitzkrieg (German: lightning war) A military tactic aiming to shock and disorganize enemy forces by swift surprise attacks using tanks and aerial bombardment. It was extensively used by the Germans in *World War II in Poland, Belgium, the Netherlands, France, and Africa. It was also used by the US general Patton, in Europe in 1944. The **Blitz** refers to the intensive German air raids on London during the battle of Britain in *World War II. Between July and December 1940, 23,000 civilians died.

Blixen, Karen. *See* Dinesen, Isak.

Bloch, Ernest (1880–1959) Swiss-born composer of Jewish descent. He lived in various countries before taking up residence in the US in 1916. His opera *Macbeth* (1903–09), a rhapsody for cello and orchestra entitled *Schelomo* (1916), *Concerto Grosso* (1925), and *Sacred Service* (1930–33) incorporate Jewish musical elements into a cosmopolitan 20th-century style.

Bloch, Felix (1905–83) US physicist, born in Zurich. After working in Germany he left Europe when Hitler came to power and emigrated to the US, becoming a citizen in 1939. He developed the *nuclear magnetic resonance technique for magnetic field measurements in atomic nuclei, for which he shared the Nobel Prize (1952) with the independent discoverer, E. M. *Purcell. Bloch's concept of magnetic neutron polarization (1934) enabled him, in conjunction with L. *Alvarez, to measure the neutron's magnetic moment. During World War II he worked on the development of the atomic bomb.

Block Island 41 11N 71 35W An island in S Rhode Island, in the Atlantic Ocean at the beginning of Long Island Sound and separated from the mainland by Block Island Sound. The island was discovered by Adriaen Block in 1614; it was settled in 1661, joined the colony in 1664, and became the town of New Shoreham in 1672. Tourism and fishing are its main industries. Length: 7 mi (11.5 km); width: 1.5–3.5 mi (2.5–6 km).

Bloemfontein 29 07S 26 14E The judicial capital of South Africa and the capital of the Orange Free State. Founded in 1846, it is an important transportation and agricultural center. Industrial development is being encouraged with the opening of new gold mines nearby. It has the University of the Orange Free State (1855) and the US universities of Harvard and Michigan have observatories here to take advantage of the dry clear atmosphere. Population (1985): 204,000.

Blois 47 36N 1 20E A city in France, the capital of the Loir-et-Cher department on the Loire River. It has a famous chateau, begun in the 13th century, and trades in wine, brandy, and grain. Population: 51,950.

Blok, Aleksandr Aleksandrovich (1880–1921) The leading Russian symbolist poet. His early poetry, notably *Verses about the Beautiful Lady* (1901–02), celebrated the spiritual fulfillment of his love for Liubov Mendeleyeva, whom he married in 1903. But his love for Russia was the deeper theme, and in *Scythians* (1918) and *The Twelve* (1918) he expressed a revolutionary optimism that soon turned to deep disillusion.

Blondel, Maurice (1861–1949) French philosopher. He invented a philosophy of action, seeking a compromise between intellectualism and pragmatism. His chief works are *Action* (1893), *The Process of Intelligence* (1922), and *Being and Beings* (1935).

Blondin, Charles (Jean-François Gravelet; 1824–97) French acrobat and tightrope walker. In 1859 he walked across a tightrope suspended over Niagara Falls and later repeated the feat several times with various acrobatic variations.

blood The red fluid contained within the arteries and veins and pumped around the body by the *heart. Blood consists of a watery fluid (*see* plasma) in which are suspended various blood cells—the red cells (*see* erythrocyte), containing the red oxygen-carrying pigment hemoglobin, and several kinds of white cells (*see* leukocyte), concerned with the body's defense mechanisms. The *platelets are small particles involved in blood clotting. Blood acts as a medium for transporting oxygen, carbon dioxide, digested food, hormones, waste materials, salts, and many other substances to and from the tissues. An average adult has about 2.3 fl oz (70 ml) of blood per pound (0.45 kg) of body weight (i.e. about 4.5 qt [5 l] in an average man). Blood is present in all animals with a circulatory system: its functions are similar to that of human blood although its composition varies. *See also* blood clotting; blood groups; circulation of the blood.

Blood, Council of (*or* Council of Troubles; 1567–74) A court established in the Low Countries during the *Revolt of the Netherlands by the Spanish governor, the Duke of *Alba, to suppress Protestantism and particularism. Thousands were imprisoned or executed without proper trial and, following the arrest of two prominent magnates, *Egmont and *Horn, many others fled abroad. Alba used the threat of the council to impose the tenth penny, an unpopular tax that united Catholics and Calvinists against Spain. After Alba's departure (1573), the council was abolished.

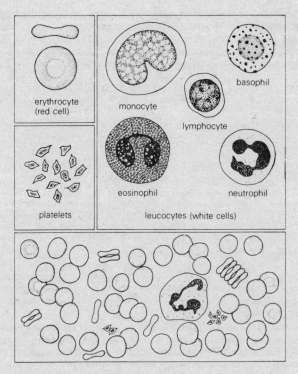

BLOOD *Blood cells and platelets, showing surface and side views of a red cell and five types of white cell (above). Human blood, magnified about 1500 times (below), containing a single white cell, a mass of red cells, and two clusters of platelets.*

blood clotting The mechanism by which blood is converted from a liquid to a solid state, which normally occurs after injury to blood vessels and prevents loss of blood. The process involves a number of chemical reactions between certain soluble proteins (clotting factors) in the blood, resulting in the formation of a fibrous protein (fibrin), which forms the basis of the blood clot. *Platelets accumulate at the site of the injury, their presence being essential for the reactions to occur. *See also* thrombosis.

blood fluke A parasitic flatworm of the genus *Schistosoma* (3 species), which causes the disease *schistosomiasis among human populations in many parts of the world. The flukes are carried by freshwater snails and enter their human hosts to inhabit blood vessels, feeding on blood and causing severe debilitation. *See also* fluke.

blood groups The different types into which blood can be classified on the basis of the presence or absence of certain proteins (*see* antibody) on the surface of the red cells, which is genetically determined. The major grouping is the ABO system, which was the first human blood system to be discovered—in 1900, by Karl Landsteiner (1868–1943). It consists of four groups: A, B, AB, and O. Group A cells carry the A antigen and the plasma contains *antibodies against B antigen (anti-B antibodies); the converse applies to group B blood. Transfusion of blood between these groups will cause destruction of the donor blood cells (*see* blood transfusion). Group O blood contains neither antigen and can therefore be used in transfusions to people of groups A and B. Group AB blood contains neither anti-A nor anti-B antibody: people of this blood group can accept both A and B blood during transfusion. There are numerous other minor blood-group systems of which the rhesus system is the most important (*see* rhesus factor).

bloodhound An ancient breed of dog with a keen sense of smell, widely used for tracking purposes. It has a sturdy frame and a large dome-shaped head with long drooping ears and wrinkled skin around the eyes. Bloodhounds are black and tan, liver and tan, or red in color. Height: 25–27 in (63–69 cm) (dogs); 23–26 in (58–64 cm) (bitches).

blood poisoning (*or* septicemia) The presence of bacteria or bacterial toxins in the blood. The symptoms include fever, rigors, and various aches and pains. The bacteria may come from any infected region (such as an abscess) and they may be carried to other parts of the body, including the brain and kidneys. Treatment consists of the injection of large doses of antibiotics.

blood pressure The pressure that blood exerts on the walls of the arteries, due to the pumping action of the heart. Blood pressure is at its lowest between heartbeats (i.e. at diastole) and at its highest when the ventricles of the heart are contracting (i.e. systole). It is recorded, using an instrument called a *sphygmomanometer, as the height in millimeters of a column of mercury (mmHg). Blood pressure varies with age and individual variations are common within each age group depending on such external factors as stress, but a healthy adult might have a systolic pressure of about 120 mmHg and a diastolic pressure of 80 mmHg. This is normally expressed as 120/80. Abnormally high blood pressure (*see* hypertension) may be associated with various diseases or it may arise without any obvious cause. Abnormally low blood pressure occurs in *shock.

bloodstone A mineral of a green color speckled with red. It is a variety of *chalcedony. Birthstone for March.

blood test An analysis of a blood sample. Such tests may be useful in the diagnosis of disease. A common test is the measurement of the erythrocyte sedimentation rate (ESR)—the rate at which red blood cells settle out of plasma, which increases in rheumatic disease, cancer, and some infections. Other tests include plasma viscosity, red-cell counts (in the diagnosis of anemia), blood-sugar estimation (when diabetes mellitus is suspected), and the determination of alcohol, drugs, or bacteria in the blood or the individual's blood group. The blood is usually taken from a vein using a hypodermic needle.

blood transfusion The transfer of blood from one individual (the donor) to another (the recipient). As blood of a different *blood group from that of the recipient may cause a serious reaction, the blood groups of both the donor and the recipient must be determined beforehand. Direct person-to-person transfusion is now rarely performed; the donor blood is usually stored, at a temperature of 34°F (4°C), in a **blood bank** and should be used within 3–4 weeks of collection. Blood transfusion is performed when there has been extensive loss of blood; for example, during surgery or following an accident. Some people (e.g. Jehovah's Witnesses) object to transfusions on religious grounds.

bloodworm The larva of nonbiting *midges of the genus *Chironomus*. It lives in stagnant water and is red owing to the pigment *hemoglobin, which it uses to help increase its supply of oxygen.

Bloomfield, Leonard (1887–1949) US linguist, whose book *Language* (1933) outlines a strictly scientific behaviorist framework for the description of language, on which modern American structural *linguistics is based. He also did pioneer descriptive fieldwork in both Malayo-Polynesian and American Indian languages.

Bloomington 39 10N 86 32W A city in SW Indiana, founded in 1815. Indiana University was established here in 1820. Industries include electrical equipment and limestone quarrying. Population (1990): 60,633.

Bloomsbury group A group of English writers and artists active in the 1910s and 1920s who met in private houses in Bloomsbury, London, for aesthetic and philosophic discussions. The group included the writers Virginia *Woolf (and her sister Vanessa Bell; 1879–1961), E. M. *Forster, and Lytton *Strachey, the art critics Clive Bell (1881–1964) and Roger *Fry, and the economist J. M. *Keynes. Most of them had studied at Cambridge University and were influenced by G. E. *Moore's *Principia Ethica* (1903) in their belief in the overriding importance of personal relationships and aesthetic experience.

blowfly A large buzzing fly belonging to the family *Calliphoridae*. Some blowflies lay their eggs in human food, but more commonly the larvae develop in dung or decaying organic material. The larvae of certain species (e.g. of the American genus *Cochliomyia*)—known as screwworms—are serious pests of sheep and cattle, eating away the flesh at wounded areas. Chief genera: *Calliphora* (bluebottles), *Lucilia* (greenbottles).

Blücher, Gebhard Leberecht von, Prince of Wahlstatt (1742–1819) Prussian general, known as Marshal Forward. He fought in the campaigns against Revolutionary France and subsequently held command in the War of Liberation against Napoleon, whom he defeated at Leipzig (1813). In 1814 he crossed the Rhine and marched to Paris. His pursuit of Napoleon's forces at Waterloo contributed to the allied victory.

Bluebeard A European folktale character who murders successive wives and locks their bodies in a forbidden room. His new wife discovers the bodies and is herself threatened with death, but is rescued by her brothers. The story may have been based on the crimes of Gilles de *Retz or of an ancient Breton chieftain.

bluebell One of several plants having bell-shaped blue flowers. In England the bluebell is *Endymion non-scriptus,* a perennial herb, up to 20 in (50 cm) high, very common in woods and shady places. It overwinters as a bulb and produces blue (sometimes white or pink) flowers in spring. Family: *Liliaceae.* In Scotland the name is applied to the *harebell.

bluebird A songbird of the New World genus *Sialia* (3 species). The eastern bluebird (*S. sialis*) of E North America is about 6.5 in (17 cm) long and has a blue back and red-brown breast. Family: *Turdidae* (thrushes). *Compare* fairy bluebird.

bluebottle. *See* blowfly.

Bluefields 12 00N 83 49W The chief Caribbean port of Nicaragua, in the SE near the Escondido River. A 17th-century base (as Blewfeldt) of Dutch pirates, it was the capital of the British Mosquito Coast until 1850. Population (1978 est): 18,252.

bluefish A food fish, *Pomatomus saltator* (or *P. saltatrix*), also called tailor or snapper. The only member of the family *Pomatomidae*, it is found in all warm seas. It has a blue-green elongated body, up to 4 ft (1.2 m) long, with a whitish belly, a large mouth, and two dorsal fins. It lives in large schools and preys voraciously on other fish. Order: *Perciformes*.

blue fox. *See* Arctic fox.

bluegrass A perennial grass, *Poa pratensis*, also called meadow grass, native to Europe, Asia, and North America. It has erect stems, 12–35 in (30–90 cm) high, soft smooth leaves (which may be blue-tinged or green), and flower clusters 2–8 in (5–20 cm) long. It is widely cultivated for pastures and lawns.

blue-green algae Microscopic *algae of the division *Cyanophyta* (1500 species), which contain a blue pigment (phycocyanin), in addition to the green chlorophyll. They are single cells or filaments and resemble bacteria in their primitive structure (e.g. the genetic material is not organized into a distinct nucleus). Reproduction is asexual. Blue-green algae are widely distributed on land and in water. They occur on moist surfaces of rocks and trees, and in the soil, where they contribute to *nitrogen fixation. Aquatic blue-green algae are a constituent of plankton, sometimes forming dense concentrations (blooms), which color the water.

blue gum A fast-growing evergreen Australian □tree, *Eucalyptus globulus*, up to 130 ft (40 m) high with patchy gray and fawn bark. It has sickle-shaped blue-green leaves up to 10 in (25 cm) long. The timber is used for construction work and pulp, and eucalyptus oil is distilled from the leaves. Family: *Myrtaceae*. *See also* Eucalyptus.

Blue Mountains A mountain range in Australia, in New South Wales. Part of the *Great Dividing Range, it reaches 3871 ft (1180 m) at Bird Rock and contains the Blue Mountains National Park. It is a popular tourist area.

Blue Rider, The A group of artists formed in Munich in 1911 by *Marc and *Kandinsky when the latter's work was rejected by an exhibition committee. Their manifesto *Der Blaue Reiter Almanac* (1911) and their exhibitions illustrated their diverse influences: primitive and naive art, children's pictures, and religious paintings on glass. Their aim was to unite in an expressionist style (*see* expressionism) the symbolic and spiritual elements manifest in the art of all ages. The group, which also included Paul *Klee and August *Macke, disbanded during World War I.

Blue Ridge Mountains A mountain range that extends NE from N Georgia to E West Virginia and W Virginia, part of the Appalachian Mountains. The highest point is Mount Mitchell (6684 ft; 2038 m) in North Carolina. Noted for their scenic beauty, the Mountains include Shenandoah National Park (Virginia), Great Smoky Mountains National Park (North Carolina), the Appalachian Trail, and the Blue Ridge Parkway.

blues A type of American folk music that evolved from the African-American spirituals and work songs of the 1860s and became a song form used in jazz, rhythm and blues, and rock. A blues song is often slow and bittersweet; the syncopated melodic line and harmonies contain "blue" notes, which are flattened versions of certain notes in the major or minor scale. In origin it always consisted of three sets of four bars, in which the second set is a repetition of the first. The final line is improvised. The first published blues were "Memphis Blues" (1912) by W. C. *Handy and Jelly Roll Morton's "Jelly Roll Blues" (1915). The blues influenced the development of jazz and rock music and influenced classical composers such as George Gershwin, who wrote the orchestral *Rhapsody in Blue* (1924). Famous blues singers include Blind Lemon Jefferson (1897–1930), Bessie Smith (?1898–1937), and Billie Holiday (1915–59).

blue shark A *shark, *Prionace glauca*, that is abundant in warm-temperate and tropical seas. It has a slender dark-blue body, up to 13 ft (4 m) long, with a white belly and long sickle-shaped pectoral fins. It is found usually near the surface and feeds voraciously on shoaling fish, squid, and other sharks. Family: *Carcharhinidae*.

Blue Sky Law A term referring to any law that protects those who buy stocks and bonds from unscrupulous schemes that promise "the blue sky." The first law was passed by Kansas in 1911 and upheld by the US Supreme Court in 1917. Usually, blue sky laws provide for dealer licensing, issue registration, and penalties for fraudulent practice.

Bluestockings A group of intellectual society hostesses in 18th-century England. They included Lady Mary Wortley *Montagu and the novelist Fanny *Burney; their guests were Samuel *Johnson, Horace *Walpole, David *Garrick, and others, some of whom were accustomed to wearing ordinary blue, rather than formal dress, stockings to the meetings. The term is still used to describe intellectual women.

bluetit A European tit, *Parus caeruleus*, formerly a woodland species but now common in towns and gardens. It has a blue crown and wings, a yellow breast, white face and wing bars, and a black collar and eyestripe. Bluetits are acrobatic birds and feed chiefly on insect larvae.

bluets A tufted herb of the genus *Houstonia* (about 25 species), native to North America but often grown in rock gardens. The small white, blue, or purple funnel-shaped flowers are borne singly or in clusters. Some creeping species form mats, providing a close ground cover in shade. Family: *Rubiaceae* (madder family).

blue whale The largest living *whale, *Balaenoptera musculus*, probably the largest animal ever. It grows to over 98 ft (30 cm) and weighs over 150 tons. Widely distributed in world oceans, blue whales are approaching extinction due to overhunting. Family: *Balaenopteridae* (*see* rorqual). □mammal.

Blum, Léon (1872–1950) French socialist, statesman, and writer; prime minister (1936–37, 1938, 1946–47). His *popular front government of 1936–37 brought about radical reforms in labor organizations and nationalized the Bank of France. After the fall of France to the Germans in 1940 Blum was arrested by the Vichy government and spent the remainder of the war in prison. From 1946 until his death he led the moderate socialist wing in France. His books include *L'Exercice du pouvoir* (1937) and *À l'échelle humaine* (1945).

blunderbuss A short-range smoothbore gun with a bell-shaped muzzle, firing many balls. In use from the 17th to 19th centuries, its name is derived from the Dutch word *donderbus*, thunder gun. It ranged in size from the pistol to the small artillery piece.

B'na-i B'rith (Sons of the Covenant) An international Jewish organization devoted to the betterment of life in the Jewish community. Founded in 1843 as a fraternal order, it included women by 1897 and now has over 500,000 members in almost 50 countries. It promotes civil rights and fights anti-Semitism through its Anti-Defamation League (1913), educates its youth through the Hillel Foundation on college campuses, and has many vocational services, hospitals, and philanthropic organizations.

boa A snake belonging to the subfamily *Boinae* (40–60 species) of the *constrictor family and occurring in Old and New World regions. 8 in–15 ft (20–760 cm) long, boas may be terrestrial, semiaquatic, or arboreal and are usually green, brown, or yellowish with a camouflaging pattern of blotches and diamonds. They kill their prey by biting and then constricting. The boa constrictor (*Boa constrictor*), occurring from Mexico to Argentina, is about 12 ft (3.5 m) long, hunts birds and small mammals at night, and bears live young.

Boadicea (Latin name: Boudicca; d. 60 AD) Queen of the *Iceni. Her husband Prasutagus ruled in what is now Norfolk (England). At his death in 60, Roman officials attempted to seize his wealth and maltreated Boadicea and her daughters. She led the Iceni into open rebellion and they sacked Colchester, London, and St Albans. The Roman governor Suetonius Paulinus defeated the rebels at or near Fenny Stratford on Watling Street. Boadicea committed suicide.

boar, wild A Eurasian wild *pig, *Sus scrofa*, once common in forests throughout Europe. Up to 5 ft (1.5 m) long and 40 in (1 m) high at the shoulder, wild boars have a rough bristly coat colored grayish brown. The ancestors of domestic pigs, they are still hunted for sport in some regions. Males have four tusks.

Boas, Franz (1858–1942) German-born US anthropologist. In 1886 Boas left his post of assistant curator of the Berlin Royal Ethnological Museum and embarked upon extensive research among the Indians of the NW American coast. In 1899 he became the first professor of anthropology at Columbia University. His most famous books are *The Mind of Primitive Man* (1911), *Primitive Art* (1927), and *Race, Language and Culture* (1940). Boas was concerned not only with the physical features of ethnic groups, but also with cultural and psychological aspects. He strongly opposed the racial theories propounded by the Nazis.

boatbill A nocturnal heron, *Cochlearius cochlearius*, occurring in tropical American swamps. It is about 20 in (50 cm) tall and has a gray plumage with black markings on the head and neck. It closely resembles the *night heron but has a characteristic broad flattened hook-tipped bill.

bobcat A short-tailed cat *Felis rufa*, resembling a lynx, found in North America from S Canada to Mexico. About 35 in (90 cm) long, it is brown with gray or white markings and has large ears tipped with a tuft of hairs. Bobcats feed at night on a wide variety of small birds, rodents, and deer.

Bobo-Dioulasso 11 11N 1 18W A city in SW Burkina Faso. It is the country's main trade, industrial, and communications center. Industries include food processing and handicrafts. Population (1985): 228,668.

bobolink An American *oriole, *Dolichonyx oryzivorus*, that nests in Canada and the northern states of the US and migrates to South America in winter. It is black below and white above and nests on the ground, foraging for insects and seeds.

Bobruisk (*or* Bobruysk) 53 08N 29 10E A port in Belarus on the Berezina River. It has an 18th-century fortress and its industries include engineering, timber, and tire manufacturing. Population (1987): 232,000.

bobsledding The sport of racing bobsleds (also called bobsleighs or bobs), which was developed by British sportsmen at St Moritz (Switzerland) in the late 19th century. A bobsled is a steel-bodied toboggan with two pairs of runners, the front pair steerable, and a rear brake, holding two or four people. In a race, the bobsleds slide one at a time down a narrow icy chute some 1640 yd (1500 m) long with high walls and banked turns, reaching speeds of over 81 mph (130 km per h).

Boccaccio, Giovanni (1313–75) Italian writer and poet. Son of a merchant of Florence, he was sent to Naples about 1328 to learn business. Literature interested him more, however; between then and 1341, when he returned to Florence, he wrote *Filocolo*, a prose romance, *Filostrato*, which supplied the plot of Chaucer's *Troilus and Criseyde*, and *Teseida*, the source of Chaucer's *Knight's Tale*. Between 1348 and 1353 he composed the *Decameron*, a collection of a hundred stories told by a party of young people escaping from plague-stricken

Florence in 1348. He met *Petrarch in 1350 and was much influenced by him. In later life he chiefly wrote scholarly works in Latin and lectured on Dante's *Divine Comedy*. He also founded the first chair of Greek in W Europe, at the University of Florence.

Boccherini, Luigi (1743–1805) Italian violoncellist and composer. He became famous in Rome while still a boy. Boccherini produced his first opera *La confederazione* (1765) in Lucca. His large output includes cello concertos and sonatas, symphonies, choral works, and string quintets and quartets.

Boccioni, Umberto (1882–1916) Italian futurist painter and sculptor. He trained under *Balla before settling in Milan (1907), where, influenced by the poet *Marinetti, he aimed to express the violence and speed of modern life in such paintings as *The City Rises* (1910; New York). His manifesto of futurist sculpture (1912) advocated the use of materials such as glass, cement, light-bulbs, etc.

Bochum 51 28N 7 11E A city in NW Germany, in North Rhine-Westphalia. It is the site of the Ruhr University (1965). The manufacture of cars, textiles, and chemicals has replaced coal mining and iron and steel production. Population (1988): 381,000.

Bodawpaya (d. 1819) King of Burma (1789–1819). His aggressive policies ensured considerable expansion of Burmese territory during his reign. He annexed Arakan (1785), Manipur (1813), and Assam (1816) and almost precipitated an Anglo-Burmese war by demanding the surrender of Chittagong, Dacca, and Murshidabad from the British Indian government. His sudden death averted a confrontation. The *Burmese Domesday Book* (1784), a survey of Burma, was compiled during his reign.

Bodensee. *See* Constance, Lake.

Bode's law (*or* Titius-Bode law) A relationship between the distances of the planets from the sun. Take the number sequence 0, 3, 6, 12, 24, . . ., add 4 to each number, and divide each sum by 10. The resulting sequence is in good agreement with observed planetary distances (in astronomical units) out to Uranus, provided the belt of *minor planets is considered a single entity. Formulated by Johann Titius (1729–96) and popularized in 1772 by Johann Bode (1747–1826), it is still unexplained by theory.

Bodhidharma (6th century AD) Indian Buddhist patriarch from Conjeeveram, near Madras. He entered China about 520. Teaching a form of meditation called *dhyana* (Chinese *ch'an*, Japanese *zen*), he is credited with founding *Zen Buddhism.

Bodhisattva In Mahayana Buddhism, the title of a person who is to become a Buddha. The term is also used to describe the Buddha (Gautama) before his enlightenment. The Bodhisattva ideal is that of the individual who seeks enlightenment not for himself alone but for all beings. In Indian art the Bodhisattvas are depicted as youthful and represent various aspects of the nature of Buddha.

Bodin, Jean (1530–96) French philosopher and jurist. Although a Protestant, he was a successful lawyer and became parliamentary representative of Vermandois (1576). He visited Britain in 1581 where his belief in witchcraft, propounded in *Démonomanie des sorciers* (1580), later influenced James I. His greatest work, *La République* (1576), is a comprehensive political philosophy.

Bodleian Library The major *library of Oxford University, first established in 1409 and restored and enlarged by Sir Thomas Bodley from 1598 to 1602. Since 1610 it has been entitled to receive a free copy of every book published in Britain; it contains well over 2.5 million volumes.

Bodoni, Giambattista (1740–1813) Italian printer. In 1768 he became the Duke of Parma's printer and, influenced by François-Ambroise Didot (1730–1804), began to design his own typefaces. The best known, designed in 1790 and named for him, is still in use.

Boehm, Theobald (1794–1881) German flautist. He invented the **Boehm System**, a keyed mechanism for the flute that is still in use today and has been applied successfully to the clarinet and the oboe.

Boehme, Jakob. *See* Böhme.

Boeotia A region of central Greece, N and W of *Attica. Its main geographical features are rich central plains, surrounded by hills and mountains, and Lake Copaïs (now drained). The dozen or so city states that shared the territory formed a federal state dominated by *Thebes in 446 BC. The Boeotians had a reputation for good living and stupidity, belied by the military success of Thebes and the poetry of *Hesiod and *Pindar, among others. Boeotians took no part in Greek colonization overseas.

Boer. *See* Afrikaner.

Boer Wars (*or* South African Wars) The wars fought against the British by the Boers or *Afrikaners of South Africa. In the first (1880–81) the Boers of the Transvaal under *Kruger rebelled against British rule. After inflicting a massive defeat on the British garrison at *Majuba Hill, the Transvaal regained its independence under the *Pretoria Convention. In the second Boer War (1899–1902) the Boer forces of the South African Republic (previously the Transvaal) and Orange Free State were initially successful, besieging Ladysmith, Mafeking (held courageously by *Baden-Powell from October, 1899, until his relief in February 1900), and Kimberley. They suffered reverses during 1900 but, using guerrilla tactics, were able to hold off the British under *Kitchener and F. S. *Roberts. The British devastated the countryside, rounded up Boer women and children, of whom some 20,000 died in concentration camps, and finally defeated the Boers, who lost their independence in the Peace of Vereeniging (1902).

Boethius, Anicius Manlius Severinus (c. 480–524 AD) Roman statesman and philosopher. A patrician by birth, Boethius was consul in 510 during the Gothic occupation of Rome under *Theoderic, to whom he became chief minister. His championing of Roman traditions and institutions earned Theoderic's displeasure, and Boethius was imprisoned, tortured, and eventually executed. His translations of Aristotle and treatises on music and mathematics were standard texts in medieval Europe but his most famous work is *The Consolation of Philosophy*, written while he was in prison. A dialogue between the author and the personification of philosophy, the *Consolation* seeks to prove that virtue alone remains constant and the knowledge of God is the only true wisdom.

Bogart, Humphrey (1899–1957) US film actor. He achieved international success in the 1940s with his portrayals of tough heroes whose cynicism masked a romantic idealism. His films include *The Petrified Forest* (1936), *The Maltese Falcon* (1941), *Casablanca* (1942), *To Have and Have Not* (1944), in which Lauren Bacall, whom he subsequently married, made her screen debut; *The Big Sleep* (1946), *The African Queen* (1951), for which he won an Academy Award, and *The Harder They Fall* (1956).

Boğazköy (*or* Boğazkale). *See* Hattusas.

Bogomils. *See* Cathari.

Bogor (former name: Buitenzorg) 6 34S 106 45E A city in Indonesia, on W Java. It is famed for its botanical garden (1817) and former Dutch governor gen-

BOER WAR On Cronjé's Heels (1900), by the British war artist H. Seppings Wright. The tactics of the Boers and the unfamiliar terrain caused problems for the conventionally trained British troops.

eral's residence (1745). It is an agricultural center with an agricultural university (founded 1963) and an important research institute. Population (1980): 247,409.

HUMPHREY BOGART *With Rod Steiger (right) in* The Harder They Fall *(1956).*

Bogotá, Santa Fé de 4 38N 74 15W The capital of Colombia, on a fertile central plateau of the E Andes at an altitude of 8600 ft (2640 cm). Founded by the Spanish in the early 16th century on the site of the conquered Indian settlement of Bacatá, it became capital of the viceroyalty of New Grenada and an important cultural center. Today it possesses a university (1867), a number of colleges, and several notable technical schools. Regular airlines have helped to improve its rather isolated position from the rest of the country. Population (1985): 3,985,000.

Bohai. *See* Chihli, Gulf of.

Bohemia (Czech name: Čechy; German name: Böhmen) An area and former province (1918–49) of W Czechoslovakia. It consists chiefly of a plateau enclosed by mountains. The most industrialized part of Czechoslovakia and, since 1993, of the Czech Republic, Bohemia possesses important mineral resources, including uranium, coal, and iron ore. Agriculture is well developed. It is renowned for its many mineral springs. *History*: Bohemia derives its name from the Boii (the first known inhabitants), who were displaced by the Czechs (1st–5th centuries AD). Bohemia became part of the greater Moravian empire in the 9th century, during which period Christianity was introduced. St Wenceslas was the first great Bohemian ruler but his brother, Boleslav I (d. 967; reigned 929–67), was forced to acknowledge the rule of Emperor Otto I and for many centuries thereafter Bohemia was linked with the Holy Roman Empire. During the 11th century there was a successful expedition into Moravia, which was linked from then on with Bohemia. It achieved the height of its power following the acquisitions of the Přemyslid Otakar II (1230–78; reigned 1253–78). The Přemyslid dynasty came to an end with the assassination of Wenceslas III (1289–1306; reigned 1305–06) and John of Luxemborg was subsequently elected king (1310). The golden age of Bohemia was established by his son

Charles I (Emperor *Charles IV), who founded the university at Prague in 1348. The reigns of his successors were marked by religious upheavals inspired by Jan Hus (*see* Hussites). The accession (1526) of Archduke Ferdinand began the long Habsburg domination of Bohemia. It was laid waste during the Thirty Years' War and after the Peace of Westphalia (1648) forcible Germanization and oppressive taxation reduced most Czechs to misery. There was a rebirth of Czech nationalism during the 19th century but full independence was only attained at the end of World War I, when Bohemia became part of the Republic of Czechoslovakia.

Bohemond I (*or* Bohemund; c. 1056–1111) Prince of Antioch (1099–1111). He fought (1080–85) with his father Robert Guiscard against Alexius I Comnenus and was a leader of the first Crusade, during which he took Antioch (1098). He was captured by the Turks (1100–03) and after renewed warfare with Alexius became his vassal (1108).

Böhm, Karl (1894–1981) Austrian conductor, who was noted particularly for his performances of operas by Mozart and Richard Strauss. He was conductor of the Dresden State Opera (1934–43) and the Vienna State Opera (1943–45).

Böhme, Jakob (*or* Boehme; 1575–1624) German Lutheran theosophist, who lived most of his life as a shoemaker in Silesia. His first work, the *Aurora* (1612), was condemned by the local authorities. Although forbidden to write, he later published such works as *Der Weg zu Christo* and *Mysterium magnum* (both 1623). He was influenced by *Paracelsus, alchemy, and astrology but also claimed divine inspiration for his writings. His central belief was that God was the source of everything, including evil, since he had two wills, one good and the other evil. He has influenced many thinkers, notably * Hegel and *Schelling.

Bohr, Niels Henrik David (1885–1962) Danish physicist. He made an immense contribution to atomic theory by combining *Rutherford's nuclear model with Planck's quantum theory. The model of the atom he proposed (the *Bohr atom) was modified by *Sommerfeld but is essentially the basis for modern atomic theory. Bohr also invented the concept of complementarity to combine the particle and wave aspects of subatomic particles. He was awarded a Nobel Prize in 1922. During the 1930s his Institute of Theoretical Physics in Copenhagen became a haven for many Jewish and other physicists expelled by Hitler. In 1939 he took news of Meitner's and Hahn's uranium fission work to the US and started the process that culminated in the manufacture of the atomic bomb. Bohr himself later worked at Los Alamos on the bomb, after escaping from German-occupied Denmark. A fervent advocate of atomic energy for peaceful uses, he organized the first Atoms for Peace Conference in 1955. His son **Aage Bohr** (1922–   ) shared the 1975 Nobel Prize for Physics for his work on atomic theory.

Bohr atom A model of the atom, put forward by Niels *Bohr in 1913. His model assumes that electrons move around a central nucleus in circular orbits. The electrons are confined to fixed orbits at fixed distances from the nucleus, each orbit corresponding to a specific energy level. If the electron gains or loses the right amount of energy, in the form of a photon of electromagnetic radiation, it jumps or falls into another orbit. The jumps are quantized (*see* quantum theory), the energy associated with each jump being equal to hf, where h is the Planck constant and f is the frequency of the radiation. The model gives a good explanation of the spectral emission of the hydrogen atom and was later modified by *Sommerfeld to explain the fine structure of the hydrogen lines, by assuming that the electrons move in precessing elliptical orbits.

Boiardo, Matteo Maria, Conte di Scandiano (1441–94) Italian poet. He served the Dukes of Ferrara as governor of Modena (1480–82) and Reggio

(1487–94). His chief work was the unfinished *Orlando innamorato* (1483), a chivalrous epic about Roland (*see* Charlemagne) and the precursor of the more famous *Orlando furioso by* *Ariosto.

boil An inflamed pus-filled swelling on the skin, usually caused by the infection of a hair follicle with the bacterium *Staphylococcus aureus*. Boils are more likely to develop when constitutional resistance is low or when the diet is inadequate. The application of a warm poultice will bring the boil to a head and allow the pus to drain. A **carbuncle** is a collection of boils situated close together; it is slightly more difficult to treat and may require the use of antibiotics.

Boileau(-Despréaux), Nicolas (1636–1711) French poet and critic. After the publication of his satires in 1666 he became friendly with *Molière, *Racine, and other leading writers. *L'Art poétique* (1674) was received as a definitive guide to the classical principles in literature and had a powerful contemporary influence in France and England. He also wrote a mock epic, *Le Lutrin* (1674), and translated *Longinus' treatise *On the Sublime*.

boiling point The temperature at which the *vapor pressure of a liquid is equal to the atmospheric pressure. The boiling point of a liquid is usually given at standard atmospheric pressure (101,325 pascals).

Bois de Boulogne A park in W Paris, France, bordering on the Seine River. It was presented to the city in 1852 by Napoleon III and contains the Auteuil and Longchamp racecourses. Area: 2125 acres (860 ha).

Boise 43 38N 116 12W The capital and largest city of Idaho. The center of a gold rush in 1862, it has timber, food-processing, and agricultural industries. Population (1990): 125,738.

Bokassa I (Jean Bedel B.; 1921–   ) Emperor of the Central African Empire from 1977 until his overthrow in 1979. He seized power in the Central African Republic in 1966, becoming president and later proclaiming himself emperor.

Bokhara. *See* Bukhara.

Boleslaw (I) the Brave (c. 966–1025) The first King of Poland, who extended the territory of the Polish principality, which he inherited in 992, and was crowned king (1000) by Emperor Otto III. He reorganized the Polish church, making it responsible directly to the pope and independent of the German church.

Boleslaw (II) the Generous (1039–81) King of Poland (1058–79), recognized by the pope in 1076. Boleslaw successfully pursued Polish interests at the expense of German influence until a revolt of the clergy and nobility led to his excommunication and deposition.

Boletus A genus of mushrooms (about 50 species). The undersurface of the cap bears a series of vertical tubes (instead of gills), in which the spores are formed. Most grow near trees and they are generally edible or harmless (*see* cèpe). An exception is Satan's boletus (*B. satanas*), which is poisonous but not deadly. It has a short stalk and a gray or grayish-green cap 4–8 in (10–20 cm) in diameter. Family: *Boletaceae*; class: *Basidiomycetes*.

Boleyn, Anne (c. 1507–36) The second wife (from 1533) of Henry VIII of England and the mother of Elizabeth I. Henry soon tired of Anne, who was accused of adultery and executed.

Bolger, James Brendan (1935–   ) New Zealand political leader; prime minister (1990–   ). A farmer, he became involved with National Party politics on the local level before winning election to Parliament in 1972. He held several cabinet posts (1977–84) under Prime Minister Robert Muldoon and assumed leadership of the party in 1986. Although elected prime minister handily, Bolger faced diminishing public support as the country's economy slumped.

Bolingbroke, Henry St John, 1st Viscount (1678–1751) English states-man and philosopher. A Tory, he became a member of parliament in 1701 and was secretary of war (1704–08) before becoming secretary of state for the north in 1710. A supporter of the *Jacobites, he fled to France (1715–25) after their failed rebellion. There, he encountered the major thinkers of the *Enlightenment (including Voltaire) and wrote *Reflections upon Exile* and *Reflections Concerning Innate Moral Principles*. He became the bitter opponent of Robert *Walpole and wanted to create a Country Party of Whigs and Tories united by their opposition to Walpole. In 1735 he returned to France. He also wrote *The Idea of a Patriot King* (1749).

Bolívar, Simón (1783–1830) South American soldier and statesman, known as the Liberator. The son of a wealthy Venezuelan creole family, his childhood tutor and subsequent travels in Europe instilled in Bolívar a lasting admiration for the ideas of the Enlightenment. He returned to Latin America in 1807 and devoted the rest of his life to its liberation from Spain. In 1813 he seized Caracas but after defeat in 1814 went into exile until 1817. His victory at the battle of *Boyacá (1819) achieved the liberation of New Granada, which was renamed Colombia. Bolívar became its president after liberating Venezuela and Quito (Ecuador) in 1821, and organized a federation of the three newly independent states. Latin America was finally freed of the Spanish by campaigns in Peru, and Upper Peru took the name Bolivia in honor of Bolívar, who became its president. His dream of a united Andean republic was never realized and he died disillusioned by the political bickering that thwarted this goal.

Bolivia, Republic of An inland country in central South America consisting of low plains in the N and E, crossed by the Madre de Dios, Bené, and Mamoré river systems; in the W, ranges of the Andes rise to over 21,000 ft (6400 m) and the Altiplano, a plateau averaging about 13,000 ft (3900 m), contains Lakes Titicaca and Poopó. Bolivia has some of the world's highest inhabited regions, most of the population, which is of mixed Indian and Spanish descent, living at altitudes of over 10,000 ft (3000 m). *Economy*: Bolivia is one of the poorest South American countries. Tin mining has long been of the first importance to Bolivia's economy and remains the principal industry. The main tin producers have been nationalized in recent years. Other minerals include zinc, lead, antimony, and copper. Silver is much less important than previously. Agriculture is being improved in the E part and the main crops are sugar cane, potatoes, maize, rice, and wheat. Livestock, including llamas, is raised and forestry is being developed. Main exports include tin and other minerals, oil (through a pipeline to Arica on the Chilean coast), natural gas (to Argentina), hides and skins, and vicuña wool. Poor transportation is a detriment to growth. *History*: ruins near Tiahuanaco indicate the existence of a pre-Inca civilization (the Aymaras) going back to the 10th century. The area later became part of the Inca Empire and was conquered by the Spanish in the 16th century, when it became known as Alto Peru. The discovery of tin and silver at Potosí soon after the Spanish conquest led to great prosperity. In 1776 it became part of the viceroyalty of Buenos Aires. After a long war it gained its independence with the help of Simón Bolívar in 1825 and became a republic with Antonio José de *Sucre as first president. During the remainder of the century as a result of civil wars and struggles with neighboring countries Bolivia lost much territory, including access to the Pacific coast. Political unrest and violent changes of government have continued into the 20th century and in 1971 a military coup brought Gen. Hugo Banzer Suárez to power. He achieved a measure of political stability, remaining in office until overthrown in a coup in 1978. Since then frequent political upheavals have resumed with a resulting succession of presidents. Disputes with Peru and Chile continued over the question of access to the Pacific coast. The programs that Pres. Jaime Paz Zamora, elected in 1989, instituted to curb drug trafficking were not very successful. He was succeeded by Gonzalo Sanchez de Lozada in 1993. Official languages: Spanish, Quechua, and Aymara. Official currency: peso boliviano of 100 centavos. Area: 424,160 sq mi (1,098,580 sq km). Population (1990 est): 6,730,000. Capital: La Paz (legal capital: Sucre).

Böll, Heinrich (1917–85) German novelist. After infantry service in World War II, he eventually settled down as a full-time writer in 1951. His novels and stories include *The Train Was on Time* (1949), *The Clown* (1963), *The Lost Honor of Katharina Blum* (1975), and *The Safety Net* (1982). His writing frequently depicts ironically the moral degeneration of postwar German society. He won the Nobel Prize in 1972.

boll weevil A stout brownish *weevil, *Anthonomus grandis*, also called cotton boll weevil. Originally a native of the New World tropics, it is now a major insect pest of cotton crops in the W hemisphere. The female lays a single egg within each cotton boll, which thus fails to develop.

Bologna 44 30N 11 20E A city in N Italy, the capital of Emilia-Romagna. The history of the site of Bologna dates from Etruscan times. It became a free city in the Middle Ages and the Emperor Charles V was crowned here in 1530. It has an ancient university (1088) and a 14th-century gothic church. Its industries include engineering and food processing. Population (1988 est): 427,000.

Bologna, Giovanni da. *See* Giambologna.

Bolsheviks One of the two factions into which the Russian Social Democratic Workers' Party split in 1903 in London (the other was the *Mensheviks). The Bolsheviks, which means those in the majority, were led by *Lenin, who believed that the revolution must be guided by a single centralized party of professional revolutionaries (*see also* Leninism). The Bolsheviks came to power in the *Russian Revolution (1917) and from 1918 until 1952 the Soviet Communist Party was termed Communist Party (Bolsheviks).

Bolshoi Ballet The principal Russian ballet company, based at the Bolshoi Theater in Moscow. It originated from a dancing class established by the Moscow orphanage in the late 18th century and moved into its present premises in 1856 after fire had destroyed the first Bolshoi Theater. Known for its dramatic style and its realistic and elaborate scenery, it first appeared in the West in 1956 in London and has since become one of the world's leading ballet companies.

Bolton 53 35W 2 26W A city in NW England, in Greater Manchester. Traditionally a cotton-spinning town (Samuel Crompton, inventor of the spinning mule, was born here), Bolton also manufactures textile machinery and chemicals and is involved in engineering. Population (1985): 261,000.

Boltzmann, Ludwig Eduard (1844–1906) Austrian physicist, who developed statistical mechanics with J. C. *Maxwell and J. W. *Gibbs, notably the Maxwell-Boltzmann statistics of particle systems obeying classical laws. He also linked thermodynamics with molecular physics by showing that increasing entropy is related to increasing disorder among particles. Working with his teacher Josef Stefan (1835–93), he showed that Stefan's law could be derived thermodynamically and it is now usually known as the *Stefan-Boltzmann law.

Boltzmann constant (k) A constant, obtained by dividing the *gas constant by *Avogadro's number, equal to 1.3806×10^{-23} joule per kelvin. Named for Ludwig *Boltzmann.

Bolyai, János (1802–60) Hungarian mathematician, who (with *Loba-chevski) was the first to study the properties of spaces with *non-Euclidean geometry.

Bolzano 46 30N 11 22E A city in Italy, in Trentino-Alto Adige. It has a 14th-century gothic cathedral. Bolzano is a center for tourism and trades in fruit and wine. There are steel and textile industries. Population (1988): 101,000.

Boma 5 50S 13 03E A port in SW Zaïre, on the Zaïre River. It was formerly the capital of the Congo Free State, later the Belgian Congo (1886–1926). Forest products, such as palm oil, are exported. Population (1991 est): 246,000.

bombardier beetle A blue-gray and orange beetle, about 0.35 in (9 mm) long, belonging to a widely distributed genus (*Brachinus*) of *ground beetles. It has an efficient means of chemical defense, emitting puffs of an irritant secretion from the anal glands. Similar beetles of the genus *Pherosophus* occur in Africa, Asia, and the East Indies.

Bombay 18 56N 72 51E A city in India, the capital of Maharashtra and the country's main seaport on the W coast. The city proper occupies a group of islands that are united by a system of causeways and breakwaters; the site, known as Bombay Island, is linked with Salsette Island in the N. Its natural harbor, 7 mi (11 km) wide, is the focus of most of India's international trade. Bombay is also the financial and commercial center of the country. Industry includes cotton textiles, food processing, and oil refining. The city is also the site of the country's first nuclear reactor. The harbor is dominated by the monumental Gateway of India arch (1911). The University of Bombay (1857) and numerous government buildings are situated in the center of the city and the many temples (dating from the 8th century AD and earlier) reflect the cultural and religious diversity to be found in the city. The population is mainly Hindu but there are large Muslim, Christian, and Jewish minorities. The city's island location has led to problems of overcrowding and a twin city on the mainland is planned. *History*: ceded to the Portuguese in 1534, it passed to Charles II of England in 1661 and to the British East India Company in 1668. The arrival of the railroads, the opening of the Suez Canal, and land reclamation led to considerable expansion in the 19th century. Population (1991): 9,909,547.

Bombay duck A fish, *Harpodon nehereus*, found in the estuaries of N India, where it is widely used for food. It has a gray or brown body, about 16 in (40 cm) long, with small dark speckles and large pectoral and pelvic fins. Order: *Myctophiformes*.

Bon The pre-Buddhist religion of Tibet, characterized by the belief in a supreme sky god and a hierarchy of good and evil spirits, gods, demons, and ghosts. Elaborate ritual, including animal or even human sacrifice, abounded; religious practice was presided over by a class of shamans (*see* shamanism), priest-magicians who could influence the spirits by means of white or black magic, even being able to open the gate between earth and heaven. It was absorbed into Tibetan Buddhism, to which it lent a very individual character.

Bon, Cape 37 05N 11 02E A peninsula in NE Tunisia, extending into the Mediterranean Sea. Its fertile plains produce oranges, olives, and market-garden produce. Length: about 46 mi (75 km). Width: 22 mi (35 km).

Bonaparte (*or* Buonaparte) A Corsican family that included the French emperors, *Napoleon I and *Napoleon III, and the nominal emperor, *Napoleon II. **Carlo Bonaparte** (1746–85), a lawyer, had four sons. **Joseph Bonaparte** (1768–1844) was a diplomat of indifferent qualities who rose to high office by virtue of the position of his brother Napoleon I, from whom he received the thrones of Naples (1806) and Spain (1808). After Napoleon's defeat at Waterloo

(1815) Joseph lived in exile. **Lucien Bonaparte** (1775–1840) was president of the Council of Five Hundred under the Directory and became a critic of Napoleon's policies. The brothers were reconciled, however, on the eve of Waterloo and after Napoleon's defeat Lucien lived in exile in Italy. **Louis Bonaparte** (1778–1846) was created King of Holland by Napoleon in 1806 but, exasperated by Louis's inability to enforce the *Continental System, Napoleon obliged him to relinquish the crown in 1810. He too died in exile. His son by Hortense de *Beauharnais became Napoleon III. **Jérôme Bonaparte** (1784–1860) was created King of Westphalia in 1807 and was a commander in Napoleon's Russian invasion and at Waterloo. He survived to become a dignitary in the Second Empire (1852–70), established by his nephew Napoleon III.

The exploits of these and other members of the Bonaparte family formed the iconography of **Bonapartism**, a movement that sought to recreate the Napoleonic empire and to establish the dynasty in France. Louis Napoleon's *Des idées napoléoniennes* (1839) typified the romantic and conservative nature of Bonapartism.

Bonaventure, St (Giovanni di Fidanza; c. 1221–74) Italian Franciscan theologian, known as Doctor Seraphicus. He studied and lectured at Paris, in 1257 receiving the degree of doctor and becoming minister general of the Franciscan Order. He wrote the official biography of St Francis. As a theologian, he supported the traditional teachings of St Augustine, as opposed to the new Aristotelian thought that influenced his contemporary St Thomas *Aquinas. Feast day: July 14. Emblem: a cardinal's hat.

bond A security issued by a government, local authority, or public company as a means of raising capital. Most bonds pay a fixed rate of interest and are redeemable on a stated day. *See also* gilt-edged securities.

bone A rigid tissue that forms most of the skeleton of higher animals and man. The shape of individual bones is governed by their function (*see* skeleton). Most bones have a central cavity filled with *marrow. Bone is composed of a matrix of fibers of the protein collagen, responsible for the strength of bones, and bone salts, chiefly calcium salts (*see* apatite). This tissue is formed by activity of bone cells (osteoblasts), which become enclosed in the matrix when they have ceased to function. Bone formation starts during embryonic life. Most bones (including the long bones) develop from cartilage and the process is complete at birth. Membrane bones (e.g. the skull bones) are formed directly in connective tissue, the process being completed after birth (hence the gap [called a fontanelle] in a newborn baby's skull). The branch of medicine concerned with the diagnosis and treatment of diseases of bones is called **osteology**.

Bône. *See* Annaba.

boneset A plant of the genus *Eupatorium*, also called thoroughwort, found in tropical South America, Mexico, and the West Indies but grown elsewhere as greenhouse or border plants. Boneset is a perennial herb, shrub, or small tree. The flat-topped flower heads consist of disk florets, usually rose or white, with protruding styles. Family: *Compositae. See also* comfrey.

bongo An antelope, *Boocerus euryceros*, of dense tropical central African forests. About 48 in (120 cm) high at the shoulder, bongos are red-brown with vertical white body stripes and white markings on the head and legs. The male has spiraled horns up to 40 in (100 cm) long. Bulls are solitary; cows and calves live in small herds. They feed on leaves and shoots.

Bonhoeffer, Dietrich (1906–45) German pastor and theologian. As a young theological lecturer and pastor, Bonhoeffer identified himself with the German *Confessing Church, which opposed the pro-Nazi part of the Lutheran church, and during the war became involved with anti-Hitler conspirators. He was arrested in 1943, sent to Buchenwald concentration camp, and finally hanged. His posthumous *Letters and Papers from Prison* (1953) and radical theological writings continue to be influential.

Boniface, St (*or* St Wynfrith; c. 680–754 AD)   English missionary, known as the Apostle of Germany. He was born in Crediton, Devon, and entered the Benedictine Order. He visited Frisia in 716 and in 718 was granted papal authority to evangelize the Germans. He successfully established Christianity in several German states and instituted church reforms elsewhere, culminating in his appointment as Archbishop of Mainz in 751. He was martyred with 53 companions in Frisia. Feast day: June 5.

Boniface VIII (Benedict Caetani; c. 1234–1303)   Pope (1294–1303). He was elected after a long career in papal administration. An expert in canon law, he repeatedly clashed with *Philip IV of France concerning papal supremacy and the royal claim to judge and tax the clergy (which he also disputed with *Edward I of England). The bull *Unam Sanctam* (*One Holy*; 1302) proclaimed papal supremacy over temporal powers. In 1304 he was captured in Italy by Philip's forces and although soon released died shortly afterward.

Bonin Islands   A Japanese group of about 30 forested volcanic islands in the central Pacific Ocean, the most important being Chichi-jima. Strategically important during World War II, they were captured by the US in 1945 (returned 1968). Sugar cane, cocoa, and bananas are produced, timber is exported, and there is offshore whaling. Area: 40 sq mi (103 sq km). Population (1985 est): 700. Chief settlement: Omura.

bonito   A swift marine food and game fish, belonging to the worldwide genus *Sarda*, which is related to *mackerel and *tuna. About 30 in (75 cm) long, bonitos are greenish blue above, with dark longitudinal stripes, and silvery below. Other related fish called bonito include the leaping bonito (*Cybiosarda elegans*), plain bonito (*Orcynopsis unicolor*), and *skipjack tuna. □oceans.

Bonn   50 43N 7 07E   The capital of the Federal Republic of Germany in North Rhine-Westphalia on the Rhine River. The old part of the town contains the cathedral (12th–13th centuries) and Beethoven's birthplace (now a museum). The university was founded in 1786. *History*: originally settled by the Romans, it was destroyed by the Normans in the 9th century AD, and was the seat of the Electors of Cologne from the 13th to the 16th centuries. It passed from France to Prussia in 1815 and was made the federal capital in 1949. Berlin was proclaimed capital of the reunited Germany in 1990, but many government functions remained in Bonn. Population (1988): 292,000.

Bonnard, Pierre (1867–1947)   French painter. He took up art in Paris in the 1880s, after studying law, and as a member of the *Nabis, he painted decorative domestic scenes, influenced by Japanese prints. More original works of this period were his lithographs, *Aspects of the Life of Paris* (1895), and illustrations for Verlaine's book *Parallèlement* (1900). After 1900 his paintings of interiors, landscapes, and bathing women were treated increasingly with dazzling color and light.

Bonnet, Charles (1720–93) Swiss naturalist, noted for his speculations about evolution. He demonstrated that aphid eggs could develop without fertilization (*see* parthenogenesis). This led him to propose that every organism contained a sequence of preformed individuals corresponding to successive generations. His catastrophe theory of evolution argued that periodic destruction of most life forms was followed by evolutionary advancement of the survivors.

Bonneville Salt Flats (*or* Bonneville Flats) A barren salt plain in the US, in NW Utah. The flats form part of the Great Salt Lake Desert and are a relict feature of an ancient lake. Several world land speed records have been established here since 1935.

Bonnie Prince Charlie. *See* Charles Edward Stuart, the Young Pretender.

Bonny, Bight of (name until 1975: Bight of Biafra) An inlet of the Atlantic Ocean, bordering on Nigeria and Cameroon. It is the innermost bay of the Gulf of Guinea.

bonsai An ordinary shrub or tree, such as a conifer or flowering cherry, that is developed as a miniature (up to about 24 in [60 cm] high). The technique was first practiced as an art form in China over 700 years ago, probably using weather-beaten trees, which were considered aesthetically pleasing. It was later perfected by the Japanese (who treat good specimens as heirlooms) and has now spread to the W hemisphere. Bonsais grow from seeds or cuttings planted usually in earthenware pots with one or more drainage holes and containing a compost with a limited nutrient and water supply. Both branches and roots are trained and pruned. The trees may take ten years or more to acquire an aged appearance, and some live 300–400 years. Good hardy species may be kept outdoors for most of the year.

bontebok. *See* blesbok.

Bonus Army (1932) Unemployed veterans who marched on Washington, DC to demand payment of adjusted compensation certificates voted them in 1924, but deferred until 1945. After much rioting and violence, the veterans were given travel money and persuaded to leave the city, and by 1936 had received their compensation.

bony fish Any fish belonging to the class *Osteichthyes* (or *Pisces*), which includes the majority of food and game fishes (*see* teleost). They have bony skeletons and their gills are covered by a structure called an operculum. Many species use a swim bladder for buoyancy control and even for breathing air (*see* lungfish). Fertilization of the eggs occurs outside the body. Subclasses: *Actinopterygii*; *Sarcopterygii*.

booby A large tropical seabird belonging to the family *Sulidae* (gannets, etc.; 9 species) characterized by a large head, a long stout tapering bill, large webbed feet, and a wedge-shaped tail. Boobies are 26–33 in (65–85 cm) long and typically have a white plumage with brown markings. Boobies soar high over the sea, diving to catch fish and squids.

boogie-woogie A piano blues in which the left hand establishes a driving repetitive pattern with eight beats to the bar, while the right provides a variety of syncopation. Originating in the SW US, it was popular in the 1930s.

book A set of sheets of paper or similar material, usually bearing printed or handwritten words, folded and bound together between protective covers. The handwritten book (the codex), combining compactness, strength, and ease of use, began to oust its predecessor, the cumbersome papyrus scroll, during the 2nd century AD. Vellum (or parchment), being more durable than papyrus, became the preferred writing surface until the use of *paper spread slowly across Europe from 11th-century Byzantium. Printing at first brought no radical changes in book production, the sheets still being folded and bound by hand. Development of more efficient presses and cheaper paper production in the late 18th and early 19th centuries gradually brought the price of books within reach of the general public. During the 20th century paper binding (paperbacks) brought about a revolution in publishing so that in the US alone over 32,000 new titles are published each year. In response to this deluge libraries have evolved new methods of data storage, using microfiche and microfilm (*see* microcopy).

BOOBY *Blue-footed boobies* (Sula nebouxii) *of the Galapagos Islands in courtship display. The male (left) can be distinguished from the female by its smaller eye pupil.*

bookbinding The practice of sewing or gluing together the pages of a *book along one edge and securing them between protective covers (boards) joined across the back (spine) by a flexible hinge. Utilitarian in purpose, bookbinding has nonetheless long been practiced as a decorative art. In the Middle Ages wooden boards were common and elaborate examples were encrusted with precious metals and gems. The advent of printing encouraged diversification in the types of material used for binding, with leather and vellum becoming paramount. Gold tooling, the commonest form of decoration, reached a peak of elaboration in the 17th and 18th centuries. The spread of literacy caused a demand for still cheaper binding materials; cloth bindings (1822), and in the 20th century paper and plastics, have catered to this need.

Nowadays books are bound by machinery first invented in the late 19th century. The bindings are similar to hand bindings except in paperbacks, which are simply glued together. Hand binding remains a specialist craft employed in the production of luxury books.

Booker McConnell Prize An annual prize of £10,000 for a work of British fiction. It was set up in 1968 by the British engineering and trading company Booker McConnell, in conjunction with the Publishers Association, on the lines of the French Prix Goncourt (*see* Edmond de Goncourt). Since 1971 it has been administered by the National Book League. It is Britain's most prestigious literary prize.

booklouse A soft-bodied wingless insect 0.04–0.28 in (1–7 mm) long, also called dustlouse, belonging to the order *Psocoptera* (about 1600 species). Booklice inhabit buildings, often feeding on old books, papers, and entomological collections. *See also* bookworm.

bookmaking The occupation of accepting bets, chiefly involving horse racing and professional and college sports events, but also other sports, current events, etc. The bookmaker (bookie) lays odds against a particular horse winning a race, which the bettor accepts. Licensed betting shops have been established in some states. *See also* Totalizator.

Book of Changes. *See* I Ching.

Book of the Dead A collection of ancient Egyptian texts dating from the 16th century BC. They consist of charms, formulas, and spells written on papyrus and placed inside mummy cases for use by the dead in the afterlife.

bookworm Any insect that damages books by gnawing the bindings and boring holes in the paper. Bookworms therefore include *silverfish, booklice, moth and beetle larvae, etc.

Boole, George (1815–64) British mathematician, who applied the methods of algebra to logic. Replacing logical operations with symbols, Boole showed that the operations could be manipulated to give logically consistent results. His method, known as Boolean algebra or symbolic logic, led to mathematics being given a logically consistent foundation. The subject was further developed by G. Frege, B. A. W. *Russell, and A. N. *Whitehead.

boom The phase in the *trade cycle in which output reaches a peak. Booms are characterized by full employment, rising prices, high profits, and high investment that goes with business confidence. *Compare* depression; recession.

boomerang A curved hand-thrown wooden missile used by Australian Aborigines to kill game, as a weapon of war, or in play. The angled shape and the spin given to the missile when thrown enables the light types to return to the thrower if they miss their target. Up to 30 in (75 cm) long, they can be effective to a distance of 50 yd (45 m).

boomslang A venomous green snake, *Dispholidus typus*, occurring in African savanna and reaching 6 ft (1.8 m) in length. It feeds on birds and chameleons, lying in wait and often holding its body erect and motionless before striking. Small amounts of its venom can cause fatal hemorrhaging in man. Family: *Colubridae*.

Boone, Daniel (1734–1820) American pioneer. Born in Pennsylvania, he left home at an early age and became a hunter in North Carolina and later served in the *French and Indian War. In 1767 he led a group of settlers along the Wilderness Road through the Cumberland Gap into Kentucky. After several years of exploration there, he guided another group of settlers into Kentucky in 1775 to found a colony for the Transylvania Company. The settlement was later named Boonesboro. During the Revolutionary War, Boone was taken prisoner by the Shawnees, but he was adopted by the tribe and set free. After the war, he was appointed to several public offices in Kentucky but lost all his land holdings, due to a failure to register them properly. Late in his life he moved to Missouri, where he received a small land grant from Congress.

Boonesboro (*or* Boonesborough) A former fort in central Kentucky, SE of Lexington, on the Kentucky River. Settled by frontiersman Daniel Boone in 1775, it was the end of a branch of the Wilderness Road.

Boötes (Latin: herdsman) A large constellation in the N sky near Ursa Major. The brightest star is *Arcturus.

Booth, Edwin (1833–93) US actor. Born in Maryland, the son of the prominent actor Junius Brutus Booth (1796–1852) and older brother of John Wilkes *Booth, he first appeared on stage at age 16. He was best known for his performances in Shakespearean tragic roles, especially Hamlet, which he performed for one hundred consecutive nights in 1864. As a result of his great popularity and commercial success, he constructed Booth's Theater in New York in 1869, appearing there frequently until its closure in 1874. Financial difficulties forced him to spend the rest of his life touring the United States and Europe. He was the founder and first president of the Player's Club in 1889.

DANIEL BOONE *A renowned frontiersman who explored Kentucky and helped open the area for American settlers.*

Booth, John Wilkes (1838–65) US actor and assassin of Pres. Abraham *Lincoln. Born in Maryland, he was the younger brother of Edwin *Booth and achieved considerable success during his brief dramatic career. A partisan of the South during the Civil War, he masterminded a plot to assassinate the leading members of the Lincoln cabinet. On April 14, 1865, he shot and fatally wounded President Lincoln in Ford's Theater in Washington, DC. Booth fled Washington but was cornered and killed by federal troops near Bowling Green, Va. two weeks later.

Booth, William (1829–1912) British preacher and founder of the *Salvation Army. An itinerant Methodist preacher, he left the Methodists in order to do evangelistic work among the poor. The reluctance of established churches to accept his slum converts led to the foundation of the Salvation Army, with Booth as General (1877). His eldest son **William Bramwell Booth** (1856–1929) was chief of staff of the Salvation Army from 1880 and later General (1912–29). His daughter **Evangeline Booth** (1865–1950) was also a leading officer and then General (1934–39).

Boothia Peninsula A peninsula of N Canada projecting into the Arctic Ocean, in Franklin district. The northernmost part of the North American mainland, it is sparsely populated, with a police post and trading post. Area: 12,500 sq mi (32,375 sq km).

Bootle 53 28N 3 00W A city in NW England, on the River Mersey adjacent to N Liverpool. Bootle's docks are extensive and modern and its industries include engineering, tanning, tin smelting, and flour milling. Population (1981): 62,463.

bootlegging The illegal distribution or production of highly taxed goods, especially liquor or cigarettes. During *Prohibition (1919–33), when the manufacture, sale, and transportation of alcohol was banned, a well-organized illegal industry developed. Gangsters, such as Al *Capone, controlled both speakeasies (illegal bars) and private distribution systems. Other illegal activities (graft, extortion, protection rackets, prostitution) accompanied bootlegging and became the basis of an organized crime empire still active. Bootlegging, including the use of illegal stills, continues in certain areas of the US, especially "dry" areas (where liquor is not sold).

bootstrap theory The theory in which no elementary particle is regarded as being more fundamental than any other. Each particle exists by virtue of the existence of all the others. Its name derives from the phrase "to pull oneself up by the bootstraps." The theory avoids the problem of a series of classes of particles, each more fundamental than the last. *See also* particle physics.

bop (*or* bebop) A type of *jazz that originated in the US in the 1940s as a reaction against swing. Bop emphasized the art of melodic improvisation neglected during the swing era, but was also characterized by harmonic and rhythmic experimentation. In New York City, Dizzy Gillespie and Charlie "Bird" Parker established small bop bands that required the audience to listen rather than dance.

Bophuthaswana, Republic of A small country in S Africa, consisting of several separate landlocked areas. The majority of the population is Tswana. *Economy*: chiefly subsistence agriculture, especially livestock; much is being done to improve production by means of irrigation schemes. Rich mineral resources include chrome, platinum, asbestos, and iron. *History*: in 1972 it became the first *Bantu Homeland to receive self-government under the Bantu Homelands Constitution Act (1971). It was granted independence in 1977, but this is recognized only by South Africa; the granting of independence in effect wrested South African citizenship from its people. Official currency: South African rand. Area: 14,769 sq mi (38,261 sq km). Population (1985): 1,627,000, of whom 65% lived in South Africa. Capital: Montshiwa.

borage A widely grown annual Mediterranean herb, *Borago officinalis*. Borage is a stiff hairy plant, up to 24 in (60 cm) high, with terminal clusters of small blue flowers with backward-pointing petals. It is used in herbal remedies, potpourri, beverages, and salads and the flowers may be candied. Family: *Boraginaceae*.

Borah, William Edgar (1865–1940) US politician and lawyer. After successfully practicing law and chairing the Idaho Republican State Central Committee, he became a US senator (1907–40) and headed the Senate Foreign Relations Committee (1925–33). While in office he was responsible for the creation of the Department of Labor (1913), for the US not joining the League of Nations after

World War I, and for the Washington Disarmament Conference (1921–22). Although known as an isolationist, he advocated recognition of the Soviet Union.

boranes Compounds of boron and hydrogen. The simplest is diborane B_2H_6, which is made by reacting sodium borohydride ($NaBH_4$) with *sulfuric acid. The formulas of boranes are not accounted for by classical theories of valence and their molecules contain electron-deficient bonds.

Borås 57 44N 12 55E A city in S Sweden. It is an important center of the textile industry. Population (1985 est): 100,000.

borax (or sodium tetraborate; $Na_2B_4O_7$) A natural substance, usually occurring in hydrated crystalline form. It is found in some salt lakes and in alkaline soils and is used in the manufacture of glass and enamel.

Bordeaux (Latin name: Burdigala) 44 50N 0 34W A city in SW France, the capital of the Gironde department on the Garonne River. It is a major seaport and wine center. Industries include shipbuilding, engineering, oil and sugar refining, and chemicals. There are many fine 18th-century buildings and squares, a cathedral (12th–15th centuries), and a university (1441). *History*: an important commercial center under the Romans, it became the capital of Aquitania (*see* Aquitaine) but declined following the collapse of the Roman Empire. It flourished once again under English rule (1154–1453). It became a center of the Fronde in the 17th century and of the Girondins during the French Revolution. It was the seat of the French government for a brief period in 1914 and again in 1940. Population (1975): 226,281.

Borden, Lizzie (Andrew) (1860–1927) US murder suspect. Thought to have axed to death her well-to-do father and stepmother in Fall River, Mass., in 1892, she was acquitted by a jury in 1893. The mystery that still surrounds the case has long been talked, sung, and written about.

Borden, Sir Robert Laird (1854–1937) Canadian statesman; Conservative prime minister (1911–20). An advocate of economic independence, he opposed a reciprocal trade agreement with the US and came to power after defeating the Liberals on this issue. He formed a coalition government to introduce conscription in 1917 and gave women the vote in 1918. Borden supported British policies but claimed more independence for Canada in world affairs, winning separate Canadian representation at the League of Nations.

Border States Slave-holding states (Delaware, Maryland, West Virginia, Kentucky, Missouri) that bordered the South and stayed in the Union during the US Civil War. During the war they continued slavery, having been exempted from the Emancipation Proclamation (1863) by Pres. Abraham *Lincoln, while fighting for the Northern cause.

border terrier A breed of working dog originating in the border region of England and Scotland. It has a deep narrow body, triangular forward-falling ears, and a short strong muzzle. The coat is red, yellowish-brown, gray and tan, or blue and tan. Weight: 13–15 lb (6–7 kg) for dogs; 11–13 lb (5–6 kg) for bitches.

Bordet, Jules Jean Baptiste Vincent (1870–1961) Belgian bacteriologist, who discovered (1895) the two factors (antibody and complement) in blood serum responsible for the rupture of bacterial cells. This fundamental discovery paved the way for diagnostic tests for many bacterial diseases, including syphilis. Bordet founded the Pasteur Institute, Brussels (1901), and was awarded the 1919 Nobel Prize for Medicine.

bore In oceanography, a tidal flood wave with a steep front occurring in certain estuaries and traveling upstream at great speed, sometimes to a distance of several kilometers. It occurs when the spring flood tide brings sea water into an estuary more quickly than it can travel up the river, so that a ridge of water builds up.

Borelli, Giovanni Alfonso (1608–79) Italian physicist and physiologist, who attempted to explain the workings of the body in purely mechanical terms (*De Motu Animalium*, 1680–81). A friend of *Galileo, Borelli made contributions to astronomy, including ideas concerning the attractive forces between planets, their orbits, and the path taken by comets through space.

Borg, Bjorn (1956–   ) Swedish tennis player, the world's leading player in the late 1970s. In 1980 he won the men's singles at Wimbledon for the fifth consecutive year, thus beating the record of three consecutive wins. He retired from world class competition in 1983.

Borgå. *See* Porvoo.

Borges, Jorge Luis (1899–1986) Argentinian writer and scholar. Educated in Europe, he joined the Spanish avant-garde Ultraist movement in 1920. In 1921 he returned to Argentina, where he founded three literary journals and published a book of poems in 1923. His best-known works are collections of intricate, fantastic, and paradoxical stories, especially *Fictions* (1944, 1966) and *The Aleph* (1949, 1970). He became director of the National Library in 1955, when already almost totally blind.

Borghese An Italian family that originated in Siena and rose to wealth and fame following its move to Rome in the 16th century and the election in 1605 of **Camillo Borghese** (1552–1621) as Pope Paul V. He advanced his family's fortunes, particularly those of his adopted nephew **Scipione Caffarelli** (1576–1633), an astute church politician and lavish art patron, who sponsored *Bernini and built the Villa Borghese (now an art gallery) in Rome. In 1803 **Camillo Filippo Ludovico Borghese** (1775–1832) married Napoleon's sister, Marie Pauline (1780–1825). The family split into two branches later in the 19th century.

Borgia, Cesare (c. 1475–1507) Duke of Romagna and captain general of the armies of the Church. The illegitimate son of Pope *Alexander VI, Borgia became Archbishop of Valencia and a cardinal following his father's election to the papacy (1492). He surrendered his cardinalship to marry the sister of the King of Navarre and to become captain general of the Church. He won the Romagna, with French help, in three campaigns (1499–1502), for which Machiavelli regarded him as the savior of Italy. Borgia was forced to relinquish the Romagna after Alexander's death (1502) and was imprisoned. He escaped and died in the employ of the Navarrese king. His sister **Lucrezia Borgia**, unfairly notorious for immorality, was married three times by her father Alexander VI to further his political aims. Her third husband Alfonso (1486–1534) became Duke of Este and she presided over a culturally distinguished court at Ferrara.

Borglum, Gutzon (1867–1941) US sculptor, famous for his gigantic sculptured heads of US presidents, inspired by similar ancient Egyptian monuments. Best known are those carved on rocks of the *Mount Rushmore National Memorial, the head of Lincoln in the US Capitol rotunda, and the 12 apostles in the cathedral of Saint John the Divine in New York City.

Boris (I) of Bulgaria (d. 907 AD) Khan of Bulgaria (852–89). Boris was converted to Orthodox Christianity in 865 and encouraged the spread of Christianity among the Bulgars. His reign gave birth to Slavonic-Bulgarian literature and civilization. In 889 he abdicated and entered a monastery.

Boris III (1894–1943) King of Bulgaria (1918–1943). Boris ruled as a dictator from 1938 and supported the Axis Powers in World War II. He apparently died of a heart attack but may have been assassinated.

BJORN BORG *Playing at Wimbledon, England, in 1979.*

Borlaug, Norman (1914–) US plant breeder, who developed new strains of wheat and rice for underdeveloped countries. Working in Mexico since 1944, he received the Nobel Peace Prize (1970) for his role in the "green revolution." His miracle grains have had their greatest impact in Mexico and India.

Bormann, Martin (1900–45) German Nazi leader. Prominent in the Nazi Party from 1925, he became Hitler's personal secretary in 1942. He was sentenced to death in absentia at Nuremburg. In 1973 it was established that he had committed suicide in May 1945.

Born, Max (1882–1970) British physicist, born in Germany. He shared the 1954 Nobel Prize with W. Bothe for his work in statistical mechanics. Born and *Heisenberg developed matrix mechanics, which *Schrödinger was able to show was equivalent to his own wave mechanics. Born was professor of natural philosophy at Edinburgh University from 1936 to 1953.

Borneo An island SE of Peninsular Malaysia, in the Greater Sunda Islands, the third largest island in the world. During the 19th century Borneo was settled and virtually partitioned by the Dutch and British to protect their East India companies from piracy. It now consists politically of the Indonesian territory of *Kalimantan (about 70%), the Malaysian states of *Sabah and *Sarawak, and the independent nation of *Brunei. It is mountainous with coastal swamps and dense jungle. The chief population groups are the coastal Malays and indigenous Dyaks. It possesses valuable resources of oil, coal, and gold. Area: 290,000 sq mi (750,000 sq km).

Bornholm 55 02N 15 00E A Danish island in the Baltic Sea, SE of Sweden. Dairy farming is practiced and industries include pottery, using locally worked clay, and watchmaking; tourism is important during summer. Area: 227 sq mi (588 sq km). Chief town: Rønne.

Bornu A former Muslim kingdom in West Africa. It existed from the 11th century until the late 19th century, when it was divided among Britain, France, and Germany. Most of the area was incorporated into the protectorate of Northern Nigeria in 1900 and the modern Nigerian state of Bornu encompasses part of the former kingdom.

Borobudur A huge Buddhist stupa (shrine) complex in central Java, Indonesia, built about 800 AD and abandoned, unfinished, about 1000. It has five square terraces of diminishing size, one on top of the other, on the vertical surfaces of which is carved a continuous relief depicting the Buddha's life and doctrine. On top, three circular terraces support 72 stupas around a crowning central stupa, all with a Buddha icon.

Borodin, Aleksandr Porfirevich (1833–87) Russian composer, one of the *Five. A professor of chemistry and medicine, he had little formal training and lacked time to compose. Nevertheless, he produced two symphonies (1867 and 1876), the tone poem *In the Steppes of Central Asia* (1880), three string quartets, and the opera *Prince Igor* (completed by *Rimsky-Korsakov and Glazunov in 1890), which contains the famous *Polovtsian Dances*.

boron (B) A nonmetallic element isolated (1808) by Sir Humphry Davy. It has two forms: an impure brownish amorphous powder and pure brown crystals. The main source, kernite ($Na_2B_4O_7.4H_2O$), is mined in California. Boron is used in semiconductors and in hardened steel. Boron fibers are used in lightweight composite materials. The isotope boron-10 absorbs neutrons: boron carbide (B_4C) and boron alloys are used in the control rods and shielding of nuclear reactors. Other compounds include borax ($Na_2B_4O_7.10H_2O$), used in glass manufacture, and boric acid (H_3BO_3), used in ceramics and fireproofing. At no 5; at wt 10.81; mp 4144°F (2300°C).

Borromeo, St Charles (1538–84) Italian churchman, Cardinal and Archbishop of Milan. He was appointed to his offices in 1560 by his uncle, Pope Pius IV. He played a leading part in the third convocation of the Council of Trent (1562–63) and actively supported the evangelization of Switzerland. These activities and the capable reforms he carried out in his archdiocese made him an important Counter-Reformation figure. Feast day: Nov 4.

Borromini, Francesco (1599–1667) Italian baroque architect. Born in N Italy, he settled in □Rome, where all his work was executed. With his rival *Bernini, he brought the baroque style in Rome to its peak. His highly individual approach expressed the classical architectural style in forms never before achieved. Although much less successful than Bernini, he was in many ways a greater genius as an architect. His main buildings, S Carlo (1641), S Ivo (1660), and the oratorio of S Filippo Neri (1650), showed a virtuosity of decoration and a command of complex spatial effects that Bernini never approached.

Borstal system An English penal system established (1908) for the rehabilitation and training of offenders aged between 15 and 21. They may be detained in an institution called a Borstal for between six months and two years. Following release, the offender remains under supervision for two years and may be recalled to a Borstal if he commits an offense. The name derives from the prison at Borstal, where the system was introduced in 1902.

borzoi A breed of large □dog originating in Russia, also called Russian wolfhound and used originally for hunting wolves and for hare coursing. The borzoi is a lightly built swift runner with a long silky coat, which is usually white with black to light-brown patches. Height: about 28 in (70 cm).

Bosanquet, Bernard (1848–1923) British philosopher. His early neo-Hegelian philosophy saw the individuality of persons, institutions, and works of art as a combination of abstract general concepts (universals). His *Philosophical Theory of the State* (1899) presents a solution to the problem of communal will and individual liberty. *Bradley influenced his later work.

Bosch, Carl (1874–1940) German chemist, who developed the *Haber process for the conversion of atmospheric nitrogen into ammonia, so that it could be used industrially. This Haber-Bosch process has been used to manufacture enormous quantities of nitrates for both explosives and fertilizers. He shared the 1931 Nobel Prize for Chemistry for his work on high-pressure reactions.

Bosch, Hieronymus (Jerome van Aeken; c. 1450–c. 1516) Dutch painter. He was born in 's-Hertogenbosch (hence his name), where from 1486 he belonged to the Roman Catholic Brotherhood of Our Lady. His allegories have been interpreted variously as forerunners of *surrealism or as expressions of heretical beliefs but as his patrons, including Philip II of Spain, were devout Catholics, they were probably intended as sermons on evil and its consequences. The often inexplicable symbolism and fantastic imagery of half-animal half-human creatures and devils was inspired by contemporary proverbs and writings. Among his major works are *The Haywain* (El Escorial) and *Garden of Earthly Delights* (Prado).

Bose, Sir Jagadis Chandra (1858–1937) Indian plant physiologist and physicist. His research into plant behavior, in which he showed how plants responded to external stimuli (such as injury), revealed parallels between plant and animal tissues. He also invented the crescograph (a device for measuring plant growth) and founded the Bose Research Institute, Calcutta.

Bose, Subhas Chandra (c. 1897–c. 1945) Indian nationalist leader. He was a civil servant before joining Gandhi's movement of noncooperation with the British. He became president of the *Indian National Congress in 1938 but resigned in 1939 because of disagreement with Gandhi over policy. Arrested and imprisoned in Calcutta (1940), he left India in 1941. With Japanese help he organized in Singapore the Indian National Army to free India from British rule (1943). He was said to have been killed in an air crash in 1945.

Bose-Einstein statistics One of two statistical approaches to quantum mechanical problems: it assumes that any number of identical particles may occupy the same energy level. The other statistical method is called *Fermi-Dirac statistics. Particles that obey Bose-Einstein statistics are called *bosons. Named for S. N. Bose (1894–1974) and A. *Einstein.

Bosnia and Hercegovina (Serbo-Croat name: Bosna I Hercegovina) A country in SE Europe, formerly a constituent republic of Yugoslavia. It consists of a chiefly mountainous triangular-shaped area with karst topography. It is primarily agricultural, producing mainly cereals, vegetables, fruit, and tobacco; sheep are also raised. *History*: part of ancient Illyria, the region was inhabited by Slavs from the 7th century AD onward. Bosnia became a separate political entity in the 10th century but later came under the control of Hungary. It became an independent kingdom in the late 14th century and annexed Hercegovina but fell to the Turks in 1463, remaining under their control for four centuries. In 1908 it was annexed to Austria-Hungary; Serbian opposition to this led to the assassination of Archduke Francis Ferdinand, precipitating World War I. After the war, when Austria-Hungary was dissolved, it became part of the kingdom that was to become Yugoslavia in 1929. In 1992, Bosnia and Hercegovina's declaration of independence precipitated civil war among the country's various ethnic factions, particularly the Serbs who were opposed to breaking away from Yugoslavia. The capital, Sarajevo, was devastated. Area: 19,737 sq mi (51,129 sq km). Population (1986): 4,360,000. Capital: Sarajevo.

boson A class of elementary particles with integral spin. Bosons always obey *Bose-Einstein statistics and include all the *mesons and the *photon. *See* particle physics.

Bosporus (Turkish name: Karadeniz Boğazi) A strait separating Europe and Asia and connecting the Black Sea with the Sea of Marmara. It has Istanbul at its S end and it is spanned by one of the world's longest suspension bridges. Length: about 19 mi (30 km). Width: about 0.4–2.5 mi (0.6–4 km).

boss In architecture, a small projection in a roof vault, covering the crossing of the supporting ribs. Although sometimes plain, medieval bosses were frequently carved into elaborate decorative shapes. *See also* gothic architecture.

Bossuet, Jacques Bénigne (1627–1704) French Roman Catholic bishop and preacher. He became famous for several funeral orations on prominent persons, such as that on *Henrietta Maria delivered in 1669. He became Bishop of Meaux in 1681, having first been tutor to the dauphin, and later attempted to bring about a compromise between Louis XIV and the pope on the issue of *Gallicanism. He wrote a number of devotional and apologetic works.

Boston 42 20N 71 05W The capital of Massachusetts, on Massachusetts Bay. It is an important port and market for fish and a major financial center. Its industries include publishing, food processing, and the manufacture of machinery. An architecturally exceptional city, its most notable buildings are the old State House (1748), Faneuil Hall (1762), and the State Capitol (1798). Boston is a major cultural and educational center. It is the site of Boston University (1869), Northeastern University (1898), and Boston Latin School (established in 1635 and one of the country's first free secondary schools). Harvard Medical School is also situated here. Notable residents have included Nathaniel Hawthorne, Henry Thoreau, Ralph Emerson, and Longfellow. *History*: founded in 1630 by Puritan Englishmen, it prospered as the main colony of the Massachusetts Bay Company. It became a center of opposition to the British prior to the American Revolution (*see* Boston Tea Party). Often dubbed the "Hub of the Universe," Boston flourished as the commercial, industrial, and financial center of the New England states during the early 19th century. It was a leading force in the anti-slavery movement during the 1830s. Population (1990): 574,283.

Boston Massacre (1770) An incident in which five Americans, part of a crowd protesting the quartering of British soldiers in their homes, were killed by the British. Crispus *Attucks was the first fatality. The British soldiers were arrested, tried, and acquitted, due to the efforts of American lawyers, who then turned around and used the incident to promote the cause of the patriots. Eventually, the troops were moved from the city to islands in the harbor.

Boston Tea Party (1773) An expression of colonial hostility toward Britain before the *American Revolution. A group of Americans dressed as Indians, objecting to the import of cheap tea, enforced by the Tea Act to rid the East India Company of its surplus stocks, threw a cargo of tea into Boston harbor. Britain retaliated with the *Intolerable Acts. *See also* Stamp Act.

Boston terrier A breed of □dog originating in the US from crosses between bulldogs and terriers. It is compactly built with a short square muzzle and a short tail. The short smooth coat is brown to brownish-yellow with white markings. Height: about 15 in (38 cm).

Boswell, James (1740–95) Scottish writer, the biographer of Samuel *Johnson. Son of an Edinburgh advocate, he came to London in 1760 and first met Johnson in 1763. He traveled widely on the Continent from 1764 to 1766, meeting other famous men, such as Voltaire and Rousseau. Although he practiced law in Edinburgh from 1766 to 1788, he maintained a close relationship with Johnson. The biography, published in 1791, was widely acclaimed but in later years he suffered from severe depression and alcoholism.

Bosworth Field, Battle of (Aug 22, 1485) The battle fought near Market Bosworth, Leicestershire, in which Henry Tudor defeated Richard III, thereby ending the Wars of the *Roses. Richard was killed in the battle and Henry became the first *Tudor monarch, as Henry VII.

botanic gardens Collections of growing plants designed to display both familiar native plants and more unusual alien species, particularly ornamentals. Often the plants are grouped to demonstrate their evolutionary and geographical relationships or their similar ecological requirements. Some gardens concentrate on certain types of plants: an arboretum is one specializing in trees and shrubs. Botanic gardens originated in ancient China, as collections of fruit, vegetables, and medicinal plants, but it was not until the 16th and 17th centuries that they became popular in Europe, the first being established in Italy, at Pisa (1543) and Padua (1545). Today the larger botanic gardens have extensive herbaria, where dried labeled specimens are kept for reference. Many have their own laboratories and libraries, providing facilities for research scientists, and often hold courses in horticultural techniques for trainee gardeners. Most also concentrate on preserving and propagating rare species, with greenhouses and culture techniques for those with specialized needs. *See also* Kew Gardens.

botany The scientific study of plants. From ancient times plants have figured prominently in human cultures as man is dependent on them for food, shelter, drugs, and many other purposes. Scientific botany dates from the 4th century BC, with the studies of the ancient Greeks—notably *Theophrastus, who is said to have founded the science, and *Dioscorides, who published one of the first herbals. Until the 17th century botany was almost entirely restricted to the description and properties of medicinal plants. The basic principles of modern plant classification were laid down by John *Ray at the end of the 17th century, and by the middle of the 18th century *Linnaeus had published his works on the naming and classification of plants, which established the principles of *taxonomy still used today for both plants and animals. The invention of the microscope in the 16th century enabled detailed studies of plant structure, culminating in *Schleiden's theory of the cellular nature of plants in the 1830s. The 18th century saw important advances in plant physiology with the discovery of *photosynthesis, the food-manufacturing process of green plants. During the 19th century the origin of plant species was elucidated in Charles *Darwin's theory of evolution and Gregor *Mendel—working with plants—established the mechanisms of inheritance.

Botany in the 20th century has been revolutionized by advances in physiology, biochemistry, and breeding techniques, which have greatly increased the economic importance of plants and enabled a scientific approach to the related disciplines of *horticulture, *agriculture, and forestry. *See also* biological sciences.

Botany Bay An inlet of the Tasman Sea, in SE Australia. It was the site of Capt Cook's first landing in Australia (1770). The bay is now surrounded by the suburbs of Sydney. Industries, located chiefly on the N shore, include chemicals, plastics, and fiberglass, with an oil refinery on the SE shore. Area: about 16 sq mi (42 sq km).

botfly A hairy beelike fly belonging to the families *Gasterophilidae* (horse botflies), *Calliphoridae* (e.g. the deer botfly), or *Oestridae* (e.g. the sheep botfly). The larvae are parasitic in mammals, often living within nasal and sinus cavities or in the digestive tract to cause irritation, weakening, and vertigo. When mature the larvae pass out with the feces. *Compare* warble fly.

Botha, Louis (1862–1919) South African statesman; the first prime minister of the Union of South Africa (1910–19). Botha grew up in the Orange Free State, where his parents had settled after the Great Trek from Natal. In 1897 he became a member of the Transvaal Volksraad (parliament) and commanded the Transvaal's forces during the second *Boer War. He became prime minister of the Transvaal in 1907 and of the newly formed Union in 1910.

Botha, P(ieter) W(illem) (1916–) South African statesman; prime minister (1978–84) and state president (1984–89). As defense minister (1966–78) under his predecessor, Vorster, he was largely responsible for South Africa's intervention in 1975 in the civil war in Angola. Following a 1983 referendum, Botha's government began a policy of allowing some nonwhites limited participation in the political process, although blacks would not be included. In 1984 he signed a joint security pact with Mozambique intended to end conflict between the two countries. He resigned his office in 1989 due to illness.

Bothe, Walther Wilhelm Georg Franz (1891–1957) German experimental physicist, who (with H. *Geiger) developed the coincidence method for particle counting. The use of this technique in cosmic radiation research brought him a share (with Max *Born) in the Nobel Prize for 1954. During World War II he built Germany's first cyclotron. He was responsible for discovering the particle later identified by *Chadwick as the neutron.

Bothnia, Gulf of A shallow section of the Baltic Sea, between Sweden and Finland. It remains frozen for about five months of the year because of its low salinity. Its many small islands restrict navigation. Area: about 45,200 sq mi (117,000 sq km).

Bothwell, James Hepburn, 4th Earl of (c. 1535–78) The third husband of Mary, Queen of Scots. He was almost certainly responsible for the murder of her former husband *Darnley in 1567, after which he allegedly abducted Mary and married her; they may already have been lovers. Following their defeat at Carberry Hill, Bothwell escaped to Denmark, where he died, insane, in captivity.

bo tree An Indian tree, *Ficus religiosa*, up to 98 ft (30 m) high, also called the peepul or pipal. It has heart-shaped leaves, the tips of which are drawn out into a long narrow tail, and globular fleshy purple fruits. Related to the fig, the bo tree is sacred to Buddhists, as it was the tree under which Buddha sat when he attained enlightenment. Family: *Moraceae* (mulberry family).

Botswana, Republic of (former name until 1966: Bechuanaland) A country in the center of S Africa, lying between the Zambezi and Molopo Rivers. It is largely an arid plateau, with the Kalahari Desert in the S and W and some hills in the E. The Okavango River in the N, with its marshy basin, is important for irrigation. The majority of the population, consisting mainly of the Bantu-speaking Tswana group, lives along the E border. The original inhabitants, the Bushmen, now comprise only a small minority. *Economy*: chiefly agricultural, with livestock, especially cattle, taking precedence over crops, which are still largely dependent on the rather sparse rainfall. In 1975 land ownership was reformed to permit more modern use of land. Large quantities of minerals, discovered in the 1960s, are now being developed and these include diamonds, nickel, copper, and coal. The main exports are beef and by-products of cattle but minerals are rapidly becoming an important source of export revenue. *History*: the area became the British Protectorate of Bechuanaland in 1885 and was annexed to the Cape Colony in 1895. It later became a British High Commission Territory, gaining internal self-government in 1965 and full independence in 1966 as the Republic of Botswana within the Commonwealth of Nations. Until 1980 it was under the democratic rule of Sir Seretse *Khama, who maintained a delicate balance in his opposition to the policies of neighboring countries, in spite of being dependent on them for communications and trade. He was succeeded by Quett K. J. Masire. Official language: English; the main African language is Tswana. Official currency: pula of 100 thebe. Area: 222,000 sq mi (575,000 sq km). Population (1990 est): 1,218,000. Capital: Gaborone.

Botticelli, Sandro (Alessandro di Mariano Filipepi; c. 1445–1510) Florentine *Renaissance painter, named for his brother's nickname, meaning "little barrel." He trained under Filippo *Lippi. His chief patrons were the Medici, for whom he produced illustrations for Dante's *Divine Comedy* and allegorical paintings, influenced by humanist writers, such as *Primavera*, *Birth of Venus* (both Uffizi), and *Mars and Venus* (National Gallery, London). They are notable for their graceful draftsmanship. In 1481–82 he worked on frescoes for the Sistine Chapel, in the Vatican. Probably under the influence of the religious leader *Savonarola, his later works, e.g. *Mystic Nativity* (1501; National Gallery, London), became more religious and emotional.

bottlebrush An evergreen Australian shrub or tree of the genus *Callistemon* (25 species). Growing to a height of about 20 ft (6 m), it has stiff narrow leaves, 2 in (5 cm) long. The flower heads consist mainly of bunches of fluffy red or yellow stamens, resembling bottle brushes. The fruits are woody. Bottlebrushes may be grown as ornamental hedges and shrubs. Family: *Myrtaceae*.

bottlenose A *dolphin, *Tursiops truncatus*, with a short beak. Gray-blue and growing to 13 ft (4 m), bottlenose dolphins are a shallow-water species and have become popular in dolphinariums. They have been the subject of research into the social behavior and language of whales. □mammal.

Bottrop 51 31N 6 55E A city in western Germany in North Rhine-Westphalia in the *Ruhr. Its main industries are coal mining and the manufacture of by-products. Population (1988): 112,000.

botulism A rare and serious form of *food poisoning from foods containing the toxin produced by the bacterium *Clostridium botulinum*. The toxin can affect the cardiac and respiratory centers of the brain and may result in death by heart or lung failure. The bacterium thrives in improperly preserved foods, such as canned raw meats. The toxin is invariably destroyed in cooking.

Botvinnik, Mikhail Moiseivich (1911–) Soviet chess player, who was world champion (1948–57, 1958–60, 1961–63), losing the title to *Petrosian (1963). He was also a successful electrical engineer.

Bouaké 7 42N 5 00W A city in the central Ivory Coast. It is an important trade center, linked by rail and road to Abidjan, with a trade in coffee, cocoa, and rice. Population (1984 est): 200,000.

Boucher, François (1703–70) French *rococo painter, born in Paris, the son of a lacemaker. He studied in Italy (1727–31) but was chiefly influenced by *Watteau, many of whose drawings he engraved. He worked for Louis XV, and Madame de Pompadour, whom he painted (Wallace Collection, London), and to whom he gave art lessons. He became director of both the Gobelins tapestry factory (1755), for which he produced designs, and of the French Academy (1765). His paintings are mainly mythological and pastoral scenes and nudes.

Boucher de Perthes, Jacques (1788–1868) French antiquary. In the Somme valley he discovered stone implements together with extinct animal remains; these made him challenge contemporary theories about human origins. His *De la création* (1838–41) and *Antiquités celtiques et antédiluviennes* (1847) argue for the human race's great antiquity.

Boudicca. *See* Boadicea.

Boudin, Eugène (1824–98) French painter and forerunner of *impressionism, born in Honfleur. He painted his coastal scenes in the open air instead of the studio and encouraged *Monet in this practice.

Bougainville A volcanic forested island in the SW Pacific Ocean, the largest in the *Solomon Islands archipelago and a province of Papua New Guinea. Copra, cocoa, timber, and tortoise shell are exported. Area: about 4000 sq mi (10,360 sq km). Chief town: Kieta.

Bougainville, Louis Antoine de (1729–1811) French navigator. After service in the Seven Years' War in Canada he joined the navy. Between 1766 and 1769 he circumnavigated the world and wrote an account of the journey in *A Voyage round the World* (1771). He was later a successful commander in the American Revolution. Several geographical features, including the island Bougainville, and the plant genus *Bougainvillea* are named for him.

Bougainvillea A genus of tropical South American shrubs (18 species) climbing by means of hooked thorns. The shrubs bear numerous showy "flowers," usually reddish-purple, for most of the year. The colored parts are actually large bracts, which surround the small inconspicuous flowers. *Bougainvillea* is grown as an ornamental throughout the tropics and subtropics. Family: *Nyctaginaceae*.

Boulanger, Nadia (Juliette) (1887–1979) French composer, teacher, and conductor. Lennox *Berkeley and Aaron *Copland have been among her pupils. Her works include the cantata *La Sirène* (1908; awarded the Prix de Rome), the opera *La Ville morte* (1911), choral works, and instrumental pieces.

NADIA BOULANGER *Rehearsing the Boston Symphony Orchestra in 1962.*

Boulder 40 01N 105 17W A city in N central Colorado, on the E edge of the Rocky Mountains. The town was settled in 1858, and the University of Colorado was established in 1876. It is a center of scientific research; mining, agriculture, and tourism are other important activities. Population (1990): 83,312.

boules A French game similar to *bowls, often played on rough ground. The players aim small metal bowls at a target ball (*cochonnet*).

Boulez, Pierre (1925–   ) French composer and conductor, a pupil of Messiaen. Boulez has been active as a conductor of contemporary music and his own work reflects the influence of Schoenberg, Webern, and Cage. He has used total *serialism in such works as *Structures I and II* (for two pianos; 1951–52 and 1956–61) and has set poems by René Char in *Le Marteau sans maître* (for contralto and 6 instruments; 1953–55) as well as poems by Mallarmé in *Pli selon pli* (for soprano and orchestra; 1957–60) and *Répons* (1981).

Boulle, André Charles (*or* Buhl; 1642–1732) French cabinetmaker in the service of Louis XIV. He gave his name to the technique of boullework (*or* buhlwork), a style of marquetry using brass, tortoiseshell, mother-of-pearl, etc., inlaid on ebony.

Boulogne-sur-Mer 50 43N 1 37E A port and resort in N France, in the Pas-de-Calais department on the English Channel. It was severely damaged in World War II. It is the country's main fishing port and has a ferry service to England. Industries include boat building, textiles, and steel. Population (1983): 99,000.

Boulton, Matthew. *See* Watt, James.

Boumédienne, Houari (Mohammed Boukharouba; 1925–78) Algerian statesman; president (1965–78). In 1960 he became chief of staff of the nationalist forces fighting the French. After independence in 1962 he became minister of defense and then vice president under *Ben Bella. In 1965 he overthrew Ben Bella to become president.

Bourbons A European ruling dynasty that originated in Bourbonnais (now Allier, central France). It acquired ducal status in 1272, when Agnès Bourbon married the sixth son of Louis IX. The first Bourbon king of France was *Henry IV (reigned 1589–1610) after whom the house continued to rule until the *French Revolution (1792). The Bourbons were briefly restored under *Louis Philippe (1830–48), a member of a cadet branch.

The Bourbon Louis XIV's grandson became (1700) *Philip V of Spain, where the Bourbons ruled almost continuously until the abdication of *Alfonso XIII in 1931. His grandson *Juan Carlos was restored to the Spanish throne in 1975. In Naples and Sicily, Bourbons ruled between 1734 and 1860.

Bourdelle, Émile (1861–1929) French sculptor. Influenced by his teacher *Rodin, Bourdelle initially relied on vigorous surface carving for expressive effect. After 1910 he became popular and influential with his sculptures inspired by classical Greek art.

Bourgeois, Léon (1851–1925) French statesman; prime minister (1895–96). He was the chief theorist of solidarism, the concept that an individual's rights in society must be balanced by his responsibility to it. Prominent in the League of Nations, he won the Nobel Peace Prize in 1920.

bourgeoisie Originally, the urban merchants who developed trade at the end of the Middle Ages and who led the struggle against the feudal aristocracy for the rights of citizenship. The meaning was later extended to include the whole middle class. In the 19th century, *Marx used the concept within his theory of class struggle to describe the propertied entrepreneurs who created industrial capitalism and liberal democracy; conflict between the bourgeoisie and the *proletariat would ultimately lead to revolution. *See* Marxism.

Bourges (Latin name: Avaricum) 47 05N 2 23E A city in central France, the capital of the Cher department. An important town of Aquitaine, it became the capital of Berry in the 12th century and the French center of power following the battle of Agincourt (1415). It has a fine gothic cathedral. Industries include textiles and armaments. Population (1982): 92,000.

Bourguiba, Habib (1902–) Tunisian statesman; president (1956–87). A leading figure in the struggle for Tunisian independence, he formed the Neo-Destour Party in 1934. He spent ten years between 1934 and 1955 in French prisons. On independence in 1956 he became president, being reelected three times (1959, 1964, 1969), and in 1974 became life president; he was, however, overthrown in a coup in 1987.

Bournemouth 50 43N 1 54W A resort in S England, in Dorset on Poole Bay. It is a large all-year-round resort with many tourist attractions, including 6 mi (10 km) of beach. It has a famous symphony orchestra. Population (1981 est): 144,803.

Boutros-Ghali, Boutros (1922–) UN secretary general (1992–), an Egyptian diplomat who was the first African to head the UN. He attempted to focus world attention on the problems of the Third World, such as Somalia's civil war, while also dealing with civil war among Balkan nations and with tensions in the Middle East in the wake of the Persian Gulf War. He was a law professor before becoming a diplomat and was Egypt's foreign minister from 1977, when Egypt and Israel made their first moves toward peace.

Bouvines, Battle of (July 27, 1214) The battle in which *Philip II Augustus of France defeated the Holy Roman Emperor *Otto IV. The failure of the planned diversionary attack by King John of England facilitated Philip's victory, which increased the baronial opposition to John in England (*see* Barons' Wars).

Boveri, Theodor Heinrich (1862–1915) German cell biologist, noted for his studies of chromosomes. Boveri showed that the egg nucleus and the sperm nucleus both contribute hereditary material during the formation of a new cell (zygote) and that irregular distribution of chromosomes leads to abnormal development. These findings led *Sutton to propose his chromosome theory of inheritance in 1903.

Bovet, Daniel (1907–92) Swiss pharmacologist, who discovered pyrilamine, the first of the allergy-relieving antihistamine drugs (1944). He also made various synthetic substitutes for the muscle-relaxing drug curare (1947). For his discoveries he received the 1957 Nobel Prize for Physiology.

Bovidae A family of hoofed *ruminant mammals (about 128 species), comprising antelopes, cattle, sheep, and goats. Most live in herds and graze on the plains, although some inhabit mountainous regions. Several species have been domesticated by man for meat, milk, hides, and wool. Order: *Artiodactyla*.

Bow, Clara (1905–65) US film actress. She personified the vivacious spirit of the 1920s in such films as *Mantrap* (1926) and *It* (1927), after which she became known as the "It" girl. She retired from acting in the 1930s, after being unsuccessful in sound films.

Bowdler, Thomas (1754–1825) British doctor and editor. His *Family Shakespeare* (1818) expurgated all words, expressions (and even plots) "which cannot with propriety be read aloud in a family." He similarly "bowdlerized" Gibbon's *History of the Decline and Fall of the Roman Empire* (1826).

Bowdoin, James (1726–90) US politician, governor of Massachusetts (1785–87). He played an active role in Massachusetts politics before, during, and after the American Revolution; he headed the state constitutional convention (1779). As governor he was responsible for containing *Shays' Rebellion (1786–87). He founded the American Academy of Arts and Sciences (1780); Bowdoin College was named for him posthumously.

Bowen, Elizabeth (1899–1973) British novelist. Born in Dublin, daughter of an Anglo-Irish landowner, she was brought to England as a child. Her novels, in which themes of loneliness and personal relationships are delicately explored, include *The Death of the Heart* (1938) and *The Heat of the Day* (1949).

bowerbird A songbird belonging to a family (*Ptilonorhynchidae*; 18 species) found in Australasian forests. About 8–14 in (22–35 cm) long, it is closely related to the bird of paradise but has a duller plumage, often gray or black. Male bowerbirds court females by building typically dome-shaped bowers with twigs, moss, and stones, often decorating them with feathers, flowers, and shells.

BOWERBIRD *The male satin bowerbird* (Ptilonorhynchus violaceus), *which has a blue-black plumage, builds an avenue of upright sticks to attract the female.*

bowfin A *bony fish, *Amia calva*, also called grundle or mudfish, found in fresh waters of E North America. It has a mottled green body, up to 24 in (60 cm) long, a long dorsal fin, and feeds on fish and invertebrates. Family: *Amiidae*; order: *Amiiformes*.

Bowie, David (David Jones; 1947–) British pop singer. Both his style of singing and his theatrical public image have undergone several changes during the course of his career in progressive pop music. His albums include *Ziggy Stardust* (1972) and *Stage* (1978). He has also acted in films, notably *The Man Who Fell to Earth* (1976).

Bowie, James (c. 1796–1836) US soldier, pioneer, and popularizer of the Bowie knife. After engaging in some land deals in Louisiana, he settled in Texas, married the daughter of the Mexican vice-governor and became active in the movement to free Texas of Mexican rule. A colonel in the Texas army, he was one of the officers in charge at the Alamo, where he died. It is thought that he or his brother invented the Bowie knife that was widely used in the West.

bowling (*or* tenpin bowling) A game in which two players or teams compete by attempting to knock down standing pins with rolling balls. The ten pins, 15 in (38.1 cm) high and each weighing about 3.5 lb (1.5 kg), are placed in a triangle 20 yd (18.29 m) distant at the end of a wooden lane. The balls, which have a thumb hole and two finger holes, have a maximum circumference of 27 in (68.5 cm) and a maximum weight of 16 lb (7.26 kg). Each player has two tries to knock the pins down, points being awarded accordingly. The pins are then reset for the next frame. Ten frames comprise a game.

bowls A game in which biased bowls ("woods") are rolled toward a smaller one (the "jack"). **Flat green bowls** is played on a level grass surface 40–44 yd (36.6–40.2 m) square (for championship greens). Matches are usually played between two sides of four, each player using two bowls; a contest consists of three to six simultaneous matches. The jack is rolled onto the green by the first player and is followed by the other bowls in turn, the object being to position them as near the jack as possible. Playing all the bowls constitutes one "end." Scoring is determined by the closeness of the balls to the jack. *See also* boules.

box A small evergreen tree, *Buxus sempervirens*, up to 30 ft (9 m) high, native to S Europe, Africa, and S England. The leaves are small and glossy and the flowers and seedpods inconspicuous. Being slow growing, box is widely grown as hedges for topiary or screening. The hard fine-grained wood is used for decorative inlay work and engravings. Family: *Buxaceae*.

box elder A *maple tree, *Acer negundo*, up to 65 ft (20 m) high, native to North America but widely planted in Europe as a street ornamental. Also called ash-leafed maple, it has compound pale-green leaves with five toothed leaflets.

boxer A breed of working dog originating in Germany. It has a powerful frame with long straight legs and a broad muzzle. The short glossy coat is fawn to yellowish-brown or brindle, sometimes with white markings, and the mask is black. Height: 22–24 in (56–61 cm) (dogs); 21–23 in (53–58 cm) (bitches).

Boxer Rebellion (1900) An uprising in China so called because the rebels belonged to a secret society named the Fists of Righteous Harmony. They opposed the western presence in China and engaged in violence against foreign missionaries and Chinese Christians. Wearing yellow sashes and believing themselves invulnerable to foreign weapons, they marched on Beijing, killing and pillaging as they went. The rebellion was eventually suppressed by an international force of troops from seven nations and a crippling indemnity was imposed on China.

boxing Fist-fighting between men wearing gloves in a roped-off ring. Organized boxing in modern times began in 18th-century England, where it became an aristocratic pastime. The basis of modern boxing rules are the **Queensberry Rules**, drawn up under the patronage of the Marquess of Queensberry (1844–1900), published in 1867, and first used in 1892. They established the use of gloves as opposed to fighting with bare fists, which was the custom in the prize fights of the time. In professional boxing the ring is 14 × 20 ft (4 × 6 m) square. The weight limits for professional boxers are: flyweight, 112 lb (50.8 kg); bantamweight, 118 lb (53.5 kg); featherweight, 126 lb (57.2 kg); lightweight, 135 lb (61.2 kg); light welterweight, 140 lb (63.5 kg); welterweight, 147 lb (66.7 kg); light middleweight, 154 lb (69.8 kg); middleweight, 160 lb (72.6 kg); light heavyweight, 175 lb (79.4 kg); heavyweight, unlimited. A bout consists of up to 15 3-minute rounds, separated by 1-minute intervals, and is presided over by a referee. A boxer is assisted by cornermen. A fight may be decided on points (scores awarded by the referee or judges after each round), by disqualification, or by knockout. A boxer is deemed to be knocked out if he cannot rise within 10 seconds (he is considered down if any part of his body besides his feet is touching the ground) or if the referee decides that he is not in fit condition to continue.

box turtle A terrestrial turtle belonging to the North American genus *Terrapene* (6 species). Up to 7 in (18 cm) long, box turtles have a high-domed rounded carapace patterned with brown and yellow and a hinged plastron, which allows tight closure of the shell, forming a protective box. They feed on worms, insects, and berries. Family: *Emydidae*.

Boyacá, Battle of (August 7, 1819) The victory, after a heroic crossing of the Andes, of Simón *Bolívar's army of 3000 men over a Spanish force. It assured the liberation of Venezuela and Colombia.

Boycott, Charles Cunningham (1832–97) British estate manager in Ireland. Boycott clashed with the *Land League over its request for rent reductions and as a result the local community refused to associate with, or "boycotted," him.

Boyd-Orr of Brechin Mearns, John, 1st Baron (1880–1971) Scottish scientist and expert on nutrition. In the 1930s he identified nutritional problems among the British population and helped formulate adequate nutritional standards. First director general of the United Nations Food and Agriculture Organization (1945–48), he was awarded the Nobel Peace Prize (1949).

Boyer, Charles (1899–1977) French film actor. He went to Hollywood in 1929 and specialized in the roles of romantic lovers in such films as *Mayerling* (1937) and *Love Affair* (1939). □Dietrich, Marlene.

Boyle, Robert (1627–91) British physicist and chemist, born in Ireland. Boyle showed that air possesses weight, that it is necessary for sound propagation, and that its pressure affects the boiling point of water. His chemical work, summarized in *The Skeptical Chymist* (1661), distinguished between elements, compounds, and mixtures and dismissed the Aristotelian concept of the four elements. His work on gases and vacuums, with Robert *Hooke, led to the law that bears his name. Boyle published his law in 1663, but in France the law is known as Marriotte's law, after Edmé Marriotte (1620–84), who did not publish it until 1676.

Boyle's law At constant temperature, the pressure of unit mass of a gas is inversely proportional to its volume. This law is only approximately true for real gases. A gas that obeys Boyle's law exactly is called an *ideal gas. Named for Robert *Boyle.

Boyne, Battle of the (July 1, 1690) The victory of William III of England over the former King James II in Ireland. The battle was fought at the River Boyne, N of Dublin, where James hoped to halt the Williamites' advance southward. It was not an overwhelming victory, losses being comparatively slight on both sides, but the sensation of two kings fighting in Ireland for an English throne ensured its fame. The battles of the Boyne and of *Aughrim are still celebrated by Ulster Unionists on the latter's anniversary, July 12.

Boyoma Falls (former name: Stanley Falls) A series of seven cataracts in NE central Zaïre, on a 62 mi (100 km) stretch of the Lualuba River, where it becomes the Zaïre River, close to Kisangani.

Boy Scouts. *See* Scouting.

Bo Zhu Yi (*or* Po Chü-i; 772–846) Chinese poet, imperial official, he became a governor in the provinces and eventually president of the imperial board of war (841). His many poems and ballads deal with the social problems of his age.

Their lasting popularity rests on their lucid language, which, according to tradition, he achieved by reading his work to a peasant woman and deleting anything she did not understand.

Brabant 1. A former duchy in the Low Countries, between the Meuse and Scheldt Rivers. On Belgian independence (1830) it was divided, forming the Belgian provinces of Antwerp and Brabant and the Dutch province of *North Brabant. 2. A province in central Belgium. It is densely populated with large industrial areas, including Brussels. Agriculture is highly developed, with dairy farming and the production of cereals, fruit, and vegetables. Area: 1268 sq mi (3284 sq km). Population (1991): 2,235,890. Capital: Brussels.

Brabham, Jack (John Arthur B.; 1926–) Australian automobile racer, who won 14 Grand Prix races between 1955 and 1970 and was world champion in 1959, 1960, and 1966. From 1961 he built his own cars.

Brachiopoda A phylum of primitive marine invertebrate animals (about 250 species) called lamp shells because of their resemblance to ancient Roman oil lamps. The body is protected by two shell valves, usually attached to the sea bed by a fleshy stalk (peduncle). Ciliated tentacles filter food particles from the water and propel them into the mouth. Eggs and sperm are discharged into the sea and produce free-swimming ciliated larvae.

bracken (*or* brake) A *fern, *Pteridium aquilinum,* that is abundant almost throughout the world. Its black underground rhizome creeps extensively, producing aerial fronds, up to 16 ft (5 m) high, with stout erect stalks bearing triangular blades made up of branches of paired leaflets. Spore capsules occur in brownish clusters (sori) around the margins on the underside of the leaflets. Bracken is sometimes considered a pest by farmers; the roots have been used in tanning and the fronds in thatching and as fodder. Family: *Dennstaedtiaceae.*

bracket fungus A fungus that forms a fruiting body resembling a shelf or bracket, usually on trees or timber. The spores are produced in fine tubes that open at pores on the surface. A common species is *Coriolus versicolor,* the semicircular brackets of which, 1–2 in (3–5 cm) across, are found on stumps and branches of deciduous trees. The brackets are marked with concentric colored zones of brown, yellow, gray, or green. Family: *Polyporaceae*; class: *Basidiomycetes.*

bract A modified leaf, often small and scalelike, found at the base of a flower or inflorescence (flower cluster). Occasionally bracts are large and brightly colored, resembling petals, as in the poinsettias. Smaller bracts (bracteoles) may be found on the flower stalk.

Bradbury, Ray (1920–) US science-fiction writer. Many of his works of fantasy and science fiction deal essentially with the themes of conventional fiction, and his literary style has been much admired. His novels include *The Illustrated Man* (1951) and *Fahrenheit 451* (1953) and his many collections of stories include *The Golden Apples of the Sun* (1953), *I Sing the Body Electric* (1969), and *The Stories of Ray Bradbury* (1980).

Braddock, Edward (1695–1755) British general in command of British troops in North America (1755) at the beginning of the French and Indian War. While on an expedition to take Fort Duquesne (Pittsburgh, Pa), his army was ambushed by Canadian and Indian forces, whose fighting tactics were unlike any the British had seen. Defeated and in retreat, Braddock was killed near Fort Duquesne.

Bradford 53 48N 1 45W A city in N England, in West Yorkshire near Leeds. It is the foremost wool textile town in the UK and a world center for the raw-wool market. Besides woolens and worsteds, many other fabrics are manufactured and engineering is important. Bradford has a university (1966) and is the birthplace of J. B. Priestley. Population (1991): 449,100.

Bradford, William (1663–1752) British printer, who emigrated to Pennsylvania in 1682. In 1725 he founded the *New York Gazette,* the first New York newspaper.

Bradley, Bill (1943–) US basketball player and politician. He was an All-American basketball player for Princeton University (1963–65) and later played professionally for the New York Knickerbockers (1967–77). A Rhodes scholar (1965–67), he studied at Oxford. Upon retirement from basketball he served in the US Senate (1970–) as a Democrat from New Jersey.

Bradley, Francis Herbert (1846–1924) British philosopher. He lived as a semi-invalid, holding a sinecural fellowship at Oxford. Indebted to *Hegel, his idealist metaphysics are often brilliant in detail and grandiose in conception, but unwieldy in overall effect. In his greatest work, *Appearance and Reality* (1893), he argues against the acceptance of any general categories as absolutely real. Truth is relative and reality is unknowable and transcendent.

Bradley, Omar Nelson (1893–1981) US general. In World War II, he was in command in North Africa and at the invasion of Sicily. He later commanded the First US Army in the invasion of France (1944). In 1948 he became army chief of staff and was then the first chairman of the joint chiefs of staff (1949–53) until his retirement.

Brady, "Diamond Jim" (James Buchanan B.; 1856–1917) US financier. An entrepreneur who earned his fortune through selling of railroad equipment, he was known for the collection of diamonds he amassed and wore. He was responsible for funding, in great part, Johns Hopkins University Hospital and New York Hospital.

Brady, Mathew B. (1823–96) US photographer. He was one of the first to learn daguerreotype methods from Samuel F. B. *Morse. By 1854 he had two studios in New York City and one in Washington, D.C., where he photographed most of the famous people of his time, including Abraham Lincoln. Throughout the Civil War (1861–65) he and his team of photographers were active on the battlefields, recording war in pictures for the first time.

Braga 41 32N 8 26W A city in N Portugal. It has a cathedral (12th–17th centuries) and is the seat of the primate of Portugal. A nearby holy sanctuary is visited by many pilgrims. Industries include jewelry and cutlery. Population (1981): 63,100.

Bragança (*or* Braganza) The ruling dynasty of Portugal from 1640 to 1910 and of Brazil from 1822 to 1889. The family was descended from Alfonso, illegitimate son of *John I and 1st Duke of Bragança. The first Bragança king was *John IV (1640–56) and the last was Manuel II (1889–1932; reigned 1908–10), after whose deposition Portugal became a republic. When Brazil became independent (1822), it was ruled by two members of the family, *Pedro I (1822–31) and *Pedro II (1831–89), before becoming a republic (1889).

Bragg, Braxton (1817–76) US Confederate general. He graduated from West Point in 1837 and served in the US Army until 1856. At the outbreak of the Civil War in 1861, he was given command of the Confederate Army of Tennessee and fought an indecisive battle at Murfreesboro (1862–63). He was victorious at Chickamauga (1863), but his defeat at Chattanooga (1863) forced the Confederate Army to leave Tennessee. Relieved of his command in late 1863, he became military advisor to Confederate Pres. Jefferson *Davis and then commanded troops in North Carolina until the end of the war.

Bragg, Sir William Henry (1862–1942) British physicist, who worked in Australia from 1886 to 1908. His early research, described in *Studies in Radioactivity* (1912), concerned the passage of alpha and beta particle and gamma rays through matter. He invented the Bragg diffractometer for measurement of X-ray wavelengths (1912) and with his son **Sir (William) Lawrence Bragg** (1890–1971) discovered the law of X-ray diffraction that bears their name. Together they wrote *X-rays and Crystal Structure* (1915) and were jointly awarded the Nobel Prize for 1915.

Bragg's law A law stating that, if two parallel X-rays of wavelength λ are reflected by adjacent planes, distance d apart, in a crystal lattice and the rays then constructively interfere, then $2d\sin\theta = n\lambda$, where n is an integer and θ the angle between the X-rays and the planes. θ is called the Bragg angle. If n is half-integral, then destructive *interference is observed. Named for Sir William and Sir Lawrence *Bragg.

Brahe, Tycho (1546–1601) Danish astronomer, who made accurate astronomical instruments and used them to make observations enabling him to revise the existing, often inaccurate, astronomical tables. He first attracted attention by observing a nova in 1572. As a result, King Frederick II had two observatories built for him on the island of Hveen, where he worked from 1580 to 1597. During this period he made extensive observations, which led him to support *Copernicus's theory that the planets revolve around the sun. However, he believed the earth to be immovable, with the sun and planets revolving around it. After Frederick's death, he quarreled with his successor and moved to Prague: there he met *Kepler, who became his student. After Brahe's death, Kepler used his teacher's observations to test his laws of planetary motion.

Brahma The creator god of later Vedic religion. Arising from the cosmic Golden Egg, he brings into existence the cyclical process of the creation and destruction of the world. His four heads and arms represent the four *Vedas, castes, and yugas (ages of the world). Brahma represents the creative aspect of supreme deity in the *trimurti triad but since the 7th century his worship has been superseded by that of *Siva and *Vishnu, the other members of the triad.

Brahman (Hinduism) In the *Upanishads, the absolute unmanifest changeless source of the phenomenal universe, seen as self-existent, extra-temporal Being, all-pervading and infinite. Brahman is both the basis of existence and the state of one who has achieved release (*see* atman). Brahman originally meant "the sacred Word," and as such was the exclusive domain of the literate priestly caste. In its extended significance it therefore came to be considered the proper spiritual object of that class alone. *See* Brahmanism.

Brahman (cattle). *See* zebu.

Brahmanas Commentaries on the *Vedas, written in Sanskrit between about 1000 and 600 BC. They systematically explore Aryan legends and folklore in order to account for traditional rituals and are major sources of Indian philosophy, theology, and myth.

Brahmanism An early speculative rather than devotional form of *Hinduism, derived from the *Vedas and characterized by the veneration of an elite priestly caste, who, as the privileged keepers of religious knowledge, were seen as actually embodying the sacred word. *See also* Brahman.

Brahmaputra River A river in S Asia. Rising in SW Tibet as the Tsangpo, it flows generally E across the Himalayas before turning S into the Assam Valley of NE India as the Dihang. From here, as the Brahmaputra, it flows WSW across NE India to join the *Ganges River N of Gaolundo Ghat. Together they enter the Bay of Bengal in a large delta. The floodplains are highly cultivated. Length: 1800 mi (2900 km).

brahmin (*or* brahman) The first of the four major Hindu castes, that of the priests. Observing many social taboos and being innately more ritually pure than the warrior, merchant, or peasant classes, brahmins alone are able to perform the most important religious tasks, to study and recite the scriptures. Since in India spiritual and secular knowledge are virtually inseparable, brahmins frequently hold considerable intellectual and political power. After India achieved independence in 1947, opposition to brahminical elitism strengthened, but this has not yet significantly weakened their sacerdotal role.

Brahmo Samaj A Hindu revivalist movement, arising in response to contact with Christianity. Founded by Rammohan Ray (1772–1833), it intended to restore monotheistic Hinduism and the authority of the *Upanishads. Unlike the *Arya Samaj, it set out to be a universal religion. Disagreements between advocates of devotion or asceticism, rather than rational theism, led to schisms and the incorporation of Christian elements and in some cases to wholly new philosophical formulations.

Brahms, Johannes (1833–97) German composer, born in Hamburg. Brahms's precociousness was demonstrated by his youthful piano compositions; as a young man he became a friend of the violinist Joseph Joachim (1831–1907), Liszt, and the Schumanns. Brahms moved to Vienna in 1863 and later became musical director of the Gesellschaft der Musikfreunde (Society of Friends of Music; 1872–75). Musically conservative, Brahms composed in traditional forms and was unsympathetic to the progressive ideas espoused by Wagner and Liszt, although his compositions abound in lyrical melodies and rich harmonies. His main orchestral works comprise four symphonies, two piano concertos, a violin concerto, and a concerto for violin and cello. His choral works include *A German Requiem* (1868) and the *Alto Rhapsody* (1869). He wrote a large quantity of chamber music, including a piano quintet, three piano quartets, and three piano trios; string sextets, quintets, and quartets; a clarinet quintet and trio; and sonatas for violin, cello, and clarinet. He also composed much piano music and many songs.

Brăila 46 82N 27 58E A port in E Romania, situated at the limit for oceangoing ships on the Danube River. Following the Turkish occupation of the city (1544–1828), it was rebuilt with radiating and concentric streets. It is a major grain center. Population (1992 est): 234,700.

Braille, Louis (1809–52) French teacher, who, blinded by an accident at the age of three, published a system of writing that allows the blind to read by touch. He later applied the Braille system to the reading of music. Modern Braille consists of 63 characters, each of which is made up of one to six embossed dots.

brain The mass of nervous tissue that lies within the skull and is ensheathed by three membranes (meninges). It is the organ of the mind and it controls many bodily activities. The hindmost part of the brain, joining the *spinal cord, is the medulla oblongata: this ascends to the pons, which joins the midbrain. These parts are together called the brainstem, which contains the vital centers controlling breathing and heartbeat and also regulates the level of consciousness and conveys information to and from the cerebrum. The cerebellum is connected to the brainstem and is important in the coordination of movements. The upper end of the brainstem is connected to the largest and most highly developed part of the brain—the cerebrum. This consists of two cerebral hemispheres connected to each other by a tract of nerve fibers. Its surface is intricately folded and is made up of an outer layer of nerve cell bodies (gray matter) and an inner mass of nerve fibers (white matter). The cerebrum is largely responsible for understanding the environment, language, rational thought, and the voluntary control of movements. The hemispheres differ in function: one hemisphere controls the dominant side of the body (normally the left hemisphere in right-handed people) and that hemisphere controls speech. The nondominant hemisphere specializes in analyzing how things are arranged in space. Deep within the cerebrum and brainstem lie cavities (ventricles) filled with *cerebrospinal fluid. The brain of vertebrate animals is similar but less highly developed than the human brain; in lower animals a collection of ganglia (nerve cell bodies) functions as the brain. *See also* electroencephalography; hypothalamus; nervous system; neuron.

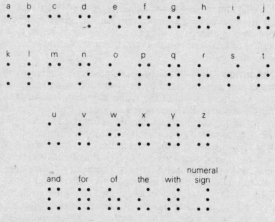

BRAILLE *The alphabet*

Brain Trust (1932) A group of US academics, advisers to Franklin D. Roosevelt's first campaign for the presidency. Consisting of Columbia University professors Adolph A. *Berle, Jr., Rexford G. Tugwell (1891–1979), and others, the group formulated social and economic policies and were instrumental in developing the president's *New Deal programs.

brake **1.** A device used to slow down or stop the rotation of a shaft. An essential component of all vehicles, modern braking systems depend either on the friction between a pair of expanding shoes and the inside of a drum attached to the wheel (**drum brakes**) or between two caliper-operated pads and the two sides of a disk (**disk brakes**). **2.** A device that absorbs and measures the power developed by an engine or motor. Brake horsepower is the power so measured. 1 brake HP = 746 watts.

Bramante, Donato (1444–1514) Italian Renaissance architect. Bramante started his career as a painter and later executed his first building projects in Milan. He spent his last 16 years in Rome, however, where most of the buildings for which he is remembered were erected, showing as they do a much more sophisticated handling of classical forms. His earlier buildings, such as S Maria delle Grazie (1480s) in Milan, although competent, do not show the same assur-

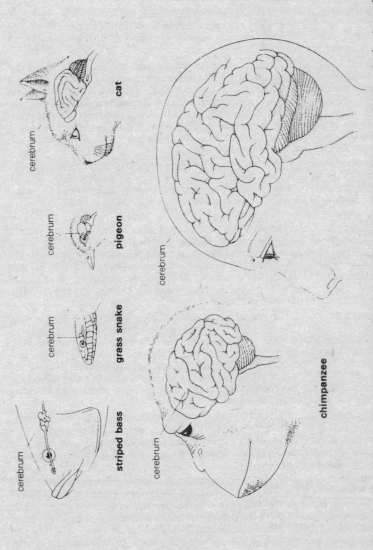

BRAIN *The brains of these representative vertebrates (drawn to the same scale) show a progressive increase in the size and complexity of the cerebrum. In man this development is such that the cerebrum covers or encloses all the other parts of the brain.*

ance that he exhibited in, for example, the Tempietto di S Pietro in Montorio (1502). The Palazzo Caprini (1514) had a lasting influence on secular architects and Bramante's designs for St Peter's can be seen strongly reflected in the later designs of *Michelangelo.

brambling A finch, *Fringilla montifringilla,* 6 in (14.5 cm) long, that breeds in Asia and N Europe and migrates south in winter. It has a brown-speckled plumage with white wing bars and orange underparts but in winter the male has a black head and back.

Bran A legendary Celtic god-king of Britain, whose story is told in the medieval Welsh collection of tales, the *Mabinogion.* Of giant stature, he once waded across the sea between Britain and Ireland. His severed head lived on for some 80 years, renowned for the good advice and entertainment it gave his followers. In accordance with his wish, Bran's head was finally buried at a spot in London in order to protect Britain from invasion. It gave this protection until it was dug up by King Arthur, who believed that the protection of the country was better served by the valor of individuals.

Branchiopoda A subclass of small *crustaceans (over 800 species) that, except for the brine shrimp, occur in fresh water. They include the *fairy shrimps, *tadpole shrimps, *water fleas, and clam shrimps, all bearing flat fringed appendages used for locomotion, respiration, and filter feeding. *Parthenogenesis is common.

Brancusi, Constantin (1876–1957) Romanian sculptor. At first locally trained, he moved to Paris in 1904, where he developed a highly individual style. His stone and metal sculptures show a search for abstract simplicity and surface polish, such as the *Sleeping Muse* series beginning in 1906 and the *Birds* variations (1912–40). In contrast, his wood sculptures, such as the *Prodigal Son* (1915), utilize complex angular forms inspired by *African art and are often mythological or religious in theme.

Brandeis, Louis (Dembitz) (1856–1941) US lawyer, associate justice of the Supreme Court (1916–39). Known as "the people's attorney" during his days as a practicing lawyer (1878–1916), he espoused the causes of the common man. His appointment as the first Jew to sit on the Supreme Court caused much controversy. His court decisions reflected his strong feelings about civil rights, and he defended freedom of expression. He applied sociology to the hard facts of the law and favored experimentation in regard to laws governing ever-changing economic practices and institutions.

Brandenburg 52 24N 12 31E A city in east-central Germany, on the Havel River. It was the former capital of the Prussian province of Brandenburg. The city was severely damaged during World War II and has been largely rebuilt. Its industries include steelworks and machinery and textile manufacturing. Population (1981): 94,700.

Brandenburg A former state corresponding to the present-day districts of Magdeburg, Potsdam, Neubrandenburg, and Frankfurt in Germany and to part of W Poland. The region was conquered by the Germans between the 10th and 12th centuries and in 1157 *Albert (I) the Bear became margrave, and then *elector, of Brandenburg. Under *Frederick William, the Great Elector (1640–88), Brandenburg gained suzerainty of Prussia and became a leading German power. In 1701 the Elector of Brandenburg became *Frederick I of Prussia.

Brandenburg Gate A ceremonial gateway in □Berlin. The Brandenburg Gate was built (1789) in the neoclassical style by the architect C. G. Langhans (1732–1808). Situated at the W end of Unter den Linden, it became the symbol of the modernized city.

Brando, Marlon (1924–) US film actor. Deeply influenced by his training in the "method" style of acting developed by Lee Strasberg at the New York Actors' Studio in the 1950s from the theories of Konstantin *Stanislavsky, Brando was recognized early in his career as one of the most talented and innovative American actors. His films include *A Streetcar Named Desire* (1951), *On the Waterfront* (1954), *Mutiny on the Bounty* (1962), *Last Tango in Paris* (1971), *The Godfather,* for which he won the Academy Award in 1972, *Apocalypse Now* (1979), and *The Freshman* (1990).

MARLON BRANDO *In the title role of* The Godfather.

Brandt, Willy (1913–92) West German statesman; chancellor (1969–74). In Norway from 1933, he was a leader of the resistance movement against the Nazis throughout World War II, after which he was Norwegian press attaché in Berlin (1945–48). A member of the Social Democratic Party from 1931, he became its chairman in 1964. As chancellor he negotiated treaties with Russia, Poland, and East Germany and in 1971 was awarded the Nobel Peace Prize. He resigned the chancellorship when it was revealed that one of his aides was an East German spy. He subsequently chaired an international commission on the state of the world economy (the Brandt Commission), which published its report in 1980.

brandy A *spirit distilled from fermented grape juice (wine); the term also denotes drinks distilled from the fermented juices of other fruits. The best types of wine brandy are matured in oak casks and named for the Cognac and Armagnac districts of France where they are made. Marc (French) or grappa (Italian) brandy is made from the refermented grape pips, skins, and stems left after pressing for wine. VSOP—very superior old pale—brandy is usually 20–25 years old.

Brandywine, Battle of the (Sept. 11, 1777) A battle fought in SE Pennsylvania during the *American Revolution. In an attempt to capture Philadelphia, British Gen. William *Howe landed with 15,000 troops at the head of Chesapeake Bay and encircled Gen. George *Washington's force, which had taken up a defensive position on the eastern bank of Brandywine Creek. Coordinating his attack with the forward movement of the Hessian troops under Gen. William von Knyphausen and of the forces of Gen. Charles *Cornwallis, Howe forced the Americans to retreat but was unable to capture the road to Philadelphia.

Brant, Joseph (1742–1807) Mohawk Indian chief. He went to a mission school, where he became an Anglican, and commanded the Mohawks on the British side in the American Revolution. He subsequently settled them in Canada and in 1785 he visited England to claim compensation for war losses. He later resisted the taking of Mohawk lands by speculators.

Brant, Sebastian (?1458–1521) German poet. He studied and taught law at Basle, and was made an imperial councillor by Maximilian I. His most important work was *The Ship of Fools* (1494), a series of satires on contemporary vices (with illustrations ascribed to Dürer). It became popular throughout Europe.

Brantford A city in SE Ontario in SE Canada. Situated on the Grand River, which empties into Lake Erie, it serves as a distribution center, and also produces such items as farming tools, lumber, construction machinery, and paper products. The first long-distance (8 mi; 13 km) telephone call was (1878) made from here by Alexander Graham Bell. Population (1981): 74,315.

Branting, Karl Hjalmar (1860–1925) Swedish statesman; prime minister (1920, 1921–23, 1924–25). His domestic policy pioneered welfare state legislation in Sweden. An enthusiastic supporter of the League of Nations, he was awarded, with the Norwegian pacifist, Christian Lange (1869–1938), the Nobel Peace Prize in 1921.

Brantôme, Pierre, Abbé and Seigneur de Bourdeille (c. 1540–1614) French chronicler. Only nominally a priest, he was a courtier under Marguerite de Valois and Henry II and traveled throughout Europe as a soldier. He began writing when crippled in a riding accident. His *Mémoires* (1665–66) chronicle the lives of illustrious men and women of his time.

Braque, Georges (1882–1963) French painter, who with *Picasso developed *cubism. He was initially influenced by impressionism and later fauvism before painting his earliest cubist landscapes (1908–09) at L'Estaque and Guyon, inspired by *Cézanne. His favorite subjects were still lifes, which during their period of close collaboration, sometimes looked identical to those of Picasso. Notable among Braque's innovations were the use of lettering in compositions, e.g. *The Portuguese* (1911; Basle), mixing paint with sand to produce interesting textures, and papiers collés (paper pasted on canvases). After World War II he painted independently in large flat planes instead of small fragmented cubes. In his later years he produced sculpture and eight paintings of studio interiors (1948–55).

Brasília 16 0S 48 10W The capital and a federal district of Brazil, situated on the central plateau. The idea of a capital in the interior was first suggested in 1789, but it was not until 1956 that the present site was chosen. It was inaugurated in 1960, the chief designer being Lúcio Costa and the principal architect, Oscar *Niemeyer. Its fine modern buildings include the National Congress Building and the cathedral. The university was founded in 1962. Population (1980): 411,305.

Braşov (German name: Kronstadt) 45 39N 25 35E A city in E central Romania, surrounded by the Transylvanian Alps. It has many historic buildings and the first book printed in Romanian appeared here in the 16th century. Its varied industries include motor vehicles, chemicals, and textiles. Population (1992 est): 324,000.

brass An *alloy of copper and zinc. Brasses containing less than 36% zinc are ductile when cold and can be easily worked into complex shapes. Those with more than 36% zinc are harder and stronger. Brass is easy to machine and stamp into shape and is used for screws, hinges, and a wide variety of articles. It does not rust but exposure to sea water causes dezincification (leaching out of the zinc). This is partially prevented by the addition of tin (1%) in Naval Brass, sometimes with about 0.05% of arsenic. *See also* Muntz metal.

Brassica A genus of mainly annual or biennial herbs (about 40 species, especially in the Mediterranean region), with erect clusters of four-petaled yellow flowers. Many species have basal rosettes of large simple leaves, but in others the leaves are spaced out up the main stem. The genus includes many important vegetables, mostly cultivated varieties of native species; the leaves, buds, stems, or roots may be eaten. *See also* broccoli; Brussels sprout; cabbage; cauliflower; kale; rape; rutabaga; turnip.

BRASILIA *The dramatic interior of the cathedral, which was designed by Oscar Niemeyer.*

brass instruments Wind instruments made of brass. The *French horn, *trumpet, *trombone, and *tuba are commonly used in the symphony orchestra; brass bands use a greater variety, including *bugles and *cornets. Brass instruments have either a cup-shaped or cone-shaped mouthpiece, the shape of which influences the tone quality, as does the type of bore, which may be conical (horn) or cylindrical (trumpet). A brass instrument plays the harmonic series natural to its length; additional series are made available by the use of crooks, slides, or valves.

Bratislava 48 10N 17 10E The capital of Slovakia, on the Danube River. It was the capital of Hungary (1526–1784). Notable buildings include the gothic cathedral (13th century), where many of the kings of Hungary were crowned, and its castle. The university was founded in 1919. It is an important industrial center; oil is refined here. Population (1987 est): 425,000.

Brattain, Walter Houser (1902–87) US physicist, who shared the 1956 Nobel Prize for his part in the invention of the transistor (with W. B. *Shockley and John *Bardeen) while working at the Bell Telephone Laboratories in 1948.

Brauchitsch, Walther von (1881–1948) German general. He became commander in chief of the German army in 1938, but was dismissed (1941) by Hitler after the failure of the Moscow campaign. He died awaiting trial for alleged war crimes.

Braun, Eva (1910–45) The mistress and finally the wife of Adolf Hitler. Their relationship probably began in 1933, and they were married shortly before their suicides on Apr 30, 1945.

Braun, Wernher von *See* von Braun, Wernher.

Braunschweig. *See* Brunswick.

Brazil, Federal Republic of (Portuguese name: Brasil) A country comprising almost half the area of South America, situated in the NE. The N of the country is dominated by the Amazon basin with its tropical rain forests. The land rises to the Guiana Highlands in the N and the Brazilian Highlands in the S, with large tracts of grassland in between. The Mato Grosso Plateau in the SW is arid savanna. The population is largely of European descent, with some African and Asian minorities and a very small and dwindling Indian minority. Most of the inhabitants live along the coast, especially in the S and SE, although the government has launched ambitious road and regional plans in an attempt to open up and develop the interior. The building of *Brasília was the most impressive single attempt to draw the population away from the overcrowded coastal areas. *Economy*: despite a remarkably high annual growth rate (especially in the period 1960–70) and recent industrialization, Brazil is still mainly an agricultural country, the chief crops being sugar cane, manioc, maize, rice, and beans. Brazil was formerly the world's largest producer of coffee but overproduction has led to a decline in its position. Severe frosts in 1975 caused a 60% loss in the coffee crop. Cocoa, bananas, and oranges are also important. Numbers of livestock have increased and Brazil is now ahead of Argentina as a cattle producer. The fishing industry has been nationalized and in 1971 territorial waters were extended to 200 mi (320 km). Brazil is exceptionally rich in mineral resources, many of them as yet untapped, although more mines are now being opened up as the government attempts to exploit the vast regions of the interior. The iron-ore reserves are estimated to be the largest in the world. There are gold deposits in most parts of the country and the large mine at Minas Gerais was discovered in the late 17th century. Recently large deposits of phosphates have been discovered there, as well as uranium, manganese, and copper. The country's many other minerals include high-grade quartz crystal. Efforts to encourage industrial development since the 1960s have included an increase in steel production, which in turn is designed to encourage ship building. The most important manufacturing industry, however, is textiles, although motor-vehicle production is on the increase. Hydroelectric sources provide 90% of power. There is now an agreement with Germany, based on Brazil's rich uranium deposits, to build eight nuclear power stations. Oil production only provides a fraction of Brazil's domestic needs although new offshore fields have been found near Campos. Main exports include sugar, coffee, cotton, and minerals, especially iron ore. *History*: claimed by the Portuguese in 1500, it became a Portuguese settlement. During the Napoleonic Wars, the Portuguese court was transferred to Brazil and in 1815 it was made a kingdom. In 1822 independence was declared by *Pedro I, son of John VI of Portugal, with a constitution that proclaimed him emperor. In 1889 his son *Pedro II was deposed and Brazil became a republic. From 1930 to 1945 it was ruled under the benevolent dictatorship of Getúlio *Vargas. Less stable governments followed, including a further period under Vargas. In 1964 the left-wing president, João Goulart, was overthrown in a military coup led by Gen. Humberto Castelo Branco. In 1966 Marshal Artur da Costa e Silva was elected president and in 1968 he assumed absolute power. He resigned in 1969 and the government was taken over by a junta comprising the three heads of the armed forces. The transition from military to democratic rule in the early 1980s was marked by civil disruptions resulting from severe economic measures imposed on the country to satisfy Brazil's foreign creditors. The demand for stringent economic cutbacks by the International Monetary Fund, Brazil's chief lending agent, led to riots and looting. In an attempt to avoid default by Brazil and the chaos it would create in international banking, the IMF softened its demands. In 1992, Brazil hosted the Earth Summit, a meeting of the world's nations called to address environmental issues. Amid widespread financial scandals, Pres. Fernando Collor de Mello resigned at the end of 1992. Head of state: Pres. Itamar Franco. Official language: Portuguese. Official currency: cruzeiro of 100 centavos. Area: 3,286,000 sq mi (8,511,965 sq km). Population (1990 est): 153,770,000. Capital: Brasília. Main port: Rio de Janeiro.

Brazil nut The seed of a tall forest tree, *Bertholletia excelsa,* up to 145 ft (45 m) high, native to tropical South America. The tree produces showy fluffy flowers that develop into hard woody fruits, up to 6 in (15 cm) in diameter, each containing 12–24 seeds (the nuts). Commercial supplies come entirely from wild trees. Family: *Lecythidaceae.*

brazilwood An evergreen tree, *Caesalpinia brasiliensis,* of tropical South America. The leaves are bipinnate—each leaflet is divided into smaller leaflets—and the irregular orange flowers develop into seed pods. The tree yields a very hard wood from which a red dye is extracted; the wood is also used for cabinetwork. Family: *Leguminosae.*

brazing. *See* solder.

Brazos River A river in central Texas that flows E and mainly S past Houston to the Gulf of Mexico at Freeport. Several dams on the river provide power for electricity and irrigation. Length: 850 mi (1369 km).

Brazza, Pierre Paul François Camille Savorgnan de (1852–1905) French explorer of Italian descent. In 1878 he explored, claimed, and colonized French Equatorial Africa, founding Brazzaville. He was the first governor of the French Congo (1886–97).

Brazzaville 4 07W 15 15E The capital of the People's Republic of Congo, situated in the S on the Zaïre River opposite Kinshasa (Zaïre). Founded in the 1880s, it developed as a European center and an important riverport, and became capital of French Equatorial Africa in 1910. During World War II it was the center of the Free French forces in Africa. It became capital of the newly independent Republic of Congo in 1960. The Marien-Ngouabi University was founded in 1972. Population (1992 est): 992,000.

bread A staple food made basically by baking a mixture of *flour and water. Ordinary leavened bread is made by mixing a dough of flour, water, yeast, sugar, salt, and sometimes other ingredients. The dough is kneaded and left to rise twice, a process that can take several hours, before being baked. White loaves, rolls, French sticks, and brown bread are made from different types of wheat flour. Rye bread is another variety, which has a stronger, more bitter flavor and can be black, brown, or white.

Bread has been baked since the earliest times, evidence of barley cakes having been found in Neolithic dwellings.

breadfruit The starchy fruit of a tropical tree *Artocarpus communis.* When roasted it forms a staple part of the diet in the Pacific islands, to which it is native, and it is widely cultivated elsewhere. The tree grows to a height of 98 ft

(30 m) and has thick shiny divided leaves. The large round fruits, as much as 12 in (30 cm) across, have a thick warty rind and develop from long female catkins. Family: *Moraceae.*

bread mold A fungus that grows on bread, especially one of the genera *Rhizopus* or *Mucor*. Black bread mold (*R. stolonifer*) forms a filamentous branching structure from which arise erect stalks bearing black spore cases resembling pinheads. It also grows on fruit, manure, and other decaying organic matter. Class: *Phycomycetes.*

bream One of several *teleost fishes, especially *Abramis brama,* a food and game fish related to *carp that occurs in European lakes and slow-moving rivers. Its deep body, 12–28 in (30–70 cm) long, is bluish gray or brown above and silvery below. It lives in schools in deep water and feeds on invertebrates or small fish. *See also* sea bream.

Bream, Julian Alexander (1933–) British guitarist and lutenist. Taught by his father, Bream gave his first public performance at the age of 12. His outstanding talent attracted Andrés Segovia's attention. His repertoire includes arrangements of baroque and Renaissance pieces as well as works written for him by Britten and Henze.

breast The milk-producing (mammary) gland of women. Each of the two breasts consists of a mass of fatty tissue in which are embedded milk-secreting lobes, which drain through a series of ducts to the nipple. Breast cancer is the commonest form of cancer in women. Treatment usually involves surgical removal of the breast (*see* mastectomy), sometimes with radiotherapy or *cytotoxic drugs. The activity of the gland is controlled by the hormone prolactin, secreted by the pituitary gland (*see* lactation).

breathalyzer A roadside test used by the police to estimate the amount of alcohol in the breath, which reflects the level of alcohol in the blood.

breathing. *See* respiration.

Brébeuf, St Jean de (1593–1649) French Jesuit missionary and patron saint of Canada. Ordained in 1623, he evangelized the Huron Indians in New France in several expeditions, until he was captured and tortured to death by the Hurons' enemies, the Iroquois. Feast day: Sept 26.

breccia A sedimentary rock consisting of relatively large (over 0.08 in [2 mm] in diameter) angular fragments of preexisting rocks. These fragments have usually undergone little transport from their source and are poorly sorted. Scree material cemented together forms one kind of breccia.

Brecht, Bertolt (1898–1956) German dramatist and poet. He first studied medicine, serving briefly as a medical orderly in 1918. He abandoned the exuberant expressionism of his early plays after his conversion to Marxism in 1928, producing his best-known work the next year, *Die Dreigroschenoper,* an adaptation of John Gay's *The Beggar's Opera* with music by Kurt *Weill. In 1933 he left Germany and lived in Scandinavia and the US (1941–47). During these years he wrote his most powerful plays, notably *Galileo* (1938), *Mother Courage* (1939), and *The Caucasian Chalk Circle* (1949). These exploit his "distancing" technique, in which by emphasizing the unreality of the play he increases its didactic impact. In 1949 he returned to East Berlin and founded his famous Berliner Ensemble Company.

Breckinridge, John Cabell (1821–75) US politician, vice president (1857–61), and Confederate general. Before becoming vice president in Pres. James *Buchanan's administration he was a congressman from Kentucky (1851–57). He worked to fend off secession by the South prior to the outbreak of the Civil War, but favored slavery in the territories. A senator for a short time in 1861, he was expelled when he accepted a commission of general in the Confederate Army. Later in the war he served as the Confederate secretary of war.

Breda 51 35N 4 46E A city in the SW Netherlands, in North Brabant province. Occupied several times, its capture by the Spanish in 1625 is depicted in Velázquez's famous painting, *The Surrender of Breda*. Its industries include textiles and engineering. Population (1988 est): 120,500.

breeder reactor. *See* fast reactor.

breeding The controlled mating of selected animals or plants, usually in order to produce offspring with improved performance, such as a higher milk yield in dairy cattle, or certain desirable characteristics, such as a particular flower color in garden plants. Based on careful selection of parents (often over many generations) and a knowledge of genetics, modern plant and animal breeding is aimed at improving yield, resistance to disease, hardiness to climate, consumer appeal of the product, etc., and has helped meet increased world demand for food.

Brehon Laws A collection of ancient Irish laws, dating back to the 8th century, which constitute one of the most important sources for the history of contemporary Irish society. The Brehon was an official who pronounced upon the law. The Laws describe conditions of tenure and transfer of land and the legal status and responsibilities of clan members, besides fixing penalties and fines for criminal acts.

Breitenfeld, Battles of Two battles fought in Germany during the *Thirty Years' War and won by Sweden. *Gustavus II Adolphus led the Swedish-Saxon army to victory against the Catholic and imperial forces under *Tilly in 1631. The second battle (1642) was a Swedish victory against the imperial army in a campaign to win Saxony.

Bremen 53 05N 8 48E The second largest port in Germany, capital of the *Land* of Bremen on the Weser River. Its cathedral (founded 1043) was restored following damage during World War II. Its industries include ship building, oil refining, and food processing. Population (1988): 522,000.

Bremen The smallest *Land* in Germany, comprising the cities of *Bremen and *Bremerhaven enclosed by the *Land* of Lower Saxony. Area: 156 sq mi (404 sq km). Population (1988): 652,000.

Bremerhaven 53 33N 8 35E A city in N Germany, in Bremen, on the Weser estuary. A major fishing, freight, and passenger port, its industries include fish processing and ship building. Population (1987): 132,194.

bremmstrahlung Electromagnetic radiation emitted by a charged particle when it is decelerated on passing close to a nucleus. The effect is most often observed with electrons since they are light and therefore easily decelerated. The radiation from one particle is emitted as a single photon. It is an important method by which *cosmic rays dissipate their energy on entering the earth's atmosphere.

Brendan, St (484–c. 578 AD) Irish abbot. He is traditionally credited with founding the monastery at Clonfert (Cluain Fearta), Co Galway. The Latin *Navigation of St Brendan* (c. 1050) recounts his legendary voyage to "northern and western islands," which may refer to the Orkneys and Hebrides. Feast day: May 16.

Bren gun A gas-operated light machine gun with interchangeable barrels first built at *Br*no, Czechoslovakia (1933), and later manufactured at *En*field, UK (1935). Widely used in World War II, it was accurate, reliable, easily maintained, and used 0.303 caliber ammunition.

Brennan, William J(oseph), Jr. (1906–   ) US jurist and lawyer; Supreme Court associate justice (1956–90). He graduated from Harvard Law School (1931) and entered private practice, specializing in labor law. He was a judge of New Jersey Superior Court (1949–52) and on the New Jersey Supreme Court (1952–56). He was appointed to the US Supreme Court in 1956 by President *Eisenhower and confirmed by the Senate in 1957. A defender of the First Amendment and known as a moderate liberal, he championed civil rights, especially in *NAACP* v. *Button* (1963), *New York Times Co.* v. *Sullivan* (1964), and *US* v. *Eichman* (1990).

Brenner Pass (German name: Brenner Sattel; Italian name: Passo del Brennero) 47 02N 11 32E The lowest of the chief passes in the Alps, on the Austrian-Italian border. Important since Roman times, it links Innsbruck (Austria) with Verona (Italy) by road and rail.

Brentano, Clemens (1778–1842) German writer, a member of the Heidelberg School of Romantic writers. With Achim von Arnim he published the influential folksong collection, *Des Knaben Wunderhorn* (1805–08). Emotionally unstable in early life, he became a Roman Catholic in 1817, and for six years was a monk.

Brentano, Franz (1838–1916) German psychologist and philosopher. He trained as a priest but resigned over the doctrine of papal infallibility. Thinking psychology a necessary foundation for philosophy, he suggested distinguishing marks for psychic phenomena, chief among which was intentionality ("directedness-to-an-object") adopted by *Russell and *Moore. His main works are *Psychology from an Empirical Standpoint* (1874) and *The Origin of Ethical Knowledge* (1889).

brent goose A dark-colored *goose, *Branta bernicla*. 21–23 in (53–58 cm) long, it breeds in the Arctic and winters in temperate N Atlantic coastal regions, feeding chiefly on eelgrass on mudflats. The pale-bellied form occurring in Canada and the E US and the dark-bellied form of Arctic Russia and European coasts are both geographic races.

Brescia 45 33N 10 13E A city in Italy, in Lombardy. It has Roman remains, 9th-century and 17th-century cathedrals, and a 12th-century palace. A railroad junction, its manufactures include metal goods, firearms, machinery, and textiles. Population (1988): 200,000.

Breslau. *See* Wroclaw.

Brest (name until 1921: Brest-Litovsk; Polish name: Brześć nad Bu-giem) 52 08N 23 40E A port in Belarus on the Bug and Mukhavets Rivers near the Polish border. The Treaties of *Brest-Litovsk were negotiated here in World War I. It is a major industrial, commercial, and transportation center. Population (1987): 238,000.

Brest 48 23N 4 30W A port and naval base in NW France, in the Finistère department on the Atlantic Ocean. A German U-boat base in World War II, it was almost entirely destroyed by Allied bombing. It is the site of the University of Brittany. Industries include fishing, chemicals, and clothing. Population (1983): 201,000.

Brest-Litovsk, Treaties of (1918) The peace treaties between the Central Powers and, respectively, the Ukraine and Soviet Russia toward the end of World War I. An independent Ukraine was recognized by the first treaty. By the second, Russia acknowledged Ukrainian independence and also lost its Polish and Baltic possessions. The treaties were annulled following the ultimate defeat of the Central Powers.

Brétigny, Treaty of (1360) The treaty that concluded the first phase of the *Hundred Years' War. Never fully effective, it promised a large ransom by France for *John II of France (captured at Poitiers in 1356) and granted territories, including Aquitaine, to Edward III of England. In return, Edward was to renounce his claim to the French throne.

Breton A Celtic language with four distinct dialects spoken in Brittany by about one million people. It was originally introduced to this area by immigrants from SW England, who had been displaced by invading Anglo-Saxon tribes. It is related to *Cornish and *Welsh but has been strongly influenced by French. It has a literature that dates from the 15th century. Official encouragement of French has tended to decrease the number of Breton speakers.

Breton, André (1896–1966) French poet. After involvement with *dada, he became the leader of French *surrealism in 1922 and wrote three manifestos (1924, 1930, 1942) defining its aims. His many essays explore surrealist themes, such as the relationship between dreams and reality. His novel *Nadja* (1928) freely blends real and surreal; *Poèmes* (1948) seeks to express the unconscious mind. Briefly a Communist Party member, he lived in the US from 1938 to 1946.

Brett, George Howard (1953–   ) US baseball player who played (1973–93) for the American League's Kansas City Royals. Primarily a third baseman, he was a frequent All-Star and was voted the league's most valuable player in 1980. He won the league's batting title three times, including a .390 average in 1985, and reached 3000 career hits in 1992. He retired after the 1993 season.

Bretton Woods Conference (1944) A conference held at Bretton Woods, N.H., at which the US, Britain, and Canada established a system of international financial rules, which led to the setting up of the *International Monetary Fund (IMF) and the *International Bank for Reconstruction and Development (World Bank). The chief features of the system were, first, an obligation for each country to maintain the exchange value of its currency within 1% of a value fixed in terms of gold; and, secondly, the provision by the IMF of finance to bridge temporary payments imbalances. In the face of increasing strain, the system eventually collapsed in 1971, following the US government's suspension of convertibility from dollars to gold.

Breuer, Josef (1842–1925) Austrian physiologist and pioneer of psychoanalysis. After successfully treating hysteria in one of his patients, Breuer collaborated with Sigmund *Freud in writing *Studies in Hysteria* (1895). Earlier, working with Ewald Hering (1834–1918), Breuer described the Hering-Breuer reflex involved in the nervous control of breathing movements.

Breuer, Marcel Lajos (1902–81) US architect, furniture designer, and teacher, born in Hungary. In the 1920s he taught at the *Bauhaus, designing the first tubular steel chair (1925). After 1937 he practiced in the US as an architect. One of the best-known buildings on which he worked is the UNESCO headquarters in Paris (1958).

Breuil, Henri (1877–1961) French archaeologist, famous for his work on *Paleolithic art. Although ordained an abbé (1900), Breuil devoted his outstanding talents as a draftsman to copying cave paintings all over Europe (*see also* Altamira) and in N Africa, China, and S Africa. He was professor at the Collège de France (1929–47) and published over 600 books and articles.

brewing. *See* beer and brewing.

Brewster, Sir David (1781–1868) Scottish physicist, who studied the polarization of light, double refraction in crystals, and relations between crystalline forms and optical properties (*see* Brewster's law). He also invented and patented the kaleidoscope. In 1831 he helped to found the British Association for the Advancement of Science.

Brewster, William (1567–1644) US Pilgrim leader. Educated in England, he broke from the Anglican Church in 1606 and formed the Separatists, a group that went to Holland to avoid persecution in 1608 and finally to America in 1620 aboard the *Mayflower.* He was a signer of the *Mayflower Compact* (1620) and served as Plymouth Colony's spiritual leader.

Brewster's law Light reflected from a solid surface is plane polarized, with maximum polarization occurring when the tangent of the angle of incidence is equal to the refractive index. Named for Sir David *Brewster.

Brezhnev, Leonid Ilich (1906–82) Soviet statesman; secretary of the Soviet Communist Party (1964–82) and president of the Soviet Union (1977–82). Brezhnev, a metallurgist, was a political leader in the Red Army during World War II. After holding offices in the Ukraine and Moldavia, he became a member of the presidium in 1957 and its chairman in 1960. He and *Kosygin forced Khrushchev to resign in 1964 and Brezhnev became first secretary of the Communist Party. By the late 1960s he had become the most powerful Soviet leader and in 1977 became president.

Brian Boru (926–1014) High King of Ireland (1001–14) after victories over the Danes and the other Irish. He was murdered after his victory at the battle of Clontarf. Brian was the last high king with effective jurisdiction over most of Ireland.

Briand, Aristide (1862–1932) French socialist statesman; prime minister (1909–11, 1913, 1915–17, 1921–22, 1925–26, 1929) and foreign minister (1925–32). The crisis of Verdun in *World War I precipitated the fall of his government in March 1917, when Clemenceau's attacks upon Briand for his attempt to negotiate peace forced him to retire. From 1919 he was a leading advocate of international cooperation and was instrumental in securing the *Locarno Pact (1925) and *Kellog-Briand Pact (1928). With Gustav *Stresemann, he shared the Nobel Peace Prize in 1926.

briar A shrubby rambling *rose with arching prickly stems, found in hedgerows and scrub in many parts of Europe. The principal species are *Rosa rubiginosa, R. micrantha, R. agrestis,* and *R. elliptica. See also* sweet briar.

Briar is also the name of a shrubby white *heath (*Erica arborea*), the roots and knotted stems of which are used for making briar pipes.

bribery and corruption The giving of a gift to a person in a position of trust, particularly a public official, to induce him to act contrary to his duty. If such a gift is secretly given and received it is presumed to be corrupt. The federal statute defines an official to include "any officer or employee or person acting for or on behalf of the United States, or any department or agency or branch of government thereof. . . ."

brick A traditional building material in the form of a rectangular block usually measuring 9 × 4½ × 3 in (225 × 112 × 75 mm). They are normally made from clay and baked or fired in a kiln at about 1650°F (900°C). Water is driven off, organic matter becomes oxidized, and some of the clay minerals fuse and fill the gaps between the clay particles. Iron oxide gives the brick its reddish color. Bricks are laid in various patterns, known as bonds. Refractory bricks made from fireclay are used to line furnaces.

Bride, St. *See* Bridget, St.

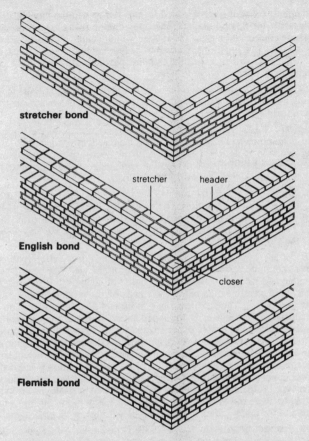

stretcher bond

stretcher   header

English bond

closer

Flemish bond

BRICKS *The factors of cost, strength, and decorative effect influence a bricklayer's choice of bond.*

bridge A card game deriving from *whist. **Straight bridge** was first played about 1880; having overtaken whist in popularity, about 1911 it was displaced by its descendant, **auction bridge**, in which the opposing pairs of partners competed to decide the trump suit. By 1929 the American game of **contract bridge**, popularized by Ely *Culbertson and putting greater emphasis on skill, supplanted other forms of bridge. Two pairs of partners (referred to as North-South and East-West in bridge notation) bid to name the trump suit (or to play without a trump suit, i.e. in "no trumps") and "contract" to win a specified number of tricks (e.g. "four spades") above the six tricks of the "book." A game consists of 100 points, with each spade or heart trick counting 30, each diamond or club 20, and for a bid in no trumps 40 for the first trick and 30 for subsequent tricks. Only the tricks contracted for in the bidding are counted toward game; extra points are awarded separately for "honors" (ace to ten of trumps), overtricks, and for slams (when the partners have bid for and won all the tricks or all but one trick in a hand). Penalty points are awarded to the opponents for undertricks (when the partners who have declared trumps fail to win the number of tricks they contracted for in the bidding). The side winning two games consecutively or two games out of three wins the rubber, which counts as either 500 or 700 extra points. The playing of the hand after the bidding is similar to whist, except that the declarer's partner, called the dummy, puts his entire hand face upward on the table to be played by the declarer.

Bridge of Sighs (Italian name: Ponte dei Sospiri) A covered bridge in Venice (Italy) linking the Doge's Palace with the state prison. Its name derives from the sighs of the prisoners who were conducted over it.

Bridgeport 41 11N 73 11W A city in SW Connecticut, on the Poquonock River at its entrance to Long Island Sound. Connecticut's largest city, Bridgeport was settled in 1639. The University of Bridgeport was established in 1927. Products manufactured include electrical appliances, brass hardware, drugs, clothing, and plastics. Population (1990): 141,686.

Bridger, Jim (James B; 1804–81) US fur trapper, explorer, and scout. In his travels looking for furs, he discovered Great Salt Lake (1824) and what is now Yellowstone Park. He led many expeditions through unexplored territory and established Fort Bridger, a trading post, in Wyoming in 1843. He also acted as a scout for the US Army.

bridges Structures that provide a means of crossing a river, valley, road, or railroad. There are three basic designs, which differ in the way they bear the weight of the bridge and its load; some bridges consist of composite structures. **Beam** (*or* girder) **bridges** are supported at their ends by the ground, with the weight thrusting downward. The cantilever is a more complex form of girder. **Arch bridges** thrust outward as well as downward at their ends and are in compression. **Suspension bridges** use cables under tension to pull inward against anchorages in the ground. The roadway, or a truss supporting it, hangs from the main cables by a network of vertical cables. In certain bridges, there is insufficient room to allow traffic to pass underneath them. In these cases the bridges are designed with movable parts. Swing bridges can rotate horizontally. **Bascule bridges** are cantilever-type bridges with a counterweight and hinge to rotate the bridge vertically. **Drawbridges** and **vertical lift bridges** have towers that lift the whole of one section of the bridge upward. *See also* Bailey bridge; pontoon bridge.

Bridges, Robert Seymour (1844–1930) British poet. Educated at Oxford, he worked as a doctor until 1882. He published several volumes of lyrics and a long philosophical poem, *The Testament of Beauty* (1929), but an even greater contribution to literature was his edition of the poems of his friend Gerard Manley *Hopkins. He was made poet laureate in 1913.

Bridget, St (St Bride *or* St Brigit; died c. 523 AD) Irish abbess and second patron saint of Ireland. The traditions regarding her life are various, but she is believed to have founded the first Irish convent, at Kildare. Feast day: Feb 1.

Bridgetown 14 05N 59 35W The capital of Barbados, a port in the SW on Carlisle Bay, founded in 1628. The main industries are sugar, rum, and tourism. The University of the West Indies was founded in 1963. Population (1990): 6070.

Bridgman, Percy Williams (1882–1961) US physicist, whose experiments with high pressures led to the invention of a seal the efficiency of which increased with pressure, enabling him to attain pressures of up to 20,000 atmospheres. Bridgman studied the effects of such pressures on solids and, in 1955, his methods were used by the General Electric Company to synthesize diamonds. For this work he was awarded the Nobel Prize in 1946. In *The Logic of Modern Physics* (1927) he made an important contribution to the (operational) concept of scientific meaning.

Brie An area in N France, between the Seine and Marne Rivers. Predominantly agricultural, it produces wheat and sugar beet and is noted for its cheese. Area: 2510 sq mi (6500 sq km).

brig A sailing vessel with two masts, both carrying square sails.

brigantine A sailing vessel with two masts, square-rigged on the foremast, with a fore-and-aft mainsail and square topsails.

Briggs, Henry (1561–1630) English mathematician. On hearing of *Napier's use of *logarithms, which have a base of e, Briggs realized that logarithms to the base ten, known as common or Briggsian logarithms, would make calculations simpler. Common logarithms are now widely used although Napierian logarithms are used for some purposes.

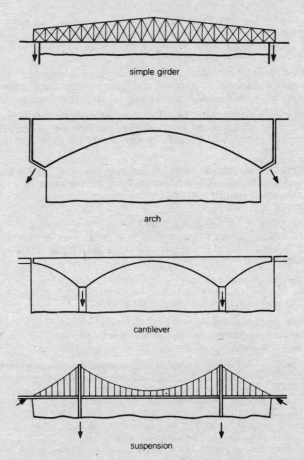

simple girder

arch

cantilever

suspension

BRIDGES *The arrows show how forces are exerted onto or away from the foundations in each of the basic structural types.*

Bright, Richard (1789–1858) British physician, who described many disorders, particulary the group of symptoms, including edema (retention of body fluid), that he showed to be due to kidney disease. This is sometimes called **Bright's disease** (*see* nephritis).

Brighton 50 50N 0 10W A resort in S England, on the East Sussex coast. Originally a fishing village, its growth began with the development of sea bathing in the 1750s. The Prince Regent (later George IV) had the Royal Pavilion redesigned by John Nash in oriental style. Other notable features include the Lanes and the boating marina (completed in 1979). Brighton is also a conference center and site of the University of Sussex (1961). Population (1981): 146,134.

Brigit A Celtic goddess of fire, fertility, learning, culture, and crafts. Elements of her cult were passed into the traditions surrounding St *Bridget, notably the burning of a sacred fire by her shrine.

brill An edible *flatfish, *Scophthalmus rhombus,* related to *turbot, that occurs in European coastal waters, down to depths of 230 ft (70 m). Its smooth body, up to 28 in (70 cm) long, is sandy to gray or dark-brown with light and dark spots above and white with darker blotches below.

Brillat-Savarin, Anthelme (1755–1826) French lawyer and writer. His *Physiologie du goût* (1825) is a collection of gastronomical anecdotes and aphorisms. After the Revolution he became a judge of the French supreme court.

brilliant cut A method of cutting diamonds and other gems to impart maximum brilliance. The upper and lower halves of the stone are cut into 33 and 25 polished facets respectively. These facets meet around the girdle or perimeter of the circular stone.

brimstone A lemon-yellow butterfly, *Gonopteryx rhamni,* found in Europe, N Africa, and parts of Asia. Adults hibernate, flying early in spring. The next generation emerges in June or later, the caterpillars feeding on buckthorn. Family: *Pieridae.*

Brindisi (Latin name: Brundisium) 40 37N 17 57E A seaport in SE Italy, in Apulia. It was an important Roman naval base and a center of the Crusades in the Middle Ages. It has a 12th-century cathedral and a castle. Virgil died here. Population: 79,784.

brine shrimp A crustacean belonging to a genus (*Artemia*) of *fairy shrimps that lives in salty pools and lakes. The widely distributed species, *A. salina,* 0.40 in (10 mm) long, is often cultivated for fish food.

briquette A block of compressed coal dust bound with pitch or a similar substance. Briquetting converts fuel that would otherwise be of little use into one of higher quality that can be sold.

Brisbane 27 30S 153 00E The third largest city in Australia, the capital and chief port of Queensland on the Brisbane River. The chief industries are engineering, ship building, oil refining, food processing, and wool scouring. Exports include wool, meat, mineral sands, and wheat. The University of Queensland was established in 1910 and Griffith University in 1975; other notable buildings include Parliament House (1869), two cathedrals, the Observatory (1829), built by convicts, and the Queen Elizabeth II Stadium, built for the 1982 Commonwealth Games. *History*: originally a penal colony, the settlement was opened to colonists in 1842. It became the state capital when Queensland was formed in 1859. Population (1991 est): 1,327,000.

brisling. *See* sprat.

Brissot, Jacques-Pierre (1754–93) French journalist and revolutionary. A legal reformer and humanitarian before the French Revolution, he became leader of the Brissotins, later called the *Girondins, in 1789. A proponent of revolutionary war, his policies led to the French declaration of war on Austria in 1792. Internal rivalries and disputes over the conduct of the war produced a power struggle between the *Jacobins and Girondins. After the defeat of the Girondins, Brissot was executed.

bristlecone pine A *pine tree, *Pinus aristata,* native to mountainous regions of Colorado, Arizona, and New Mexico. Up to 49 ft (15 m) tall, it has needles grouped in clusters of five, and cones about 3 in (7.5 cm) long with distinctive bristles on each scale. Bristlecone pines are among the longest-lived trees: it has been estimated that some trees have reached an age of 5000 years and they have been used to date archeological sites (*see* dendrochronology).

bristletail A slender wingless insect, 0.20–0.80 in (5–20 mm) long, that has two or three long tail bristles and belongs to the order *Thysanura* (three-pronged bristletails) or *Diplura* (two-pronged bristletails). Most bristletails live in damp sheltered places, e.g. under stones and logs, and feed on plant detritus. However, a few species feed on books and papers or anything containing starch (*see* silverfish; firebrat).

bristle worm. *See* annelid worm.

Bristol 51 27N 2 35W A port and industrial city in SW England, the administrative center of Avon on the Avon River, 7 mi (11 km) from the Bristol Channel. An important port in the 17th and 18th centuries, concentrating on trade with the Americas, its docks on the Bristol Channel now handle much of British import and export trade. Bristol University dates from 1909. Bristol's industries include engineering (particularly aircraft manufacture), chemicals, tobacco, soap, paper manufacture, chocolate, printing, and nonferrous metal refining. Population (1981): 387,977.

Bristol Channel An inlet of the Atlantic Ocean in the UK, between South Wales and SW England. It forms an extension of the Severn Estuary and has the greatest tidal range in England. Length: about 85 mi (137 km).

Britain, Battle of. *See* World War II.

Britannia metal An *alloy of tin (80–90%) with variable amounts of antimony and copper. It resembles silver and was formerly used for tableware instead of *pewter.

British Academy A learned society formed in 1901 and incorporated in 1902. The Academy aims to promote the study of languages and literatures, history, archaeology, philosophy, religion, law, economics, and the visual arts, from which academic fields its Fellows are elected.

British Antarctic Territory A British colony established in 1962 that consists of the South Orkney and South Shetland islands and a part of the Antarctic. It is used as a base for the British Antarctic Survey stations.

British Blue A breed of short-haired cat originating in the UK. They have a powerful body, a short thick tail, and a broad head with slightly rounded ears. The coat is an evenly shaded blue and the eyes are copper, orange, or yellow.

British Broadcasting Corporation (BBC) A radio and television broadcasting network in Britain. The BBC was first set up as a private company in 1922 and was incorporated in 1927; it is responsible to Parliament and is politically neutral and independent. It relies on revenue from television licenses as it is not permitted to carry advertising.

British Columbia The westernmost province of Canada, on the Pacific Ocean. Mostly in the mountainous Cordilleran region, it is bounded by the *Rocky Mountains in the E and the *Coast Range, including islands, in the W. The main rivers (the Fraser, Kootenay, Thompson, and Columbia) and their tributaries are swift flowing and there are many lakes and waterfalls. Forests cover over 55% of the surface and provide the basis for most manufacturing. Fishing, hydroelectricity, and tourism are also economically important. There are rich mineral resources; gold, silver, lead, zinc, copper, coal, and oil are all produced. Although only a small area is farmed, dairy produce, mixed farming, and fruit are valuable. Prosperous and urbanized, British Columbia is Canada's fastest-growing province; half the population lives in the Lower Mainland. *History*: visited by Captain Cook (1778), British Columbia also attracted Russians, Spaniards, and Canadians. A British colony established on Vancouver Island (1849) spread to the mainland when gold was discovered (1858). Entry into Canada (1871) and the transcontinental railroad (1885) provided the basis for economic development. Area: 359,277 sq mi (930,528 sq km). Population (1991): 3,282,061. Capital: Victoria.

British Empire Britain's overseas possessions from the 16th to early 20th centuries. The Empire's origins lay in the discovery by John *Cabot of Cape Breton Island (1497) but permanent settlements in North America were not established until the early 17th century, when colonists, some escaping religious persecution, were granted royal charters to settle Virginia, Maryland, and New England. The loss of the American colonies in 1783 (*see* American Revolution) was a major blow. In Canada the English came into conflict with the French and only established control in the *Seven Years' War (1756–63) from which they also emerged victorious in India. The East India Company had received its charter in 1600 but its interests in India had remained commercial until the decline of the Mogul Empire provided the chance for territorial expansion. Robert Clive's victory at Plassey (1757) assured British, rather than French, dominance there and the East India Company continued to govern until 1857, when its authority was replaced by the crown's.

The Napoleonic Wars in the early 19th century brought possessions in the West Indies (Trinidad, Tobago, St Lucia) as well as Mauritius, Sri Lanka, and in South Africa. Britain's first settlement in Africa had been on James Island in the Gambia River (1661) but substantial possessions were not obtained until the late 18th century with the acquisition of what are now Sierra Leone, Ghana, and Nigeria. The 19th-century colonial expansion in Africa was fired by missionary zeal, which motivated such explorers as *Livingstone, as well as by commercial activities. The late 19th century saw the establishment of British dominance in Egypt and the Sudan but in South Africa it was undermined by *Afrikaner hostility.

Colonies in Australia were initially (18th century) penal settlements. During the 19th century, New Zealand was controlled by the British from 1840, and Hong Kong (1841) and Burma (now Myanmar; 1886) were acquired. In the mid-19th century, following the 1839 *Report on the Affairs of British North America* by Lord *Durham, the self-governing colonies in Canada, Australia, New Zealand, and South Africa received responsible government, whereby governors were advised by local ministers. In 1907 Canada, Australia, and New Zealand (and in 1910 South Africa), by now federated, were termed dominions and regular *Imperial Conferences were instituted. In 1931 the *Commonwealth of Nations was established, giving the dominions autonomy, and in the following decades Britain's other colonies gradually achieved full independence.

British Expeditionary Force (BEF) Army formations that helped France counter German invasions in World Wars I and II. In World War I, its 6 divisions had increased to 65 by 1918 and it suffered almost 3 million casualties, of which 900,000 were fatal. In World War II it consisted of 10 divisions until its evacuation from Dunkirk (1940).

British Guiana. *See* Guyana, Republic of.

British Honduras. *See* Belize.

British Indian Ocean Territory A British colony established in 1965 consisting of Chagos Archipelago, largest island of which is Diego Garcia, claimed by Mauritius. Aldabra, Farquhar, and Desroches were returned to the Seychelles in 1976. Although the islands are at present leased to companies that run copra plantations, they were acquired as a base for military activities.

British Isles An archipelago separated from the mainland of NW Europe by the North Sea and the English Channel. It consists of Great Britain, Ireland, the Isle of Man, and the Channel Islands. Area: about 121,577 sq mi (314,950 sq km).

British Museum The national museum containing one of the finest collections of antiquities in the world. Founded in 1753, its Egyptian, Assyrian, Greek, Roman, Chinese, and Cambodian collections are unique and include a number of Egyptian mummies, the Elgin Marbles, and the Rosetta Stone. The natural history exhibits were transferred to a separate building (built 1873–80) known as the Natural History Museum.

British North America Act (1867) An act passed by the British Parliament uniting the colonies of Nova Scotia, New Brunswick, Canada West (now Ontario), and Canada East (now Quebec) as the Dominion of Canada.

British thermal unit (btu) A unit of energy equal to the amount of heat required to raise the temperature of 1 lb of water through 1°F. It is equal to 1055.06 joules (251.997 calories).

British Virgin Islands. *See* Virgin Islands.

Britons The indigenous inhabitants of Britain before the Anglo-Saxon settlements. They spoke languages of the Brythonic branch of the *Celtic language family. At the Roman conquest (1st century AD) Britain was divided into a number of tribal kingdoms with a common Celtic culture (*see* La Tène). Religious affairs were conducted by priests known as *Druids. *See also* Belgae.

Brittan, Leon (1939–) British Conservative politician; home secretary (1983–86); commissioner of European Community (1989–). Trained as a lawyer, he entered politics in 1974, becoming minister of state at the Home Office (1979–81) and chief secretary to the Treasury (1981–83). As a commissioner of the European Community, he directed its competition policy.

Brittany (Breton name: Breiz; French name: Bretagne) A planning region and former province in NW France. It consists of a peninsula between the Bay of Biscay and English Channel. It was part of ancient Armorica and in 56 BC was conquered by Julius Caesar. During the 5th–6th centuries AD Celts from Britain migrated here to escape the Anglo-Saxon invasion. Finally incorporated into France in 1532, it has retained its own distinctive culture. An important area for tourism, Brittany suffered from oil pollution on many beaches following the *Amoco Cadiz* oil tanker disaster in March 1978. Area: 10,494 sq mi (27,184 sq km). Population (1991 est): 2,805,400.

Britten, (Edward) Benjamin, Baron (1913–76) British composer and pianist. He spent the years 1939–42 in the US and subsequently founded the English Opera Group (1947) and the Aldeburgh Festival (1948). He wrote many works, as well as leading roles in his operas, for his lifelong friend, the tenor Peter Pears. Among Britten's best-known compositions are the operas *Peter*

Grimes (1945), *Billy Budd* (1951), and *Death in Venice* (1973); the orchestral works *Variations on a Theme by Frank Bridge* (1937) and the *Cello Symphony* (1964); choral works, such as the *Spring Symphony* (1949) and *A War Requiem* (1962); and many chamber and instrumental works.

BENJAMIN BRITTEN *His opera* Gloriana *(1953), on the story of England's Queen Elizabeth I and her courtier, the Earl of Essex, was written for the coronation of Elizabeth II.*

brittle star A marine invertebrate animal, also called sand star or serpent star, belonging to a class (*Ophiuroidea*) of *echinoderms. It has a small disklike body bearing five long fragile arms, used for locomotion. Brittle stars sometimes occur in large numbers on soft muddy sea beds and are active at night, feeding on small crustaceans, mollusks, and bottom debris. □oceans.

Brno (German name: Brünn) 49 12N 16 40E The second largest city in the Czech Republic, in S Moravia, formerly the capital of the province of Moravia. A fortified town in the Middle Ages, it contains the Spilberk fortress, an Austrian political prison (1621–1857). Other notable buildings include the 15th-century cathedral; its university was founded in 1919. The botanist Gregor Mendel devised his fundamental principles of heredity here (1865). Brno is now an important industrial center specializing in engineering and textiles; the *Bren gun was originally developed here. Population (1985 est): 385,000.

broad bean A stiff upright annual plant, *Vicia faba*, 24–60 in (60–150 cm) tall, with a ribbed stem and compound gray-green leaves composed of a few large leaflets. The flowers have white petals and dark-purple blotches on the wings. The large pod has a woolly lining surrounding large flat edible beans, for which the plant is cultivated throughout Europe, both as a vegetable and as an animal feed. *See also* bean.

broadbill A brightly colored passerine bird belonging to a family (*Eurylaimidae;* 14 species) of tropical African and Asian forests. It is about 5 in (12 cm) long with a large head, partly joined toes, and a very broad short bill. Most species are insectivorous, feeding in trees or on the wing.

Broadway A major street in New York City, along and near which are sited most of the leading commercial theaters. The word is used to refer to commercial theater in the US in general. *See also* Off-Broadway theaters.

broccoli A cultivated variety of wild *cabbage (*Brassica oleracea*) with a stout upright stem and a loose cluster of flower heads at the top. The leaves are narrow and curly; the lower ones are shed as the plant grows, leaving a scarred stem. Sprouting broccoli has purple or white flowers. Calabrese or green sprouting broccoli is an Italian variety, often with fused parallel stems. Both are eaten as vegetables while the flowers are in bud. *See also* Brassica.

Broch, Hermann (1886–1951) Austrian novelist. In 1927 he sold the family textile business to return to the University of Vienna. His trilogy *The Sleepwalkers* (1931–32) is a historical study of Europe in a variety of literary forms. Briefly imprisoned by the Nazis, he emigrated to the US in 1940. There he continued to experiment with innovative literary techniques, most notably in *The Death of Virgil* (1945).

Brocken 51 48N 10 37E A mountain in central Germany, the highest of the Harz Mountains. According to legend, this bare granite peak is the scene of the witches' sabbath (*see* witchcraft) on Walpurgis Night (May 1). The **Brocken specter** (*or* Brocken bow), first observed here, is a magnified shadow of the observer cast against mist or cloud below the level of the summit and surrounded by colored fringes resulting from the diffraction of light.

Broglie, Louis Victor, 7th Duc de. *See* de Broglie, Louis Victor, 7th Duc de.

Broken Hill 31 57S 141 30E A mining city in Australia, in W central New South Wales. The rich silver, lead, and zinc deposits were discovered in 1883. Population (1981): 26,913.

Broken Hill (Zambia). *See* Kabwe.

Bromfield, Louis (1896–1956) US writer. He wrote about rural life in such novels as *The Green Bay Tree* (1924), *Possession* (1925), *Early Autumn* (1926), for which he won a Pulitzer Prize, *The Rains Came* (1937), *Wild is the River* (1941), and *Malabar Farm* (1948).

bromine (Br) A dense reddish-brown liquid element, discovered by A. J. Balard (1802–76) in 1826. It is extracted from sea water and other natural brines by electrolysis or by displacement with chlorine. The liquid element is volatile and its vapor has a pungent smell reminiscent of chlorine with severe irritating effects on the eyes and throat. Compounds include silver bromide (AgBr), used in photography, and ethylene dibromide ($C_2H_4Br_2$), used to scavenge lead in making additives for motor fuel. Other compounds are used as fumigants, dyes, flameproofing agents, and in medicine. At no 35; at wt 79.904; mp 19°F (-7.2°C); bp 137.9°F (58.78°C).

bronchial tubes. *See* lung.

bronchitis Inflammation of the bronchi, the tubes conducting air to the lungs. Acute bronchitis is often due to a virus infection, particularly a cold or influenza. Chronic bronchitis is common in middle-aged and elderly men, being aggravated by cigarette smoking and air pollution. Irritation of the mucus-secreting glands in the bronchi results in a persistent cough, with the production of large amounts of sputum. The patient is breathless and liable to chest infections. Treatment consists of stopping smoking (and reducing exposure to other irritants) and the prompt management of any chest infection.

Bronowski, Jacob (1908–74) British mathematician, science writer, and broadcaster, born in Poland. He became widely known for his highly successful television series *The Ascent of Man* (1973), a history of the development of science and technology. His writings include commentaries on poetry, particularly that of William *Blake, and the importance of the scientific method, especially in *The Commonsense of Science* (1951).

Brontë sisters Three British novelists, daughters of the rector of Haworth, an isolated village in Yorkshire. After briefly attending a local boarding school, **Charlotte Brontë** (1816–55) and **Emily Brontë** (1818–48) rejoined their sister **Anne Brontë** (1820–49) at home. Their early writings chronicled the imaginary kingdoms of Angria and Gondal. All the sisters worked for brief periods as governesses and teachers to help pay off the debts of their artist brother, **Patrick Branwell Brontë** (1817–48), an alcoholic and opium addict who died of tuberculosis. In 1846 the sisters published *Poems by Currer, Ellis, and Acton Bell* and in 1847, under the same pseudonyms, the novels *Jane Eyre* (by Charlotte), *Wuthering Heights* (by Emily), and *Agnes Gray* (by Anne). In 1848 Emily died of tuberculosis, as did Anne in 1849. Charlotte published *Shirley* (1849) and *Villette* (1853). She married her father's curate in 1854 and died in pregnancy a year later.

Brontosaurus A huge herbivorous dinosaur, also called *Apatosaurus,* of the late Jurassic period, which ended about 135 million years ago. Up to 68 ft (21 m) long and weighing up to 30 tons, it had massive pillarlike legs, a long neck and tail, and spent most of its time in swamps, coming ashore to lay eggs. With its nostrils placed high on its head, it was able to stand almost fully submerged. Order: *Saurischia.* □fossil.

Brontotherium A genus of extinct North American hoofed mammals—*titanotheres—that lived during the Oligocene epoch (between 38 and 26 million years ago). Standing 8 ft (2.5 m) at the shoulder, *Brontotherium* had a large skull with a pair of bony horns.

Bronx, the 40 50N 73 52W One of the five boroughs of New York City, US, situated NE of the Harlem River. It is mainly residential but has an industrialized waterfront. Problems of overcrowding and poor housing conditions have made it the object of local and federal urbanization programs. Area: 41 sq mi (107 sq km). Population (1976 est): 1,255,500.

bronze An *alloy of copper and (4–11%) tin. Because it melts between 1650°F and 1835°F (900°–1000°C), about the temperature of an ordinary wood fire, it was one of the first metals to be used for making weapons and utensils, being known around 2000 BC in Britain. It is harder than pure copper and "copper" coins are usually made of bronze containing 95% copper, 4% tin, 1% zinc, and occasionally other metals. Phosphor bronze contains 0.5% phosphorous. *See also* gun metal.

Bronze Age The cultural phase during which metallurgical technology, based first on copper (in the Chalcolithic period) and then on bronze (copper alloyed with tin), replaced the stone technology (*see* Stone Age) of the *Neolithic period. In Eurasia the development of international trade, literacy, the plow, and the wheel took place during this phase, which began at varying dates according to locality (the earliest being about 6500 BC in Anatolia); it gave way to the

*Iron Age in about 1000 BC. In Africa, iron, discovered about 800 BC, replaced stone without an intervening Bronze Age. In the Americas, copper, discovered about 100 AD, was followed rapidly by iron, while in Australasia, the introduction of metallurgy occurred in the colonial period.

BRONTË SISTERS *A family portrait (c. 1834) of (from left) Anne, Emily, and Charlotte by their brother Branwell.*

Bronzino, Il (Agnolo di Cosimo; 1503–72) Florentine mannerist painter (*see* mannerism). His religious and allegorical works, such as *Venus, Cupid, and Folly* (National Gallery, London), were influenced by *Michelangelo and Bronzino's teacher *Pontormo. As court painter to Cosimo I de' Medici, he painted many portraits, including *Eleanor of Toledo and Her Son Giovanni* (Uffizi), a characteristic work having a cold detached dignity and a marblelike finish.

Brook, Peter (1925–   ) British theater director. His work for the Royal Shakespeare Company, of which he became a director in 1962, included experimental productions of Shakespeare. Since 1970 he has worked with the International Center for Theater Research in Paris, where he has developed acting techniques evolved during a tour of Africa and Asia. He has also directed films, including *Lord of the Flies* (1963) and *King Lear* (1971).

Brooke, Rupert (Chawner) (1887–1915) British poet and critic. His scholarship, charm, and good looks gained him many influential friends in literary and political circles. He received a naval commission in 1914 but died of blood poisoning on a hospital ship in the Aegean, without having seen action. His romantic image and the idealistic patriotism of his wartime poetry, *1914 and Other Poems* (1915), made him a national hero.

Brookeborough, Basil Stanlake Brooke, 1st Viscount (1888–1973) Northern Irish statesman; prime minister of Northern Ireland (1943–63). He became a Unionist MP in 1929 and was minister of agriculture (1933–41) and then minister of commerce (1941–43). He was firmly committed to union with Great Britain.

Brook Farm (1841–47) US utopian community in W Roxbury, Mass. It was established by George *Ripley, a Unitarian minister who had become a transcendentalist. He wanted to experiment with the intellectual and the worker living a simple life together, earning equal pay. Charles A. Dana (1819–97), Nathanial *Hawthorne, Ralph Waldo *Emerson, Theodore Parker (1810–60), Amos Bronson *Alcott, and Margaret Fuller (1810–50), among others participated at Brook Farm in one way or another. Poor farming land, lack of water, natural disasters, and failing finances forced its closing in 1847.

Brooklyn 40 40N 73 58W One of the five boroughs of New York City, situated at the SW end of Long Island. Settled by Dutch farmers in 1636, it has many colonial buildings and is the site of Pratt Institute (1887), Brooklyn Institute of Arts and Sciences (1823; comprising Brooklyn Museum, Brooklyn Children's Museum, and Brooklyn Botanic Garden and Arboretum), and branches of four New York universities. The New York Naval Shipyard, which was established here in 1801, was converted to civilian use in the 1960s. Three bridges, including the famous Brooklyn Bridge (1869–83), span the East River connecting Brooklyn with Manhattan. A major port, it handles a vast amount of shipping and its waterfront is 33 mi (53 km) long. Area: 81 sq mi (210 sq km). Population (1976 est): 2,313,200.

Brooks Range A mountain range in N Alaska, just below the Alaskan North Slope, crossing the state to the Canadian border and including the De Long, Baird, Endicott, and Davidson mountains. The highest point is Mt Michelson (9239 ft; 2816 m).

broom A bushy deciduous shrub, *Sarothamnus scoparius* (or *Cytisus scoparius*), 24–80 in (60–200 cm) high, with shiny green five-angled stems and small pointed compound leaves. The bright-yellow flowers are clustered at the ends of the twigs. Broom is found in heaths and woodland glades in Europe. It is poisonous to livestock but is often grown as an ornamental. The branches are used for brooms and thatching. Family: *Leguminosae*.

broomrape A parasitic plant of the worldwide genus *Orobanche* (about 100 species), lacking chlorophyll but having underground tubers attached to the roots of the host plant. The flowering shoots rise 2–28 in (5–70 cm) above ground on scaly stems topped by spikes of tubular two-lipped flowers, which may be white, yellow, or purple. The fruit is a capsule. Family: *Orobanchaceae*.

brotulid A fish, also called brotula, belonging to the family *Brotulidae* (it is sometimes placed with the cusk eels in the family *Ophidiidae*). Brotulids have an eel-like body, up to about 35 in (90 cm) in length, and most live in deep marine waters. Order: *Perciformes*.

Brough, Louise (1923–) US tennis player, who in 1948 and 1950 won all three titles at Wimbledon (singles, doubles, and mixed doubles). She also won all 22 of her *Wightman Cup matches. (1946–57).

brougham A compact four-wheeled carriage light enough to be drawn by one horse. The original brougham was designed by Lord Brougham (1778–1868) in 1838.

Brouwer, Adriaen (c. 1605–38) Flemish painter, who worked in Holland, initially as a pupil of *Hals, and later in Antwerp. He excelled in small paintings of brawling and drunken peasants, the somber coloring of which was increasingly influenced by Dutch art.

Brouwer, L(uitzen) E(gbertus) J(an) (1881–1966) Dutch mathematician, who made important contributions to the development of *topology. He is often regarded as the founder of the subject in its modern form. He is also the founder of a school of mathematics known as intuitional mathematics, which holds that mathematics is a mental construction in which laws should be self-evident and derived by intuition.

Brown, Sir Arthur. *See* Alcock, Sir John.

Brown, Ford Madox (1821–93) British painter, born in France. After studying in Belgium, Paris, and Rome, he returned to England, where he was influenced by the Pre-Raphaelites. He painted chiefly historical themes, although his most famous paintings, *Work* and *The Last of England*, are contemporary subjects.

Brown, Jerry (Edmund Gerald B., Jr.; 1938–   ) US politician and lawyer. After graduation from Yale Law School (1964) he went into private practice, but, by 1970, was California's secretary of state. Elected Democratic governor of the state in 1974, a position his father "Pat" had also held (1959–67), he served until 1983. He was unsuccessful in seeking the presidential nomination in 1976 and 1980 and in his bid for the US Senate in 1982. He again unsuccessfully sought the Democratic presidential nomination in 1992.

Brown, John (1800–59) US abolitionist. Believing that the slaves of the US should be encouraged to rise up against their masters, Brown established an antislavery colony in Kansas and carried out the massacre of five local slave owners in 1856. In 1859, supplied with funds by northern abolitionists, Brown and his followers raided the federal arsenal at Harper's Ferry in order to acquire arms for an expected slave rebellion throughout the South. Brown and his men were quickly captured by US Army troops under the command of Lt. Col. Robert E. *Lee. Brown was later tried and convicted of insurrection, treason, and murder. He was hanged on Dec 2, 1859, and was considered by many to be a martyr to the abolitionist cause.

Brown, Robert (1773–1858) Scottish botanist, who in 1831 first recognized the *nucleus as a fundamental constituent of cells. Four years earlier, while observing a solution of pollen grains in water under a microscope, he discovered, but was unable to explain, the effect now known as the *Brownian movement.

brown algae *Algae of the division *Pheophyta* (1500 species), which contain a brown fucoxanthin (pigment) in addition to and sometimes masking the green chlorophyll. Brown algae include all the larger *seaweeds, such as wracks and kelps. They are mainly marine and are abundant along coasts in colder regions. Many show an *alternation of generations.

brown bear A large bear, *Ursus arctos,* of the N hemisphere. Brown bears have a thick shaggy coat, humped on the shoulders and varying in color from blackish-brown to gray, and they take a wide variety of food including fish, fruit, and cattle. There are many local races and subspecies, including the North American grizzly and Kodiac bears. The reputedly ferocious grizzly bear (*U. arctos horribilis*), mostly restricted to N Canada and Alaska, reaches a length of 8 ft (2.5 m) and a weight of 1213 lb (550 kg); the Alaskan Kodiac bear—a giant race of grizzly—is the largest living land carnivore, reaching a length of 9 ft (2.8 m) and a weight of 1675 lb (760 kg).

Browne, Hablot Knight (1815–82) British artist, better known as Phiz. He is renowned mainly for his illustrations of books by Charles Dickens, notably *The Pickwick Papers*. He also produced cartoons for *Punch* and watercolors.

Brownian movement The continuous random movement of very small particles (less than about 0.001 mm in diameter) when suspended in a fluid. It is caused by collisions between the particles and the atoms or molecules of the fluid. Brownian movement can be observed in smoke suspended in air and in a suspension of pollen grains in a liquid. Named for Robert *Brown.

Browning, Robert (1812–89) British poet. The son of a bank clerk, his early education consisted chiefly of wide reading in his father's library. After the failure of his autobiographical poem *Pauline* (1833) he wrote several verse dramas and dramatic monologues, including the famous "My Last Duchess" (1842). The epic but uneven poem cycle *The Ring and the Book* was his last major work. His wife **Elizabeth Barrett Browning** (1806–61) was also a poet. A spinal injury when she was 15 made her a lifelong semi-invalid. She met Robert Browning in 1845 and in 1846 she defied her domineering father and eloped with Browning to Italy. Here she wrote her most famous work, *Sonnets from the Portuguese* (1850). In later years she became involved in Italian politics, the abolition of slavery, and spiritualism.

Browning Automatic Rifle (BAR) A gas-operated shoulder-fired automatic *rifle designed in 1917 by John Moses Browning (1855–1926). The standard automatic weapon in the US army until the Korean War, it weighed over 19 lbs (8.6 kg), including its 20-round magazine.

Brownshirts The colloquial name for the Nazi Sturmabteilung (SA; stormtroopers). Their name refers to their brown uniforms. They were founded in 1921 and reorganized by Ernst *Röhm in 1930. Squads of thugs, who molested and murdered the Nazis' opponents, they numbered two million by 1933. In 1934 Hitler eliminated Röhm and greatly reduced the power of the Brownshirts. *See also* SS.

Brownsville 25 54N 97 30W A city and port on the S tip of Texas at the Mexican border, on the Rio Grande, just E of the Gulf of Mexico. Originally a fort, it was important during the Mexican War and to the Confederacy during the Civil War. The oil industry, the processing of foods and chemicals, the production of machinery, and tourism are important. Population (1990): 98,962.

Brown v. Board of Education (of Topeka) (1954) US Supreme Court case that held that segregation in public schools on the basis of race is unlawful. The "separate but equal" doctrine was overturned in a majority opinion written by Chief Justice Earl *Warren who said, "Separate educational facilities are inherently unequal."

Brown v. Board of Education (1955) US Supreme Court ruling that directed implementation of the *Brown v. Board of Education (of Topeka) ruling "with all deliberate speed." Local courts were ordered to find solutions to individual problems as they arose.

Brubeck, Dave (1920–) US jazz pianist and composer, who studied composition with Darius Milhaud and Arnold Schoenberg. Brubeck introduced complex rhythms into jazz and formed a quartet in 1951. Among his most famous pieces are "Take Five," and "Blue Rondo à la Turque."

Bruce, James (1730–94) British explorer, who in the course of an arduous expedition that set out from Cairo in 1768 reached Lake Tana, source of the Blue Nile (1770). He described his experiences in *Travels to Discover the Source of the Nile* (1790).

Bruce, Robert. *See* Robert (I) the Bruce.

brucellosis (*or* undulant fever)   An infectious disease of cattle and other
farm animals that is caused by the bacterium *Brucella abortus* and can be contracted by man through drinking unpasteurized contaminated milk. Symptoms
include fever (which may be intermittent), sweating, weakness, cough, joint
pain, and sometimes swelling of the lymph nodes. Tetracycline usually cures the
disease. The slaughter of infected animals has reduced the incidence of brucellosis.

Bruce of Melborne, Stanley Melborne, 1st Viscount (1883–1967) Australian statesman; prime minister (1923–29). He fought with the British Army in
World War I and entered politics as a member of the National Party in 1918. His
coalition government of National and Country Parties implemented social and
welfare legislation in the areas of public health and devised a scheme of national
insurance against unemployment. He represented Australia in the British war
cabinet (1942–45).

Bruch, Max (1838–1920) German composer. He wrote in a romantic but conservative style. He is best known for his first violin concerto (1868) and *Kol
Nidrei* (1880) for cello and orchestra, based on a Jewish hymn.

Brücke, Die (German: The Bridge) An organization of German artists
founded in 1905 to promote modern art. Its members, notably *Kirchner, were
influenced, like their French contemporaries, the fauves (*see* fauvism), by *Van
Gogh, *Gauguin, *Munch, and primitive art. However, unlike the fauves, their
crudely painted and vibrantly colored figure studies and landscapes expressed an
underlying anxiety more typical of such early German artists as *Grünewald.
Although the group broke up in 1913, it has had a lasting influence on the
graphic arts, particularly the *woodcut. *See also* expressionism.

Bruckner, Anton (1824–96) Austrian composer and organist. He was a professor at the Vienna conservatory (1871–91). In 1891 he was granted a pension
and apartments in the Belvedere palace in Vienna, where he revised his compositions and worked on his ninth symphony (1887–96), which remained unfinished at his death. His symphonies, which exhibit the influence of Wagner and
Schubert, had a mixed reception during his lifetime and were frequently performed in shortened versions. Bruckner also composed choral music in a poly-
phonic style, chamber music, organ music, and a *Te Deum* (1881–84) for orchestra, soloists, and chorus.

Brueghel the Elder, Pieter (*or* Bruegel; 1525–69) Flemish painter, noted
for his often satirical scenes of peasant life and his landscapes. Although popularly called Peasant Brueghel, he was a learned man, whose patrons included
Cardinal de Granvelle (1517–86). He studied under Pieter Coecke van Aelst
(1502–50), whose daughter he later married, but was chiefly influenced by
*Bosch in such works as the macabre *Triumph of Death* (Prado). He visited Italy
(c. 1551–53) but Italian art influenced his style only in his last years. In 1563 he
settled in Brussels, where he executed his best-known works, e.g. *Peasant Wedding* (Kunsthistorisches Museum, Vienna), and a landscape series entitled the
Labors of the Months. Many of his paintings were copied by his eldest son
Pieter the Younger (?1564–1638?). His younger son **Jan the Elder**
(1568–1625), popularly called Velvet Brueghel, is noted for his flower and landscape paintings. He was a friend and sometimes assistant of Rubens.

Bruges (Flemish name: Brugge) 51 13N 3 14E A city in NW Belgium. It was
the capital of Flanders in the 12th century and during the 13th and 14th centuries
it became the center of the Hanseatic League in N Europe. It has many fine
gothic buildings, including the 14th-century cathedral, the Church of Notre
Dame (containing Michelangelo's marble statue, the Virgin and Child), and the

bruise

Market Hall (13th–15th centuries) with its famous belfry and 47-bell carillon. It is linked by canal to many European ports. The traditional industry is lace; newer industrial developments include the manufacture of ships and electronic equipment. Population (1991): 117,063.

bruise An area of discolored skin caused by the leakage of blood from damaged blood vessels beneath the skin. Bruises are usually caused by a blow to the skin and are always more pronounced where the blood vessels are loosely suspended in the tissue (e.g. around the eye). They change from bluish to greenish yellow, as the blood pigment is chemically broken down and absorbed.

Brummel, George Bryan (1778–1840) British dandy, known as Beau Brummel. He was a prominent member of fashionable society and a close friend of the Prince Regent, later George IV. He fled to France to evade his creditors in 1816 and died in an asylum.

Brunei, State of A small sultanate in NW Borneo, on the South China Sea. It consists of two separate areas, entirely bounded (except for its coast) by the Malaysian state of Sarawak. It is mainly low lying with some hills in the S; the interior is largely dense forest. The people are mainly Malays, while about a quarter of the population are Chinese or other small minorities. *Economy*: dominated by oil (the main export) since the discovery of the Seria oil field in 1929, production is being maintained by the addition of offshore oil rigs. Recent efforts to diversify the economy include the construction of a deepwater port and a natural-gas liquefaction plant. Agriculture is also being encouraged in an attempt to make Brunei more self-sufficient in food production. *History*: a powerful state in the 16th century controlling the whole of Borneo, as well as parts of the Philippines, it became a British protected state in 1888. In 1962 there was a revolt, mainly in protest against the proposal to join the Federation of Malaysia, and since then the sultan has ruled by decree. In 1967 Hassanal Bolkia Mu'izuddin Waddaulah succeeded his father as sultan. In 1971 internal self-government was achieved and full independence was attained in 1984. Official language: Malay; Chinese and English are also widely spoken. Official religion: Islam. Official currency: Brunei dollar of 100 cents. Area: 2,230 sq mi (5,776 sq km). Population (1990 est): 372,000. Capital and main port: Bandar Seri Begawan.

Brunel, Isambard Kingdom (1806–59) British engineer, who was one of the most original inventors of the 19th century. His most famous works were the Clifton suspension bridge, which spanned the Avon Gorge, near Bristol, England, completed in 1864, and his ships the *Great Western* (1837), the *Great Britain* (1843; □ship), the first large ship to be driven by screw propellers and now preserved in Bristol, and the *Great Eastern* (1858). Much of his work was done for the Great Western Railroad, for which he built over 990 mi (1600 km) of track, using the 7 ft (2 m) broad gauge rather than the 4 ft 8½ in (1.5 m) standard gauge. His father **Sir Marc Isambard Brunel** (1769–1849) was also an engineer. Born in France, he worked in New York after fleeing the French Revolution in 1793. He moved to England in 1799, where he became famous for his work on tunneling. In 1818 he patented the tunneling shield, which allowed tunnels to be dug below water.

Brunelleschi, Filippo (1377–1446) Italian architect. The founder of Renaissance architecture, Brunelleschi began his career as a goldsmith, only taking up architecture in his thirties, after spending some time studying Roman remains. His taste for classical architecture probably arose from a desire to understand Roman building techniques. This is demonstrated by his most famous construction, the dome of Florence cathedral (1430s), which used classical methods of construction. The Ospedale degli Innocenti (1419–26) is often regarded as the first architectural expression of the Renaissance.

Brunhild (*or* Brynhild) A heroine of Norse and Germanic legend. In the *Volsungasaga* she is the daughter of Odin, doomed to sleep on a fire-encircled rock until wakened by a mortal (*see* Siegfried). In the **Nibelungenlied* she is the queen of Issland.

Brüning, Heinrich (1885–1970) German statesman. As chancellor without a majority in the Reichstag, he governed by decree from 1930 to 1932. His deflationary policies brought him unpopularity and he resigned. In 1934 he left Germany, holding academic posts at Harvard (1937–52) and then at Cologne Universities.

Brünn. *See* Brno.

Brunner, Emil (1889–1965) Swiss Protestant theologian. A professor at the University of Zurich from 1924 to 1953, he became a supporter of the theological views of *Barth. However, he differed from Barth in allowing that God's image in mankind survived the Fall, despite man's fundamental sinfulness.

Bruno, Giordano (1548–1600) Italian philosopher. He became a Dominican (1563) but in 1576 his heretical opinions forced him to flee, first to Geneva, then to France, England, and Germany. Returning to Italy (1592) he was tried by the Inquisition, refused to recant, and was burned. His pantheistic philosophy, viewing all creation as one life, animated by God as "world-soul," influenced *Spinoza, *Descartes, and *Leibniz among others.

Bruno of Cologne, St (c. 1032–1101) German founder of the Carthusian order. He was educated at Cologne and Rheims, where he later taught at the cathedral school. He eventually withdrew with six companions to the mountainous region near Grenoble and built a monastery on the site of the present Grande Chartreuse, which became the mother house of the Carthusians. Called to Italy by Pope Urban II, his former pupil, he founded the monastery of La Torre in Calabria, where he died. Feast day: Oct 6.

Brunswick (German name: Braunschweig) 52 15N 10 30E A German city in Lower Saxony on the Oker River. It was the capital of the former duchy of Brunswick. Notable buildings include the castle and the romanesque cathedral (both 12th-century), the old town hall (14th–15th centuries), and the ducal palace (1768–69). It also has the oldest technical university in Germany (1745). Its industries include metal working and the manufacture of motor vehicles and pianos. Population (1988): 248,000.

brush turkey A *megapode bird, *Alectura lathami,* occurring in dense rain forests of New Guinea and E Australia. It is 26–28 in (65–70 cm) long with a black plumage and builds a huge mound of fermenting plant material in which the eggs are incubated.

Brussels (Flemish name: Brussel; French name: Bruxelles) 50 51N 4 22E The capital of Belgium, situated in the center of the country on the Senne River. As headquarters of the EEC and NATO, it is an important international center. Its varied industries include the manufacture of machinery, chemicals, and lace. Fine buildings include the 15th-century gothic town hall, the 13th-century Maison du Roi, the church of St Gudule, the 18th-century Palais de la Nation (parliament building), and the Royal Palace. The Free University was founded in 1834 and a Flemish-speaking counterpart became independent in 1970. *History*: settled by the French in the 7th century AD, it developed into a center of the wool industry in the 13th century. It became the capital of the Spanish Netherlands in the 15th century and later of the Austrian S Netherlands. In 1830 it was chosen as capital of the new kingdom of Belgium. It was occupied by the Germans in both World Wars. Population (1991): 954,045.

Brussels sprout A variety of wild cabbage, *Brassica oleracea* var. *gemmifera,* cultivated for its large edible buds. The stout erect shoots, up to 31 in (80 cm) high, have long-stalked curly leaves arranged spirally up the stem; in the angle between the leaf bases and the stem are large buds, like miniature cabbages up to 2 in (5 cm) in diameter. The lower leaves gradually fall, leaving the stem densely covered with buds. *See also* Brassica.

BRUSSELS *The European Economic Community building.*

Brutus, Marcus Junius (?85–42 BC) Roman soldier and one of the assassins of Julius Caesar. Brutus, who supported Pompey against Caesar in the civil war, was pardoned by Caesar and made governor of Cisalpine Gaul (46) but subsequently joined the conspiracy to murder Caesar (44). He committed suicide after his defeat by Antony and Octavian at Philippi (42).

Bryan, William Jennings (1860–1925) US politician, orator, and lawyer. A Democrat from Illinois, he served as a congressman (1891–95), ran for president three times (1896, 1900, 1908) but was defeated each time, and served as secretary of state (1913–15) under Pres. Woodrow Wilson. He was a strong proponent of *Free Silver; his "Cross of Gold" speech (1896) led to his endorsement by four political parties in the 1896 presidential election. Called the "Great Commoner," he championed liberal causes; advocated an income tax, prohibition of alcohol, and women's rights; and worked for the creation of a federal department of labor. In 1925, just before his death, he was the prosecutor in the anti-evolution Scopes trial, which was won by defense attorney Clarence *Darrow.

Bryansk 53 15N 34 09E A city in W Russia. It dates from at least the 12th century and is a communications center with varied industries. Population (1987): 445,000.

Bryant, William Cullen (1794–1878) US poet, journalist, and literary critic. He wrote his most famous poems, "Thanatopsis," when he was 17. The success of his *Poems* (1821) enabled him to abandon his law practice and move to New York. From 1829 he was editor of the newspaper *Evening Post* which became, over the next fifty years, an advocate of many liberal causes.

Bryce Canyon National Park A national park in SW Utah, just N of Arizona. Established as a national park in 1928, it is noted for its naturally carved limestone cliffs, horseshoe-shaped amphitheater-like eroded rock structures, and glowing colored rocks. Area: 56 sq mi (145 sq km).

bryony Either of two unrelated Eurasian plants. **Black bryony** (*Tamus communis*) is a herbaceous climber with heart-shaped leaves that turn yellow in autumn. The bell-shaped yellow flowers are borne in separate male and female spikes. The fruits are scarlet berries, and the plant overwinters as a tuber. Family: *Dioscoreaceae* (yam family).

White bryony (*Bryonia dioica*) is a perennial herb climbing by means of tendrils. The hairy stem arises from a large rootstock and the leaves are palmately lobed. Greenish male and female flowers occur on separate plants and produce poisonous scarlet berries. Family: *Cucurbitaceae* (gourd family).

bryophyte A small flowerless green plant of the division *Bryophyta* (about 25,000 species), comprising the *liverworts and *mosses. The plant body is either differentiated into stems and leaves or is a flat branching structure (thallus). Bryophytes range in size from microscopic to over 40 in (1 m) long; they lack true vascular (conducting) tissues and roots (the rootlike rhizoids serve mainly for anchorage). Bryophytes show *alternation of generations: the plant itself is the sexual (gametophyte) phase, which bears male and female sex organs (antheridia and archegonia, respectively). Fertilization of an egg cell results in the development of a spore capsule—the asexual (sporophyte) phase—which remains attached to the gametophyte and largely dependent on it. The spores are dispersed by wind, insects, or water and germinate to form new plants.

Bryozoa (*or* Ectoprocta) A phylum of aquatic colonial invertebrate animals (about 6000 species), called moss animals, found chiefly in seas as matlike encrustations on rocks. A colony consists of individuals, each up to 0.12 in (3 mm) long and with a chitinous or gelatinous case and a ring of ciliated tentacles around the mouth. These are extended, creating a feeding current that brings food particles into the U-shaped digestive tract. Ciliated larvae establish new colonies by budding off more individuals.

Brythonic languages. *See* Celtic languages.

Brześć nad Bu-giem. *See* Brest.

btu. *See* British thermal unit.

Bubastis (modern name: Tall Bastah) A ruined temple city in Lower Egypt. Bubastis was the capital of the 18th nome (province) and attained importance when the pharaohs of the 19th dynasty (1320–1200 BC) moved their capital to the Nile Delta. It became a royal residence when Sheshonk I was pharaoh (952 BC). After the Persian conquest (525 BC) the city declined. Bubastis was sacred to the cat goddess Bast.

bubble chamber An instrument that makes visible the tracks of ionizing particles, used for observing particle decays and interactions. It contains a liquid, usually hydrogen, helium, or deuterium, under pressure and at a temperature slightly above its normal boiling point. The particle induces boiling along its path and the bubbles are photographed to record the particle's track and those of any charged decay or reaction products.

Buber, Martin (1878–1965) Austrian-born Jewish religious philosopher. He wrote on *Hasidism, to which he was deeply sympathetic, and from 1925 produced, with F. *Rosenzweig, a remarkable German translation of the Bible. However, his best-known and most influential work was *I and Thou* (1923), which sets out his philosophy of religious faith in the form of a dialogue between man and God. Buber was a committed Zionist (he settled in Palestine in 1938), and advocated a joint Arab-Jewish state.

bubonic plague. *See* plague.

Bucaramanga 7 08N 73 10W A city in N Colombia. Situated in mountainous country, it is the commercial center for an area producing coffee and tobacco; manufactures include cigarettes and textiles. The Industrial University of Santander was founded here in 1947. Population (1985): 341,513.

buccaneers Bands of pirates who lived by plunder in the Caribbean in the second half of the 17th century. Most were English or French and they preyed primarily on Spanish shipping and settlements. They were often hired by the French governors of Tortuga and the English of Jamaica. By 1670 they had become, under the leadership of Henry *Morgan, a major problem for all countries, and a number of treaties promised to bring them under control. In 1685 the English navy began to hunt buccaneers and after 1697 no European country employed them.

Bucer, Martin (1491–1551) German Protestant reformer. A Dominican friar, Bucer abandoned his vows and married in 1522, settling in Strasbourg. He advised Henry VIII on his divorce from Catherine of Aragon and tried to mediate between *Luther and *Zwingli in their debate concerning the Eucharist. In 1549 he went to England and became professor of divinity at Cambridge.

Buchanan, James (1791–1868) US statesman; 15th president of the US (1857–61). Trained as a lawyer, Buchanan served as a member of the US House of Representatives (1821–31), US minister to Russia (1832–33), and US senator from Pennsylvania (1835–45). Buchanan resigned from the Senate to become secretary of state in the cabinet of Pres. James *Polk (1845–49) and US minister to Great Britain during the administration of Pres. Franklin *Pierce (1853–56). As the 1856 presidential nominee of the *Democratic Party, Buchanan defeated the Republican John *Fremont and attempted to effect a compromise over the issue of slavery during his single term in the White House. Hoping to prevent the secession of the southern states, he supported the legalization of slavery in Kansas and proposed a Constitutional amendment that would recognize the rights of slave owners. Buchanan's efforts were ultimately unsuccessful; less than a month after leaving office, the southern states seceded from the Union and the *Civil War began.

Bucharest (Romanian name: Bucureşti) 44 25N 26 07E The capital of Romania, in the SE on a tributary of the Danube. As well as being the administrative and cultural center of the country, Bucharest has many industries, including flour milling, textiles, chemicals, and oil refining. *History*: there is evidence of human settlement from prehistoric times. A fortress was built against Turkish invasion in the 15th century and it became capital of Walachia in 1659. During the 19th century Bucharest played an important role in revolutionary movements, becoming capital of Romania in 1862. The university was founded in 1864. It was badly damaged by German bombing in World War II and since then has developed considerably. Population (1992 est): 2,064,000.

Bucharest, Treaties of 1. (1812) The treaty ending the Russo-Turkish war of 1806–12. It assigned Bessarabia to Russia and Walachia and Moldavia to Turkey; the Serbs were to receive autonomy. **2.** (1886) The treaty ending the Serbian-Bulgarian war (1885–86) over Eastern *Rumelia, which was kept by Bulgaria. **3.** (1913) The treaty ending the second *Balkan War, which partitioned Macedonia between Serbia, Greece, Romania, and the defeated Bulgaria. **4.** (1918) The treaty in which Romania acknowledged its defeat by the Central Powers in World War I. It was annulled after their defeat by the Allies.

Büchner, Georg (1813–37) German dramatist. A medical student, he fled to Zürich after publishing a revolutionary pamphlet in 1834. He wrote three plays, the tragedies *Danton's Death* (1835) and *Woyzeck* (1836) and the comedy *Leonce und Lena* (1836), and a fragment of a novel, *Lenz* (1836). His innovative techniques influenced later expressionist writers.

Buck, Pearl S(ydenstricker) (1892–1973) US novelist. The daughter of Presbyterian missionaries, she grew up in China and later returned there as a teacher. Her novels about China include *The Good Earth* (1931), *A House Divided* (1935), *Dragon Seed* (1942), and *The Three Daughters of Madame Liang* (1969). She won the Nobel Prize in 1938.

Buckingham, George Villiers, 1st Duke of (1592–1628) A favorite of James I of England. He replaced Robert Carr, Earl of *Somerset, in the king's favor (1615), becoming Earl of Buckingham (1617), Lord High Admiral (1619), and Duke of Buckingham (1623). James resisted Parliament's attempts to demote Buckingham, who was assassinated after his unsuccessful expedition to relieve the Huguenots at La Rochelle (1627). His son **George Villiers, 2nd Duke of Buckingham** (1628–87) was a member of the powerful political group the *Cabal, under Charles II. After his father's death he was brought up in the royal family, with whom he went into exile after the final royalist defeat in the Civil War (1651). Becoming a privy councillor at the Restoration, he was overshadowed by *Arlington when the Cabal came to power. Also a playwright, he wrote the satirical *The Rehearsal* (1671).

Buckingham Palace The London residence of the British monarch. It was built about 1705 for the Duke of Buckingham, becoming a royal residence in 1761. It was completely redesigned by Nash for George IV, although its main façade was not added until 1913.

Buckinghamshire A county in the South Midlands of England, bordering on Greater London. It is known appropriately as Leafy Bucks because of the many trees throughout the county. It is mainly agricultural, the chief crops being barley, wheat, and oats; sheep, cattle, poultry, and pig farming are also significant. Industry includes the manufacture of furniture based on the extensive beech woods. Area: 725 sq mi (1878 sq km). Population (1991): 619,500. Administrative center: Aylesbury.

Buckley, William F(rank) Jr. (1925–) US journalist and writer. A conservative, he founded and edited *National Review* (1955) magazine. He also writes a syndicated newspaper column. His works include *God and Men at Yale* (1951), *The Unmaking of a Mayor* (1966; about his unsuccessful bid to be mayor of New York City), *Saving the Queen* (1976), *Overdrive* (1983), *Right Reason* (1985), and *High Jinx* (1986).

buckthorn A small thorny deciduous tree or shrub of the genus *Rhamnus* (about 13 species), widespread in the N hemisphere. The leaves are oval, with attractive autumn colors. The small green flowers produce blue-black berries. The wood is used for charcoal and slow fuses, and the bark for dyes. The alder buckthorn (*Frangula alnus*) is a similar and related shrub that lacks thorns. Family: *Rhamnaceae*.

buckwheat A herbaceous plant of the genus *Fagopyrum,* especially *F. esculentum.* Up to 24 in (60 cm) tall, they have arrow-shaped leaves and clusters of densely packed small pink or white flowers. Buckwheats are native to Asia but widely cultivated for their seed, used as a cereal substitute, or as green fodder. Family: *Polygonaceae* (dock family).

Budapest 47 33N 19 03E The capital of Hungary, situated in the N of the country on the Danube River. Most of Hungary's industry is sited here and includes machinery, iron and steel, and chemicals. The university was founded in 1635. *History*: from the 14th century the fortress of Buda, on the W bank of the

Buddha

Danube, was the seat of the Magyar kings. After occupation by the Turks, it came under Habsburg rule in the 17th century. In 1872 it united with Pest, on the E bank of the river, to form the modern city that became the capital of Hungary in 1918. In 1956 it was the scene of a popular uprising, suppressed by Soviet troops. Population (1990): 2,016,000.

Buddha, title of **Gautama Siddhartha** (c. 563–c. 483 BC) Indian prince, whose teachings formed the basis of Buddhism. The son of Suddhodana and his queen, Maya, in Kapilavastu (Nepal), Gautama was reputed to have been a child of exceptional intelligence and beauty about whom many stories and legends have been told. At the age of 16 he married his cousin Princess Yasodhara, who some 13 years later bore him a son, Rahula. Soon after this event Gautama, renouncing his life of indolence and luxury, abandoned his family and set out to seek solutions to the problems of the transience and suffering of human existence. He was then about 29. After six years of emaciating asceticism he reluctantly concluded that austerity was as unlikely as triviality to provide the solution he sought. Abandoned now by his five companions for his rejection of mortification, he determined to seek enlightenment, alone, within himself. According to tradition, this he achieved while seated beneath a banyan tree, in what is now called Buddh Gaya, in Bihar (his title, *Buddha,* is Sanskrit for the Awakened One). Probably 35 years old at this time, he devoted the rest of his life to teaching the principles (*see* dharma) of this enlightenment, first moving to Benares, where he founded the Buddhist order of monks, and thereafter teaching in various places in N India. He died at Kusinagara in Uttar Pradesh. *See also* Buddhism.

Buddhaghosa (5th century BC) Buddhist scholar. A Brahman convert from Buddh Gaya, he wrote the *Visuddhi-magga* (*Path of Purity*), a collation of Sinhalese Buddhist commentaries that he collected in Ceylon and translated into Pali.

Buddh Gaya (*or* Bodh Gaya) 24 42N 85 00E A village in India, in Bihar. It was here that Gautama Buddha attained enlightenment under the sacred bo (*or* bodhi) tree.

Buddhism The nontheistic religion and philosophical system founded in NE India in the 6th century BC by Gautama Siddhartha (the *Buddha). His followers seek to emulate his example of perfect morality, wisdom, and compassion, culminating in a transformation of consciousness known as enlightenment. Buddhism teaches that greed, hatred, and delusion separate the individual from the true perception of the nature of things, causing him to remain tied to the *bhavachakra. The apparent substantiality of all objects, including the self, is illusion; everything mundane is impermanent and ultimately unsatisfying. The central beliefs of Buddhism are based on the Buddha's *Four Noble Truths, the last of which is the *Eightfold Path by which enlightenment may be attained and the individual self annihilated in *Nirvana. Buddhism is not dogmatic, but through its long history has developed into many schools (*see* Mahayana; Theravada; Zen Buddhism). With more than 500 million followers in Sri Lanka, Nepal, Japan, and elsewhere in the Far East, Buddhism is currently gaining adherents in the West.

budding In biology, a method of asexual reproduction in lower plants and animals, for example liverworts and coelenterates, in which new individuals develop from outgrowths of cells (buds) on the parent. The process also occurs in single-celled fungi, for example yeasts. In horticulture the term is used for the *grafting of a bud onto a stock.

Buddleia A genus of trees and shrubs (about 100 species), mostly native to tropical or warm temperate regions but widely introduced. The small four-petaled flowers are usually clustered in dense heads; the fruit is a capsule or berry. Many species are grown as ornamentals, especially *D. davidii* (butterfly bush) 13–16 ft (4–5 m) high, the long purple flower heads of which attract many butterflies; and *B. globosa,* which has round orange flower heads. Family: *Buddleiaceae.*

BUDDHA *A sculptured head from Gandhara, NW Paki-stan, made in the 4th or 5th century* AD.

Budé, Guillaume (1467–1540) French Renaissance scholar. Budé wrote many important Greek commentaries and philological works. He founded the Collège de France (1530) and as royal librarian built the library that formed the nucleus of the Bibliothèque Nationale.

Budge, (James) Don(ald) (1916–   ) US tennis player, the first to win all four major singles titles (Australian, French, US, and Wimbledon) in one year (1938). He was also an outstanding doubles player.

budgerigar A small *parakeet, *Melopsitticus undulatus,* occurring in large flocks in arid regions of Australia. It is 7.6 in (19 cm) long and has a green and yellow plumage with barred upper parts. Since its introduction to Britain in

1840 it has become a popular cagebird; white, violet, yellow, blue, and gray forms have been produced by selective breeding.

budget A prediction of the financial behavior of a firm, government, etc., over a specified period. Careful budgeting enables any deviation from a plan to be noted early and the appropriate action to be taken.

Buena Vista, Battle of (1847) Battle during the *Mexican War. US Gen. Zachary *Taylor's forces met the much larger forces of Mexican Gen. Antonio Lopez de *Santa Anna near Monterrey, Mexico. After several days of fighting, the Mexicans retreated, leaving NW Mexico in possession of the Americans.

Bueno, Maria (Esther) (1939–) Brazilian tennis player. She won the US singles title four times, the US doubles four times, the Wimbledon singles three times, and the Wimbledon doubles five times.

BUENOS AIRES *Avenida 9 de Julio, one of the world's widest streets.*

Buenos Aires 34 50S 58 37W The capital of Argentina, the largest city in South America and one of the world's largest ports, situated on the Río de la Plata estuary. It is the financial, commercial, and industrial center of the country. Its chief exports are beef and wool. A cultural center, Buenos Aires possesses many universities (including the University of Buenos Aires, 1821), the national library, and a famous opera house (the Teatro Colón). There are several fine avenues, including the Avenida de Mayo and the Avenida de Julio. Notable buildings include the cathedral (completed in 1804). *History*: founded in 1580, after Indian attacks on earlier settlements, it became capital of the newly created viceroyalty of the Río de la Plata in 1776 and of the new Republic of Argentina in 1880. In the late 19th and early 20th centuries its population was greatly swelled by European immigrants, especially Spanish and Italian. Population (1991): 2,960,976.

buffalo A large African hoofed mammal, *Syncerus caffer,* also called Cape buffalo. Weighing over 1543 lb (700 kg) and measuring 44–60 in (110–150 cm) at the shoulder, buffaloes have massive curved horns and a smooth black coat. They live in large herds in grassy areas where both tree cover and water are available. Once numerous, their numbers have been reduced by hunting and disease. Family: *Bovidae. Compare* bison; water buffalo.

Buffalo 42 52N 78 55W A city in New York state on Lake Erie and the Niagara River. The state's second largest city, it is linked to New York City by the New York State Barge Canal (formerly Erie Canal). A major port, its industries include the manufacture of iron and steel, motor vehicles, and electrical equipment. Population (1990): 328,123.

Buffalo Bill. *See* Cody, William F(rederick).

buffer solution A solution the *pH of which is insensitive to dilution or the addition of moderate amounts of acid or base. Generally it consists of a mixture of a weak acid or base and its salt. If, for example, acid is added to an acetic acid-acetate mixture, the hydrogen ions will combine with acetate ions to form acetic acid molecules, thus lowering the acidity. Buffers are present in many living organisms, as fluctuations in pH would destroy the activity of enzymes, etc.

Buffet, Bernard (1928–   ) French painter. Precociously talented, he established his reputation by 1948. His realistic paintings are notable for their strong black lines, melancholy colors, and elongated forms.

Buffon, Georges Louis Leclerc, Comte de (1707–88) French naturalist, who formulated a crude theory of evolution and was the first to suggest that the earth might be considerably older than suggested by the Bible. He estimated the age of the earth to be 75,000 years, with life emerging some 40,000 years ago.

bug A common name for any insectlike animal. Specifically, the term refers to insects of the order *Hemiptera* (the true bugs), especially the *bedbug and insects of the suborder *Heteroptera* (plant bugs, water bugs, etc.).

Bug River 1. (*or* Western Bug) A river in E central Europe, rising in the SW Ukraine, and flowing NW as part of the border with Poland to the Vistula River. Length: 450 mi (724 km). 2. (*or* Southern Bug) A river rising in the W Ukraine and flowing SE to the Dnieper estuary on the Black Sea. Length 530 mi (853 km).

Buganda A former kingdom in East Africa, now comprising an administrative region of Uganda bordering on Lake Victoria. The UK government assumed responsibility for Buganda in 1893. When Uganda became a republic (1963) the kabaka (king) of Buganda became president of Uganda. His arrest (1966) by the former prime minister Dr. Milton Obote caused widespread rioting in Buganda.

Bugatti, Ettore (Arco Isidoro) (1881–1947) Italian □car manufacturer. In 1909 he founded a factory in Molsheim, Alsace, to produce cars to race at Le Mans. His finest car was probably the Type 41—the Golden Bugatti.

bugle A high-pitched brass (or copper) instrument with a wide conical tube, a cup-shaped mouthpiece, and a small bell. It lacks valves and so can only play a single harmonic series (usually having the fundamental of C). Formerly much used for military signaling, it is also used on ceremonial occasions and in the brass band.

bugloss A biennial herb of the Eurasian genus *Echium* (about 30 species), e.g. viper's bugloss (*E. vulgare*). Up to 35 in (90 cm) high, the plants are covered with bristly hairs and produce spikes of funnel-shaped flowers, about 0.8 in (2 cm) long, usually bluish with several protruding stamens. Another plant called bugloss is *Lycopsis arvensis,* an annual similar to *Echium* species but with smaller flowers. Family: *Boraginaceae.*

Bujumbura (former name: Usumbura) 3 30S 29 20E The capital of Burundi, a port on the NE shore of Lake Tanganyika. Founded in the 19th century, it became the capital of Ruanda-Urundi after World War I. The university was founded in 1960. Population (1989 est): 240,500.

Bukavu (name until 1966: Costermansville) 2 20S 28 52E A port in E Zaïre, on Lake Kivu. A commercial center, it has local agricultural and brewing industries. Population (1991 est): 209,500.

Bukhara (*or* Bokhara) 39 47N 64 26E A city in Uzbekistan. The Bukhara region (*oblast*) of which it is the capital was the center of a powerful kingdom, which was ceded to Russia in 1868. It grew rapidly in the 1950s after the discovery of natural gas. It has textile industries, and the traditional crafts of gold embroidery and metalworking are still practiced. Population (1987): 220,000.

Bukhari, al- (810–70 AD) Muslim scholar and historian. After extensive travels, he collected more than 600,000 traditional records (*see* Hadith) of the words and deeds of the prophet Mohammed. He published a selection of these, arranged by subject, which he considered authentic teachings. The resulting collection is revered by orthodox Muslims as second in authority only to the Koran.

Bukharin, Nikolai Ivanovich (1888–1938) Soviet politician and communist theoretician. In exile after 1911, Bukharin edited the socialist newspaper *Novy Mir,* in New York. He returned to Russia during the Revolution and became editor of the newspaper *Pravda.* He believed that Russia should achieve socialism slowly and therefore supported Lenin's New Economic Policy (1924). He was chairman of the Comintern until dismissed by Stalin in 1929. He helped draft the 1936 constitution but was expelled from the Communist Party shortly afterward and died in Stalin's purges.

Bukovina (*or* Bucovina) An area in E Europe, in the NE Carpathian Mountains. As part of the principality of Moldavia, it fell to the Turks in 1512 and was ceded to Austria in 1775. Occupied by the Romanians in 1918, the N part was ceded to the Soviet Union (1940), later becoming part of the Ukraine. S Bukovina remained a Romanian province until it was abolished in 1952.

Bulawayo 20 10S 28 43E The second largest city in Zimbabwe. It was founded on its present site in 1894 by the British, near to its original site of the kraal of Lobengula, the center of the Ndebele tribe. Nearby are the popular tourist attractions of Rhodes Matapos National Park and the Khami Ruins. The city is the country's chief industrial center with metal, tire, and cement industries. Population (1987 est): 495,000.

bulb A modified underground stem of certain perennial herbaceous plants, for example onions, daffodils, and tulips, that serves as an overwintering organ. Food is stored in overlapping fleshy leaves or leaf bases, borne on a very short stem, and is used to produce one or more plants the following season. When a bulb produces two or more plants it acts as an organ of vegetative reproduction. East Anglia (UK) and the Netherlands are centers for the commercial production of spring-flowering bulbs.

bulbul A gregarious forest-dwelling songbird belonging to an Old World family (*Pycnonotidae*; 120 species). 5–9 in (12–22 cm) long, bulbuls are yellow, green, or brown, sometimes with bright patches on the head and beneath the tail. They have a slender bill surrounded by stiff bristles and feed largely on fruit and berries.

Bulfinch, Charles (1763–1844) US architect. Strongly influenced by architecture in England and Italy, he introduced the Federal style in the US. His buildings include the state houses in Boston, Mass. (1787–88), Hartford, Conn. (1792–96), and Augusta, Maine (1828–31). He was responsible for designing the east portico of the US Capitol building (1817–30).

Bulganin, Nikolai Aleksandrovich (1895–1975) Soviet statesman; prime minister (1955–58). Bulganin began his career in 1918, when he joined

*CHEKA. In World War II he became (1944) a member of Stalin's war cabinet and, in 1947, defense minister. As prime minister, Bulganin participated in the attempt to oust Khrushchev in 1957 and was subsequently dismissed.

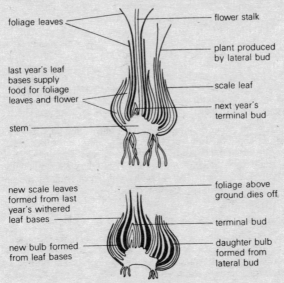

BULB *A section through a daffodil bulb in spring (above) and summer (below) to show growth cycle.*

Bulgaria, People's Republic of A country in SE Europe, in the E Balkans on the Black Sea. The low-lying Danube basin in the N rises to the Balkan Mountains in the center of the country; further S, beyond the valley of the Maritsa River, the Rhodope Mountains reach heights of almost 10,000 ft (3000 m). The inhabitants are mainly Bulgars, with minorities of Macedonians, Turks, and Gypsies. *Economy*: industrialization has proceeded rapidly since World War II, following the introduction of a centrally planned economy. Particular emphasis has been given to heavy manufacturing industries. The industrial sector has recently been reorganized into several large combines. Coal, iron, and other minerals are mined and hydroelectricity and nuclear energy contribute to power supplies. Oil has been found offshore in the Black Sea and natural gas is also being produced. Agricultural production, the traditional mainstay of the economy prior to 1945, has been mechanized and organized on a cooperative basis, the main crops being wheat, maize, beet, and barley. Tourism has been considerably developed in recent years. Main exports include machinery, chemicals, food products, textiles, tobacco, and nonferrous metals. *History*: following the invasion of the Bulgars in the 7th century AD and their gradual adoption of the culture and language of the conquered Slavs, Bulgaria became a significant power in SE Europe. Despite coming under Turkish rule in 1396, the Bulgars succeeded in retaining their national identity over the centuries until they once again became independent in 1908 under the Saxe-Coburg ruler *Ferdinand, who took the title of tsar. Bulgaria aligned itself with Germany in both World Wars. In 1944 it was occupied by the Soviet Union and power was seized by the Fatherland Front, a left-wing alliance, which formed a pro-Soviet government that declared war on Germany. In 1946 a People's Republic was proclaimed and Bulgaria remained one of the most loyal of the Soviet Union's satellite states. Under a new constitution in 1971 Todor *Zhivkov became chairman of the Council of State and first secretary of the Communist Party. He ran a strict regime, even insisting that the Turkish minority in the country adapt to Bulgarian ways. In the late 1980s, hundreds of thousands of Bulgarian Turks fled to Turkey. As political reform toppled Communist governments in eastern Europe in 1989, Zhivkov was ousted. He was succeeded by Peter T. Mladenov. In a 1990 election, Mladenov, a former Communist, won, but he resigned several months later and Zhelyu Zhelev of the opposition party succeeded him. In 1992, in the first free elections, Zhelev was reelected. Official language: Bulgarian. Official currency: lev of 100 stotinki. Area: 42,823 sq mi (110,912 sq km). Population (1990 est): 8,978,000. Capital: Sofia. Main port: Varna.

Bulgarian A language belonging to the South *Slavonic group spoken by eight million people in Bulgaria, Greece, Romania, and other areas. It differs from other Slavonic languages in several respects as it lacks case declensions for nouns and shares grammatical features and vocabulary elements with other non-Slavonic Balkan languages. The literature written in Bulgarian dates from the establishment of Christianity (9th century).

Bulge, Battle of the. *See* World War II.

bulk modulus. *See* elastic modulus.

bull (from Latin: *bulla,* seal) Originally, the seal attached to papal edicts. The term was later used for the documents themselves, but now refers only to the most important missives. Named by their opening word or phrase, for example *Pastor Aeternus* (Eternal Father; 1870), they are issued to assert doctrine.

bullace A type of *plum, *Prunus insititia,* cultivated for centuries but probably originating in SW Asia. The young branches are very hairy and have few thorns. The blue-black fruit is similar to that of the blackthorn but larger and sweeter.

bulldog A breed of dog originating in England, where it was used in bull- and bear-baiting. It has a compact rounded body with short sturdy legs and a short tail. The relatively large head has an undershot jaw (i.e. the lower jaw projects in front of the upper) and loose folds of skin. The fine short coat can be of any color except black. Weight: 55 lb (25 kg) (dogs); 51 lb (23 kg) (bitches).

bulldozer A powerful caterpillar tractor equipped with a blade or shovel for moving or digging earth and often used for preliminary clearing and leveling of building sites, roads, etc. The blade can be raised or lowered hydraulically or set at an angle for sideways shifting of earth.

bullfighting Subduing and killing bulls. The national spectator sport of Spain, it is also popular in parts of France and Latin America, and mounted bullfighting in practiced in Portugal. The bulls are specially bred. At a normal *corrida de toros* (bullfight) three matadors kill two bulls each. Following the initial ceremonial procession the first bull enters the ring. Preliminary passes are made by the *banderilleros* (assistants) with their capes to attract the bull's attention and allow the matador to assess the bull's reactions. The matador then makes his first series of passes with his cape, controlling the direction and extent of the bull's charge. During the next stage, the matador makes the bull charge at a mounted picador, who uses a form of lance to stab the bull's neck, weakening the muscle so that it lowers its head. This procedure is repeated up to three times, each of the three matadors taking turns to draw the bull away from the horse and continue the capework. During the following stage the neck muscle is further weakened by pairs of barbed sticks (*banderillas*) thrust into it by the *banderilleros*. In the final stage the matador performs a series of passes with his *muleta* (a small red cape folded over a stick) to weaken the bull further until he can reach over its head to thrust his sword in at the right angle to sever its aorta.

bullfinch A plump woodland *finch, *Pyrrhula pyrrhula,* of N Eurasia. It is about 6 in (14 cm) long and has a gray back, a pinkish breast, and black head, wings, and tail. Bullfinches have strong stout bills and strip buds and flowers from trees, for which they are often regarded as pests.

bullfrog A large frog, *Rana catesbiana,* of North America. Dull green with a slightly warty skin, bullfrogs grow to about 8 in (20 cm) and can jump up to 7 ft (2 m). Females are larger than males. They are the only common American frogs large enough to be used as food.

Other large frogs—*Pyxicephalus adspersus* in Africa and *Rana tigrina* in India—are also called bullfrogs.

bullhead One of several predatory bottom-dwelling fish, also called sculpin, belonging to the family *Cottidae,* including the Eurasian miller's thumb (*Cottus gobio*). Bullheads have a tapering conical body, up to 12 in (30 cm) long and often covered with spiny bony plates, a broad spiny head, and two dorsal fins. They are found in fresh water and shallow seas of the N hemisphere. Order: *Perciformes. See also* catfish.

bull market A stock or commodity market in which there is a continuing upward movement in prices. An initial rise in prices, caused by favorable economic factors, is often magnified by consequent buying by investors. *Compare* bear market.

bull mastiff A breed of dog resulting from crosses between bulldogs and mastiffs. It is sturdily built with a short broad muzzle and folds of skin surrounding the face. The short coat is red, fawn, or streaked brown. Height: 25–27 in (63–68 cm) (dogs); 24–26 in (61–66 cm) (bitches).

Bull Run, Battles of (*or* Battles of Manassas) Two battles in the *Civil War fought in NE Virginia. Both were Confederate victories. In the first (July 21, 1861) Union forces failed to prevent the unification of Confederate forces under Gen. P. G. T. Beauregard (1818–93) and Gen. Joseph E. Johnstone (1807–91) at Manassas Junction near a stream named Bull Run. The untried Union troops were repulsed after an unsuccessful attack. The second battle (August 29–30, 1862) followed an unsuccessful Union attempt to capture Gordonsville, a rail junction near Richmond, the Confederate capital. The 70,000 Union troops had withdrawn to await reinforcements when Stonewall *Jackson attacked and forced their retreat to Washington.

bull terrier A breed of dog originating in the UK from crosses between bulldogs and terriers. It is strongly built with a courageous temperament. The coat is either pure white (with darker head markings) or colored. Height: 19–23 in (48–56 cm). (Miniature bull terriers must not exceed 14 in [36 cm] in height.)

Bülow, Bernhard Heinrich, Fürst von (1849–1929) German statesman and diplomat; chancellor (1900–09). He pursued aggressive foreign policies that contributed to German isolation in Europe. He alienated France over the Moroccan crisis in 1905 and Russia over the Bosnian crisis in 1908. He resigned after losing the confidence of Emperor William II and of the Reichstag and served from 1914 to 1915 as ambassador to Italy.

Bülow, Hans Guido, Freiherr von (1830–94) German pianist and the outstanding conductor of his time. Bülow championed Wagner until his wife Cosima (Liszt's daughter) eloped with Wagner in 1866. From that time he championed the works of Brahms.

bulrush A widely distributed perennial herbaceous plant, *Scirpus lacustris,* growing in ponds, lakes, and rivers; 40 in–10 ft (1–3 m) high, it has cylindrical leafless stems bearing branched clusters of small reddish-brown flowers. Family: *Cyperaceae* (sedges, etc.). The name is also applied to the *reedmace, and the biblical bulrush is the *papyrus.

Bultmann, Rudolf (Karl) (1884–1976) German New Testament scholar. A professor at Marburg University (1921–51), he allied himself with the anti-Nazi *Confessing Church during the Third Reich. In his influential writings he argued that the New Testament message must be "demythologized" (or stripped of its no longer acceptable mythical concepts) if it was to have any relevance to contemporary man.

Bulwer-Lytton, Edward George Earle. *See* Lytton, Edward George Earle Bulwer-Lytton, 1st Baron.

bumblebee A social *bee, also called humblebee, belonging to a genus (*Bombus*) found mainly in temperate regions. Bumblebees, 0.6–1 in (15–25 mm) long, are usually black with yellow or orange bands. They live in colonies, on or below the ground, containing 100–400 workers in the summer. Their life cycle is like that of the *honeybee, although only young fertilized queens survive the winter. Solitary parasitic bumblebees belong to the genus *Psithyrus.* Family: *Apidae.*

Bunche, Ralph (1904–71) US political scientist and UN official. As a government official Bunche specialized in colonial areas during World War II and became the first African American to hold an important position in the State Department. He was a founder of the UN and director of its trusteeship division. Bunche won the Nobel Peace Prize for negotiating the 1949 Arab-Israeli truce and supervised the UN Congo peace force in 1960.

Bundelkhand A region in present-day Madhya Pradesh state, in N central India, taking its name from the Bundela Rajputs, a dynasty that ruled here from the 14th to the 18th centuries. The area is rich in architectural history; in the 10th and 11th centuries the Candella kings built many beautiful temples at Khajuraho and a fine fortress was erected later at Jhansi.

Bunin, Ivan Alekseevich (1879–1953) Russian poet and novelist. He published his first book of poems in 1891, and translated works by *Byron and *Longfellow. His prose works include novels (*The Village,* 1910), short stories (*The Gentleman from San Francisco,* 1916), and autobiographical works (*The Well of Days,* 1910). In 1920 he emigrated to Finland. He won the Nobel Prize in 1933.

bunion A deformity and swelling at the joint at the base of the big toe. It is usually caused by pressure from ill-fitting shoes: the toe becomes bent toward the others and a fibrous fluid-filled sac (bursa) develops over the affected joint. Bunions may require surgical treatment.

Bunker Hill, Battle of (June 17, 1775) A battle of the *American Revolution actually fought on Breed's Hill (next to Bunker Hill) in Charlestown, near Boston. The Americans defended the strategic hill from two British attacks but Sir William *Howe displaced the Americans at the third attempt. The American defense helped raise support for the Revolutionary cause.

Bunsen, Robert Wilhelm (1811–99) German chemist, after whom the Bunsen burner is named. He did not, however, invent the Bunsen burner although he did popularize it. In collaboration with *Kirchhoff, Bunsen developed the technique of *spectroscopy, using a Bunsen burner to heat the substance. In 1860 they used the technique to discover the elements *rubidium and *cesium. He also invented a carbon-zinc electric cell (1841).

Bunsen burner A gas burner for laboratory use, popularized by R. *Bunsen. It consists of a vertical metal tube with a variable air inlet at the bottom. Gas is led into the bottom of the tube and the gas-air mixture burned at the top. Adjustment of the air inlet allows control of combustion intensity, temperature, sooting, and other flame properties.

bunting A sparrowlike bird belonging to a subfamily (*Emberizine*) of the *finches. Buntings are 5–8 in (12–20 cm) long and usually have a brownish or grayish plumage. They live on the ground or in bushes and thickets and scratch for seeds with their characteristically large feet. The subfamily includes the *yellowhammer and the *snow bunting.

Buñuel, Luis (1900–83) Spanish film director. He worked mainly in France and Mexico. His films are characterized by surrealist techniques and by their anticlericalism and satire on social hypocrisy. They include *Un Chien Andalou* (1928), *Viridiana* (1961), *The Discreet Charm of the Bourgeoisie* (1972), and *That Obscure Object of Desire* (1977).

bunya bunya. *See* Araucaria.

Bunyan, John (1628–88) British writer. Son of a tinker, he fought in the parliamentary army during the Civil War. From 1650 to 1656 he underwent a spiritual crisis, finally resolved by his conversion to religion. He became the leader of a group of Baptists in Bedford and in 1660 he was imprisoned for preaching without a license. During his 12 years in prison he wrote his spiritual autobiography, *Grace Abounding* (1666), and began his major work, *The Pilgrim's Progress* (1678). An imaginative allegory written in plain but majestic prose, it has been widely read and admired for centuries.

Bunyan, Paul US legendary giant of the frontier logging camps; a symbol of bigness and American ingenuity. Paul Bunyan and his companions—Babe the Blue Ox, Johnny Inkslinger, and Shot Gunderson—all larger than life, grew out of the lumber camps of the 1800s and were credited with creating Puget Sound, the Grand Canyon, and the Rocky Mountains. His legend was highly publicized, and he appeared in the works of poets and composers such as Carl *Sandburg, Robert *Frost, W. H. *Auden, and Benjamin *Britten.

Burbage, Richard (c. 1567–1619) English actor. He played leading roles in the first productions of many of Shakespeare's plays. He also acted in plays by Kyd, Webster, and Ben Jonson, and was a shareholder in the Blackfriars and the Globe theaters.

Burbank, Luther (1849–1926) US plant breeder. Largely self-taught and using methods he devised himself, primarily the cross-breeding of different varieties, he developed many new varieties of agricultural importance. His first commercial success, the Burbank potato, enabled him to settle in California, where, by skillful selection and breeding techniques, he originated more than 800 new strains and varieties of fruit, vegetables, and flowers.

Burbank 34 12N 118 18W A city in SW California, just NW of Los Angeles. Established in 1887, it is home to major television and movie studios, among them Walt Disney Productions. Burbank also has a large aerospace industry. Population (1990): 93,643.

burbot A food fish, *Lota lota,* that is similar and related to the *ling. Up to 3.6 ft (1.1 m) long, it lives on the bottom in cold fresh waters of Europe, Asia, and North America and feeds voraciously on other fish.

Burckhardt, Jacob Christoph (1818–97) Swiss art and cultural historian. The son of a Protestant clergyman, he studied at the Universities of Berlin and Bonn. From 1843 he lectured at Basle University, becoming professor of history

burdock 420

there in 1858, after three years at Zürich. His most important work, *The Civilization of the Renaissance in Italy* (1860), was a model for later cultural histories, with its thorough and systematic analysis of the period.

burdock A tall stiff biennial plant of the genus *Arctium* (about 5 species), 25–52 in (60–130 cm) high, found in Europe and Asia. They have broad heartshaped leaves and reddish-purple thistlelike flower heads, surrounded by many large stiff hooked bracts, which are retained by the fruits. Family: *Compositae*.

Burgas 42 30N 29 29E A city in E Bulgaria, on the Black Sea. Bulgaria's second largest port (after Varna), its industries include fishing, mining, and oil refining. Population (1991 est): 205,000.

Bürge, Joost (1552–1632) Swiss mathematician, who invented *logarithms independently of, and probably before, John *Napier. He also contributed to the exponential notation (i.e. y^x to indicate y multiplied by itself x times).

Burgenland A federal state in E Austria, bordering on Hungary. It was ceded to Austria by Hungary following World War I. Predominantly agricultural, it produces cereals, root crops, and fruit and vegetables; livestock are also extensively raised. Area: 1531 sq mi (3965 sq km). Population (1987 est): 266,000. Capital: Eisenstadt.

Burger, Warren Earl (1907–) US jurist and lawyer; Supreme Court chief justice (1969–86). He practiced law in St Paul, Minn., and taught at St Paul's Mitchell College of Law. In 1953 he was appointed US assistant attorney general and then, in 1955, to the US Court of Appeals for the District of Columbia by President *Eisenhower. Chosen by President *Nixon to replace Earl *Warren as chief justice on the Supreme Court in 1969, Burger presided over a court more conservative than Warren's, while upholding certain rights of criminals and aliens. Burger himself was a strong advocate of reforming the judicial system. Upon his retirement, he was succeeded as chief justice by Associate Justice William *Rehnquist.

Burgess, Anthony (John Burgess Wilson; 1917–93) British novelist and critic. A teacher and lecturer in English literature and phonetics, he became a full-time writer in 1959. His novels include the sinister tragicomedy *A Clockwork Orange* (1962), which was filmed by Stanley *Kubrick, *Inside Mr. Enderby* (1963), *Nothing like the Sun* (1964), *Napoleon Symphony* (1974), *Earthly Powers* (1980), *Enderby's Dark Lady* (1984), *Any Old Iron* (1989), and *A Dead Man in Deptford* (1993).

Burghley, William Cecil, Lord (1520–98) English statesman; close adviser to Elizabeth I. A moderating influence on Elizabeth, his pragmatism is evident in her religious settlement (*see* Reformation). He helped to bring about the Treaty of Edinburgh (1660) with Scotland, which undermined French influence there. He influenced Elizabeth's pro-Protestant foreign policy, aiding the Revolt of the Netherlands against Spain, and helped to prepare England for the threatened Spanish invasion (*see* Armada, Spanish). He was instrumental in securing the execution of Mary, Queen of Scots, in 1587. He was succeeded as royal adviser by his son **Robert Cecil, 1st Earl of Salisbury** (c. 1563–1612), who negotiated the accession of James VI of Scotland to the English throne as James I (1603). As lord treasurer (1608–12), he was James' chief adviser.

burglary In law, entering a building, ship, or other inhabited vehicle without leave or right to, intending to commit serious crimes, such as theft, rape, grievous bodily harm, or unlawful damage. A person is not guilty of burglary if the premises at the time are open to the public.

Burgos 42 21N 3 41W A city in N Spain, in Old Castile. Its fine cathedral (13th–16th centuries) contains the remains of the legendary hero El Cid. Population (1986): 164,000.

Burgoyne, John (1722–92) British general. In the American Revolution he commanded the British force in the N, ordered in conjunction with a column from New York under Sir William *Howe to divide the Americans along the Hudson River. Howe's progress was blocked and Burgoyne was defeated by *Gates at Saratoga (1777).

Burgundian school A group of musicians working at the court of the Dukes of Burgundy in the 15th century. Under Philip the Good, who reigned from 1419 to 1467, there was a great flowering of the arts. Two composers are outstanding: Guillaume *Dufay and Gilles Binchois (c. 1400–60). Their compositions include chansons with French texts, motets, masses, and magnificats. The composers of the Burgundian school were influenced by such English composers as John *Dunstable.

Burgundy A region in France, E of the Rhône and Saône Rivers. The Burgundians were a Scandinavian people who occupied the region in the 4th century AD, establishing a powerful kingdom that was conquered by the Franks in 534. The NW part of the former kingdom became a duchy in the 9th century and passed to the French crown in the mid-14th century. John the Good transferred it to his fourth son, Philip the Bold, and after the death (1477) of his descendant Charles the Bold it was annexed by the crown.

Burke, Edmund (1729–97) British political philosopher and politician. A member of Parliament from 1765, he attacked George III's exalted view of the monarch's political role. In the pamphlet *Thoughts on the Cause of the Present Discontents* (1770) and in two famous speeches, "On American Taxation" (1774) and "On Moving His Resolutions for Conciliation with the Colonies" (1777), he blamed the unrest in the American colonies on British misgovernment. He also campaigned against the corrupt Indian administration of the *East India Company. An opponent of democracy, he believed that the common good was best secured by responsible aristocratic government. He thus condemned the French Revolution (*Reflections on the Revolution in France,* 1790). He has been regarded as the foremost Conservative philosopher. He also wrote a widely read work on aesthetics, *A Philosophical Enquiry into the Origin of Our Ideas of the Sublime and Beautiful* (1757).

Burkina Faso (former name: Republic of Upper Volta; French: République de Haute-Volta) A landlocked country in West Africa, bordered by Mali (W and N), Niger (NE), Benin (SE), Togo, Ghana, and Ivory Coast (S). It consists mainly of a low-lying plateau, crossed by the headwaters of the Volta River: the Black, Red, and White Voltas. The population is almost entirely African, the largest groups being the Mossi and Fulani. *Economy*: chiefly agricultural, the main food crops being millet and sorghum; livestock is important and is the main export. Production of rice, groundnuts, cotton, and sugar is being increased by means of schemes to improve water supplies, although these advances were hampered by the severe droughts affecting the Sahel region in the early 1970s. Some minerals, including manganese, have been found but lack of communications makes their exploitation difficult. *History*: the area was occupied by powerful Mossi states from the 14th century. It became part of the French protectorate of Soudan in 1898 and in 1919 the separate protectorate of Upper Volta was formed. In 1932 it was divided between Niger, Ivory Coast, and Soudan but was reconstituted in 1947. In 1958 Upper Volta became an autonomous republic, gaining full independence outside the French Community in 1960. A military coup in 1966 brought Lt. Col. (later Gen.) Sangoulé Lamizana (1916–   ) to power. Lamizana

was elected president in 1978 but was overthrown in a coup in 1980. Another
military coup (1982) brought Maj. Jean-Baptiste Ouédraogo to power. He was
ousted by Capt. Thomas Sankara (1983), supported by paratroopers, who then
set up a military government. In 1984 the name was changed from Upper Volta
to Burkina Faso (Land of the Incorruptible Men) to reflect better the nation's
African heritage. Sankara was ousted in 1987 by Capt. Blaise Campaore. A
more democratic constitution took effect in 1991. Official language: French. Official currency: CFA (Communauté financière africaine) franc of 100 centimes.
Area: 105,764 sq mi (274,002 sq km). Population (1990 est): 8,941,000. Capital: Ouagadougou.

Burlington 44 29N 73 13W A city and port in NW Vermont, on the E shore of
Lake Champlain. Vermont's largest city, it served as a naval base during the War
of 1812 and is the home of the University of Vermont (1790). Wood, maple
syrup, and electrical, metal, and cereal products are some of its manufactures.
Tourism is an important industry. Population (1990): 39,127.

Burma, Socialist Republic of the Union of. *See* Myanmar.

Burmese A language of the Tibeto-Burman branch of the *Sino-Tibetan language family spoken by 30 million people in Myanmar (formerly Burma),
where it is the official language. Written in an alphabet derived from the *Pali
script of India, Burmese literature dates from the 11th century AD.

Burmese cat A breed of short-haired cat originating from an Asian hybrid im-
ported into the US in 1933. The Burmese has a long slender body, a small head
with large ears and greenish-yellow eyes, and usually a dark-brown coat. Other
recognized colors include silvery-gray (the Blue Burmese), lilac, red, and cream.

Burne-Jones, Sir Edward Coley (1833–98) Pre-Raphaelite painter and designer. After meeting *Rossetti (1856) he abandoned his studies for an art career
but only established his reputation in an exhibition in 1877. Typical of his
dreamy romantic paintings, inspired by Botticelli's style, medieval legends, and
classical mythology, is *King Cophetua and the Beggar Maid* (Tate Gallery).
More influential for the 20th century were his designs for stained glass and
tapestries.

burnet A slender perennial herb of the genera *Sanguisorba* (about 3 species)
and *Poterium* (about 25 species), of N temperate regions; 20–40 in (50–100 cm)
high, they have pinnate toothed leaves and oval heads of crimson or greenish
petal-less flowers borne on long stems. The leaves are used to flavor salads and
soups. Family: *Rosaceae*.

Burnet, Sir Frank Macfarlane (1899–1985) Australian physician, who advanced understanding of virus diseases and immunology. Burnet discovered the
phenomenon of acquired immunological tolerance to foreign tissue transplants,
for which he shared a Nobel Prize (1960) with Sir Peter *Medawar. He did important work in the identification of bacteria and in the culture of viruses.

Burnet, Gilbert (1643–1715) English bishop and historian, born in Edinburgh. He was a minister in the Church of Scotland and a professor at Glasgow
University before settling in England in 1674. While abroad during James II's
reign, he became a friend of William of Orange, with whom he sailed to England in 1688 and who appointed him Bishop of Salisbury in 1689. His books
include *History of My Own Time* (1723–34).

Burnett, Frances (Eliza) Hodgson (1849–1924) British novelist. The
daughter of a Manchester manufacturer, she moved to the US in 1865. Her best-
known works are the children's books *Little Lord Fauntleroy* (1885), *The Little
Princess* (1905), and *The Secret Garden* (1909).

Burnley 53 48N 2 14W A city in N England, in Lancashire in the Calder Valley. Traditionally a cotton-weaving town (with some spinning and dyeing), there has been some diversification of industry in recent years (light engineering, chemicals). Population (1983): 92,000.

burns Damage to the skin caused by heat, electricity, chemicals, or radiation. In order of increasing severity, burns may cause reddening of the skin, as in sunburn (first-degree burn), blistering (second-degree burn), and finally damage to the tissues beneath the skin (third-degree burn). The extent rather than the thickness of the burn determines its effect. Both second- and third-degree burns cause fluid loss, which may be extensive enough to lead to *shock. Treatment consists of the application of wet dressings and later the administration of intravenous fluids and transfer of the patient to clean surroundings, where the burns are exposed and allowed to heal. The danger of infection can be prevented by the use of antibiotics. Skin grafting may be necessary to replace the skin destroyed by severe burns.

Burns, Robert (1759–96) Scottish poet. Son of a poor farmer in Ayrshire, in 1783 he began writing poems in traditional styles. *Poems, Chiefly in the Scottish Dialect* (1786), published in Kilmarnock, won him immediate fame; from 1786 until 1788 he was lionized by Edinburgh society, which was little to his taste (he was a lifelong radical) or his profit. His return to farming was a failure and from 1789 he worked for the excise service. His poems range from sentimental love lyrics, often patterned on traditional songs, to broad humor, as in "Tam o'Shanter" (1788), and scathing satire, as in "The Twa Dogs" (1786) and "Holy Willie's Prayer" (1785). He collected and wrote numerous songs for inclusion in *The Scots Musical Museum* (1787–1803) and *Select Scottish Airs* (1793–1818).

Burnside, Ambrose Everett (1824–81) US military leader and politician. Appointed commander of the Union's Army of the Potomac in 1862, in the Civil War, he was defeated at Fredericksburg (1862) and removed from command. He participated in the early stages of the Wilderness Campaign (1864–65) but resigned when his tactics at Petersburg were criticized. He was governor of Rhode Island (1866–69) and was a senator from Rhode Island (1875–81). Sideburns were named for him.

Burr, Aaron (1756–1836) US statesman; chosen by the Senate to be Republican vice president (1801–05) after tying with Jefferson in the election of 1800. In 1804, after killing his political rival Alexander *Hamilton in a duel, Burr fled to Philadelphia and plotted to establish an empire in the West. Arrested for treason but acquitted (1807), after further intrigues, including a scheme for Napoleon to conquer Florida, Burr gave up politics for law.

Burra, Edward (1905–76) British painter. His early watercolors were chiefly scenes of Mediterranean lowlife. Later, in response to the horrors of the Spanish Civil War and World War II, he began to paint sinister subjects in a realistic style. His works include *Soldiers* (1942).

Burroughs, Edgar Rice (1875–1950) US novelist. After a variety of unsuccessful jobs he gained wealth and international fame from his fantasy fiction. *Tarzan of the Apes* (1914) introduced his most famous character, an English nobleman's child, abandoned in the African jungle and reared by apes. Among the approximately 70 works he published were western, crime, and science fiction adventures.

Burroughs, William (1914–   ) US novelist. He graduated from Harvard in 1936 and wandered in the US and Europe. In 1944 he became a drug addict. *Junkie* (1953) and *The Naked Lunch* (1959) were influential novels of the *Beat movement. He lived mostly in Paris, London, and Tangiers, continuing his literary experiments in such novels as *Nova Express* (1964), *Queer* (1985), and *Mind Wars* (1985).

ROBERT BURNS *A portrait of the 18th-century Scottish poet by Alexander Nasmyth.*

burrowing owl A long-legged ground-dwelling *owl, *Speotyto cunicularia,* of grasslands from Florida and the western US to Argentina; 9 in (22 cm) long, it nests in colonies, often in disused rodent burrows, and feeds at night on frogs, lizards, mice, and insects.

Bursa 40 12N 29 04E A city in NW Turkey. It was the capital of the Ottoman Turks for most of the 14th century and contains notable mosques and sultans' tombs and a university (1975). Population (1990 est): 835,000.

Burton, Sir Richard (1821–90) British explorer, diplomat, and translator. After military service in India he traveled in Arabia (entering the sacred city of Mecca in 1853 disguised as a Muslim) and Somaliland. He made two attempts (1855, 1857–58) to discover the source of the Nile and on the second, with *Speke, discovered Lake Tanganyika. The two men later quarrelled over Speke's claim to have discovered the Nile source in Lake Victoria. Apart from his many travel books, he published superb translations of oriental erotica, including *Kama Sutra of Vatsyayana* (1883) and the *Arabian Nights* (16 vols, 1885–88). After his death his wife burned almost all his diaries.

Burton, Richard (R. Jenkins; 1925–84) British actor, born in Wales. He first achieved success as a stage actor, especially in Shakespearian roles, but since the 1950s acted almost exclusively in films. These include *Look Back in Anger* (1959), *Becket* (1964), and *Who's Afraid of Virginia Woolf?* (1966). His two marriages to Elizabeth Taylor were highly publicized.

Burton, Robert (1577–1640) British scholar. He was educated at Oxford and spent his life there as a don. *The Anatomy of Melancholy* (1621, revised five times) is a vast, witty, and erudite miscellany of Jacobean knowledge on what is now called depression; it includes folklore, superstitions, and the learning of the ancient Greeks and Arabs.

Burundi, Republic of A small inland country in central Africa, bordering on Lake Tanganyika in the SW. It consists chiefly of high plateau along the main Nile-Congo dividing range, descending rapidly to the Great Rift Valley in the W. Most of the population belongs to the Hutu, a Bantu tribe, but the rulers are Tutsi and there are other tribal minorities. *Economy*: mainly subsistence agriculture; coffee is the main export and tea is also being developed. Minerals have been found including gold, cassiterite, and nickel, and there has been considerable development in recent years, although industry still provides only a very small proportion of the revenue. *History*: the area (with present-day Rwanda) became part of German East Africa in 1890 and from 1919, as the S part of Ruanda-Urundi, it was administered by Belgium, first under League of Nations mandate and then as a UN trust territory. It became independent in 1962 and in 1964 a monetary and customs union with Rwanda was dissolved. In 1966 the hereditary Mwami Mwambutsa IV was deposed by his son, who was enthroned as Mwami Ntare V. In the same year, following military coup, Capt. (later Lt. Gen.) Michel Micombero (1940–83) set up a republic with himself as president. In 1972 he assumed absolute powers and fighting broke out in which thousands were killed, including the deposed king. Further intertribal killings took place in 1973. In 1976 Micombero was overthrown in a coup. Burundi held its first democratic elections in June 1993. An attempted military coup in October resulted in the death of the new president and severe inter-tribal warfare. Official languages: French and Kirundi; Swahili is also used commercially. Official currency: Burundi franc of 100 centimes. Area: 10,759 sq mi (27,834 sq km). Population (1991 est): 5,800,000. Capital: Bujumbura.

Bury 53 36N 2 17N A city in NW England, in Greater Manchester on the River Irwell. A textile town concentrating on cotton spinning and weaving, the woolen and felt industries are important. John Kay and Sir Robert Peel were born here. Population (1986): 174,000.

Buryatia (formerly Buryat Autonomous Soviet Socialist Republic) An administrative division in SE central Russian Federation. Over half its area is covered by forest. The Buryats, who comprise about 35% of the population, are traditionally nomads and speak a Mongolian language. The region is one of Siberia's most prosperous, having valuable mineral deposits, including coal, molybdenum, and gold. The main industries are mining, timber, and food processing; spring wheat and fodder crops are grown and stock breeding is also important. Area: 135,650 sq mi (350,300 sq km). Population (1991 est): 1,050,000. Capital: Ulan Ude.

burying beetle A strong beetle, also called a sexton beetle, belonging to a genus (*Necrophorus*) occurring chiefly in N temperate regions. Burying beetles are 0.05–0.41 in (1.5–35 mm) long and feed and lay their eggs on the dead bodies of small animals, which they first bury: the larvae use the same food source. Family: *Silphidae* (carrion beetles).

Bury St Edmunds 52 15N 0 43E A city in E England, in Suffolk. Its ruined abbey, which was built to house the shrine of St Edmund, last King of East Anglia, became a famous place of pilgrimage. Bury St Edmunds is a market town with brewing, sugar refining, and agricultural machinery industries. Population (1985): 29,500.

Bush, George (Herbert Walker) (1924–   ) US politician and statesman, president (1989–93). The son of Prescott Bush, a Connecticut senator, he served in World War II, graduated from Yale University (1948), and went to Texas, where he was successful in the petroleum industry. A Republican, he served Texas in the US House of Representatives (1967–71), was ambassador to the United Nations (1971–72), chaired the Republican National Committee (1972–73), and was director of the Central Intelligence Agency (CIA) (1976–77). His unsuccessful bid for the Republican presidential nomination in 1980 eventually brought him the vice presidency (1981–1989) under Ronald *Reagan. He won the nomination in 1988 and decisively defeated Michael *Dukakis. In 1990–91, Bush's leadership in the Middle East crisis that followed Iraq's invasion of Kuwait greatly enhanced his status. In *Operation Desert Storm, US-led UN coalition forces completely defeated the Iraqi troops of Saddam *Hussein. In 1992, as the United States fought a stubborn recession, Bush was defeated for reelection by Bill *Clinton.

Bush, Vannevar (1890–1974) US electrical engineer and inventor of the differential analyzer, an electronic analog computer. He was a professor (1919–38) at Massachusetts Institute of Technology and then became president (1938–55) of the Carnegie Institution of Washington.

bushbaby A small nocturnal *prosimian primate belonging to the genus *Galago* (4 species), of African forests and bush. They are 11–31 in (27–80 cm) long including the tail (6–16 in [15–40 cm]). Common bushbabies (*G. senegalensis*) have soft dense grayish fur and a long bushy tail. They live in small groups and climb acrobatically among the trees in search of large insects; they also eat fruit and leaves. Family: *Lorisidae*.

bushbuck A small antelope, *Tragelaphus scriptus,* of tropical African bush and forest, also called harnessed antelope; 26–43 in (66–109 cm) high at the shoulder, bushbucks are red with white spots and stripes on the flanks and legs. Males have black-tipped horns with a single spiral turn. They are shy and nocturnal, living in pairs.

bush cricket A *cricket belonging to the family *Tettigoniidae* (over 4000 species), having a green or brown body and short tail appendages (cerci). Bush crickets rarely fly or jump, but crawl among bushes and trees in fields and meadows. The swordlike ovipositor with which the female inserts eggs into plant tissues can cause considerable damage. Many species are carnivorous, usually eating small insects.

bushel A unit of capacity (dry or liquid) equal to 2150.42 cubic inches in the US and 8 gallons or 2219.36 cubic inches in the UK.

Bushido The military and ethical code of the Japanese *samurai class. It originated in about the 13th century, although the term was not used until the 17th. Obedience to one's lord and fearlessness were its main virtues, along with austerity, honesty, and kindness. In the 13th–14th centuries it was influenced by Zen Buddhism and in the 17th–19th centuries, by Confucianism. In the mid-19th century it became the basis of Japanese emperor worship and nationalism. *See also* martial arts.

GEORGE BUSH *President (1989–93) succeeding Pres. Ronald Reagan, whose vice president he had been.*

Bushire (*or* Bandar-e Bushehr) 28 59N 50 50E A city in SW Iran, on the N shore of the Persian Gulf. The port serves inland Iran but has lost trade to Abadan. Population (1986): 120,787.

Bushman. *See* Khoisan.

bushmaster A *pit viper, *Lachesis muta,* occurring in scrub and forests of Central and South America. The longest venomous snake of the New World, it reaches a length of 6 ft (1.8 m) and is brownish pink with dark diamond-shaped blotches. Its venom can prove fatal to man.

Bushnell, David (1742–1824) US inventor, who in 1776 built the first sub-marine, nicknamed the Turtle. It was intended to be a combat vessel, laying mines on the hulls of enemy ships, but it lacked the necessary maneuverability.

bushrangers Outlaws in the Australian outback in the late-18th and 19th cen-turies. They robbed farmsteads and stagecoaches, murdered, and plundered, but while some were ruthless and cruel, others shared their gains with the poor. The most famous of the Australian bushrangers is probably Ned *Kelly.

Busoni, Ferruccio (1866–1924) Italian virtuoso pianist and composer. An admirer of Liszt, he exploited the extreme possibilities of the piano in both his playing and in his transcriptions and compositions for the instrument. Among his works are a piano concerto (1903–04), the *Fantasia contrappuntistica* (for piano; 1910), and the opera *Doktor Faust* (1916–24).

Bustamante y Sirvén, Antonio Sánchez de (1865–1951) Cuban lawyer. He is best known for the Bustamante Code, a system of international law regarding the security of people and property. It was ratified by the sixth Pan-American Congress in 1928.

BUSHBABY *The enormous eyes and large sensitive ears of the common bushbaby make it well suited to a nocturnal existence.*

bustard A large omnivorous bird belonging to a family (*Otididae*; 22 species) occurring in grassland regions of the Old World and having long legs adapted for running. Bustards have a long stout neck, broad wings, and a gray or brown mottled plumage, often with ornamental plumes. The great bustard (*Otis tarda*), 48 in (120 cm) long and weighing 31 lb (14 kg), is the largest European land bird. Order: *Gruiformes* (cranes, rails, etc.).

butadiene ($H_2C:CHHC:CH_2$) A colorless flammable gas made from *butanes and butenes. It is used in making synthetic rubbers.

butane (C_4H_{10}) A colorless flammable gaseous *alkane found in crude oil. It is used in the manufacture of synthetic rubber and, in its pressurized liquefied form, as a fuel.

butcherbird. *See* shrike.

butcher's broom A small evergreen European shrub, *Ruscus aculeatus,* up to 31 in (80 cm) high. The leaves are reduced to small brown scales, but the plant has oval flattened branches that function as leaves. There are separate male and female flowers, which are small and greenish and grow on separate plants. The fruit is a red berry. Family: *Liliaceae.*

Bute, John Stuart, 3rd Earl of (1713–92) British statesman; prime minister (1762–63). A close friend of George III and extremely unpopular, he was forced to resign after securing the passage of a cider tax. He continued unofficially to influence the king until 1765.

Butler, Benjamin Franklin (1838–93) US statesman; Republican congressman (1866–75, 1877–79). A Union general, Butler was hated by southerners for his military governorship of New Orleans during the Civil War. As a Radical

Republican congressman, he advocated the impeachment of Pres. Andrew *Jackson and harsh Reconstruction policies. After several attempts he became governor of Massachusetts for one year (1882) and ran unsuccessfully for the presidency on a populist ticket in 1884.

Butler, Reg(inald) Cotterell (1913–81) British sculptor. Butler trained as an architect and practiced as an engineer (1939–50) before devoting himself to sculpture. Influenced by Henry *Moore and Alexander *Calder, he produced iron and stainless-steel constructions suggestive of plant and insect forms.

Butler, Samuel (1835–1902) British novelist. Son of a village rector and grandson of a bishop, he rejected his family, religion, and prospects, emigrating to New Zealand from 1859 to 1864, when he returned wealthy. After failing as an artist, he turned to literature and engaged in the Darwinian controversy. *Erewhon* (1872), which made him famous, satirizes Victorian utopian ideals. The autobiographical *The Way of All Flesh* (1903) recounts his painful liberation from his claustrophobic family background.

Butor, Michel (1926–) French experimental novelist and critic. He studied philosophy at the Sorbonne and has taught in Egypt, Thessalonika, Geneva, and Manchester. His novels, employing the techniques of the anti-novel (*see* nouveau roman), include *Passing Time* (1956), *Second Thoughts* (1957), *Degrees* (1960), *Mobile* (1962), and *Third Below* (1977).

butte A small steep-sided mass of rock left upstanding after the erosion of a *mesa. It usually consists of a resistant rock capping that protects the underlying rock from erosion.

buttercup An annual or perennial herbaceous plant of the worldwide genus *Ranunculus* (about 300 species), usually with much divided leaves. The flowers are usually yellow, with spirally arranged petals and stamens. The fruit is a head of small nutlets (achenes). A common Eurasian species, widely introduced, is the perennial meadow buttercup (*R. acris*), up to 28 in (70 cm) high. The genus, which is poisonous to livestock, also includes the *crowfoots. Family: *Ranunculaceae*.

butterflies and moths Insects belonging to the order *Lepidoptera* (about 100,000 species), distributed worldwide. The adults have two pairs of scale-covered wings, which are often highly colored and patterned. They range in size from the smallest moths, with a wingspan of only 0.16 in (4 mm), to butterflies with wingspans of up to 12 in (300 mm). They all undergo a complete metamorphosis comprising a four-stage life cycle: egg, larva (*see* caterpillar), *pupa (chrysalis), and adult (imago). The caterpillars feed mainly on plants, eating leaves or boring into stems and roots, in some cases becoming serious crop pests (e.g. the cabbage white butterfly and the spruce budworm). Some species pupate by spinning silken cocoons (*see* silkworm moth). The adults are often strong fliers, seeking out a mate and migrating long distances. They feed mainly on nectar and other plant juices using a long tubular proboscis and may aid plant pollination in the process (*see* yucca moth). The forewings and hindwings of moths are locked together by a "bristle-and-catch" device (frenulum). Butterflies generally are active by day and rest with their wings held together vertically; moths, which are mainly nocturnal, generally rest with their wings flat. Another differentiating feature is the antennae, which are smooth and club-shaped in butterflies and plumed or feathery in moths.

butterfly bush. *See* Buddleia.

butterwort A *carnivorous plant of the genus *Pinguicula* (about 30 species), found in the N hemisphere and South America. These perennial herbs, 5–6 in (12–15 cm) high, have a rosette of yellow-green leaves covered with sticky glands on which insects are trapped. The single spurred funnel-shaped violet or pink flower arises on a slender stalk. Family: *Lentibulariaceae.*

button quail A small ground-dwelling bird belonging to a family (*Turnicidae*; 15 species) found in warm Old World grassland regions. Button quails are 5–8 in (13–19 cm) long with a brown streaked plumage, short wings, and a small slender bill. The female courts the male and leaves him to incubate the eggs and tend the young. Order: *Gruiformes* (cranes, rails, etc.).

buttress A projecting mass of masonry strengthening a wall. The huge vaults of Roman and Byzantine public buildings caused buttresses to be built to counteract the outward thrust of the roof. In *gothic architecture, the graceful but highly functional **flying buttress** developed to support the upper walls of large churches.

butyl rubber A synthetic *rubber made by copolymerization of isobutylene with small amounts of *isoprene. It is less permeable to gas than natural rubbers and is used in tire inner tubes.

Buxtehude, Dietrich (1637–1707) Danish organist and composer. He settled in Germany in 1668 as organist at the Marienkirche, Lübeck. In 1673 he started his famous *Abendmusiken* ("evening concerts"); J. S. Bach walked 200 miles to Lübeck to hear Buxtehude's music. One of the most influential of the North German school of organists, he composed much organ music and sacred music.

buzzard A *hawk belonging to a widespread genus (*Buteo*) characterized by broad wings, a large rounded tail, and a brown plumage. Buzzards hunt in open country for small mammals, reptiles, insects, and carrion and soar gracefully at great heights. The common Eurasian buzzard (*B. buteo*), 22 in (55 cm) long, occurs in a number of races; the migratory rough-legged buzzard (*B. lagopus*) is distinguished by its feathered legs.

buzz bomb. *See* V-1 missile.

Byblos 34 08N 35 38E A *Phoenician city-state on the E Mediterranean coast, now Jubeil (Lebanon). Egyptian records from the 14th to the 10th centuries BC attest a thriving trade with Byblos; excavations here have revealed strong cultural links with Egypt. Under Greek and Roman rule Byblos dwindled in relative commercial importance but remained famous as the center of orgiastic worship of Astarte (*see* Aphrodite) and her lover *Adonis. *See also* Sidon; Tyre.

Bydgoszcz (German name: Bromberg) 53 16N 17 33E A city in N Poland. It is an important inland port on a canal linking the Vistula and Oder Rivers. Industries include engineering, printing, and the processing of forest products. Population (1992 est): 392,000.

Bylot, Robert. *See* Baffin, William.

Byng, George, Viscount Torrington (1663–1733) English admiral. A supporter of William III, he gained rapid promotion and in the War of the Spanish Succession captured Gibraltar (1704). He defeated the fleet of *James Stuart off Scotland (1708) and crowned his career by destroying a Spanish fleet off Messina (1717).

Byng of Vimy, Julian, 1st Viscount (1862–1935) British field marshal. He won distinction in World War I first at *Gallipoli, then as commander of the successful Canadian troops at Vimy Ridge. After the war he was governor general of Canada (1921–26).

Byrd, Harry Flood (1887–1966) US politician. After serving as Virginia's Democratic chairman, he was elected governor (1926–30) before becoming a US senator (1933–65). As chairman of the Senate Finance Committee (1955–65) he was known as a conservative who opposed increased federal power.

Byrd, Richard E(velyn) (1888–1957) US explorer. A naval pilot, he served in World War I and in 1926 began a series of record-breaking flights over the two Poles and the Atlantic Ocean. In 1928 he set out on the first of several expeditions to explore Antarctica from the air. In 1934–35, he spent five months alone in a hut at Bolling Advance Base, describing his experience in *Alone* (1938).

Byrd Land. *See* Marie Byrd Land.

Byron, George Gordon, Lord (1788–1824) British poet. Born with deformed ankles and a clubfoot, he grew up lacking parental affection. His first book, *Hours of Idleness* (1807), was followed in 1809 by a satire aimed at its ungenerous reviewers. After two years traveling in Europe he published *Childe Harolde's Pilgrimage* (1812) to immediate acclaim and was lionized by London society. He was bisexual and among many love affairs had an incestuous relationship with his half-sister Augusta Leigh. He married Annabella Milbanke in 1815 but she left him the following year. Byron then left England forever. He stayed near Geneva with *Shelley and then went to Italy. In 1818 he began writing the witty verse satire *Don Juan*. In 1823 he became involved in the Greek struggle for independence and he died while training troops at Missolonghi.

Bytom (German name: Beuthen) 50 21N 18 51E A town in SW Poland. It is a major heavy-industry center in a coal, zinc, and lead mining area. Population (1992 est): 232,000.

LORD BYRON *Portrait by Thomas Phillips (1770–1845).*

Byzantine art and architecture The painting, architecture, and decoration that developed in the ancient city of Constantinople (formerly Byzantium; modern Istanbul) after 330 AD, when it became the new Roman imperial capital, until 1453, when Constantinople fell to the Turks. Primarily religious and often symbolic or didactic, Byzantine art suppressed both realistic portrayal and opportunities for individual artistic expression. Owing to Constantinople's position as a meeting point of Asia and Europe, the bright colors and intricacy of oriental design mingle in Byzantine mosaics and *icons with Christian symbolism. Three main phases of Byzantine art succeeded one another between 330 and 1453 AD. The first phase (330–726) came to an end with the Iconoclastic controversy (726–843), which resulted in the destruction of many works of art (*see* iconoclasm). During the second golden age (843–1204) and the final phase (1204–1453) a complicated iconography of religious pictures was evolved, wherein each divine person, prophet, saint, angel, and apostle was allocated their strict position on the wall, apse, or dome of the church. This was possible because of the design of the Byzantine *basilica with its characteristic dome rising from a square base—an innovation that greatly extended the versatility of the Roman dome, which was restricted to circular buildings. The Church of Holy Wisdom (Hagia Sophia) in Constantinople, built between 532 and 537, is the outstanding example of a Byzantine basilica with a central dome (in this case buttressed by semidomes). The characteristic brickwork, pillars, and internal mosaics of Byzantine buildings also had a profound effect on western architecture, from the spectacular St Mark's (11th century) in Venice to the somewhat surprising Westminster Cathedral in London in the 20th century.

Byzantine Empire (*or* Eastern Roman Empire) The Roman territories E of the Balkans separated from the western *Roman Empire by *Diocletian in 293 AD. An eastern emperor and magistrates coexisted with their western counterparts at Rome. Under *Constantine the Great, the Empire became Christian. Constantinople (previously Byzantium; now *Istanbul) was inaugurated as the "New Rome" in 330 AD. The Byzantine Empire survived until the fall of Constantinople to the Ottoman Turks in 1453—almost a millennium after the western Empire.

Byzantium. *See* Istanbul.

C

Cabal Five ministers of Charles II of England who dominated politics from 1667 to about 1674. They were Sir Thomas Clifford (1630–73), Lord Ashley (later 1st Earl of *Shaftesbury), the 2nd Duke of *Buckingham, the Earl of *Arlington, and the Earl of *Lauderdale. It was not a united body: the king played one minister off against another to retain control of policy. Clifford and Arlington supported a secret pro-Catholic policy of friendship with France, which, owing to parliamentary opposition, cost them their offices in 1673–74.

Caballé, Montserrat (1933–   ) Spanish soprano. She sang at La Scala, Milan, and in 1965 made her debut in New York. She became a member of the Metropolitan Opera and specialized in bel canto roles, such as the title role in Bellini's *Norma.*

cabbage A flowering plant, *Brassica oleracea* var. *capitata,* widely cultivated as a vegetable. The short stem bears a round heart, up to 10 in (25 cm) in diameter, of tightly compressed leaves. Many different cultivated varieties have been developed, of various shapes, colors, and densities, used for cooking, salads, and pickling. For example, the Savoy cabbage is a cooking variety with dark-green wrinkled leaves. All cabbages and many other brassicas—including cauliflower, broccoli, kale, and Brussels sprouts—are derived from the wild cabbage (*B. oleracea*), a perennial herb native to coastal regions of W Europe; 12–24 in (30–60 cm) high, its straggling stem bears a spike of yellow flowers. Family: *Cruciferae.*

cabbage palm A West Indian palm tree, *Roystonea oleracea,* that may grow to a height of 98 ft (30 m) but is often cut when young for its head of young leaves, which resembles a cabbage and is eaten as a vegetable. An oil and a type of sago are obtained from the fruit. The name is also given to several other palms, including *Livistona australis,* of E Australia.

cabbage root fly A plant-eating fly, *Erioischia brassicae,* whose larva is a serious economic pest. The larvae feed on the roots of cabbages, radishes, turnips, etc., having developed from eggs laid around the stems. Family: *Muscidae.*

cabbage white butterfly A white butterfly belonging to the genus *Pieris,* whose caterpillars eat cabbages and related vegetables. The species are the large white (*P. brassicae*), the green-veined white (*P. napi*), and the small white (*P. rapae*).

caber tossing An event in Scottish athletics. A competitor carries the caber, a tapering tree trunk 13–17 ft (4–5 m) long, vertically in his cradled hands and then tosses it forward. As the top end hits the ground, the other end should continue over it so that the tossed caber should lie in the direction in which it was thrown; a toss more than 90° off-line is invalid.

Cabimas 10 26N 71 27W A city in NW Venezuela, on the NE shore of Lake Maracaibo. It is an important center within the Ambrosio oil fields. Population (1976 est): 159,000.

Cabinda (*or* Kabinda) A district of Angola, forming an enclave between the Congo and Zaïre on the Atlantic coast. Extensive oil deposits were discovered offshore in 1968 and led to the expansion of the chief town, Cabinda. The area also produces coffee, palm oil, timber, and cocoa. Area: 2806 sq mi (7270 sq km). Population (1960): 58,547.

cabinet A committee of the executive heads of government. In the US, the cabinet comprises the heads of the various departments of the executive branch. They are Secretary of State, Secretary of Defense, Secretary of the Treasury, Secretary of Labor, Secretary of the Interior, Secretary of Transportation, Secretary of Education, Secretary of Health and Human Services, Secretary of Energy, Secretary of Commerce, Secretary of Agriculture, Secretary of Housing and Urban Development, and the Attorney General, who heads the Department of Justice. All cabinet members are appointed by the president and subject to confirmation by the Senate. The extent of the cabinet's influence in the formation of national policy depends on the extent to which the president chooses to consult its members. The American cabinet system was developed from the British cabinet, which originated in the 18th century with the selection of a royal adviser, called the *prime minister, from the majority party in *Parliament. Unlike the members of the American cabinet who are responsible only to the president, all British ministers also fulfill legislative functions. British cabinets consist of about 20 leading ministers, from either house of Parliament, appointed by the prime minister. They serve until dismissed by the prime minister or until their party loses its parliamentary majority. This parliamentary system has also been adopted by many other countries.

Cabora Bassa Dam 15 34S 33 00E A dam in Mozambique, on the Zambezi River. It is the largest dam in S Africa.

Cable, George Washington (1844–1925) US author and reformer. Through his novels and short stories he gave a feeling for the southern life, especially that of his native New Orleans. He was a strong advocate for the rights of the newly freed blacks and published many essays on the subject. They are collected in *The Silent South* (1885) and *The Negro Question* (1888). His short stories are collected in *Old Creole Days* (1879).

Cabot, John (Italian name: Giovanni Caboto; c. 1450–c. 1499) Italian explorer. He settled in England in about 1484 and under Henry VII's patronage discovered Cape Breton Island (which he thought to be Asia) in 1497. He set out on a second voyage in 1498 and appears to have died at sea. His son **Sebastian Cabot** (c. 1476–1557) was a cartographer to Henry VIII. In Spanish service he explored the coast of South America (1525–28).

Cabral, Pedro Álvares (?1467–1520) Portuguese navigator. In 1500, on his way to India with 13 ships, he landed in Brazil, which he claimed for Portugal. Resuming his voyage E, he landed at Mozambique, of which he later gave an interesting account, and thence reached Calicut, where he established the first commercial treaty between Portugal and India. He returned to Portugal in 1501 with only four ships.

Cabrini, St Frances Xavier (1850–1917) Italian founder of the Missionary Sisters of the Sacred Heart, known as Mother Cabrini. She sailed in 1889 to the US and established 67 houses there and in Buenos Aires, Paris, and Madrid. She worked mainly among poor Italian immigrants in the US and was the first US citizen to be canonized. Feast day: Nov 13.

cacao. *See* cocoa and chocolate.

Caccini, Giulio (c. 1545–c. 1618) Italian singer and composer. He developed the monodic style (a single vocal line supported by a chordal bass), which led to the earliest operas; his opera *Euridice* was performed in 1602.

Cáceres 39 29N 6 23W A market city in W Spain, in Estremadura. It produces textiles and cork. The old part of the town is surrounded by Roman and Moorish walls. Population: 56,064.

cachalot. *See* sperm whale.

cacomistle An arboreal nocturnal mammal of the American genus *Bassariscus* (2 species). Cacomistles are grayish brown with small faces, long ears, and pointed snouts; the long bushy tail, patterned with black and white rings, accounts for about half the total body length (24–40 in; 60–100 cm). They feed on small animals and fruit. The North American cacomistle, or ring-tailed cat (*B. astutus*) occurs from the SW US to S Mexico; the South American cacomistle extends from Central America to Peru. Family: *Procyonidae* (raccoons, etc.); order: *Carnivora*.

Cactoblastis. *See* cactus moth.

CACTUS *Two ornamental cacti:* Rhipsalidopsis *"Electra" (above) from Brazil and* Opuntia microdasys *(below) from Mexico.*

cactus A flowering plant belonging to the family *Cactaceae* (over 2000 species). These perennial herbs and shrubs grow chiefly in the drier regions of tropical America and the West Indies. Plant size and shape varies widely; the larger species may grow to a height of 33 ft (10 m) or more. Cacti show pronounced modifications to prevent water loss—their leaves or shoots are reduced to spines, they have thick waxy outer layers, and many possess succulent water-storing stems. The flowers, borne singly, are large and brightly colored. Some genera are cultivated for their soft timber or alkaloid content, and the fruits of many species are edible (*see* prickly pear). Cacti are grown as ornamentals in many regions of the world.

cactus moth A South American cactus-boring *pyralid moth, *Cactoblastis cactorum,* that was introduced into Australia in 1925 as a means of biologically controlling the prickly pear cactus, which had ruined large areas.

caddis fly A mothlike insect, also called sedge fly, belonging to the worldwide order *Trichoptera* (about 5000 species). Caddis flies—0.05–1.6 in (1.5–40 mm) long, with long antennae—are found in cool damp places and feed on nectar. The omnivorous larvae (called caddis worms) live in flowing fresh water, often in portable cases constructed from sand, stones, pieces of leaf, etc.

Caddo A North American Indian language spoken by a confederation of related tribes formerly inhabiting areas in Arkansas, Louisiana, Oklahoma, and Texas. The Caddoan group of languages takes its name from the ancient Caddo, who were a semisedentary agricultural people who established villages of conical huts around a central temple mound. Political and religious affairs were conducted by a hereditary elite. The present Caddoan population, numbering approximately 1000 members of the various member tribes, is now settled primarily in the Wichita Reservation in Oklahoma.

cade A *juniper tree or shrub, *Juniperus oxycedrus,* native to Mediterranean coastal regions and growing to a height of 26 ft (8 m). Also called prickly juniper, it has needles and rounded reddish berry like fruits, 0.24–0.40 in (6–10 mm) in diameter. Oil of cade is distilled from the wood and used in medicine and veterinary work.

Cade, Jack (d. 1450) English rebel, who led a rebellion in 1450 against Henry VI. The rebels, who were chiefly opposing high taxes and court corruption, demanded the recall of Richard Plantagenet, Duke of York, from Ireland. In spite of initial successes in Kent and London, the rebellion was soon quelled and Cade was killed.

Cádiz 36 32N 6 18W A city and seaport in SW Spain, in Andalusia on the Gulf of Cádiz. Founded by Phoenician merchants (c. 1100 BC), it was taken from the Moors by Alfonso the Wise of Castile in 1262. Following the discovery of America it prospered as a base for the Spanish treasure fleet; the harbor was burned by Sir Francis Drake in 1587, destroying many ships. It has two cathedrals and a notable collection of works by the artist Murillo. An important port and naval base, it has tuna fisheries and ship-building industries. Population (1991 est): 153,500.

cadmium (Cd) A soft dense metal, discovered in 1817 by Friedrich Strohmeyer (1776–1835). Cadmium occurs naturally as the mineral greenockite (CdS) and in zinc, copper, and lead sulfide ores. It is chemically similar to lead and is a component of low-melting-point alloys. It is used in the control rods of nuclear reactors, in light meters, television-tube phosphors, batteries, solders, and in special low-friction alloys for bearings. Cadmium and its compounds are poisonous and care should be taken in working with solders (e.g. silver solder) that contain cadmium. Compounds include several salts, the yellow sulfide (CdS) and the oxide (CdO). At no 48; at wt 112.40; mp 610°F (321°C); bp 1410°F (765°C).

Cadmus A legendary Greek hero. Obeying the oracle of Delphi, he followed a cow into Boeotia and founded the city of Thebes where it lay down. A race of fierce warriors is said to have emerged from the teeth of a dragon he had killed. He married Harmonia, daughter of Ares and Aphrodite, and is reputed to have introduced the alphabet into Greece from Phoenicia.

caecilian A limbless burrowing *amphibian of the order *Apoda,* or *Gymnophiona* (over 150 species), found in tropical and warm temperate regions of the world. Resembling earthworms, caecilians are 4–42 in (11–140 cm) long and feed on termites and earthworms.

Caedmon (died c. 680 AD) English poet, known only from the account given by *Bede in his *Ecclesiastical History.* He was an illiterate herdsman who in his old age was suddenly divinely inspired to compose a hymn on the Creation. The *Hymn* is a typical example of Old English oral verse. Caedmon later entered the monastery of Whitby, where he composed many poems on biblical themes.

Caen 49 11N 0 22W A city and port in NW France, the capital of the Calvados department on the Orne River. Situated at the center of an agricultural and horse-breeding area, Caen has iron, silk, and leather industries. Stone from nearby quarries was used to build several cathedrals and churches in England. A cultural center, its university was established in 1432 (reorganized in 1970). It has many fine churches. *History*: captured by the English in 1346 and again in 1417, it became a Huguenot stronghold in the 17th century. Caen was badly damaged during the Normandy campaign (1944) of World War II. Population (1990 est): 115,000.

Caernarfon (English name: Caernarvon) 53 08N 4 16W A town in North Wales, a tourist center, market town, and small port. Its castle (built by Edward I in 1284) is the likely birthplace of Edward II, the first Prince of Wales, and was the scene of the investiture of Prince *Charles as Prince of Wales in 1969. Population (1981): 9506.

Caerphilly 51 35N 3 14W A market city in South Wales, in Mid Glamorgan. Situated in a coal-mining area, it is best known for Caerphilly cheese (originally made here) and its castle, the largest in Wales. Population (1981): 42,736.

Caesar, (Gaius) Julius (100–44 BC) Roman general and statesman, whose career marked the end of the Roman Republic. Caesar, born of a patrician family, allied himself with the popular party by his marriage in 84 to *Cinna's daughter Cornelia. After her death in 68, he married Pompeia, whom he divorced in 62, and in 59 he married Calpurnia.

During the 60s Caesar ascended the political ladder, joining *Pompey and *Crassus in the first *Triumvirate (60) and becoming consul (59) and then governor of Gaul. Caesar's subjugation of Gaul (58–50), and his brief campaigns in Britain (55, 54), confirmed his military reputation and made him a popular hero. Crassus's death (53) and Pompey's developing association with Caesar's opponents in the Senate brought the Triumvirate to an end (50) and the Senate, with Pompey's support, asked Caesar to resign his armies. He refused and, crossing the Rubicon River into Italy (49), initiated the civil war. Caesar defeated Pompey at *Pharsalus (48) and spent the following winter in Alexandria with *Cleopatra, who became his lover. She is reputed to have had a son, Caesarion, by him. Caesar then campaigned in NE Anatolia, defeating Pharnaces II at Zela (47), the victory provoking his comment "veni, vidi, vici" ("I came, I saw, I conquered"). He went on to defeat the remnants of Pompey's party at *Thapsus (46) and Munda (45), after which he returned to Rome as dictator. There, he introduced many reforms, including the sponsorship of a revised (Julian) *calendar, but on the Ides of March (Mar 15, 44) Caesar was assassinated in the Senate

House by republicans, including *Brutus and *Cassius, who feared his monarchical aspirations.

A distinguished prose stylist, Caesar wrote outstanding accounts of his campaigns in Gaul (*De bello gallico*) and the civil war (*De bello civili*).

Caesarea 32 30N 34 54E An ancient town in Israel, on the Mediterranean coast between Tel Aviv-Yafo and Haifa. Built by Herod the Great, it had a large early Christian community and was for a time the capital of Roman Palestine. Caesarea was twice held by the Crusaders and finally destroyed by Muslims in 1265. The Israelis have excavated many Roman remains and are developing a tourist resort here.

Caesarean section A surgical operation in which a baby is delivered through an incision made in the abdominal wall and the womb, so called because Julius Caesar was said to have been born in this way. Caesarean section is employed when a baby cannot be delivered through the vagina; for instance, because it is abnormally positioned in the womb or is too large to pass through the birth canal.

Caetano, Marcello José das Neves Alves (1906–80) Portuguese statesman; prime minister (1968–74). He succeeded Salazar and initially proved a more liberal head of state. He was overthrown in a military coup.

Caffaggiolo majolica An important category of Italian pottery mainly produced from about 1504 to 1540 under Medici patronage. Its main characteristic is bold bright decoration in orange, yellow, red, and green, on a cobalt-blue background. *See* majolica.

caffeine (*or* theine; $C_8H_{10}O_2N_4$) The substance in coffee and tea that acts as a stimulant. In its pure form it is white and crystalline.

Cage, John (1912–92) Avant-garde US composer, who studied with Schoenberg and Varèse. His works include *Sonatas and Interludes* (1946–48) for prepared piano (with pieces of wood, metal, etc., fixed across its strings); *Imaginary Landscape No 4* (1951) for 12 randomly tuned radio sets; *4 minutes 33 seconds* (1954), silence in three movements for any instruments(s); *Reunion* (1968); and *Apartment Building 1776* (1976). His books, including *Silence* (1961), reflect his philosophy of indeterminism.

Cagliari 39 13N 9 08E A seaport in Italy, in Sardinia. It has Roman remains, a 14th-century cathedral, and a university (1606). There are milling, tanning, and fishing industries. Lead, salt, and zinc are exported. Population (1991 est): 212,000.

Cagliostro, Alessandro, Conte di (Giuseppe Balsamo; 1743–95) Italian adventurer. His pretended skills in alchemy and magic gained him fame throughout Europe, especially in Paris. He was arrested for promoting freemasonry and died in prison in Italy.

Cagney, James (1899–1986) US actor. He began making films in the 1930s, after working as a vaudeville singer and dancer, and became famous for his portrayals of tough gangsters. His films include *Public Enemy* (1931), *The Roaring Twenties* (1939), and *Ragtime* (1981). He won an Academy Award for *Yankee Doodle Dandy* (1942).

Caicos Islands. *See* Turks and Caicos Islands.

Caillaux, Joseph (1863–1944) French statesman; prime minister (1911–12). He was finance minister three times before World War I and introduced direct income tax into France. In 1914 his wife shot and killed Gaston Calmette (1858–1914), the editor of *Le Figaro,* who had cast aspersions on his financial dealings while in office. An advocate of a negotiated peace during World War I, Caillaux was arrested in 1917 on a charge of dealing with the enemy. His civil rights were restored in 1925.

Cain In the Old Testament, the elder son of Adam and Eve. He became jealous of his younger brother Abel, a shepherd whose burnt offerings were accepted by God in preference to his own. He murdered Abel and was banished, marked as the world's first murderer.

Cain, James M(allahan) (1892–1977) US novelist. He worked in journalism after college but left in 1931 to concentrate on writing racy, fast-paced crime novels. His first, *The Postman Always Rings Twice* (1934), became a stage play (1936) and a movie (1946). Other well-known novels that later became films were *Double Indemnity* (1936) and *Mildred Pierce* (1941).

Cainozoic era. *See* Cenozoic era.

cairn. *See* barrow.

Cairns 16 51S 145 43E A port in Australia, in NE Queensland on Trinity Bay. It is the commercial center for an agricultural, mining, and timber region; sugar is exported. Population (1991): 54,862.

cairn terrier A breed of small □dog originating in the Scottish Highlands, where it was used to flush game from cover (such as stone cairns). It has a long outer coat and a short soft undercoat; the color varies from red, sandy, or mottled gray to almost black. Height: about 10 in (25 cm).

Cairo (Arabic name: El Qahira) 80 01N 31 14E The capital of Egypt, situated in the N of the country on the E bank of the Nile River. It is the largest city in Africa and the cultural and commercial center of Egypt. Industry has developed dramatically since the 1920s and in particular since the revolution of 1952, with traditional textile manufacturing and food processing retaining importance alongside newer industries, such as metallurgy and plastics. Its many mosques include the Mosque of Omar (643 AD), Cairo's earliest remaining Arabic building, and the Mohammed Ali Mosque, housed in the 12th-century citadel. The Mosque and University of El Azhar was founded in 970 AD; three other universities were established in the 20th century. *History*: the Arabic city of El Fustat was founded in 641 AD, and from the 9th century, as El Qahira, it was successively the capital of the Fatimid, Ayyubite, and Mameluke dynasties. It was under the Mamelukes that the city enjoyed the period of its greatest prosperity. Following its conquest by the Turks in the 16th century, it declined in power, but in the 19th century its prosperity was restored under Mehemet *Ali and his successors. During World War II it was the seat of the Allied headquarters in the Middle East. Population (1990 est): 6,450,000. *See also* Giza, El.

caisson A large cylindrical or box-shaped structure sunk into the ground during excavation work. Caissons aid construction of underwater foundations, for example in the construction of piers for bridges, and may become part of the permanent structure.

caisson disease. *See* decompression sickness.

Caithness A former county of NE Scotland. Under local government reorganization in 1975 its boundaries were adjusted to form a district of the same name, in the Highlands Region.

cakewalk A ballroom dance popular in the early 1900s, originally performed by slaves satirizing the elegance of plantation society. Couples walked around in a square, being judged for the grace and inventiveness of their movements. The winners were awarded a cake, from which the expression "to take the cake" derives.

CAIRO *The Mohammed Ali Mosque now dominates Saladin's citadel, built in the 12th century.*

Calabar (former name: Old Calabar) 4 56N 8 22E A port in SE Nigeria. It was a center of the slave trade in the 18th and 19th centuries; exports now include palm oil, rubber, timber, and cocoa. Population (1992 est): 158,000.

calabash A tree, *Crescentia cujete,* 25–49 ft (7.5–15 m) tall, native to tropical America (particularly Brazil). Funnel-shaped flowers are borne on the old stems and produce gourdlike fruits, up to 20 in (50 cm) long. These fruits have woody outer layers and, after removal of the inner pulp, are used as pots, cooking utensils, etc. Family: *Bignoniaceae.*

Calabria A mountainous region occupying the southern "toe" of Italy. It is basically a poor agricultural region (producing olives, citrus fruits, vines, and cereals) with the lowest per capita income of any Italian region. Crotone is the main industrial center. Area: 5822 sq mi (15,080 sq km). Population (1991): 2,010,195. Capital: Catanzaro.

Calais 50 57N 1 52E A port in N France, in the Pas-de-Calais department. Its prosperity lies in being on the shortest sea route to England. It produces lace, tulle, and other textiles. *History*: besieged and captured by the English under Edward III in 1346, Calais remained in English hands until 1558. In World War II it was the target of savage bombardment and was heroically defended in support of the withdrawal from *Dunkirk. Population (1975): 79,369.

calamine An ore of zinc. In English usage it refers to zinc carbonate (smithsonite) and in the US it refers to zinc silicate (hemimorphite). A skin lotion of the same name contains zinc oxide.

Calamites An extinct genus of treelike pteridophyte plants, prominent during the Carboniferous period, 345–280 million years ago. Their fossilized remains form a major constituent of the Carboniferous coal seams (*see also* Lepidodendron). Class: *Sphenopsida* (*see* horsetails).

Calamity Jane (Martha Canary; c. 1852–1903) US frontierswoman, who featured in many stories and legends of the Wild West. She worked in frontier towns and camps, claimed to have been a Pony Express rider and US Army Scout, frequently dressed as a man, and was skilled in riding and shooting. She later appeared in Wild West shows.

Calas, Jean (1698–1762) French Huguenot, who was accused of the murder of his son in 1761 in order to prevent his becoming a Roman Catholic. He protested his innocence but was tried and executed. His conviction was reversed after *Voltaire, at the request of his widow, led a campaign for religious toleration and legal reform and succeeded in having the trial reviewed.

Calceolaria A genus of perennial herbs and shrubs (300–400 species) native to temperate South America. The plants grow to a height of 12–28 in (30–70 cm) and bear brightly colored slipper-shaped flowers. Some species and hybrids are grown as ornamentals. Family: *Scrophulariaceae*.

Calchas A legendary Greek prophet who foretold the length of the *Trojan War and advised the Greeks to build the wooden horse by which they gained entry to Troy. He died after being defeated by Mopsus in a trial of prophecy.

calcite A common rock-forming mineral consisting of crystalline calcium carbonate. It is usually colorless or white. It occurs in igneous, metamorphic, and sedimentary rocks. Most *limestones consist largely of calcite, sometimes in the form of fossil shells, and calcite is a common cementing material in coarse-grained sedimentary rocks. Calcite is very soluble in slightly acidic water.

calcitonin A polypeptide hormone, secreted by the thyroid gland in mammals, that reduces the level of calcium in the blood when this rises above normal. A hormone from the *parathyroid gland raises blood calcium levels and therefore acts antagonistically.

calcium (Ca) A reactive metal, first isolated by Sir Humphry Davy in 1808. It occurs in nature as *limestone ($CaCO_3$), *fluorite (CaF_2), and *gypsum ($CaSO_4.2H_2O$) and is an essential constituent of shells, bones, and teeth. The element is extracted by electrolysis of the molten chloride ($CaCl_2$). It forms many compounds. These include quicklime (CaO), which has many industrial uses as a base in additon to its role in *cement, the nitrate ($Ca(NO_3)_2$), chloride ($CaCl_2$), and carbide (CaC_2), from which acetylene is produced by the addition of water. The metal itself is reactive. It is used to clear residual gases from vacuum systems and as a reducing agent in the production of thorium and uranium. At no 20; at wt 40.08; mp 839 ± 61°F (± 16°C); bp 2731°F (1484°C).

calculator Any device for carrying out mathematical functions ($+$, $-$, $\times$, $\div$). Originally mechanical, they were later electrically operated; purely electronic calculators, based on the digital *computer, have now largely replaced all earlier types. Electronic calculators use a silicon chip *integrated-circuit package, often smaller than a dime, that contains the equivalent of hundreds of *transistors built into complex logic circuits. These logic circuits perform the basic functions of addition and subtraction using binary arithmetic (*see* binary system). Multiplication and division are performed by repeated additions or subtractions. The high speed of a modern calculator enables the solution to a problem to appear on the digital display apparently instantaneously.

Many electronic calculators have more complex functions available (percentages, square roots, trigonometric functions, etc.) by pressing a single key and some provide a memory in which the intermediate results of a chain of calcula-

calculus

tions can be stored. Advanced types enable the user to program a sequence of functions for the calculator to perform automatically.

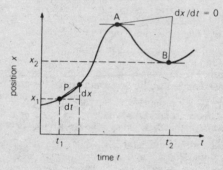

1 *The derivative* dx/dt *at* P *gives the slope of the curve at* P. *When the function has a stationary (e.g. a maximumum as at* A *or a minimum as at* B*) value,* $dx/dt = 0.$

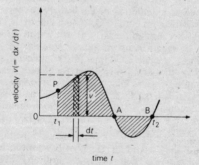

2 *The integral* $\int_{t_1}^{t_2} v.\,dt\ (= x_2 - x_1)$ *is the shaded area, i.e. it is the sum of all the areas* $v.\,dt$ *of the infinitely thin slices. The area between* A *and* B *is subtracted since* v *is negative.*

CALCULUS *The two basic techniques are (1) differentiation and (2) integration.*

calculus The mathematical techniques, developed by *Newton and *Leibniz, that are based on the concept of infinitely small changes in continuously varying quantities. For example, calculus is used to define the velocity of a moving body as the rate of change of its position at any instant. Velocity (v) is said to be the derivative of position (x) with respect to time (t); in calculus it is written $v = dx/dt$. In this notation dt is a vanishingly small time interval and dx is the distance the body travels in this time. If x is a known function of t, values for v at any time can be obtained by calculating the derivative of (differentiating) this function with respect to time. Similarly, the derivative of the velocity (or the second derivative of position) at any instant gives its acceleration (a), i.e. $d^2x/dt^2 = dv/dt = a$. The simpler notation $x'' = v$ and $x'''' = a$ is sometimes used.

The **differential calculus** is the system of rules for making such calculations. On a graph, the derivative of a function is the gradient of the curve at any point. A maximum or minimum value of the function can be found, as they occur when the gradient is zero. The **integral calculus** is concerned with the same process in reverse. If velocity is a continuously varying function of time, the change in position over a measurable time interval is calculated by summing the products of v and dt for each of the infinitely small intervals of time (dt) that make up the measurable interval. As with differential calculus, the extraction of integrals follows general rules, each type of mathematical function having a corresponding integral. The integral of v between time t_1 and t_2, written

$$\int_{t_1}^{t_2} v.dt,$$

gives the change in position in this interval. On a graph, the area between the curve of a function and the horizontal axis is the integral of the function over the specified time interval.

Equations that contain derivatives are called **differential equations**. They are solved by guessing at a general form of solution and trying it in the equation, using the rules of differential calculus. For well-known differential equations, such as those that describe wave motion and the diffusion of gases, there are standard forms of solution.

Calcutta 22 35N 88 21E A city in India, the capital of West Bengal on the Hooghly River. It is a major industrial center and the most important seaport on the E coast of India. Jute manufacturing dominates the industrial sector, while engineering, cotton textiles, and chemicals are also important. A large section of the population is employed in small workshops and handicraft industries. Calcutta is the focal point of rail, road, and air routes and its port is a major outlet for iron, coal, manganese, and mica as well as the large exports of manufactured jute goods. The city itself is part of a conurbation that has a combined population of over seven million people, many of whom live in appalling conditions; less than one-third of the conurbation is sewered, water supplies are inadequate, and many thousands of the inhabitants sleep on the streets. By way of contrast, the city center contains many imposing buildings, situated around Fort William (a British building dating from 1758). There are three universities, including Calcutta University (1857). *History*: founded in 1692 as a trading post for the British East India Company, it was the scene of much fighting (1756–57) between the British under Clive and the forces of Siraj-ud-Dawlah, Nawab of Bengal (*see* Black Hole of Calcutta). Population (1991): 4,388,262.

Calder, Alexander Stirling (1870–1945) US sculptor. His busts of John James *Audubon and William *Penn are in the Hall of Fame of Great Americans. He also sculpted fountains, sundials, and memorials. His son **Alexander Calder** (1898–1976) was also a sculptor. Trained as an engineer, Calder began his professional career as a commercial artist. During the 1920s he worked in Paris and became known for his unique moving sculptures, which were given the name "mobiles" by one of Calder's colleagues and admirers, the French artist Marcel *Duchamp. Calder's mobiles, consisting of flat metal disks suspended from wires, were influenced by the work of Joan *Miró and Piet *Mondrian. Calder later became famous for monumental freestanding constructions, which were named "stabiles" by another of his colleagues, Jean *Arp.

caldera. *See* volcano.

Calderón de la Barca, Pedro (1600–81) Spanish dramatist. He studied law and theology but rejected a career in the Church; in 1623 he began writing plays at the court of Philip IV. After the death of *Lope de Vega he became the leading Spanish dramatist. His many plays include *The Constant Prince* (1629), *Life Is a Dream* (1635), and *The Mayor of Zalamea* (1640). He was ordained priest in 1651, after which he wrote mainly masques and operas for the royal court, and religious dramas.

Caldwell, Erskine (1903–87) US novelist. After taking a wide variety of jobs he gained international fame with his novels *Tobacco Road* (1932) and *God's Little Acre* (1933). His social criticism, which in his fiction is blended with comedy and sex, is most forcefully expressed in his journalism, notably in *You Have Seen Their Faces* (1937) and *In Search of Bisco* (1965). His *Stories of Life/North and South* (1983) is a collection of short stories.

Caldwell, Sarah (1928–   ) US conductor and opera director. She began her career at the New England Opera Theater under Boris Goldovsky and at Tanglewood Music Festival under Serge Koussevitsky. Head of the Opera Workshop department at Boston University, she started to assemble the Opera Company of Boston in 1957. Her ability to search out and put together little-known operas and to bring out all phases of characterization earned her worldwide acclaim. She became the artistic director of the New Opera Company of Israel in 1983.

Caledonia The name given by ancient Roman writers to Scotland. Remote and rugged, Caledonia was scarcely known in antiquity. The Roman governor in Britain, Gneus Julius Agricola, in an exploratory expedition defeated the Caledonians in 83 AD near present-day Inverness, as did the emperor Lucius Septimius Severus in 209, but the clans and their chieftains remained independent until united under Kenneth I MacAlpine in the 9th century.

Caledonian Canal A system of lakes and canals in Scotland, linking the North Sea with the Irish Sea, via the Great Glen. Engineered by Thomas Telford, it was opened to navigation in 1822. Today it is used mainly by small craft. Length: about 60 mi (100 km).

Caledonian orogeny. *See* orogeny.

calendar Any of a variety of systems for the reckoning of time over an extended period. The period is divided into years containing a whole number of days, the days being grouped into months. Calendars are usually based on the earth's orbital period around the sun (a year), although in some systems the moon's orbital period around the earth (a month) is taken as the basis. Since the seasons recur after each tropical *year (which contains 365.2422 days), the length of the calendar year, averaged over many years, should correspond as closely as possible to that of the tropical year. This is achieved by using leap years, which contain one more day than the usual calendar year.

In 46 BC, Julius Caesar established the so-called **Julian calendar** in which a period of three years, each of 365 days, was followed by a leap year of 366 days. The average length of the year was therefore 365.25 days. Since this was over 11 minutes longer than the tropical year, an extra day appeared about every 128 years. This discrepancy was amended by the **Gregorian calendar**, which was introduced in Roman Catholic countries in 1582 by Pope Gregory XIII, was made law in Britain and its colonies in 1752, and is now in almost worldwide use. Leap years are restricted to century years divisible by 400 (e.g. 1600 and 2000) and any other year divisible by four. This reduces the average length of the calendar year to a much more acceptable 365.2425 days. *See also* French Republican calendar.

Calgary 51 05N 114 05W A city in W Canada, in Alberta. It developed with the arrival of the railroad (1884) and local oil discoveries, becoming the center of Canada's petroleum industry. Calgary is the distribution and farming center of S Alberta and is the site of the University of Calgary (1945). The Calgary Stampede, a famous rodeo, is celebrated annually. The 1988 Winter Olympic games were held here. Population (1991): 710,677.

Calhoun, John C(aldwell) (1782–1850) US statesman; vice president (1825–32), a champion of the southern states and a defender of slavery. A South Carolinian, he was a member of the House (1811–17) and then secretary of war (1817–25) before becoming vice president. He served in the Senate (1832–43; 1846–50) and as secretary of state (1844–45). His famous Nullification theory claimed the rights of states to nullify congressional laws that they considered unconstitutional. He encouraged the annexation of Texas to provide another slaveholding state and to strengthen the power of the South.

Cali 3 24N 76 30W The third largest city in Colombia. It is the industrial and commercial center for a rich agricultural area producing coffee, sugar, and cotton. Its university was founded in 1945. Population (1985): 1,351,000.

calico A simple woven cotton fabric that originated as a printed fabric from Calicut, India. Strong and serviceable with a wide range of textures, it is used mainly for dresses and domestic purposes. British calico is now usually bleached or plain white; US calico is generally printed.

Calicut. *See* Kozhikode.

California The third largest state in the US, on the W coast. California is bounded by Oregon on the N, Nevada and Arizona (whose border with California is formed by the Colorado River) on the E. Mexico lies to the S and the Pacific Ocean to the W. It consists of a narrow coastal plain rising to the Coast Range, with the fertile central valleys of the Sacramento and San Joaquin Rivers, deserts in the S, and the Sierra Nevada in the E. The Sierra Nevada contains Kings Canyon, Sequoia and Yosemite national parks, and Mt Whitney, the highest point in the state. The giant redwood is native to California. The state's spectacular scenery and favorable climate contribute to its popularity as a tourist attraction. The San Andreas Fault, extending through two-thirds of the state, has caused numerous tremors and serious earthquakes throughout the coastal area. It is the most populous state in the US and the predominantly urban population is concentrated along the coast. It has a varied economy. Oil is exploited along with natural gas, cement, sand and gravel, and borate. Aircraft and ship construction are important industries, as well as general construction and food processing; wine production is especially important. Employment is also provided by the many military bases and the film industry. Tourism is important in the many national parks throughout the state. California's agriculture is famous and the state produces grapes, tomatoes, cotton, sugar beet, strawberries, citrus fruits, hay, beef cattle, and turkeys. The state has a large number of cultural and educational institutions, many supported by public finance, such as the University of California. *History*: first discovered by Spain (1542), it became part of New Spain and was gradually settled by the Spanish and Mexicans from present-day Mexico. The Spanish established many missions, including that founded (1776) by Father Junipero Serras, a Franciscan missionary, on the present site of San Francisco. American settlers began to move westward to California in the 1840s. California remained under Spanish, and then Mexican, rule after Mexico achieved independence from Spain. Two presidents, Andrew Jackson and Alexander Polk, unsuccessfully attempted to purchase California from Mexico. In 1846 a group of Californians under the flag of the Republic of California declared themselves independent. In the meantime, Polk had set out to annex California forcibly. In the resulting conflict, the Mexican War, the US won California (1848). In the same year gold was discovered, leading to a rapid increase in the number of immigrants. The Transcontinental Railroad (completed 1869) linked the state with the East. Industry grew rapidly during World War II, and California has now become the country's center for defense-related industries. A large portion of high-technology computer firms are located in "Silicon Valley." In 1978 Californians, leading what became known as the "tax revolt," brought Proposition 13 to the voters. Its passage resulted in a 57% cut in property taxes and a $7 billion loss in revenues for the state. A devastating earthquake rocked northern California, particularly in the San Francisco Bay area, in 1989. Another earthquake hit the Los Angeles region in 1994. Area: 158,693 sq mi (411,013 sq km). Population (1990): 29,760,021. Capital: Sacramento.

California, Gulf of An inlet of the Pacific Ocean, in Mexico between the state of Sonora and the peninsula of Lower California. Length: 760 mi (1223 km).

California, University of US university, founded in 1868. Nine campuses, each with its own chancellor, are overseen by a president and board of regents. The campuses are at Berkeley (1873), San Francisco (1873), Davis (1905), Riverside (1907), Los Angeles (1919), Santa Barbara (1944), San Diego (1912), Irvine (1965), and Santa Cruz (1965).

californium (Cf) A synthetic transuranic element first isolated in 1950. Californium-252 is an intense neutron emitter. It is used as a neutron source in instruments for determining moisture contents and discovering precious metals. At no 98; at wt 251.

Caligula (Gaius Caesar; 12–41 AD) Roman emperor (37–41), son of Germanicus Caesar and Agrippina the Elder. Succeeding Tiberius, he initially enjoyed great popularity but his subsequent tyrannical and extravagant behavior brought allegations of madness, from both contemporaries and historians, and he was assassinated.

caliph The title borne by the leaders of Islam. The first caliph was *Abu Bakr, who succeeded Mohammed in 632. The *Umayyads ruled from 661 to 750 and were overthrown by the *Abbasids, who ruled in Baghdad until 1258 and then in Egypt, until ousted by the Ottomans in 1517. The title was then borne by the Ottoman sultans until 1922 and was abolished in 1924. Rival Muslim dynasties, such as the Egyptian *Fatimids (909–1171), also claimed the title.

calisaya. *See* Cinchona.

calla. *See* arum.

Callaghan, (Leonard) James (1912–   ) British statesman; Labour prime minister (1976–79). Entering Parliament in 1945, he was chancellor of the exchequer (1964–67), home secretary (1967–70), and foreign secretary (1974–76). He became prime minister when Harold *Wilson resigned and was defeated in the 1979 election by Margaret *Thatcher, but remained leader of the Labour Party, until 1980.

Callao 12 05S 77 08W A major port in W Peru, on the Pacific Ocean. It was the site of the first railroad in South America (1851) connecting Callao with Lima. Chief exports include minerals, metals, and fishmeal. Population (1990 est): 589,000.

Callas, Maria (Maria Anna Kalageropoulos; 1923–77) US-born soprano of Greek parentage. She possessed a brilliant coloratura voice and fine acting ability. From 1950 she was prima donna of La Scala, Milan, where she was famous for her interpretations of Bellini, Donizetti, Verdi, and Puccini.

Calles, Plutarco Elías (1877–1945) Mexican soldier in the post-1910 revolutionary movement and statesman. As president (1924–28) his anticlerical policies caused the rebellion of the Church's supporters (the *cristeros*) and his attempts to control oil rights brought conflict with the US. He wielded dictatorial power from 1928 to 1934, when he was succeeded by Lázaro *Cárdenas, who forced Calles into exile in 1936.

Callias (5th century BC) Athenian diplomat. He may have negotiated the so-called peace of Callias with Persia (c. 450), which established Persian and Athenian spheres of influence. He probably also helped negotiate the Thirty Years' Peace with Sparta (c. 446).

Callicrates (5th century BC) Athenian architect, chiefly famous for his collaboration with *Ictinus over the design of the *Parthenon. The temple of Athena Nike (450 BC) on the Athenian Acropolis was also his work.

calligraphy The art of handwriting. The term derives from the Greek words meaning beautiful writing. The aim of the calligrapher is to produce a script of intrinsic beauty appropriate to the subject matter, using the type of paper, ink, and writing instrument most suited to his purpose. In Europe, monks practiced calligraphy from the 6th century, at first using Roman capital letters called majuscules, but scripts using *minuscules were soon developed. From these arose the beautiful *italic and 19th-century copperplate scripts suitable for formal and commercial documents. In China, Japan, and Islamic countries calligraphy has a long history as a pure art form in which the artist combines the medium, the sentiment, and the format into an artistic composition.

Callimachus (c. 305–c. 240 BC) Greek poet and scholar. His many works, of which only fragments remain, include a catalogue of the Library of Alexandria, some fine epigrams, of which 64 survive in the *Greek Anthology,* and the *Aetia.*

Callimachus (late 5th century BC) Greek sculptor, reputedly the inventor of the Corinthian *capital and an innovator in the use of the drill in sculpture. Little is known of his work, but ancient critics accused him of overelaboration.

Calliope In Greek legend, goddess of epic poetry and the chief of the nine *Muses. She was loved by Apollo; her children included Hymen, Ialemus, and *Orpheus the musician.

Callot, Jacques (c. 1592–1635) French graphic artist, born in Nancy. In Italy (c. 1609–21) he worked for the Medici, principally on etchings of pageants. After returning to Nancy he made many etchings of beggars, hunchbacks, etc., which show his gift for caricature, but his best work is the *Miseries of War* series (1632–33) evoked by the Thirty Years' War.

callus A region of thickened hardened skin produced by constant friction or pressure. Skin calluses occur most commonly on the palms of the hands and soles of the feet. A bone callus is the mass of tissue that forms around the broken ends of a fractured bone, enabling normal healing and union. A similar tissue is produced by plants at the site of an injury.

Calmette, Albert Léon Charles (1863–1933) French bacteriologist. A pupil of Louis *Pasteur, he developed the vaccine Bacillus Calmette-Guérin (*see* BCG vaccine) in conjunction with Camille Guérin. He founded the Pasteur Institute at Lille, France (1896).

calomel. *See* laxatives.

calorie A unit of heat now being replaced by the joule. Formerly defined as the amount of heat required to raise the temperature of one gram of water through 1°C, the calorie is now defined as 4.1868 joules. The kilocalorie or Calorie (with a capital "C") is equal to 1000 calories and was formerly used to express the energy value of foods.

Calvary A hill beyond the walls of Jerusalem where Christ was crucified. The Hebrew name is Golgotha (a skull). Its precise location is unknown. Traditionally it has been taken as the spot, now within the Church of the Holy Sepulcher, where St Helena discovered a supposed relic of the Cross in 327 AD. Some have suggested that it was outside Jerusalem's Damascus Gate.

Calvin, John (1509–64) French Protestant reformer, founder of *Calvinism. He studied law and theology and in the early 1530s openly sided with Protestantism. Settling in Basle in 1536, he published the first edition of his influential *Institutes*. During a visit to Geneva in 1536 he met the Protestant reformer Guillaume *Farel, who persuaded him to stay. Their efforts to organize the Reformation in the city resulted in their exile (1538). Calvin then preached in Strasbourg, where he met other reformers, notably *Bucer. He was invited back to Geneva in 1541, remaining there as its virtual dictator until his death. He sought to shape Geneva as a model community where every citizen came under the legal discipline of the Church.

Calvin, Melvin (1911–) US biochemist, who determined the series of reactions by which green plants use carbon dioxide to manufacture starch during *photosynthesis. Calvin was awarded a Nobel Prize in 1961.

Calvinism The Christian teaching of John *Calvin, much of it published in his work *The Institutes*. On it are based the doctrines of most of the reformed Churches that are not Lutheran, including the state Churches of Holland and Scotland (*see* Presbyterianism), various Nonconformist Churches, and some Churches in North America and Germany. Calvin's systematic writings stress the transcendant power of God and man's total depravity outside God's redeeming grace. Like Luther, Calvin believed that faith must be based on Scripture alone, that justification (that is, righteousness in God's eyes) could only be achieved through faith, and that men lacked free will. Unlike Luther, he believed that some people, the elect, were predestined for salvation and the rest for damnation and also that the church should control the state.

calx. *See* phlogiston theory.

calypso A type of popular song that originated in Trinidad. The text, often containing nonsense syllables, is sung rapidly and without regard for natural word stress. Accompanied by guitars and percussion, the calypso usually satirizes local events. Calypso melodies have been popularized by steel bands playing on tuned oil drums.

calypso orchid A rare and highly prized perennial orchid, *Calypso bulbosa*, also known as the fairy slipper orchid, native to cold N temperate regions; 3–4 in (8–10 cm) high, it has a solitary pink flower with brown, purple, and yellow markings and a single crinkled dark-green leaf.

Camagüey 21 25N 77 55W A city in E central Cuba. Founded in the 16th century, it has many old buildings, including the cathedral (1617). It is the center of an area important for cattle raising and sugar. Population (1989 est): 279,000.

Camargue, la The Rhône delta area in S France, between the river channels of the Grand Rhône and the Petit Rhône. Once chiefly marshy, much land reclamation has occurred and cattle, especially bulls for the bullring, and horses are reared. Rice is also grown here. Area: about 215 sq mi (560 sq km).

Cambacérès, Jean Jacques Régis, Duc de (1753–1824) French lawyer. During the French Revolution he was a member of the National Convention and then of the Committee of Public Safety. Under Napoleon, he served as arch chancellor of the empire. His chief interest was in the development of principles of revolutionary jurisprudence and he contributed to the *Code Napoléon*.

cambium A layer of cells in woody plants that is responsible for producing additional *xylem and *phloem tissue, bringing about an increase in girth. The cambium also produces bark and protective callus tissue after injury. *See also* meristem.

Cambodia A country in SE Asia, in the Indochina peninsula on the Gulf of Thailand. It consists mainly of an alluvial plain drained by the Mekong River and enclosed by mountains. Most of the inhabitants are Khmers, with minorities of Vietnamese and Chinese. *Economy*: predominantly agricultural, the staple crop being rice. Production has been severely reduced by the recent political upheavals and there is little industry. Cambodia is rich in forests, and phosphates, gemstones, and gold are produced: there are also known quantities of unexploited iron ore and manganese. There is an abundance of freshwater fish. Exports include rubber and dried fish. *History*: the kingdom of Funan (1st–6th centuries AD) was conquered by the Buddhist *Khmers. Following the collapse of their empire in the 15th century, Cambodia was prey to attack from the Thais and Vietnamese until 1863, when it became a French protectorate. In 1887 it became part of the Union of *Indochina. In 1949 it achieved self-government as a member of the French Union, gaining full independence in 1953. Under Prince *Sihanouk Cambodia was used as a base by North Vietnamese (communist) forces (*see* Vietnam War) and, following the failure of his attempts to negotiate their withdrawal, he was deposed (1970) by Gen. Lon Nol, who was supported by the US. Shortly afterward US and South Vietnamese troops invaded the renamed Khmer Republic to support Lon Nol against the communist Khmer Rouge guerrillas. In the ensuing civil war the Khmer Rouge was finally victorious in 1974 and, after the formation of a new constitution in 1975, the Khmer Republic became Democratic Kampuchea. The Khmer Rouge government, led by Pol Pot, attempted to reshape the country's economy on cooperative lines by driving the Cambodians out of the towns, depriving them of their property, and killing some three million of the aged, sick, or dissenting. Although Pol Pot's regime maintained an uneasy relationship with the Chinese, China failed to come to its aid when the Vietnamese invaded the country on Dec 25, 1978. Pol Pot was forced from power, and a People's Revolutionary Council was set up under the pro-Vietnamese Heng Samrin. The retreating Khmer Rouge burned existing rice stocks and devastated the land, leaving behind them a trail of famine and disease, which was only partly mitigated by the efforts of international charities. Samrin was succeeded as leader by Pen Sovran. Border warfare with Vietnamese guerrillas was followed by a Vietnamese invasion in 1979. A rebel communist government backed by Hanoi was set up in opposition to Pol Pot's forces, and Cambodia was named the People's Republic of Kampuchea. Guerrilla attacks by the Khmer Rouge and other Cambodian resistance groups (both communist and anticommunist) sought to unseat the Hanoi government. Soviet military backing sustained the Vietnamese regime in Phnom Penh, the capital, whereas China supported the Cambodian resistance. In 1982 a coalition government-in-exile was formed by Sihanouk (president), Khieu Samphan, and Son Sann, former premier. In 1989, Vietnam stopped its support, leaving the former Hanoi-backed government defenseless. The UN Security Council provided a peacekeeping force in 1990. A 1991 treaty, signed by the various factions in Cambodia, as it was again known, provided for a representative ruling Supreme Council of 12 members. In 1993 elections held under UN supervision, parties supporting Sihanouk won control of the government, and he assumed the throne as king, with his son as first premier. Official language: Khmer; French is widely spoken. Official currency: riel of 100 sen. Area: 71,000 sq mi (181,000 sq km). Population (1990 est): 6,993,000. Capital and main port: Phnom Penh.

Cambrai (ancient name: Camaracum) 50 10N 3 14E A city in NE France, in the Nord department. Industries include textiles (cambric was first made here in the 16th century) and sugar refining. The town suffered damage in both World Wars. Population (1982): 37,000.

Cambrian Mountains A mountain system in Wales, extending N–S and including Snowdonia, Plynlimon, and the Black Mountains.

Cambrian period The earliest geological period of the *Paleozoic era. It began about 590 million years ago and lasted at least 70 million years, lying between the Precambrian and Ordovician periods. Rocks of this period are the first to contain an abundance of fossils, including primitive representatives of most invertebrates living today. Trilobites were very abundant, as well as brachiopods and gastropods. The Cambrian period is divided into Lower, Middle, and Upper.

Cambridge 52 12N 0 07E A city in E England, the administrative center of Cambridgeshire on the River Cam (*or* Granta). The city is dominated by its university (*see* Cambridge, University of). Cambridge has electronics and printing industries and manufactures scientific instruments. It is also an important market center. Its many historic university buildings and Bridge of Sighs make it a popular tourist center. Population (1989): 101,000.

Cambridge 42 22N 71 06W A city in Massachusetts, on the Charles River opposite Boston. A famous educational center, it is the site of Harvard University (1636) and the Massachusetts Institute of Technology (MIT). The first printing press in America was set up here (1639) and at the start of the American Revolution, George Washington established his headquarters (1775–76) in Craigie House, later the home of Longfellow. Industries include printing and publishing. Population (1990): 95,802.

Cambridge, University of One of the oldest universities in Europe. It is organized as a federation of colleges, the oldest of which, Peterhouse, dates from 1284. Kings College was founded in 1441 and its chapel is a distinctive landmark. The largest college, Trinity, was founded by Henry VIII in 1546. The first college for women, Girton, opened in 1869 (although it was not initially located at Cambridge).

Cambridge Platonists A group of 17th-century English philosophers and theologians under the leadership of Benjamin Whichcote (1609–83). Philosophically they took their ideas from *Platonism and *Neoplatonism and opposed the rationalism of *Hobbes. In religion they favored mysticism and religious tolerance and attempted to reconcile Christianity with the new ideas being produced by the rapid scientific advances made in their time. They believed in an absolute standard of morality based on reason that is independent of the divine will of God.

Cambridgeshire A county of E England. It consists chiefly of low-lying fenland, crossed by the Ouse and Nene Rivers. It is predominantly agricultural, the main products being cereals, fruit, and vegetables. Area: 1316 sq mi (3409 sq km). Population (1987): 642,000. Administrative center: Cambridge.

Cambyses II King of Persia (529–22 BC) of the Achemenian dynasty; the son of *Cyrus the Great. He conquered Egypt (525), where, according to the Greek historian Herodotus, his tyrannical disrespect for native religion caused resentment. He campaigned unsuccessfully against Carthage and Ethiopia. Cambyses died, perhaps a suicide, during a revolt against his rule.

Camden 39 52N 75 07W A city in New Jersey on the Delaware River. The former home of Walt Whitman, it manufactures textiles and radio and television appliances. Population (1990): 87,492.

Camden, Battle of (August 16, 1780) A battle of the *American Revolution. In an attempt to take the British stronghold at Camden, South Carolina, after the fall of *Charleston, the Americans were surprised and routed by Lord *Cornwallis. The Americans retreated in disorder.

camel A hoofed □mammal belonging to the genus *Camelus* (2 species). Camels are now almost entirely domesticated and are used for riding, as pack animals, and as a source of milk, meat, wool, and hides. The one-humped Arabian camel (*C. dromedarius*) is about 7 ft (2 m) high at the shoulder and generally brown in color. The dromedary is a long-legged breed of Arabian camel, developed for racing and riding. The heavier two-humped Bactrian camel (*C. bactrianus*) is native to central Asian steppes, where wild herds still exist.

Adapted to living in sandy deserts, camels can close their nostrils, have heavy protective eyelashes, hairy ear openings, and horny knee pads for kneeling. Although unable to store water, camels can replace rapidly the water that is lost from the body, drinking up to 54 qts (60 l) of water at a time. Fat is stored in the hump, which shrinks when food is scarce. Family: *Camelidae*; order: *Artiodactyla*.

Camellia A genus of evergreen shrubs and trees (80–100 species) native to India, China, and Japan. Several species are widely grown as ornamentals. The best known, *C. japonica*, grows to a height of 30 ft (9 m) and has attractive glossy oval leaves. The popular double-flowered varieties have overlapping petals ranging from white to pink and red. The genus also includes the *tea plant. Family: *Theaceae*.

Camelot The legendary capital of King Arthur's kingdom (*see* Arthurian legend). Cadbury Camp, near Yeovil, and Winchester are among the places identified with it.

Camembert 48 52N 0 10E A village in NW France, in the Orme department. Camembert is famous for the creamy cheese named for it.

cameo A semiprecious stone ornamented with a portrait or figures carved in relief. Cameo makers achieved brilliant skills during the Renaissance, when collectors paid high prices for modern gems, as well as for the earliest Hellenistic and Roman examples.

camera, photographic A device for producing a photographic image. Basically, a camera consists of a light-tight box containing a lens and light-sensitive *film or plate. The light image coming through the lens is brought into focus on the film by adjusting the distance between the film and the lens. A picture is taken by opening the shutter over the lens for a certain period to expose the film. The exposure time is determined by the shutter speed. The diameter of the opening (aperture) in front of the lens is measured by its *f-number. Shutter speed and lens aperture determine the light available to record the image on the film. In the simplest cameras they are fixed, but more sophisticated cameras have variable settings. Sometimes the aperture or the shutter speed can be controlled automatically by an *exposure meter. *See also* cinematography.

camera, television A camera for the instantaneous transmission of moving pictures. The scene to be televised is focused onto a screen in the electronic camera tube. This optical image is scanned in horizontal lines, fast enough to appear as a continuous moving picture to the human eye; in most cameras, the image is scanned 25–30 times per second. The intensity of light at each point of the image is converted to an electrical signal, which is amplified before being transmitted together with the sound and synchronization signals. *See also* television.

CAMELOT *A 19th-century romantic rendering of Arthur's capital by Gustave Doré in his illustrations of Tennyson's* Idylls.

Cameron, Julia Margaret (1815–79) British photographer, born in Calcutta. In England, she devoted herself chiefly to spiritually penetrating portrait photographs, notably of her friends Tennyson, Longfellow, Charles Darwin, and Ellen Terry. She died in Ceylon.

Cameroon, Republic of (French name: République Unie du Cameroun) A country in West Africa, on the Gulf of Guinea. Hot swampy coastal plains rise to forested plateaus in the center and to the Adamwa Highlands in the N. The main river is the Sanaga. The population consists of over a hundred different ethnic groups, the most numerous being the Bamileke. *Economy*: chiefly subsistence agriculture with varied crops; the main cash crop is coffee. Hydro-electricity is a valuable source of power and is used for aluminum smelting, which is the chief industry. Oil was discovered in 1973 and is responsible for half of the country's revenue. *History*: the area was largely uninhabited when the coast was explored by the Portuguese and others in the 15th and 16th centuries. In 1884 The German protectorate of Kamerun was established and after World War I it was divided into the French and British Cameroons, which were governed from 1922 under League of Nations mandate and from 1946 as UN trust territories. The French Cameroons attained self-government in 1957 and became independent as the Federal Republic of the Cameroon in 1960 with Ahmadou Ahidjo as its first president (1960–82). After a plebiscite in the British Cameroons in 1961, the S joined Cameroon and the N became part of Nigeria. The country is now governed on a one-party basis by the Cameroon National Union. Political and economic stability for the most part characterized the country through the 1980s, but by 1991 discontent forced President Biya to allow opposition parties and to promise revision of the constitution. In 1992 elections, boycotted by some opposition parties, Biya was reelected. President: Paul Biya. Official languages: French and English. Official currency: CFA (Communauté financière africaine) franc of 100 centimes. Area: 183,530 sq mi (475,442 sq km). Population (1990 est): 11,109,000. Capital: Yaoundé. Main port: Doula.

Camisards Protestants in the Bas-Languedoc and Cévennes regions of S France who in 1702 rebelled against the persecution of Protestants by Louis XIV. They sacked and burned churches and killed or expelled priests. The government responded with executions and the burning of villages. By 1705 the revolt was virtually over, although sporadic fighting continued until 1710.

Camões, Luís de (c. 1524–80) Portuguese poet and soldier of fortune. Few biographical facts about him are certain. After 1553 he spent 17 years wandering in the Portuguese colonies in India and China, suffering shipwreck and returning destitute to Lisbon. In 1572 he published *The Lusiads*, a national epic celebrating the 1497 voyage of Vasco da Gama and the Portuguese empire. His lyrical poetry, largely ignored in his own lifetime and published posthumously in 1595, is now greatly admired.

camomile (*or* chamomile) A perennial scented European herb, *Anthemis nobilis* (or *Chamemelum nobile*). The spreading much-branched stems (4–12 in [10–30 cm] in length) carry long-stalked daisylike flowers. An infusion of the flowers (camomile tea) is used as a general tonic. Family: *Compositae* (daisy family).

Camorra A criminal secret society, at its height in 19th-century Naples. The Bourbon kings used its members in the police, army, and civil service but after Naples became part of a united Italy (1861) the society was suppressed and eventually many of its members fled to the US, where they were ultimately absorbed by the *Mafia.

Campagna di Roma A plain in W central Italy, surrounding Rome. Well populated and fertile during classical times, it subsequently deteriorated into malarial marshes. Recently drained, it now produces fruit and vegetables for Rome. Area: about 800 sq mi (2000 sq km).

Campanella, Roy (1921–93) US baseball catcher. He played for the Brooklyn Dodgers (1948–57) and was voted most valuable player (MVP) in the National League three times (1951, 1953, 1955). An automobile accident (1958) left him paralyzed. He was inducted into the Baseball Hall of Fame in 1969.

Campania A region in S Italy. It consists of a coastal plain along the Tyrrhenian Sea and mountains in the interior and the Sorrento Peninsula. Although most of the population is urban, centered mainly around Naples, agriculture is important. The region produces fruits, vegetables, vines, olives, walnuts, tobacco, and hemp. An industrial belt stretches from Caserta along the Bay of Naples. There are many modern coastal resorts. Area: 5249 sq mi (13,595 sq km). Population (1991): 5,625,575.

Campanula A genus of annual and perennial herbaceous plants (about 300 species), often known as bellflowers, native to N temperate zones (particularly the Mediterranean region) and tropical mountains. The plants grow to a height of 6–48 in (15–120 cm) and bear spikes of blue, pink, or white bell-shaped flowers. The fruit is a capsule. Some species (including *Canterbury bell) are grown as ornamentals. Family: *Campanulaceae*.

Campbell, Kim (Avril Phaedra Campbell) (1947–   ) Canadian political leader and prime minister (1993). A lawyer, she was elected to the House of Commons in 1988 and became an ally of Progressive Conservative prime minister Brian Mulroney. She became Canada's justice minister in 1990 and defense minister in 1993. She succeeded Mulroney as party leader and prime minister after he resigned. In the fall 1993 elections, with Canada's economy suffering badly, she and the party were decisively defeated by the Liberal Party, led by Jean *Chretien.

Campbell, Sir Malcolm (1885–1949) British automobile engineer, who broke the land-speed record nine times between 1924 and 1935 and the water-speed record three times between 1937 and 1939. He was the first man to exceed 300 mph (483 km per hour; 1935). His son **Donald Malcolm Campbell** (1921–67) also set land- and water-speed records, including 403.1 mph (648.7 kph) for a wheel-driven car (1964). He was killed in an attempt to break his own water-speed record.

Campbell, Mrs Patrick (Beatrice Stella Tanner; 1865–1940) British actress. Her stage career included notable successes in plays by Shakespeare and Ibsen. She was famous for her wit as well as her passionate acting and created the role of Eliza Doolittle in *Pygmalion*, written by her friend George Bernard Shaw.

Campbell-Bannerman, Sir Henry (1836–1908) British statesman; Liberal prime minister (1905–08), whose personal popularity held together a cabinet of great talent, including *Lloyd George, *Asquith, *Churchill, and *Haldane. Campbell-Bannerman's government passed the Trades Disputes Act (1906), which gave trades unionists greater freedom to strike.

Camp David The retreat in the Appalachian Mountains, Maryland, of the president of the US. It was here that Anwar Sadat and Menachem Begin agreed in September 1978, to a framework for establishing peace in the Middle East. This agreement, mediated by Pres. Jimmy Carter, laid the foundations for the peace treaty between Israel and Egypt signed in March 1979.

Campeche 19 50N 90 30W A port in SE Mexico, on the Gulf of Mexico. Founded in 1540, its importance as a port has declined since Spanish occupation and the shallow waters hinder further development. The chief exports include timber, fish, and sugar cane and it has a university (1954). Population (1985 est): 122,000.

camphor ($C_{10}H_{16}O$) A colorless crystalline *ketone. It is obtained from the wood of the camphor tree and also made synthetically; it is used in the manufacture of celluloid and as an insect repellent.

Campina Grande 7 15S 35 53W A city in NE Brazil, in Paraíba state. It is an important commercial and industrial center and has a university (1966). Population (1980): 222,230.

Campinas 22 54S 47 06W A city in S Brazil, in São Paulo state. It is a trading center for coffee and serves an extensive agricultural area. Population (1980 est): 566,517.

campion An annual or perennial flowering plant of the genus *Silene*. Campions are native to N temperate (particularly the Mediterranean) and cold regions, grow to a height of 12–40 in (30–100 cm), and bear pink, red, or white flowers. The fruit is a capsule. Species include moss campion (*S. acaulis*) and bladder campion (*S. vulgaris*). Family: *Caryophyllaceae*.

Campion, Edmund (1540–81) English Jesuit martyr. Ordained an Anglican deacon, but uneasy about his commitment, he was received into the Roman Catholic Church (1571), and became a Jesuit. After distributing copies of an anti-Anglican pamphlet in Oxford in 1581, he was convicted of treason and hanged, refusing to deny his faith. He was beatified in 1886. Feast Day: Dec 1.

Campo Formio, Treaty of (1797) The settlement between France and Austria signed at present-day Campoformido, NE Italy, following Austria's defeat by Napoleon during his first Italian campaign. Austria gained Venice, thus ending Venetian independence, and ceded its Belgian provinces to France.

Campo Grande 20 24S 54 35W A city in SW Brazil, the capital of Mato Grosso do Sul state situated on the São Paulo–Corumbá railroad. Its university was founded in 1970. Population (1980): 282,845.

Campos 21 40S 41 21W A city in E Brazil, in Rio de Janeiro state. The chief products are cacao, sugar cane, and *aguardiente* (a form of brandy). Population (1980): 174,218.

Cam Ranh Bay 11 53N 109 10E An inlet of the South China Sea, on the coast of central S Vietnam. About 12 mi (20 km) wide and almost enclosed by two peninsulas, it makes an excellent harbor: the bay and the N peninsula were used as a vast US military, naval, and air base during the Vietnam War.

camshaft A rotating shaft equipped with a series of eccentric circular or pear-shaped disks (cams). These enable irregular or intermittent motion to be transferred to "followers" set perpendicularly to the camshaft, which move up and down as the cams rotate. Camshafts thus convert rotary motion into reciprocating motion and are used to control the valves in a four-stroke *internal-combustion engine. An **overhead camshaft** is set in the cylinder head and operates the valves directly, but in many engines the camshaft is at the base of the engine and operates the valves through pushrods.

Camus, Albert (1913–60) French novelist, an exponent of *existentialism. Born in poverty in Algiers, he won a school scholarship and studied philosophy as a university undergraduate. During World War II he edited *Combat*, a journal of the French Resistance. He published several collections of essays and plays, and three novels, notably *The Outsider* (1942), *The Plague* (1947), and *The Rebel* (1953); *The Rebel* provoked a fierce intellectual controversy with Jean-Paul *Sartre. In 1957 he won the Nobel Prize. He was killed in a car accident.

Canaan An area roughly corresponding to modern Israel, W Jordan, and S Syria, known from the Bible as the land promised by God to the Israelites before the Exodus. As early as the 18th century BC Canaan was mentioned in a document from *Mari as a political entity, probably comprising loosely allied city states. Excavations at *Jericho, Hazor, and elsewhere have revealed sophisticated Bronze Age cultures prior to the Hebrew settlement (c. 1200 BC).

Canada A country occupying the entire N half of the North American continent (except for Alaska). More than half of Canada consists of the Canadian Shield, at the center of which lies the Hudson Bay lowlands. The Western Cordillera, which is partly made up of the Coast Mountains and the Rocky Mountains, runs parallel to the Pacific coast and contains Mount *Logan, Canada's highest peak. Between the Rocky Mountains and the Canadian Shield lie the Interior Lowlands (consisting of prairies, plains, and the Mackenzie Lowlands). The SE region of Canada is dominated by the St Lawrence River and the

*Great Lakes and is the most densely populated area in the country. The N end of the Appalachian Mountains lies in the extreme SE. The N Arctic region of lakes and islands is one of the world's least populated areas. The population is mainly of British and French descent but there are several substantial minorities, including Germans, Italians, Ukrainians, and Dutch as well as the original inhabitants, the Indians and Inuit. *Economy*: both agriculture and industry are highly developed and the numerous manufacturing industries (concentrated mainly in Ontario and Quebec) include paper, iron and steel, motor vehicles, and food processing. As well as iron ore, the rich mineral resources include asbestos, nickel, zinc, molybdenum, uranium, silver, and gold. Oil production has increased considerably since the discovery of large oil fields in Alberta and an extensive pipeline system includes the Interprovincial Pipeline from Edmonton (Alberta) to Montreal (Quebec) and the Trans-Mountain pipeline from Edmonton to Vancouver. Natural gas is also produced and the Trans-Canada pipeline from the prairies to Montreal is the longest in the world. Agriculture, most of it highly mechanized, is important, with cereals in the Prairie Provinces and considerable fruit growing in British Columbia and Ontario. There is a valuable fishing industry; salmon, lobster, and cod are the most important catches. Forests cover over a third of the land and forestry has long been important to Canada's economy. The other traditional industry, the fur trade, continues, especially with mink farms and the trapping of beaver in the wild. Tourism is an important source of revenue, the majority of visitors coming from the US, with whom Canada has very close links. Almost two thirds of its trade is with the US. A 1988 agreement between the two countries providing for the gradual lifting of trade barriers was followed in 1993 by the more comprehensive *NAFTA pact. Main exports include motor vehicles, oil, wheat, wood pulp, and paper. *History*: there is evidence of Viking settlement in the NE of Canada around 1000 AD. In 1497 John Cabot reached the coasts of Newfoundland and Nova Scotia, the first of which was claimed for England in 1583. In 1534 Jacques Cartier explored the Gulf of St Lawrence. In 1605 the French established Port Royal in *Acadia and in 1608 Quebec. Known as New France, the latter settlement became a royal province in 1663. In the course of early explorations Champlain supported the *Huron Indians in their alliance with the northern tribes against the *Iroquois and later in the 17th century, when the Iroquois defeated the Huron, the French colony was almost completely destroyed. The fur trade was of extreme importance to all settlers and in 1670 the English set up the Hudson's Bay Company. By 1696 the French and English were in open conflict: in 1713 the Treaty of Utrecht gave Acadia, Newfoundland, and Hudson Bay to Britain and after the Seven Years' War, during which General Wolfe defeated the French under General Montcalm (1759), Canada was ceded to Britain by the Treaty of Paris (1763). In the late 18th century the United Empire Loyalists, fleeing from the American Revolution, settled in Canada. The ensuing ethnic tension led to the division of Quebec into French-speaking Lower Canada and English-speaking Upper Canada (1791), which were reunited again in 1841. By the British North America Act (1867) a confederation of Lower Canada (Quebec), Upper Canada (Ontario), Nova Scotia, and New Brunswick was established. In 1869 Rupert's Land was bought from the Hudson's Bay Company and the province of Manitoba was created from it in the following year. In 1871 British Columbia and in 1873 Prince Edward Island joined the confederation. Alberta and Saskatchewan were created from the NW Territories in 1905. Canada's present position as an independent constitutional monarchy in the Commonwealth of Nations was defined by the Statute of Westminster in 1931. The main political problem in recent years has been French-Canadian separatist agitation, led by the Quebec Liberation Front (Parti québecois). An accord, reached at Meech Lake, Quebec, in 1987, provided for recognition of Quebec as a distinct society, but it was not ratified by its deadline date in 1990. The Liberal Party, which had held office for 36 out of the previous 43 years (the last 11 under the leadership of Pierre *Trudeau), was ousted from power in 1979, by the Progressive Conservatives under Joseph Clark. In the 1980 elections, the Liberal Party under Trudeau was again returned to power. In 1982 a new constitution for Canada was signed by Elizabeth II. In 1984, Trudeau retired, and the Liberals lost the ensuing general election. Progressive Conservative Prime Minister Brian Mulroney formed a new government. He was reelected in 1988, and during his administration Canada was actively involved in the 1991 Persian Gulf War. His declining popularity and Canada's prolonged recession led him to announce his resignation early in 1993. He was succeeded briefly by his party's Kim Campbell, the country's first woman prime minister, but the Liberals triumphed in November 1993 elections, with Jean Chretien becoming prime minister. Official languages: English and French. Official currency: Canadian dollar of 100 cents. Area: 3,851,809 sq mi (9,976,169 sq km). Population (1990 est): 26,527,000. Capital: Ottawa. Main port: Montreal.

Canada balsam A transparent resin obtained from fir trees. It is used as an adhesive in optical instruments because its refractive index is similar to that of glass.

Canada goose A large *goose, *Branta canadensis*, that breeds in Canada and Alaska, migrating in flocks to the S US for the winter. It is 24–40 in (60–100 cm) long and has a black head and neck, white throat, dark-brown back, and pale underparts. The Canada goose has been introduced to parts of Europe as a sporting bird.

Canadian railroads Canada has two great transcontinental systems: the Canadian Pacific Limited (CP Rail) and the Canadian National Railroad (CN). The CP, running from Halifax on the Atlantic Ocean to Vancouver on the Pacific Ocean, was the first to be completed in 1885.

Canadian River A river in the S central US, flowing generally E from NE New Mexico to the Arkansas River in Oklahoma. Length: 906 mi (1458 km).

Canadian Shield. *See* shield.

Canaletto (Antonio Canal; 1697–1768) Venetian painter, famous for his views of Venice. He trained under his father, a theatrical-scenery painter, before visiting Rome (1719–20), where he designed opera sets. His popularity with English collectors led to a stay in England (1746–55), where he painted views of London. His early work, painted in the open air, was considerably freer than his later much more architectural painting, for which he used mechanical drawing instruments.

canals Man-made open water channels. They are divided into two categories: conveyance canals and navigation canals. The former carry water for irrigation, power, or drainage; the latter, to facilitate transportation, often connect two natural waterways. Canals have been dug from ancient times. The Grand Canal in China, started in 109 BC, was 620 mi (1000 km) long by the 8th century and carried 1.8 million tons of freight per annum. The completion of the Erie Canal (1825), linking the Great Lakes with the Hudson River, had an immense effect on the economy of New York and helped to open the Midwest. Some modern ship canals achieve spectacular reductions in voyage distances, especially the *Suez Canal (completed in 1869) and the *Panama Canal (1914). Others of considerable local importance include the Corinth Canal (1893), the Kiel Canal (1895), and the St Lawrence Seaway (1959) connecting the Great Lakes with the Atlantic Ocean. In canal construction, the availability of water is the primary concern. Conveyance canals are often narrow, have a high water velocity, and are earth lined and consequently are subject to erosion. Barge or ship canals are often completely lined with concrete or have concrete edges to prevent wave erosion. Variations in land or water level are common and *locks must be installed to conserve water and allow for the passage of vessels.

CANADA GOOSE *These birds pair for life and both male and female may incubate the eggs and care for the young.*

canary A small songbird, *Serinus canarius*, native to the Canary Islands, Madeira, and the Azores. Wild canaries have an olive-green plumage with yellow to gray underparts streaked with black. Popular as cagebirds since the 15th century, they have been selectively bred both for their musical song and attractive plumage—usually pure yellow but sometimes white or striped and occasionally with ornamental plumes. Subfamily: *Cardueline*; family: *Fringillidae* (finches).

canary grass An annual grass, *Phalaris canariensis*, 8–24 in (20–60 cm) high, native to the Canary Islands and N Africa and cultivated commercially in Europe for birdseed. The related reed canary grass (*P. arundinaceae*), which is widely distributed, is an important forage grass and grows 24–71 in (61–183 cm) high.

Canary Islands (Spanish name: Islas Canarias) A group of Spanish islands in the Atlantic Ocean, close to NW Africa. Since 1927 they have constituted two provinces named for their capitals of Las Palmas (including the islands of Fuerteventura, Gran Canaria, and Lanzarote) and Santa Cruz de Tenerife (including the islands of Ferro, Gomera, La Palma, and *Tenerife). The islands became Spanish possessions in the 15th century; the earliest inhabitants, the Guanches, are now extinct. The islands are of volcanic formation and, with the help of irrigation, fruits such as bananas and tomatoes are grown for export. Tourism is also a major source of revenue. Total area: 2807 sq mi (7270 sq km). Population (1991): 1,456,474.

canasta. *See* rummy games.

Canaveral, Cape (name from 1963 until 1973: Cape Kennedy) A barrier island in E central Florida separated from the mainland by lagoons. It is the site of operations by NASA at the Kennedy Space Center. The first flight to land on the moon was launched here in 1969. In 1973 Skylab, the first orbiting laboratory, was launched from here.

Canberra 35 15S 149 10E The capital of Australia, in the Australian Capital Territory on the Molonglo River. As a result of a competition in 1911, it was planned by the American architect Walter Burley Griffin, as the new federal capital, being formally inaugurated in 1927. The establishment of the National University in 1946 and the growth of government departments have led to sizable increases in population. Population (1991 est): 432,600.

cancan A boisterous dance originally performed in Parisian dance halls around 1830 as a solo or by groups of women. Tourists flocked to see its spectacular and indecorous high kicking. Famous cancan music includes the galop from Offenbach's *Orpheus in the Underworld*.

cancer A group of diseases caused by the abnormal and uncontrolled division of cells to form tumors that invade and destroy the tissues in which they arise. Such tumors are described as malignant: their cells spread through the bloodstream or lymphatic system or across body cavities to set up secondary tumors at other sites in the body (this spread is called metastasis). The cause of cancer remains uncertain, although it is known that exposure to certain substances (*see* carcinogen) will produce it. Cancer can arise in almost any tissue: in the western world the breasts, colon, lungs, bronchi, prostate gland, and stomach are common sites. Carcinomas are cancers arising in *epithelium; less common but more malignant are sarcomas——cancers of connective tissue (bone, cartilage, muscle, etc.). *Leukemia is a form of sarcoma affecting the bone marrow and other blood-forming tissues. Treatment, which varies with the type of cancer, includes *cytotoxic drugs, radiotherapy, and surgery.

Cancer (Latin: Crab) An inconspicuous constellation in the N sky, lying on the *zodiac between Leo and Gemini. It contains the star cluster *Praesepe.

candela (cd) The *SI unit of luminous intensity equal to the intensity of 1/600,000 square meter of the surface of a black body maintained at the freezing point of platinum.

Candela, Felix (1910–) Mexican architect and engineer, born in Spain. Employing a naturalistic modern style, his work is characterized by use of thin, prestressed concrete roofs, often spanning large distances, e.g. the Church of the Miraculous Virgin, Mexico City (1953).

Candia. *See* Iráklion.

Candida A genus of yeastlike fungi. They are typically spherical, ovoid, or elongated cells that reproduce by budding and spore formation; they do not undergo sexual reproduction. Several species, especially *C. albicans*, cause *candidiasis. Family: *Cryptococcaceae*; class: *Blastomycetes*.

candidiasis An infection caused by a species of yeast (*Candida albicans*). Popularly known as thrush, it affects the mouth and vagina most frequently; it may develop after treatment with certain antibiotics and with diseases (e.g.

leukemia) and drugs (e.g. steroids) that reduce the natural immunity of the body. The infection is cleared readily by such fungicides as nystatin.

Candlemas The Christian feast of the Purification of the Virgin Mary and the Presentation of Christ in the Temple (Luke 2.22–38), which is observed on Feb 2. It is so called because of the distribution of candles, symbolizing Christ's appearance as the "light of the world."

candytuft An annual or perennial flowering plant of the genus *Iberis* (about 30 species), native to S Europe and Asia and growing well in dry chalky soils. The stems (up to 6–20 in [15–50 cm] in height) bear white, pink, red, or blue flowers in flat-topped clusters. The fruits are pods containing winged seeds. Some species are grown as garden plants. Family: *Cruciferae*.

cane The stem of certain large grasses and of some palms. In some species it is hollow and jointed, e.g. *reeds (Phragmites* species), *bamboo (Bambusa* species), and *sugar cane; in others it is solid, e.g. *rattan and Malacca (Calamus* species) used for making furniture, walking sticks, etc.

Canea (Greek name: Khaniá) 35 31N 24 01E The capital of the Greek island of Crete, on the Gulf of Khaniá. Founded by Venetians in 1252, it is surrounded by massive Venetian walls. The island's main port with an important coastal trade, it exports leather, olives, olive oil, and fruit. Population (1981): 47,804.

cane rat An African *rodent belonging to the genus *Thryonomys* (2 species) common in reed beds. About 16 in (40 cm) long, cane rats have bright-orange incisor teeth, feeding on reeds, roots, bulbs, grasses, and sugar cane and can become a pest in plantations. Family: *Thryonomyidae*.

Canidae The dog family: a family of mammals belonging to the order *Carnivora*. It includes the dogs, wolves, jackals, coyote, and foxes.

Canis Major (Latin: great dog) A conspicuous constellation in the S sky near Orion. The brightest stars are *Sirius, the giants Adhara and Mirzam, and the supergiant Wezen.

Canis Minor (Latin: little dog) A small constellation in the S sky, lying near Canis Major and Orion. The brightest star is *Procyon.

canker 1. A disease of plants, especially fruit trees, caused by various fungi and bacteria. Cankers can be seen as dead, discolored, irregular, or cracked areas on the stem and branches; mechanical or climatic injury and attack by insect pests often predispose to infection. Treatment is by removal of the diseased parts. **2.** A chronic disease of horses' hooves, caused by continually wet conditions underfoot. The affected hooves become soft and swollen and eventually infected, causing inflammation and discharge. Treatment is by removing affected tissue and dressing with antibiotics. Prevention is by ensuring a dry stable floor. **3.** Inflammation of the outer ear affecting dogs, cats, and rabbits and causing irritation and itching. Treatment is by application of an antiseptic lotion or powder.

canna A genus of ornamental herbaceous plants (about 155 species), native to tropical and subtropical America. Up to 10 ft (3 m) high, they have spirally arranged leaves, which may be green, bronze, or purple, and terminal clusters of showy flowers, 6 in (15 cm) across and ranging from pale yellow to scarlet. Cannas are grown widely as bedding plants. Family: *Cannaceae*.

cannabis The resin (hashish) or crushed leaves and flowers (marijuana, "grass," or "pot") obtained from certain species of *hemp. The drug is eaten or inhaled and produces a variety of effects on the mind. These include euphoria, distortion of time sense, and increased awareness of sight, sound, and memory. Occasionally feelings of anxiety and apprehension are experienced. The long-term effects of cannabis use are obscure but may affect memory. Cannabis causes mild dependence but there is also a danger of progression to "hard" drugs, such as heroin. *See also* drug dependence; hallucinogen.

Canne, Battle of (216 BC) The battle, fought at the village of Canne in Apulia (SE Italy), in which *Hannibal and the Carthaginians killed almost 50,000 Romans. It is the worst Roman defeat on record.

Cannes 43 33N 7·00E A resort in S France, in the Alpes-Maritimes department on the French Riviera. Its development as a fashionable resort dates from the early 19th century. It has numerous hotels, sports facilities, boulevards, and casinos. The Île St Honorat contains the oldest monastery in W Europe. There are aircraft and textile industries and fruit and flowers are grown. Population (1975): 71,080.

cannibalism The practice of eating human flesh, either as food or for ritual or magical purposes. Extreme hunger has prompted modern occurrences among concentration-camp prisoners and airplane crash survivors. In ritual cannibalism certain parts of a defeated enemy may be eaten in order to absorb his strength and courage or to prevent his spirit taking revenge. In other cases (endocannibalism) it forms part of rituals performed at the death of a kinsman. The word is derived from the *Arawak term for the *Carib Indians, among whom it was common. Ritual cannibalism was practiced also by the New Zealand Maoris, the Fijian islanders, in Polynesia, in parts of Africa, in New Guinea, and among some North American Indian peoples.

canning The preservation of meat, fish, or fruit in vacuum-sealed airtight metal containers, which have been sterilized by heating followed by rapid cooling. Fruit keeps safely for at least one year, meat and vegetables for two, although in practice they may stay fresh for much longer, especially if kept cool. Canning was introduced in the 18th century and originally used pure *tin cans. Now cans are made of *tinplate. Canned foods may be reheated but do not need further cooking. *See also* food preservation.

Canning, George (1770–1827) British statesman; foreign secretary (1807–09, 1822–27) and Tory prime minister (1827). A member of Parliament from 1793, he became foreign secretary in 1807 but resigned in 1809. He again became foreign secretary and was partly responsible for the liberalization of Tory policies in the 1820s. He supported the revolt of Spain's American Colonies (1823) and the War of *Greek Independence (1825–27), before briefly becoming prime minister.

Canning Basin (former name: Desert Artesian Basin) An arid and largely unexplored sedimentary basin of NW Western Australia. It forms part of the *Great Sandy Desert and is covered chiefly by active longitudinal sand dunes. Area: about 150,000 sq mi (400,000 sq km).

Cannizzaro, Stanislao (1826–1910) Italian chemist, who resurrected *Avogadro's hypothesis, which had been neglected for 50 years, and used it to clarify the problem of representing compounds by formulas. He also discovered a method, called Cannizzaro's reaction, of converting an aldehyde into an acid and an alcohol.

cannon An early form of *artillery firearm used primarily until 1670 as a siege gun. A 14th-century invention (by the German monk, Berthold Schwarz), early cannon were made of wrought-iron rods welded together, covered with lead, and wrapped with iron bands. Some had a removable breech. Cast guns were made in England after 1500. They fired stones, cast-iron, and wrought-iron balls. Modern cannons include *guns, *mortars, and *howitzers.

Cannon, Joseph Gurney (1836–1926) US politician, Speaker of the House (1903–11). A lawyer in Illinois, he was elected to the US House of Representatives in 1872 and served 1873–91, 1893–1913, and 1915–23. During his term as Speaker, several attempts were made to break his arbitrary handling of appointments and other matters, but it was not until 1910 that fellow House members were able to pass resolutions that provided for more democratic House procedures.

Cannon, Walter Bradford (1871–1945) US physiologist, who pioneered the use of X-rays in physiological studies. By administering a suspension, or meal, of radio-opaque bismuth, the intestine could be revealed on X-rays. Cannon also investigated the body's reaction to stress, particularly the role of the sympathetic nervous system, and he identified an adrenaline-like chemical transmitter secreted by sympathetic nerve endings, which he termed "sympathin."

Cano, Juan Sebastián del (c. 1460–1526) Spanish navigator. He accompanied Magellan's expedition, taking command after Magellan's death. He successfully completed the voyage—the first around the world—in 1522. He died on a second expedition.

canoe A double-ended vessel designed mainly for propulsion by paddles, although certain kinds are equipped with sails (sailing canoe). The modern canoe is, typically, about 10–20 ft (3–7 m) long, and they are usually single or two seaters although Canadian canoes can accommodate up to four people. It is made of waterproofed canvas stretched over a ribbed frame or of aluminum, wood, or fiberglass. The modern canoe is modeled on native craft that have been in use in the Americas and in the Pacific for thousands of years. Some Pacific native war canoes, equipped with outriggers, could accommodate as many as 40 people. Other large canoes served, until the 20th century, as the chief means of transport among the islands of the Pacific. Depending on their age and location, native canoes were made by hollowing out logs or by stretching animal skins or birch bark over a ribbed frame. Canoes are much favored for recreation on lakes and rivers, being easy to maneuver and readily portable. *See also* kayak.

canonization In the Christian Church, the conferring of the status of *saint on a dead person. In the Roman Catholic Church this is done by a formal declaration of the pope after a long investigation of the person's suitability. Beatification, by which the Church permits the veneration of a person, with the title "Blessed," within a particular diocese, order, or other limited area, precedes canonization and depends on evidence of the person's exceptional virtue and authentic miracles. The Church then puts the case for the canonization and appoints someone, the *Promotor Fidei* (Latin: promoter of the faith, popularly known as the devil's advocate), to oppose it, and completes the process after proof of further miracles. In the early days of Christianity each area recognized its own saints, who were usually local martyrs. Ulrich of Augsburg (c. 890–973) is the first person known to have been canonized by a pope (in 993 AD). About 1170 Pope Alexander III decreed that only the Roman Catholic Church could add new names to the list of saints.

canon law The laws of Christian Churches, particularly the Roman Catholic, Anglican, and Orthodox Churches. They include regulations governing the clergy, the ecclesiastical courts, matters of worship and doctrine, and so on. The origins of canon law lie in the decrees of the various councils of bishops in the early Church, in authoritative pronouncements of important bishops, and in the Decretals, or letters having the force of law, of the Popes. In the 12th century many laws from these sources were included by Gratian (died c. 1179) in his *Decretum*, a collection of rules that the Roman Catholic Church recognized as authoritative. The *Decretum* in turn formed part of a later collection, the *Corpus

Juris Canonici, which in 1917 was revised to form the Codex Juris Canonici, the present Roman Catholic code of law.

Canopic jars Earthenware jars used in ancient Egypt in sets of four as containers for the internal organs removed from mummified bodies. Their lids, originally plain, were later modeled as the human, falcon, dog, and jackal heads of the four sons of the god *Horus.

Canopus A conspicuous luminous white supergiant, apparent magnitude −0.7 and 98 light years distant, that is the brightest star in the constellation Carina and the second brightest star in the sky.

Canossa A 10th-century castle near Reggio nel Emilia, in Italy. It is famous as the place in which Emperor Henry IV received absolution from Gregory VII in 1077 to end the *investiture controversy.

Canova, Antonio (1757–1822) Italian sculptor. One of the finest interpreters of the style of *neoclassicism, Canova worked first in Venice, in Rome after 1781, in Vienna, and in Paris, where he was employed by Napoleon. He achieved a wide reputation with his idealized marbles, usually of classical subjects. His best-known works are *The Tomb of Clement XIII* (1783–87; SS Apostoli, Rome) and *Pauline Borghese as Venus Victrix* (1805–07; Borghese Gallery, Rome).

Cánovas del Castillo, Antonio (1828–97) Spanish statesman and writer. Following the overthrow of the First Republic in 1874 and the restoration of the monarchy he created a system of government by two parties in rotation, which remained in force until 1923. He led the conservative party and was many times prime minister. He was assassinated by an anarchist.

Cantabrian Mountains (Spanish name: Cordillera Cantábrica) A mountain range in N Spain extending E–W along the Atlantic coast and rising to 8868 ft (2648 m).

Cantacuzino A family prominent in Romania from the 17th century. Descended from an imperial Byzantine family, the Cantacuzino settled in Moldavia and Walachia (present-day Romania) in the 16th century. Its members include **Şerban Cantacuzino** (d. 1688), who ruled Walachia from 1679 to 1688, and his nephew **Ştefan Cantacuzino**, who ruled from 1714 until ousted and executed in 1716. Serban's cousin **Dumitraşcu Cantacuzino** (1648–85) was an unpopular ruler of Moldavia (1673–75, 1684–85). A descendant **Constantin Cantacuzino** (1793–1877) governed Walachia (1848–49, 1854).

Canterbury 51 17N 1 05E A city in SE England, in Kent on the River Stour. The cathedral (11th–15th centuries), where Thomas *Becket was martyred in 1170, is the seat of the Archbishop and Primate of the Anglican Church. Canterbury is a tourist, market, and educational center; the University of Kent (1960) overlooks the city. Population (1981): 34,404.

Canterbury, Archbishop of The chief bishop of the *Anglican Communion of churches, called Primate of All England. The first of the line was St *Augustine of Canterbury. The current archbishop is Robert Alexander Kennedy Runcie (1921–   ; 102nd Archbishop 1980–   ).

Canterbury bell An annual or biennial flowering plant, *Campanula medium*, native to S Europe and frequently grown as a garden ornamental. The plant grows to a height of 30 in (70 cm) and bears spikes of pink, rose, lavender, blue, or white bell-shaped flowers, each 2 in (5 cm) or more long. Family: *Campanulaceae*.

Canterbury Plains A low-lying area of New Zealand, on E central South Island bordering on the Pacific Ocean. It is the most densely populated area of

South Island and is important agriculturally, especially for lamb raising and the production of cereals, fodder crops, and vegetables. Area: about 4000 sq mi (10,000 sq km). Chief city: Christchurch.

cantharidin. *See* Spanish fly.

Can Tho 10 03N 105 46E A port in S Vietnam, on the Mekong delta. It is the industrial center of an important rice-growing area, with a university (1956). Population (1989 est): 208,500.

Canton (Chinese names: Guangzhou *or* Kuang-chou) 23 08N 113 20E A port in S China, the capital of Guangdong province on the Zhu Jiang (Pearl River) delta. Densely populated, it is the commercial and industrial center of S China and attracts much of the country's foreign trade through its biannual trade fair. It has a university and various colleges. Its industries include steel, ship building, paper, textiles, and the manufacture of machinery and chemicals. *History*: Chinese since the 3rd century BC, it was the first Chinese city to trade regularly with Europeans (from the 16th century), having long traded with Hindus and Arabs, and was the focus of the first Opium War (1839–42). The birthplace of *Sun Yat-sen, it was the starting point of the revolution against the Qing (1911). His Guomindang (Nationalist) government was based here in the early 1920s. Canton was occupied by Japan (1938–45). Population (1990): 2,914,281.

Canton 40 48N 81 23W A city in NE Ohio. An important industrial center, it has a large iron and steel industry. It was the home of President McKinley. Population (1990): 84,161.

Canton and Enderbury Two uninhabited coral atolls in the S Pacific Ocean, in the Phoenix Islands. Claims between the US and the UK were settled in 1939, when they agreed to exercise joint control over the islands for 50 years. Canton was used as an international airport for transpacific flights until the advent of long-range jets.

Cantonese. *See* Chinese.

Cantor, Eddie (Edward Israel Iskowitz; 1892–1964) US entertainer. He began in vaudeville and then appeared in Ziegfield's *Follies* (1916–19) and the stage shows *Kid Boots* (1923–26), *Whoopee* (1928), and *Banjo Eyes* (1941). A comedian and singer, he had his own radio show in the 1930s, appeared in the films *Roman Scandals* (1933) and *Forty Little Mothers* (1940), and entertained on television's *Colgate Comedy Hour* (1950–53).

Cantor, Georg (1845–1918) Russian mathematician, born in St Petersburg. Cantor's family moved in 1856 to Germany, where he spent the rest of his life. He was the first mathematician to set the concept of infinity on a rigorous mathematical foundation. He defined different types of infinity for the set of integers, the set of real numbers, etc., each type being represented by a number known as a transfinite number. His ideas created great controversy and were viciously attacked, by Leopold Kronecker (1823–91) in particular. Cantor broke down in 1884 under the strain and died in a mental asylum.

Canute II (*or* Cnut; c. 994–1035) Danish King of England after defeating *Edmund Ironside (1016). He became King of Denmark (1019) and of Norway (1028). He defended England from Viking attacks (1017, 1026, 1028) and subjected Malcolm II of Scotland (1028). He went on a pilgrimage to Rome in 1027 to attend the coronation of Emperor *Conrad II. According to legend, he proved to flatterers the limits of his powers by demonstrating his inability to induce the waves to recede.

canyon A deep steep-sided gorge found mainly in arid and semiarid areas, the depth of which considerably exceeds its width. Canyons are often formed by rapidly eroding rivers down-cutting into soft rock in arid areas. The lack of rainfall hinders weathering and maintains the steep slope; where hard- and soft-rock bands occur, a stepped formation results. The largest and best-known canyon is the *Grand Canyon.

Canyon Lands National Park A national park in SE Utah including the area surrounding the junction of the Green and Colorado rivers. Established in 1964, it is noted for its unusual rock formations and mesas. Area: 527 sq mi (1,365 sq km).

Cao Chan (*or* Zao Zhan; ?1715–63) Chinese novelist, famous for the semi-autobiographical *Dream of the Red Chamber*, a novel written in the last years of his life. It combines a tragic love story with a description of the downfall of a great Chinese family. It mirrors the fortunes of Cao Chan's own family, which held the hereditary office of commissioner of imperial textiles in Nanking.

Capablanca y Graupera, José Raúl (1888–1942) Cuban chess player, who was world champion from 1921 to 1927. Extraordinarily gifted, he played a fast-paced game with exceptional insight. He worked as a diplomat and wrote books on chess, including *Chess Fundamentals* (1922).

capacitance The ability of an electrical component to store charge. It is measured in *farads and defined as the ratio of the stored charge in coulombs to the voltage drop across the component. Capacitance is one of the factors that control the frequency response of circuits and components to alternating currents.

capacitor An electrical component (formerly called a condenser), with an appreciable *capacitance. It consists of two conductor or semiconductor plates separated by a *dielectric. The value of the capacitance is a function of the geometry and the electrical properties of the dielectric and often also of the operating voltage and the frequency. Variable capacitors are used for tuning electronic circuits.

Cape Breton Island An island in SE Canada, in Nova Scotia, separated from the mainland by the Strait of Canso. Hilly and forested, it encloses tidal salt lakes. Coal, steel, fishing, and tourism are important. It was ceded to Britain by the French (1763). Area: 3975 sq mi (10,280 sq km).

Cape Cod A sandy peninsula in Massachusetts, between Cape Cod Bay and the Atlantic Ocean. A popular summer resort area, it also produces cranberries and asparagus. The **Cape Cod National Seashore Recreational Area** is an area on the Atlantic Ocean side of Cape Cod. It was established in 1961 to preserve the natural seashore and wildlife on the outer shores of Cape Cod. Length: 65 mi (105 km).

Cape Fear River A river rising in N central North Carolina and flowing SE to Wilmington where it empties into the Atlantic Ocean at Cape Fear. Length: 202 mi (326 km).

Cape Frontier Wars (1779–1878) The wars fought intermittently in S Africa between the white settlers moving E from the Cape and the *Xhosa people who had settled in the E Cape area. Conflict between the two groups arose mainly over land and cattle. The Xhosa had been driven back along the coast by the colonists beyond the Keiskamma River by 1819 and in 1846 the land between the Fish and the Keiskamma Rivers was annexed as British Kaffraria. The final war was in 1877–78, in which the Xhosa were defeated and their lands absorbed into the Cape Colony.

Cape Horn (Spanish name: Cabo de Hornes) The most southerly point in South America, at the S end of Horn Island, Chile. It is notorious for its stormy weather.

Capella A conspicuous yellow giant, apparent magnitude 0.1 and 45 light years distant, that is the brightest star in the constellation Auriga. It is a triple star.

Cape of Good Hope A headland in South Africa, in the SW extremity of Cape Province to which it gave its official name of Cape of Good Hope Province. It was discovered (1488) by Dias, who named it the Cape of Storms.

Cape Province (official name: Cape of Good Hope Province; Afrikaans name: Kaapprovinsie) The largest province in South Africa, in the extreme S of the African continent. It consists chiefly of plateaus separated by mountain ranges. In the diversified economy agriculture is important. The SW produces most of South Africa's fruit and vegetables for export and has many vineyards; sheep and cattle rearing is extensive and wheat and alfalfa are grown. Diamonds and copper are the chief minerals, others being asbestos, manganese, and iron ore. Industries include food processing and canning, textiles, and motor-vehicle production. *History*: first settled by the Dutch (1652), it was ceded to Britain in 1814, becoming known as the Cape Colony. The discovery of diamonds in Griqualand West led to its annexation to the Cape Colony (1871). In 1910 the colony became a province in the Union of South Africa. Area: 400,762 sq mi (646,332 sq km). Population (1991): 5,514,420.

caper A bramble-like spiny shrub, *Capparis spinosa*, native to drier regions of S Europe. The pickled flower buds are the capers used in flavoring. The fruit is a berry. Family: *Capparidaceae*.

capercaillie The largest European *grouse, *Tetrao urogallus*, of Eurasian coniferous forests, where it feeds on pine buds and needles. The male, almost 40 in (100 cm) long, is black with a blue-green gloss and red wattles above the eyes. The smaller female is brown with black and white markings.

Capernaum 32 53N 35 34E An ancient town in N Israel, on the N shore of the Sea of Galilee. It is the site of many biblical events, and a synagogue dating from about 200 AD has been excavated.

Capetians The ruling dynasty of France from 987 to 1328. It was founded by *Hugh Capet, who became King of France in 987, replacing the Carolingians. Successive kings, notably *Philip II Augustus and *Louis IX, expanded their own authority and the territory under their control (originally comprising little more than the Île-de-France). The Capetians established a royal bureaucracy, from which the *parlements developed, and were the first kings to summon the *States General.

Cape Town (Afrikaans name: Kaapstad) 33 56S 18 28E The legislative capital of South Africa and capital of Cape Province, on the Atlantic Ocean. Founded by Jan van Riebeeck in 1652 as a supply post for the Dutch East India Company, it is the oldest white settlement in South Africa. The famous National Botanical Gardens at Kirstenbosch were part of the home of Cecil Rhodes. Cape Town castle (17th century) is the oldest building in South Africa; the university was established in 1918 and has an observatory. Cape Town is a major port, with modern dockyard facilities, and is an important commercial and industrial city. Its industries include oil refining, chemicals, motor vehicles, and textiles. Population (1991): 776,617.

Cape Verde, Republic of (Portuguese name: Cabo Verde) A country occupying an archipelago in the N Atlantic Ocean, off the coast of West Africa. It consists of 10 islands and five islets, most of which are mountainous. The majority of the population is of mixed African and European descent. *Economy*: mainly subsistence agriculture. Ship refueling is important and fishing has considerable potential for development; fish and fish products are the main exports.

History: the Cape Verde Islands were settled by the Portuguese in the mid-15th century, becoming a Portuguese colony in the 19th century and gaining full independence in 1975. Plans for union with Guinea-Bissau on the African coast still meet with opposition in certain quarters, although there is already a considerable amount of cooperation. The one-party state was abolished in 1990, when the first free presidential elections were held. Aristides Pereira, president since independence, was defeated. A nonaligned nation, Cape Verde has become a center for international conferences of heads of government. President: Antonio Mascarenhas Monteiro. Official language: Portuguese. Official currency: Cape Verdean escudo of 100 centavos. Area: 1557 sq mi (4033 sq km). Population (1990 est): 375,000. Capital: Praia. Main port: Mindelo.

CAPE TOWN *The city is noted for its scenic beauty set against Table Mountain, 3550 ft (1082 m) high.*

Cape York Peninsula The most northerly part of Australia, in Queensland, situated between the Gulf of Carpentaria and the Coral Sea. It is mainly low-lying grass and scrubland in the W, rising to the Great Dividing Range in the E and contains large area that are uninhabited, although bauxite mining is important.

Cap Haïtien (*or* Le Cap) 19 47N 72 17W A port in N Haiti, on the Atlantic Ocean. The chief exports are coffee and sugar and it is the site of one of the world's largest sisal plantations. Population (1992 est): 92,000.

capillary In anatomy, a minute thin-walled blood vessel (0.005–0.02 mm diameter), networks of which connect the smallest *arteries with the smallest *veins. Nutrients and oxygen diffuse across the capillary walls to nourish the tissues. Waste products and carbon dioxide return from the tissues to the capillary blood.

capital An element of architecture used to join a column to the part of the building it supports. In classical architecture there are five orders of columns with strictly defined types of capital, of varying degrees of ornateness, for each (*see* orders of architecture). In romanesque and gothic architecture, the rules became less strict and the type of capital used depended mainly on the skill and taste of the masons involved. Thus the capital could vary from the plain (called a cushion capital) to the highly ornate, decorated with carvings of foliage, people, and animals.

capitalism An economic and political system that developed following the industrial revolution. Essential features of the system are uncontrolled free markets, based on the profit motive, and unrestricted ownership of the means of production (capital). If the system is allowed to develop without restriction it has certain undesirable attributes (*see* laissez-faire). This has led Western countries to restrict capitalism by the establishment of mixed economies, characterized by substantial government regulation. Communist countries have followed the doctrines of Karl Marx (*see* Marxism), who maintained that capitalism contains the seeds of its own destruction, and have abolished capitalism and the free-market system, replacing them with central direction of the economy by the government.

capital levy. *See* wealth.

capital punishment The punishment by death of a convicted criminal. Although execution by hanging was a sentence often applied by US courts during the 19th century and execution by the electric chair, the firing squad, and the gas chamber was common in the early 20th century, capital punishment has been infrequently applied since the Supreme Court decision of *Furman* v. *Georgia* (1967). Its questionable effectiveness as a deterrent to serious crimes such as murder, the apparent arbitrariness of its application, and the possibility that an innocent person might be put to death have given rise to serious legal and moral questions. Since 1977, however, with a reversal of the earlier Supreme Court decision, the use of capital punishment has been a matter left up to the individual states. Great Britain, which as late as the 18th century had used beheading or hanging for the punishment of many crimes, such as forgery and petty theft, abolished public execution in 1868. In 1957 the application of the death penalty in Great Britain was severely restricted, and in 1965 it was banned except in cases of treason and piracy. Many countries of Western Europe have enacted similar laws abolishing the use of capital punishment. It is still, however, applied in many countries in other parts of the world.

Capitol Reef National Park A national park in S central Utah, including an area along the Fremont River. Established in 1971, it had been a national monument since 1937. There are rock formations, cliffs, and gorges in many different colors. The reefs along the Fremont River resemble domes and are topped by white rock. Area: 60 sq mi (156 sq km).

capitulary Legal and administrative instruments of the *Carolingian kings, arranged in *capitula* (articles). These documents are concerned with many topics, both secular and ecclesiastical, including law and order, the regulation of trade, and the administration of royal estates. Although originals do not survive, copies amply illustrate the scope and power of early Carolingian administration.

Capone, Al (1899–1947) US gangster, born in Italy. He dominated the Chicago underworld of organized crime in the late 1920s. He was particularly successful in the illegal liquor traffic during Prohibition. In the St Valentine's Day Massacre of 1929, his men killed seven members of a rival gang. He was imprisoned in 1931 for income-tax evasion.

Caporetto. *See* Kobarid.

Capote, Truman (1924–84) US novelist. In his early novels and stories, such as *Other Voices, Other Rooms* (1948), he explored traditional southern literary themes of loneliness and the macabre. Later he turned to journalism, an interest reflected in *In Cold Blood* (1966), a book about an actual multiple murder. Other works include *The Grass Harp* (1951), *Breakfast at Tiffany's* (1958), and *Music for Chameleons* (1980).

Capp, Al (Alfred Caplin; 1909–79) US cartoonist. He is famous for his comic strip *Li'l Abner* depicting the hillbillies of Dogpatch, Kentucky, which first appeared in the *New York Mirror* in 1934. He continued to produce *Li'l Abner* until 1977.

Cappadocia The eastern region of Asia Minor. After early colonization by Semitic merchants, subjection to the Hittites, and invasions from the east, Cappadocia was conquered by the Persians in 584 BC but became an independent kingdom in the 3rd century BC. Feudal and isolated, Cappadocia resisted the hellenizing efforts of its ruling dynasty, which was largely pro-Roman; as the Roman Empire expanded eastward Cappadocia became strategically important and was a Roman province by 17 AD.

Capra, Frank (1897–1991) US film director, born in Italy. His best-known films highlight the ordinary man's triumph over corrupt big business or government, notably *It Happened One Night* (1934), *Mr. Smith Goes to Washington* (1939), and *It's a Wonderful Life* (1946). During World War II he directed propaganda films for the US War Department.

Capri, Island of (Latin name: Capreae) An Italian island at the SW entrance to the Bay of Naples. Its mild climate, fine scenery, and beaches have made it a popular resort since Roman times. The Blue Grotto, a cavern accessible only by sea, is a notable feature. Area: about 5 sq mi (13 sq km). Population (1990 est): 7500.

Capricornus (Latin: Goat) A constellation in the S sky, lying on the *zodiac between Aquarius and Sagittarius.

Caprivi Strip A narrow extension of NE Namibia giving the country access to the Zambezi River. Length: about 450 km (280 mi).

Capsicum A genus of annual and perennial flowering plants (about 50 species), native to Central and South America. The fruits (berries) of some species, particularly the various cultivated varieties of *C. annuum* and *C. frutescens*, are the *chilies and peppers used in cookery. Large fruits (up to about 4 in [10 cm] long) are the sweet peppers, which have a mild taste and are used in salads or cooked as a vegetable. They are usually green but may be red (the red varieties—paprika—can be ground to produce a spice). Smaller berries (about 1 in [2 cm] long) are the hot-tasting red peppers (or chilies); when dried and ground these form cayenne pepper. Dwarf varieties are grown for ornament. Family: *Solanaceae*.

capsid A delicate *plant bug belonging to the family *Miridae* (about 8000 species). Capsids are 0.08–0.24 in (2.5–6 mm) long and usually green or brown. They are found among all types of vegetation, feeding on plant juices, and are often serious crop pests. A few species prey on small arthropods.

capsule In botany, a type of dry *fruit that releases its seeds at maturity through pores, teeth, or slits: an example is the poppy capsule. The term also refers to the spore-producing structures of mosses and liverworts and the slimy envelope surrounding some bacterial cells. In zoology, it is the layer of connective issue surrounding some organs, for example the kidney.

capuchin monkey A long-tailed *monkey belonging to the genus *Cebus* (4 species), of South America. Capuchins are 28–35 in (70–90 cm) long including the tail 16–20 in (40–50 cm) and live in large troops in the treetops, feeding chiefly on fruit but also eating insects, birds, and eggs. They became familiar as organ-grinders' monkeys. Family: *Cebidae*.

Capuchins A Roman Catholic order of friars founded in 1525. They are reformed *Franciscans and are named from their adoption of the pointed cowl (capuche) worn in emulation of St Francis. Opposed by the established Franciscans, they were almost suppressed in 1542, but survived to become an important force during the Counter-Reformation, being recognized in 1619 as one of the three independent branches of the Franciscan order. From their foundation they were noted for their works of charity and their asceticism.

capybara The largest living rodent, *Hydrochoerus hydrochaeris*. Resembling giant guinea-pigs, up to 5 ft (1.25 m) long and 20 in (50 cm) high, capybaras graze on river banks in Central and South America, living in groups of up to 20 individuals. They have short coarse yellowish-brown hair and partially webbed feet (they are expert swimmers). The capybara is the only member of its family (*Hydrochoeridae*).

car. *See* automobile.

caracal A long-legged short-tailed *cat, *Felis caracal*, of African and Asian deserts, bush, and mountains. Caracals are about 26 in (70 cm) long with a reddish-brown coat, and feed mainly on birds but also catch small mammals.

Caracalla (Marcus Aurelius Antoninus; 188–217 AD) Roman emperor (211–17). Rivalry between Caracalla and his brother and coemperor Geta (189–212) threatened to divide the Empire until Caracalla procured Geta's murder. Caracalla extended Roman citizenship to all free inhabitants of the Empire, probably for financial reasons (212). In 214 he embarked on war against the Parthians, claiming to be following Alexander the Great's ambition to unite East and West, but was assassinated during the campaign.

caracara A long-legged *falcon belonging to the subfamily *Daptriine*, of Central and South America. Caracaras can run swiftly and spend much time on the ground. They are omnivorous and frequently feed on carrion.

Caracas 10 35N 66 56W The capital of Venezuela, situated near the N coast and linked by road to its port, La Guaira. Founded by the Spanish as Santiago de León de Caracas in the 16th century, it suffered damage and destruction from the English and the French in the 16th and 18th centuries and later from severe earthquakes. In the 20th century it has grown considerably, especially since the oil boom of the 1950s. The Central University of Venezuela was founded in 1725, and there are three other universities. It is the birthplace of Simón Bolívar. Population (1990 est): 1,825,000.

carat **1.** A unit of weight for precious stones, formerly defined as 4 grains (Troy), but now equal to 0.200 grams. **2.** (also karat) A measure of the fineness of gold equal to the number of parts of gold by weight in 24 parts of the alloy. Thus 18-carat gold contains $^{18}\!/_{24}$ths pure gold.

Caratacus (*or* Caractacus; 1st century AD) King of the Catuvellauni; son of *Cunobelinus (Cymbeline). Caratacus organized resistance to the Roman invasion of 43 AD. Defeated, he fled first to Wales then to the north British queen, Cartimandua, who betrayed him. He was pardoned by Emperor Claudius but died in exile.

Caravaggio (Michelangelo Merisi; 1573–1610) An influential Italian *baroque painter, whose nickname derives from his birthplace. In Rome his chief patron was Cardinal Francesco del Monte, for whom he painted scenes of the life of St Matthew in S Luigi dei Francesi. He executed numerous altarpieces, some of which, e.g. *Death of the Virgin* (Louvre), were condemned for depicting sacred personages as coarse peasants. He is also noted for his dramatic contrasts of light and shade in such paintings as *Supper at Emmaus* (National Gallery, London), which were extremely influential, particularly in N Europe. His violent temper led him to kill a man after a disputed tennis match in 1606. He spent his last years in exile in Naples, Malta, and Sicily.

caravel A sailing vessel used by the Spanish and Portuguese from the Middle Ages onward. It was usually rigged with a lateen sail on two or more masts.

CAPYBARA *These rodents are semiaquatic; they can swim underwater for considerable distances using their partly webbed feet.*

caraway A perennial flowering plant, *Carum carvi*, native to N temperate regions from Europe to the Himalayas. The much-branched stem grows to a height of 10–24 in (25–60 cm) and terminates in clusters of small white flowers. The fruit is an oblong capsule containing the familiar caraway seeds, used in cookery. Family: **Umbelliferae*.

carbohydrate One of a large group of chemical compounds containing the elements carbon, hydrogen, and oxygen and having the general formula $C_x(H_2O)_x$. Green plants manufacture carbohydrates, such as *sugars and *starch, during *photosynthesis and their cell walls consist largely of carbohydrates, predominantly *cellulose. Hence plant carbohydrates are the primary source of food energy for animals. *Glycogen is a carbohydrate energy reserve found in animals, while chitin is a structural carbohydrate occurring in arthropods (and also in fungi). Chemically, carbohydrates can be classified according to the number of sugar units they contain—one (*see* monosaccharides), several (oligosaccharides), or many (*see* polysaccharides).

carbolic acid. *See* phenol.

carbon (C) A chemical element that is unique in terms of the huge number and variety of its compounds. Carbon is the basis of organic *chemistry and of all living systems. The element occurs naturally in two forms: *graphite, which is a soft grayish-black mineral, and *diamond, the hardest substance known. *Charcoal and *coke are also composed of carbon. Large amounts of carbon are fixed as calcium carbonate ($CaCO_3$) in *limestones. The extensive and varied chemistry of carbon results from its ability to form single, double, and triple bonds with itself and other elements. Simple compounds of carbon may join together to form large polymers; for example polyethylene, $(C_2H_4)_n$, from ethylene. At no 6; at wt 12.011; sublimes at 3367 $\pm$ 32°F (25°C).

carbonaceous chondrite. *See* meteor.

Carbonari Members of a secret society in early 19th-century Italy that advocated constitutional government. The Carbonari emerged as opponents of Joachim *Murat, who ruled Naples for Napoleon. The movement spread to N Italy and was supported by those dissatisfied with the conservative regimes imposed on Italy after the fall of Napoleon. Support for the Carbonari dwindled following the formation of *Young Italy by Mazzini, but the society had helped pave the way for the unification of Italy (*see* Risorgimento).

carbon cycle (biology) The process by which carbon (in the form of carbon dioxide) in the atmosphere is taken up by plants during photosynthesis and transferred from one organism to the next in a *food chain, i.e. the plants are eaten by herbivorous animals that are themselves eaten by carnivores. At various stages carbon is returned to the environment with the release of carbon dioxide at *respiration and through decay.

carbon cycle (physics) A cycle of thermonuclear reactions in which a nucleus of carbon-12 acts as a catalyst in converting four hydrogen nuclei into a helium nucleus. The cycle produces energy and is believed to be a major source of energy in some stars. The reactions are:

$$^1_1H + {}^{12}_6C \rightarrow {}^{13}_7N \rightarrow {}^{13}_6C + {}^0_1e$$
$$^1_1H + {}^{13}_6C \rightarrow {}^{14}_7N$$
$$^1_1H + {}^{14}_7N \rightarrow {}^{15}_8O \rightarrow {}^{15}_7N + {}^0_1e$$
$$^1_1H + {}^{15}_7N \rightarrow {}^{12}_6C + {}^4_2He.$$

carbon dioxide (CO_2) A colorless odorless noncombustible gas. It is present (about 0.03% by volume) in air, being produced by combustion of carbon compounds and by respiration. Industrially, CO_2 is made from chalk or limestone and is used as a coolant in nuclear reactors, as a refrigerant, in fire extinguishers, and in fizzy drinks.

carbon fibers Black silky threads of pure carbon, made by the heat treatment of organic textile fibers (such as Courtelle) so that the side chains of the molecules are removed. They are some eight times stronger than steel and are used to reinforce resinous, ceramic, or metallic substances (with up to 600,000 fibers per square centimeter) to make components for jet engines, rockets, etc., where strength at high temperature is required.

Carboniferous period A geological period of the *Paleozoic era occurring about 370–280 million years ago, between the Devonian and Permian periods. During the period land plants increased prolifically and led to the formation of the world's major coal deposits. Amphibians became more common and by the end of the period some reptiles had evolved. The Carboniferous is divided into Lower and Upper (Mississippian and Pennsylvanian). Limestone deposits were widespread in the Lower Carboniferous; millstone grits and the Coal Measures (alternating beds of coal, sandstone, shale, and clay), in the Upper.

carbon monoxide (CO) A colorless odorless flammable gas. It is produced by the incomplete combustion of carbon compounds (e.g. coke or natural gas) and is used as a fuel (*see* water gas). CO is highly toxic, combining with red blood cells and preventing them from carrying oxygen. It is present in the exhaust fumes of internal-combustion engines.

carbon tetrachloride (CCl_4) A colorless nonflammable heavy liquid that gives off toxic fumes. It is used as a solvent but its use in fire extinguishers has been discontinued owing to its toxic products of combustion.

carborundum A dark crystalline compound (silicon carbide) manufactured by heating silica (sand) with carbon (coke). It is used as an abrasive and as a refractory material.

carboxylic acids. *See* fatty acid.

carbuncle. *See* boil.

carburetor The device in a gasoline engine that vaporizes the fuel and mixes it with air in the correct proportions. Vaporization is carried out by sucking the liquid fuel through a fine jet situated in (or near to) the throat of a tube through which the combustion air enters the engine. The carburetor also contains a choke to make the fuel-air mixture richer (i.e. contain more fuel and less air) for cold starting, a throttle valve (which controls the speed of the engine by admitting more or less of the mixture), and an air filter. In some gasoline engines the carburetor is replaced by a *fuel-injection system.

Carcassonne 43 13N 2 21E A city in SW France, the capital of the Aude department. It comprises a medieval fortified town, surrounded by towers and ramparts crowning a hill on the right bank of the Aude River, and a largely modern town, where there is a 13th-century cathedral (restored) on the left bank. A tourist center, Carcassonne is situated in a wine-producing region. Population (1975): 44,623.

Carchemish A *Hittite stronghold on the Upper Euphrates in E Turkey. After the Hittite empire's collapse (12th century BC), Carchemish survived as an independent kingdom until conquered by *Sargon II of Assyria (717 BC). In 605 BC it was the scene of a battle in which the Babylonians defeated an Egyptian army. *Woolley and T. E. *Lawrence excavated fine Hittite reliefs there (1912–14, 1919).

carcinogen An agent that causes cancer. Carcinogens can be chemicals, radiation, and some viruses. Chemical carcinogens include tar (such as that produced by cigarette smoking), aniline, and azo dyes. Large doses of radiation and the polyoma virus are known to cause cancer, particularly leukemia.

carcinoma. *See* cancer.

cardamon A perennial herb, *Elettaria cardamomum*, native to India; 5–10 ft (1.5–3 m) tall, it has large leaves, green and purple veined flowers, and small capsules filled with hard angular seeds. The spice cardamon consists of whole or ground dried fruit or seeds. It is cultivated in India, Sri Lanka, and Guatemala. Family: *Zingiberaceae* (ginger family).

Cardano, Girolamo (1501–76) Italian mathematician, who contributed to the development of negative and imaginary *numbers and, being an inveterate gambler, constructed a mathematical theory of chance. He also published a method of solving cubic equations known as Cardano's rule, although it was first derived by Niccolò Tartaglia (1500–57). His main works were *De subtilitate rerum* (1551) and *De varietate rerum* (1557).

Cárdenas, Lázaro (1895–1970) Mexican statesman. As president (1934–40) Cárdenas strove to realize many of the promises of the post-1910 revolutionary movement. He redistributed land, promoted mass education, and supported organized labor. His most famous achievement was the nationalization of the oil industry in 1938.

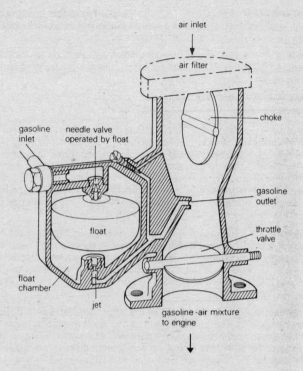

air inlet

air filter

choke

gasoline inlet

needle valve operated by float

gasoline outlet

throttle valve

float

float chamber

jet

gasoline - air mixture to engine

CARBURETOR *The level of gasoline is kept constant in the float chamber. The gasoline is atomized by passing it through the fine jet and is then mixed with air and passed to the engine. The engine speed is controlled by the throttle valve. The mixture strength is varied by the choke, a richer mixture being required for starting from cold.*

Cardiff (Welsh name: Caerdydd) 51 30N 3 13W The capital of Wales, situated in the SE of the country at the mouth of the River Taff. At the center of the city lies the Norman castle. University College, Cardiff (founded 1883), the University of Wales Registry (1893), the University of Wales Institute of Science and Technology, the Welsh National School of Medicine, and the National Museum of Wales are all located in the city. The cathedral at *Llandaff and the Welsh Folk Museum are situated on the outskirts of the city. *History*: originally a small Roman fort, the site was reoccupied by the Normans. It received its first royal charter in 1581, at which time it was a favorite haunt of pirates. It was not until 1881, however, that Cardiff expanded from a small market town to become the largest city in Wales. Its prosperity was based on coal from the valleys to the N of the city and by 1913 it was the largest coal-exporting port in the world. Trade declined rapidly, however, after World War I. Cardiff was chosen as the capital of Wales in 1955. Population (1981): 273,856.

Cardigan, James Thomas Brudenell, 7th Earl of (1797–1868) British cavalry officer. In 1824 Cardigan brought himself a command in the Hussars, where his arrogant behavior led to a notorious duel. In 1854, during the Crimean

War, he led the fatal charge of the Light Brigade at *Balaclava, made famous by Tennyson. The woolen garment known as a cardigan was named for him.

Cardin, Pierre (1922–   ) French fashion designer who, after opening a fashion house in Paris (1949), made his reputation in the 1950s with his oriental styles and slim coats with huge collars. He was the first couturier to show a collection for men (1960).

cardinal A North American *bunting, *Pyrrhuloxia cardinalis*, having a strong stout bill and a crested head. The male, about 20 cm long, has a bright scarlet plumage with a black bib; the female is yellowish brown with a red crest.

cardinals, college of (*or* Sacred College) The body of the highest dignitaries next to the pope in the *Roman Catholic Church. Originating in the advisory roles played by the parish priests and deacons of the city of Rome, the body was later extended to include six cardinal bishops responsible for the election of the pope. This function was invested in the college as a whole by the Third *Lateran Council (1179). Since then the number of cardinal bishops, priests, and deacons has increased from a total of 70 under Sixtus V (1586) to the present membership of 125 established under John XXIII and Paul VI. Cardinals from all over the world are nominated and elected by the pope, who invests them with the flat broad-brimmed red hat symbolic of their rank. They assist the pope as a privy council, conducting the temporal affairs of the Church, advising on questions of doctrine, etc.; they elect the pope from among their own number.

Cardozo, Benjamin Nathan (1870–1938) US lawyer, jurist, associate justice of the Supreme Court (1932–38). After a successful career as a courtroom lawyer (1891–1913), he served on the New York State Court of Appeals (1914–32), sitting as the chief judge from 1927. Considered a liberal, his main concern during his career as a judge was simplification of the law to fit the social needs of the case and of the times.

Carducci, Giosuè (1835–1907) Italian poet and critic. The son of a country doctor, he became professor of Italian literature at Bologna University in 1860 and won the Nobel Prize in 1906. He was elected senator in 1890. He wrote vigorous, patriotic, and anticlerical poetry but *Rime nuove* (1861–87) and *Odi Barbare* (1877–89) also contain more lyrical verse with classical influences.

cargo cults Religious cults found chiefly in Melanesia since the late 19th century. Their adherents believe that a new paradise will be heralded mainly by the arrival of a supernatural cargo of goods brought by spirits, who are variously viewed as gods, ancestors, or white foreigners. The cults probably evolved from Christian millennial teachings and native jealousy of the colonial European's material wealth.

Caria A mountainous area in SW Asia Minor under the rule of *Lydia until 546 BC, when it passed to the Persians. The Carians joined the Ionian Greeks' unsuccessful revolt against the Persians (499–493 BC). Under the Hecatomnid dynasty (395–334 BC), Caria was absorbed into the Greek world.

Carib An American Indian people of the Lesser Antilles and northern South America, after whom the Caribbean was named. The maritime island Caribs were warriors and cannibals who, before the advent of the Spaniards, expelled the *Arawak Indians from the Lesser Antilles, enslaving the women and killing and eating the men. As a consequence, in these islands men spoke Carib and women, Arawak. The mainland Caribs were less aggressive and their culture was adapted to the tropical forest region. They cultivated manioc and hunted with the blowpipe.

Caribbean Community (CARICOM) An association of 12 states in the Caribbean region (Antigua and Barbuda, Barbados, Belize, Dominica, Grenada, Guyana, Jamaica, Montserrat, St Kitts-Nevis, St Lucia, St Vincent and the Grenadines, and Trinidad and Tobago). It was established in 1973 and aims to coordinate the economic policies of member states through the Caribbean Common Market (which replaced the Caribbean Free Trade Area [CARITA] formed in 1968); to coordinate foreign policies; and generally to foster cooperation. Its headquarters are in Georgetown (Guyana).

Caribbean Sea A section of the Atlantic Ocean, between the West Indies, E Central America, and N South America. With the opening of the Panama Canal (1914) it became an important shipping route. Its tropical climate and warm waters have led to the increasing importance of tourism throughout the Caribbean islands. Area: 1,049,500 sq mi (2,718,200 sq km). Maximum depth: 25,216 ft (7686 m).

caribou. *See* reindeer.

CARICOM. *See* Caribbean Community.

caries Cavities in the teeth caused by bacterial erosion of the enamel and dentine. The bacteria feed on sugar from the diet: the sugar and bacteria become attached to the teeth to form a layer called plaque, and acid formed by bacterial breakdown of the sugar causes the damage of caries. Caries is most marked in those of Anglo-Saxon origin and it is particularly common in children and adolescents; a high-sugar diet and poor oral hygiene increase its incidence. Treatment consists of drilling away the damaged part of the tooth and replacing it with filling. Regular and adequate brushing of the teeth is the best preventive measure. The absorption of fluoride by growing teeth strengthens them against bacterial attack; *fluoridation of the public water supply is an aspect of preventive dentistry.

carillon A set of bells hung in a tower, activated from a manual and pedal console similar to that of an organ. It is a popular instrument in Belgium and Holland. Carillons vary in size from two to four octaves. The wooden keys are depressed with the closed hand. The name is also applied to an organ stop that produces a bell-like sound.

Carina (Latin: Keel) A constellation in the S sky near Crux. The brightest star is *Canopus.

Carinthia (German name: Kärnten) A federal state in S Austria. It first came into Austrian possession in 1335; following World War I parts were ceded to neighboring Italy and Yugoslavia. Chiefly mountainous, it has picturesque alpine scenery and many lakes. The main occupations are livestock rearing, forestry, mining, and tourism. Area: 3681 sq mi (9537 sq km). Population (1991): 552,421. Capital: Klagenfurt.

Carl August (1757–1828) Duke (1758–1815) and Grand Duke (1815–28) of Saxe-Weimar-Eisenach, who was the first German ruler to grant his state a liberal constitution. Carl August participated in the wars against Napoleon and made territorial gains at the Congress of Vienna (1815). He was a friend and patron of *Goethe and other German writers.

Carl XVI Gustaf (1946–) King of Sweden (1973–), succeeding his grandfather Gustaf VI (1882–1973). The Swedish monarch became little more than a figurehead under a new constitution effective from Carl's succession. In 1976 he married Silvia Sommerlath (1943–).

Carlisle 54 54N 2 55W A city in NW England, on the River Eden. Once a Roman military center (Luguvallum) and important fortress in the border wars with the Scots, it has a 12th-century cathedral and a castle (11th–13th centuries). Industries include flour milling, textiles, and agricultural engineering. Population (1981): 70,800.

Carlisle 40 12N 77 12W A city in SE Pennsylvania, SW of Harrisburg. Originally an army post, it now houses the US Army War College. The Carlisle Indian School (1879–1918) and Dickenson College (1783) are here. Manufactures include radio and electronic crystals. Population (1990): 18,419.

Carlism A Spanish conservative movement, initiated by those who supported as *Ferdinand VII's successor in 1833 his brother Don *Carlos, rather than Ferdinand's daughter *Isabella II. The Carlists wanted a more severe repression of liberals, the restoration of the Spanish Inquisition, and the maintenance of traditional regional liberties (*fueros*). In the first Carlist War (1833–39), they were supported by the small landowners in the NE but were eventually defeated. Carlism survived in its strongholds of Navarre and Aragon but in the second Carlist War (1872–76) was again defeated. During the Spanish Civil War Carlist regiments fought with Franco's armies but many Carlists became critical of Franco's government.

Carlos, Don (1788–1855) Spanish pretender. The brother of *Ferdinand VII and an ultra-Catholic reactionary, he contested the succession of his niece *Isabella II in 1833. His followers, who became known as Carlists, opposed Isabella's government in a series of Carlist wars (*see* Carlism).

Carlow (Irish name: Ceatharlach) A county in the E Republic of Ireland, in Leinster. Chiefly low lying, it rises to mountains in the E. Agriculture is intensive, producing barley, wheat, and sugar beet. Area: 346 sq mi (896 sq km). Population (1986): 41,000. County town: Carlow.

Carlsbad 32 25N 104 14W A city in SE New Mexico on the Pecos River. Founded in 1887, the nearby Carlsbad Caverns National Park (containing large limestone caves) makes it a popular tourist center. Potash, discovered in 1931, is extensively mined and it is a shipping point for cotton, alfalfa, oil, and livestock. Population (1990): 24,952.

Carlyle, Thomas (1795–1881) Scottish historian and essayist. He worked unhappily as a teacher until 1819. In 1826 he married Jane Baillie Welsh and moved to London in 1834. *Sartor Resartus*, a blend of fiction, philosophy, and autobiography, was published in 1836 and was followed by his major work, *The French Revolution*, in 1837. This and later works express his view of history as shaped by the "Hero," or inspired individual. After his wife's death in 1866 he became grief-stricken at his neglect of her and retired from public life.

Carmel, Mount 32 45N 35 02E A mountain in N Israel, extending in a ridge for 16 mi (25 km) SE from the coast at Haifa. The Carmelite religious order was founded here. Height: 1791 ft (546 m).

Carmelites A Roman Catholic religious order founded around the mid-12th century by St Berthold (died c. 1195), who claimed direct inspiration from Elijah and established a monastery at Mount Carmel. With the collapse of the Crusader kingdoms, the order moved to Europe. The original strict rule was relaxed in some respects. In 1452 an order of Carmelite nuns was instituted. In the 16th century the order was reformed by St *Teresa of Avila and emphasized the cultivation of the contemplative life, which became a distinctive feature of the order.

Carmina Burana A miscellany of lyrics, mainly in Latin, preserved together with six religious dramas in a 13th-century manuscript from Benediktbeuern, Bavaria. The work of earlier medieval wandering scholars, they encompass religious, pastoral, and erotic themes and range from satires on the Church to drinking songs. *See also* Orff, Carl.

Carnac 47 35N 3 05W A village in Brittany (NW France). It is famous for the megalithic monuments in its vicinity (*see* megalith). Chief of these, and unique of their kind, are the avenues (alignments) of monoliths, set upright in parallel rows that run continuously for hundreds of yards. The three main groups, called Ménec, Kermario, and Kerlescan, may have had both ritual and astronomical significance.

CARNAC *Nearly 3000 menhirs still stand in the Carnac alignments.*

Carnap, Rudolf (1891–1970) German-born logical positivist philosopher. A founder of the *Vienna Circle, he was professor of philosophy successively at Vienna, Prague, Chicago, and California Universities. He worked on formal logic and its applications to science and *epistemology, believing that the analysis and clarification of knowledge should be the purpose of philosophy. By developing logical syntax and *semantics, he tried to construct a formal language for the empirical sciences to eliminate confusion, ambiguity, and similar obstacles to knowledge.

Carnarvon Range A plateau in Australia, in SE Queensland. Part of the Great Dividing Range, it lies within a nature reserve and is being developed as a tourist area.

Carnatic music The music of S India as opposed to that of N India. Not having been subjected to the influences of invading cultures, the S has kept an unbroken tradition that lays stress on complex rhythmic patterns. The scale is subdivided into 12 sections similar to those of the European chromatic scale. Primarily vocal, it also employs instruments, especially drums.

carnation A large-flowered cultivated form of the clove pink (*Dianthus caryophyllus*). These perennials grow to heights of 16–24 in (40–60 cm) and have tufts of dense grasslike foliage and double flowers in white, yellow, orange, pink, red, or lavender. Hardy border carnations are suitable for outdoor cultivation, while the perpetual flowering varieties should be grown under glass. Flowers of carnations (and pinks) are noted for their clovelike fragrance. Family: *Caryophyllaceae. See also* Dianthus.

carnauba wax A hard high-quality wax gathered from the leaves of the Brazilian carnauba palm (*Copernica cerifera*) and used for making high-gloss polishes. The tree secretes the wax to prevent excess evaporation from its leaves.

Carnegie, Andrew (1835–1919) US industrialist, born in Scotland. He founded the Keystone Bridge Company (1865) to manufacture iron and, increasingly, steel. By 1888 he owned auxiliary coal and iron fields, railroads, and steamships and in 1901 his companies merged with the US Steel Corporation. A noted philanthropist, he believed that a rich man should distribute his wealth for the benefit of society and donated over $350 million to causes in the US and Britain. He founded the Carnegie Institute of Technology in Pittsburgh in 1900, the Carnegie Institution in Washington in 1902, and many libraries. He also contributed substantially to the building of Carnegie Hall.

Carnera, Primo (1906–67) Italian boxer, who was idolized during the 1930s although he was heavyweight champion only briefly (1933–34); 6.5 ft (1.98 m) tall, he was known for his knockout victories. He later took up wrestling and acted in the film *On the Waterfront* (1954).

Carnivora An order of mammals adapted for hunting and eating flesh. Carnivores have strong jaws, with sharp incisor teeth and pointed canine teeth; some of the cheek (molar) teeth, called carnassials, act as shears to chop up meat. They are the major predators and most species are terrestrial, stalking or pouncing on their prey. The 252 species are divided into seven families: *Canidae* (dogs); *Ursidae* (*see* bears); *Procyonidae* (*see* raccoons; pandas); *Mustelidae* (weasels, skunks, etc.); *Viverridae* (genets, mongooses, etc.); and *Felidae* (cats).

carnivorous plant A plant that obtains at least some of its nutrients by the digestion of insects and other small animals. Carnivorous, or insectivorous, plants show remarkable structural adaptations for their mode of life. *Butterworts and *sundews trap and digest insects by means of the sticky secretions produced by glands in the leaves. The *Venus flytrap traps its prey between bilobed hinged leaves with marginal teeth. Another common method of capture and digestion is by means of liquid-filled "pitchers" into which the insects fall (*see* pitcher plant).

Carnot, (Nicolas Léonard) Sadi (1796–1832) French scientist and soldier, whose investigations of the efficiency of steam engines led him to the concept of ideal reversible cycles, a fundamental idea in the study of *thermodynamics. He described what are now known as the *Carnot cycle and Carnot's theorem (no engine can be more efficient than a reversible engine working between the same temperatures). His father **Lazare Nicolas Marguerite Carnot** (1753–1823) was a statesman and military engineer, known as the "organizer of victory" in the French Revolutionary Wars. He was a member of the Legislative Assembly (1791), the National Convention (1792), and the Committee of *Public Safety. Carnot was exiled in 1815 and settled in Magdeburg. His *De la défense de places fortes* (1810) became a classic work on fortifications.

Carnot cycle A reversible thermodynamic cycle of changes of pressure and temperature in the gas in an ideal heat engine. The gas is compressed adiabatically (at constant heat content), thus raising its temperature, say from T_1 to T_2. It is then expanded isothermally (at constant temperature). The gas is then expanded adiabatically, lowering its temperature from T_2 back to T_1, and finally compressed isothermally at T_1, thus completing the cycle. The efficiency of this cycle depends not on the nature of the gas but only on the temperature range, i.e. it is equal to $(T_1-T_2)/T_1$, where T_1 and T_2 are absolute temperatures. Named for Sadi *Carnot.

Caro, Joseph (1488–1575) Jewish legal scholar and mystic. A refugee from Spain (1492), he settled in Safed (Galilee), an important center of the *kabbalah. His most enduring work is the legal code *Shulhan Arukh* (*The Prepared Table*; 1564–65), which is still regarded as authoritative by orthodox Jews.

carob The horn-shaped edible fruit pod of the carob tree, *Ceratonia siliqua*, an evergreen native to the Mediterranean region. The pods, sometimes known as algaroba or St John's bread, contain a sugary pulp and are used for fodder. The seeds are believed to have been the original carats of jewelers. Family: *Leguminosae*.

carol A song of a joyful nature, originally accompanied by dancing. During the Middle Ages the word was applied to a variety of different types of song. Generally written in a simple verse-plus-refrain form, carols became associated with Christmas or Easter, but often had roots in pre-Christian beliefs. The first printed carol was the *Boar's Head Carol* (1521), one of many associated with the feast of the winter solstice. Others derive from miracle and mystery plays; the few that survive in manuscripts of the 15th century celebrate the events of the first Christmas; carols continued to be written on this theme until the 19th century.

Carol I (1839–1914) The first King of Romania (1881–1914). Carol was a German prince, who was elected to the Romanian princedom in 1866 and became king when Romania gained independence from the Ottoman Empire. He introduced reforms and exploited Romania's oil fields but his economic program failed to help the peasants, who rebelled in 1907.

Carol II (1893–1953) King of Romania (1930–40). In 1925 Carol renounced his right of succession to the throne to live in Paris with his mistress Magda Lupescu and his son *Michael succeeded in 1927. Carol returned to Romania in 1930 and was proclaimed king but was forced to abdicate in 1940 by the pro-German *Antonescu. He settled finally in Mexico, where in 1947 he married Mme Lupescu.

Carolina. *See* North Carolina; South Carolina.

Caroline Affair (1837) A US-Canadian incident that strained relations between the two countries. Canadian rebels were using the American steamboat *Caroline* for delivering supplies to Navy Island, their refuge on the Niagara River. Canadians still loyal to the British sank the steamboat in American waters, and the US protested to the British minister to Canada. Although the Canadian commander was tried, he was acquitted.

Caroline Islands An archipelago in the W Pacific Ocean, part of the UN trust territory of the *Pacific Islands, administered by the US. It includes the Truk, Yap, and Palau island groups and the large volcanic islands of Kusaie and Ponape. Copra is the main export. Area: 457 sq mi (1183 sq km).

Caroline of Brunswick (1768–1821) The wife of George IV of the United Kingdom. After their separation (1796), he forbade her to see their child Charlotte. When George became king (1820), his attempt to divorce Caroline failed owing to popular support for her but she was excluded from the coronation (1821).

Carolingians The second Frankish ruling dynasty. It was founded by *Pepin the Short, who deposed the last *Merovingian king in 751, and it was named for Pepin's son *Charlemagne, who greatly expanded the Frankish territories. Crowned Emperor of the West in 800 by Pope Leo III, Charlemagne and his son *Louis the Pious were great patrons of learning, fostering the Carolingian renaissance (*see* Alcuin; Einhard). After Louis' death, the Carolingian empire was split into three kingdoms (843). The middle Frankish kingdom was divided into Italy, Lotharingia (Lorraine), and Provence; in the E Frankish kingdom (Germany) the dynasty survived until 911; and the W Frankish kingdom (France) was ruled by Carolingians until the failure of the line in 987.

carotenoids A group of yellow, orange, or red pigments manufactured by bacteria, fungi, and plants and essential in the diet of animals. There are two groups—carotenes (including beta-carotene, a precursor of *vitamin A) and xanthophylls. Carotenoid pigments are important for display and camouflage coloring in both plants and animals and also as eye pigments.

carp An omnivorous freshwater fish, *Cyprinus carpio*, native to Asia but widely introduced elsewhere and raised for food. It has an elongated body, usually about 14 in (35 cm) long, with large scales, greenish or brownish above and paler below, four barbels on the upper lip, and a long dorsal fin. During the winter it hibernates in the bottom mud. Related fish include the Crucian carp and golden carp (*see* goldfish). Family: *Cyprinidae* (about 2000 species); order: *Cypriniformes*.

Carpaccio, Vittore (c. 1460–c. 1525) Venetian painter, noted for his paintings of his native city and his narrative cycles. His works, influenced by Gentile and Giovanni *Bellini, include a cycle of *Scenes from the Life of St Ursula* and *The Miracle of the Cross* (Accademia, Venice).

Carpal Tunnel Syndrome Medical condition affecting the tendon that passes through the carpal tunnel in the wrist. Triggered by repetitive motion, such as computer keyboarding, the condition results in a swollen tendon that presses on the nerve in the carpal tunnel, which causes numbness and pain at the base of the thumb and fingers. The usual treatment includes rest and change in work techniques, but surgery is sometimes necessary.

Carpathian Mountains A mountain range in Slovakia, Poland, Hungary, Ukraine, and Romania. They form a rough semicircle about 90 mi (1450 km) long (including the Transylvanian Alps, which are also known as the **Southern Carpathians**) between Bratislava and the Iron Gate, both on the Danube River. The highest peak is Mount Gerlachovka, at 8737 ft (2663 m), in NE Slovakia.

carpel The female organ of a flower, consisting of the stigma, style, and ovary (☐plant). After fertilization, each carpel may ripen to produce a fruit containing one or more seeds. *See also* pistil.

Carpentaria, Gulf of A shallow inlet of the Arafura Sea, in N Australia, situated between Arnhem Land and Cape York Peninsula. It contains many islands, the most important being *Groote Eylandt and Wellesley. There are important bauxite and manganese deposits. Area: about 11,000 sq mi (287,500 sq km).

Carpenter, (Malcolm) Scott (1925–) US astronaut. A Navy test pilot and air intelligence officer, he joined the National Aeronautics and Space Administration (NASA) in 1959 and, in 1962, made a three-orbit flight in Project Mercury's *Aurora 7,* becoming the second American to orbit in space. He retired from the Navy in 1969, after participating in Sealab II (1965) and Sealab III (1967), experimental underwater living stations.

carpenter bee A large black solitary *bee belonging to the European genus *Xylocopa X. violacea* (1 in [25 mm long]) that excavates galleries in wood or large plant stems to make its nest. The lesser carpenter bees (genus *Ceratina*) are found mainly in Africa. Family: *Apidae*.

Carpentier, Georges (1894–1975) French boxer, who was world light-heavyweight champion from 1920 to 1922. His unsuccessful fight against Jack *Dempsey (1921) drew the first million-dollar gate. He also fought at several other weights.

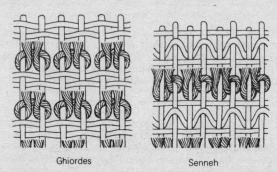

Ghiordes   Senneh

CARPET *The two varieties of knot used in oriental hand-knotted carpets are the Ghiordes (Turkish) and Senneh (Persian) knots.*

carpet A floor covering of fabric. Although tapestries were sometimes used as floor coverings in the Middle Ages, knotted carpets originated in Asia and date back to about the 3rd century BC. They are woven with tufts of wool, or sometimes silk, knotted around the warp threads as the carpet is woven or around a jute or hessian backing to form a pile. Oriental carpets traditionally have symbolic designs and colors, which distinguish them as Persian, Turkish, Indian, etc. From the 12th century onward, these designs have been used and adapted by European carpet manufacturers, the Savonnier carpets of 17th-century France being a typical example. Modern machine-made carpets, such as Wilton, have the pile formed by cut loops instead of knots, while Brussels carpet has uncut loops. In the type of carpet now called "tufted" the tufts are held in place by a foam-rubber backing. Synthetic fiber is replacing wool, especially for wall-to-wall carpet, which is made in rolls instead of the traditional squares or rectangles and cut to meet individual requirements.

Carpetbaggers Northern profiteers during the *Reconstruction of the South (1865–77) after the US Civil War, who often carried their possessions in a heavy cloth satchel (carpetbag). By manipulating the uneducated newly enfranchised African-American voters, the carpetbaggers helped the Republicans gain local and state control. A few carpetbaggers, however, were sincere advocates of equal rights for African Americans.

carpet beetle A small oval beetle, up to 0.4 in (10 mm) long, belonging to a genus (*Anthrenus*) of worldwide pests. It is the hairy red-brown or golden-brown larvae that cause the damage, by feeding on virtually all materials of animal origin, especially furs and fabrics. *A. museorum* is a major pest of museum collections. Family: *Dermestidae*.

Carpini, Giovanni da Pian del (c. 1180–c. 1252) Italian traveler in Mongolia. A Franciscan friar, at Pope Innocent IV's behest he led a remarkable mission to the Mongols, whose incursions into Christian lands were causing alarm. He departed from Lyon in 1245, reached Karakoram, where he was presented to the khan, in 1246, and then made the return trip largely in winter (1246–47).

Carracci A family of Bolognese painters who were instrumental in reviving the Renaissance art of Raphael, Titian, and Correggio after the heyday of *mannerism. They founded an influential teaching academy (1582) and collaborated on decorations for Bolognese palaces. **Ludovico Carracci** (1555–1619) devoted his life to art instruction and painting altarpieces. His cousin **Agostino Carracci** (1557–1602) was a noted engraver and assisted his brother **Annibale Carracci** (1560–1609), the most famous of the three, on decorations in the gallery of the Farnese Palace, Rome.

carrageen (*or* carageen) An edible brownish-red *seaweed, *Chondrus crispus*, also called Irish or sea moss, that grows abundantly on rocky coasts of W Britain and Ireland, N Europe, and North America. A red alga, it has thin, usually flat branching fronds, about 2–12 in (5–30 cm) long, and contains a gelatinous carrageenin (substance) used in jellies, lotions, cosmetics, food products, shoe polishes, etc.

Carrantuohill 52 00N 9 45W The highest mountain in Ireland, in Co Kerry, in Macgillicuddy's Reeks. Height: 3414 ft (1041 m).

Carranza, Venustiano (1859–1920) Mexican statesman and soldier in the post-1910 revolutionary movement. He was the first president (1917–20) under the 1917 constitution and his nationalist policies brought him into conflict with the US. He was deposed and killed in a coup in 1920.

Carrara 44 04N 10 06E A city in central Italy, in Tuscany. It is famous for its white marble, which was used by the sculptor Michelangelo.

Carrel, Alexis (1873–1944) French surgeon, who pioneered the technique for sewing (suturing) blood vessels together. He perfected this after moving to the US, where he also worked on techniques for keeping organs alive outside the body. He was awarded a Nobel Prize (1912).

Carrhae, Battle of (53 BC) The battle near Carrhae (now Haran, Turkey) in which the Roman forces under Marcus Licinius *Crassus were defeated by the Parthians.

Carrington, Peter Alexander Rupert Carington, 6th Baron (1919–   ) British Conservative politician. As foreign secretary (1979–82) he was instrumental in establishing Zimbabwe's independence (1980); he resigned following the Argentinian invasion of the *Falkland Islands (1982). Carrington was appointed secretary general of NATO in 1984.

carrion crow An omnivorous Eurasian crow, *Corvus corone corone*, about 17 in (46 cm) long with a pure-black plumage and harsh croaking call. It is a notorious egg thief, unpopular with gamekeepers. *See also* hooded crow.

carrion flower A cactus-like succulent plant belonging to the genus *Stapelia* (60 species), native to arid parts of Africa. Several are grown for their showy purplish flowers, although they have a fetid odor. *S. gigantea* has a leafless square stem, 2–12 in (5–30 cm) high, bearing a flower with a diameter of 12 in (30 cm). Family: *Asclepiadaceae*.

The name is also given to a species of *greenbrier, *Smilax herbacea*, which has small green evil-smelling flowers.

Carroll, Lewis (Charles Lutwidge Dodgson; 1832–98) British writer and mathematician. He lectured in mathematics at Oxford University (1855–81) and was ordained in 1861. The children's classic *Alice's Adventures in Wonderland*

(1865) was written for a young friend, Alice Liddell. It and the sequel, *Through the Looking-Glass* (1872), are sophisticated books that combine elements of fantasy, logic, and nonsense and have had a lasting appeal to adults as well as children. He also wrote nonsense verse, notably *The Hunting of the Snark* (1876), and was a pioneer of portrait photography.

carrot A biennial flowering plant, *Daucus carota*, found in grassy places in temperate regions from Europe to India. The stem grows to a height of 12–40 in (30–100 cm) and bears a head of small white flowers. *Daucus carota sativus* is the cultivated carrot. This is grown as an annual, and produces an orange thick fleshy edible root. Many varieties of the cultivated carrot have been developed. Family: *Umbelliferae*.

Carson, Edward Henry, Baron (1854–1935) Irish politician and lawyer, solicitor general for Ireland (1892) and England (1900–06). In 1895 Carson gained fame in his successful prosecution for homosexuality of Oscar Wilde. As a member of the English Parliament (1892–1921), he led the Ulster opposition to the Irish *Home Rule bill (1912) and raised the Ulster Volunteers to oppose its enactment. In World War I he served in Asquith's and Lloyd George's cabinets.

Carson, Kit (Christopher C.; 1809–68) US frontiersman. A saddler in Missouri, stationed on the Santa Fe trail, he joined a wagon train in 1826 and made Taos, N.M., his headquarters for a career as a guide. Well-versed in Indian ways, he was a guide in *Frémont's expeditions to the West in the 1840s and after distinguished service in the Mexican War became US Indian agent at Taos (1853). He subsequently fought for the Union in the Civil War. Illiterate, Carson dictated his memoirs (1856), published as *Dear Old Kit*.

Carson, Rachel Louise (1907–64) US science writer, who worked as a genetic biologist (1936–52) and later as editor for the US Fish and Wildlife Service. Her books, notably *The Sea around Us* (1951) and *Silent Spring* (1962), greatly increased public awareness of the natural environment and warned of the dangers of pollution.

Carson City 39 10N 119 46W The capital city of Nevada. It is named for the famous frontiersman Kit Carson. Although silver and copper are mined, the main industry is gambling. Population (1990): 40,443.

Cartagena 10 24N 75 33W A port in N Colombia, on the Caribbean Sea. It is important industrially, producing textiles, petrochemicals, and pharmaceuticals. It receives oil by pipeline from Berrancabermeja; exports include coffee and oil. The University of Cartagena was founded in 1827. Population (1985): 491,368.

Cartagena (*or* Carthagena) 37 36N 0 59W A port in SE Spain, in Murcia on the Mediterranean Sea. Founded by the Carthaginian general Hasdrubal in the 3rd century BC, it was destroyed by Ferdinand II of Castile in 1243. In the 16th century, under Philip II of Spain, it became a great naval port and remains the country's chief Mediterranean naval base. It exports minerals, olive oil, and fruits and has boat building industries. Population (1991): 166,736.

Carte, Richard D'Oyly. *See* D'Oyly Carte, Richard.

cartel An association of producers who join together to secure a higher price for their products by restricting the supply. However, a cartel is inherently unstable; all the members have an interest in producing as much as they can at the new price, in defiance of the cartel agreement. The need to enroll all producers and to maintain strict discipline explains why the highly successful oil cartel OPEC has not been followed by other primary-product cartels.

Carter, Howard (1874–1939) British archeologist. Carter worked in Egypt from 1892 and collaborated with Lord Carnarvon (1866–1923) after 1907. In

1922 they discovered the tomb of *Tutankhamen, work on which occupied Carter for the next ten years.

JIMMY CARTER *The president brings together Sadat of Egypt (left) and Begin of Israel (right) at Camp David.*

Carter, James Earl Jr. ("Jimmy") (1924–) US statesman; 39th President of the US (1977–81). A graduate of the US Naval Academy, Carter spent most of his adult life managing his family's peanut farm and warehouse in Plains, Ga. Carter later embarked on a political career, serving as governor of Georgia (1971–75) and receiving the Democratic presidential nomination in 1976. Carter defeated Pres. Gerald *Ford in the general election and soon after his inauguration attempted to implement an ambitious program of national energy conservation and environmental regulations. His greatest achievements and greatest failures, however, came in the field of foreign policy. In 1978 he sponsored negotiations at *Camp David between Egyptian president Anwar *Sadat and Israeli prime minister Menachem *Begin that led to a peace treaty between the two countries in the following year. In 1978, Carter also supported and signed a treaty relinquishing US control of the *Panama Canal. The most serious crisis of Carter's presidency came in 1979, when the US embassy in Teheran was seized by Iranian students and its staff was held hostage. Unsuccessful US appeals to the UN and the World Court and an abortive attempt at a military rescue mission in 1980 failed to gain the hostages' release. Carter's popularity declined dramatically, and he was defeated for reelection by Ronald *Reagan in 1980. A personal memoir of his presidency, *Keeping Faith*, was published in 1982.

Carteret, John. *See* Granville, John Carteret, 1st Earl.

Cartesian coordinates. *See* coordinate systems.

Carthage (Punic name: *Kart-Hadasht*, New City) An ancient city of N Africa, near modern Tunis. Traditionally founded 814 BC by *Dido and exiles from *Tyre, Carthage rapidly became leader of the *Phoenician trading cities of N Africa, waging intermittent war with the Greeks of Marseilles and Sicily. From 264 BC Carthage fought the three *Punic Wars with *Rome, her former ally, and was totally destroyed (146 BC). Refounded by Julius *Caesar (45 BC), Carthage became, in turn, the commercial, cultural, and administrative capital of Roman Africa, the capital of the *Vandal kingdom (439–533 AD), and a Byzantine outpost, until destroyed by the Muslims in 697 AD.

Carthusians A contemplative Roman Catholic religious order founded in 1084 by St Bruno and taking its name from the location of the first community, La Grande Chartreuse, near Grenoble. Although originally without a written rule, the Carthusians observed a rigorous life of fasting and solitude and were vowed to silence. The order remained fairly small but disciplined. At the time of the dissolution of the monasteries there were nine Carthusian monasteries, or *Charterhouses, in England. At present the order's English headquarters is the Charterhouse, Parkminster, Sussex. The French monks are noted for the liqueur Chartreuse, which they make.

Cartier, Jacques (1491–1557) French navigator. In 1534, under the patronage of Francis I, he sailed in search of the *Northwest Passage and explored the coast of N Canada and Newfoundland. He subsequently sailed up the St Lawrence as far as present day Montreal but failed to found a colony there (1536). His discoveries were important to French claims in Canada in the 17th century.

Cartier-Bresson, Henri (1908–   ) French photographer and pioneer of photojournalism. He studied painting before taking up photography in 1932. Although also providing a record of events on his worldwide travels, his often poignant photographs, collected in such books as *The Decisive Moment* (1952), concentrate on ordinary people and their fleeting expressions and gestures. As a filmmaker, he collaborated with Jean *Renoir in the late 1930s and returned to this medium in the 1960s.

cartilage A flexible supportive tissue consisting chiefly of a *polysaccharide—chondroitin sulfate—in which elastic or collagen fibers may be embedded. Cartilage lines the bone ends at joints and also provides the skeleton of the nose, external ear, and parts of the throat (larynx) and airways of the respiratory tract. A tough cartilage forms the intervertebral disks between the bones of the spine. During development a large amount of *bone is formed from preexisting cartilage.

cartilaginous fish Any *fish belonging to the class *Chondrichthyes*, comprising the *sharks, *rays, and *chimaeras. They have a cartilaginous skeleton, usually a ventrally situated mouth, and exposed gill slits. The males have pelvic fins modified to form copulatory organs (claspers) and fertilization occurs inside the female's body. Some species deposit their eggs on the sea bed while in others the eggs are retained and develop internally resulting in the birth of live young.

cartography The science of map and chart making. Belief in the flatness of the world, the centrality of the Mediterranean lands (or Jerusalem in Christian maps), and an all-encircling ocean dominated classical and medieval cartography. Maps and charts were individually hand drawn at first, but 15th- and 16th-century maps were printed by woodblock and colored by hand. More elaborate maps and charts, richly decorated with lettering and illustrations, were introduced by the Italians in the mid-16th century. The difficulty of accurately representing the curved surface of the earth on the plane surface of a map is dealt with by using different □map projections for different purposes. Modern map making is assisted by aerial surveying and satellite photography.

cartoon 1. A full-sized preparatory drawing or painting for a mural, easel painting, tapestry, or mosaic. Among the most famous are Raphael's cartoons for tapestries for the Sistine Chapel in the Vatican. **2.** A nonrealistic portrait or figure drawing transferring a person's most readily recognizable features into a comic likeness. Beginning in Italy as a branch of high art with *Leonardo da Vinci's grotesque heads and *Bernini's political drawings, caricatures became a favorite genre in popular art with political satires. This tradition was carried into middle-class journalism in the Victorian period and has now become the widely used cartoon strip of modern newspapers.

Cartwright, Edmund (1743–1823) British inventor and industrialist, who contributed to the mechanization of weaving and spinning. In 1785 he invented a power loom and then set up a factory for weaving and spinning yarn. Four years later he invented a machine for combing wool.

Caruso, Enrico (1873–1921) Italian tenor, born in Naples. The greatest lyric tenor of his time, he excelled in Verdi and Puccini and was acclaimed in Europe and the US, where he sang at the Metropolitan Opera in New York City.

Carver, George Washington (1864–1943) US agriculturalist, born into a slave family. Carver demonstrated to southern farmers how fertility could be restored to their land by diversification, especially by planting peanuts and sweet potatoes. He also discovered a wide range of by-products that could be obtained from these crops. At Tuskegee Institute in Alabama, he devoted most of his life to teaching and conducting research.

Cary, (Arthur) Joyce (Lunel) (1888–1957) British novelist. His early novels, notably *Mister Johnson* (1939), are mostly set in West Africa, where he worked before settling in Oxford in 1920. His best-known book, *The Horse's Mouth* (1944), is part of a trilogy about art; he also wrote a second trilogy, about politics.

caryatid A carved column in the shape of a draped female figure that first appeared in Greek architecture around 500 BC. The most notable caryatids to have survived are on the Erechtheum on the *Acropolis of Athens. Caryatids were infrequent in Roman architecture but enjoyed a limited revival in 19th-century classicism.

caryopsis A grain: the small dry *fruit of grasses and cereals. It resembles an achene, being single-seeded and indehiscent, but differs in having the seed completely fused to the fruit wall.

Casablanca (Arabic name: Dar-el-Beida) 33 39N 7 35W A port in Morocco, on the Atlantic coast. First established by the Portuguese (1515), it was taken by the French in 1907. During World War II it was the scene of the Casablanca Conference (1943), a summit meeting between Franklin D. Roosevelt and Sir Winston Churchill. The largest and most important city in Morocco, its port handles most of the country's trade, the chief export being phosphates. Its major industries include textiles, electronics, chemicals, cement, and food processing. Fishing and tourism are also important. Population (1982): 2,139,204.

Casals, Pablo (Pau C.; 1876–1973) Spanish cellist, conductor, and composer. He performed and conducted in every European country and in the US. Casals revolutionized the style and technique of cello playing and excelled as an interpreter of Bach's six suites for unaccompanied cello and of the cello concertos of Dvořák, Elgar, and Schumann. An opponent of the Franco regime in Spain, Casals settled in Prades in France, near the Spanish border; he established a chamber-music festival there in 1950.

Casanova, Giovanni Giacomo, Chevalier de Seingalt (1725–98) Italian adventurer. He lived in many European cities, working at different times as a violinist, a spy, and a librarian. His adventures, which included a dramatic escape from prison in Venice in 1756 and many romantic liaisons, are recorded in his memoirs, of which the first complete edition was published in 1960.

Cascade Range A volcanic mountain range in North America. It extends N–S, nearly parallel to the Pacific coast, between the Fraser River in British Columbia (Canada) and N California (US), where it becomes continuous with the *Sierra Nevada. It reaches 14,408 ft (4392 m) at Mount Rainier.

GEORGE WASHINGTON CARVER *Agriculturalist whose research in crop diversification and land rejuvenation aided farmers.*

case hardening A surface-hardening process in *steel manufacture, in which the metal is heated to over 900°C for several hours in the presence of carbon. The carbon is absorbed on the surface to a depth depending on the temperature and duration of the treatment. The steel is then cooled quickly (quenched) to complete the process. *See also* heat treatment.

casein The major protein present in milk. Casein is easily digested and contains a good balance of essential *amino acids, making it—in dietary terms—a high-quality protein. Cheese consists largely of insoluble para-casein, formed from casein by the action of enzymes. Casein is also used industrially to make thermoplastics (e.g. knife handles), paints, and adhesives.

Casement, Sir Roger (David) (1864–1916) British consular official and Irish nationalist, who was executed by the British for treason. Casement spent his consular career in Africa. He retired to his birthplace, Ireland, in 1912. In

World War I he tried unsuccessfully to raise German help for the Irish national-
ists. Returning to Ireland in a German submarine, he was arrested, tried, and, in
spite of opposition, hanged.

Caserta 41·04N 14·20E A market city in S Italy, in Campania. The center of
Garibaldi's campaigns for the unification of Italy in the 19th century, it has a
12th-century cathedral and a palace. Its manufactures include chemicals. Population (1990 est): 68,000.

cashew A tree, *Anacardium occidentale*, native to tropical America and cultivated widely in the tropics. It grows to a height of about 40 ft (12 m) and has
sweet-scented red flowers. The fruit is a kidney-shaped nut that develops at the
end of a hanging pear-shaped receptacle. The edible kernel—the cashew nut—is
extracted after the fruit is roasted. Family: *Anacardiaceae*.

cashmere A warm soft wool-like fabric made from the undercoat of the
*Kashmir goat, produced mainly in China, Mongolia, and Iran. Originally used
in shawls from Kashmir, it is an expensive fabric as each goat produces only
small quantities of fine soft hair and processing is costly. Imitations are common
and any soft woolen textile, natural or synthetic, is frequently called cashmere.

Casimir (III) the Great (1310–70) King of Poland (1333–70). Casimir extended Polish territory, codified laws, and founded Cracow University (1364).
He encouraged the development of Polish culture and bettered the lot of the
peasants.

Casimir IV (1427–92) Grand Duke of Lithuania (1440–92) and King of
Poland (1447–92), whose reign saw a flowering of Polish culture. Casimir
greatly enhanced the prestige of the Jagiellon dynasty by his own and his children's political marriages. After a 13-year war with the *Teutonic Knights he
won control of W Prussia (1466).

Caspian Sea The largest inland sea in the world, bounded by Iran, Azerbaijan, Russia, Kazakhstan, and Turkmenistan and fed chiefly by the Volga River.
Its surface is 93.5 ft (28.5 m) below sea level and is generally becoming lower
due to irrigation and increased evaporation from the Volga. The chief ports are
Astrakhan, Russia, and Baku, Azerbaijan. Sturgeon and seals are caught here
and oil and gas extracted. Area: about 142,827 sq mi (370,000 sq km).

Cass, Lewis (1782–1866) US politician and statesman. A lawyer and state
legislator in Ohio, he was then governor of Michigan Territory (1813–31). Appointed secretary of war in 1831 by Pres. Andrew *Jackson, he served through
the Black Hawk and Seminole wars before being appointed minister to France
(1836–42). He was a senator from Michigan (1845–48; 1849–57), ran for president in 1848, and was secretary of state (1857–60) under Pres. James
*Buchanan. During his extensive career he successfully negotiated with the In-
dians and supported the popular sovereignty doctrine of allowing the territorial
settlers to resolve the question of slavery among themselves.

Cassander (c. 358–297 BC) King of Macedon (305–297). In the wars of succession that followed the death of Alexander the Great in 323, Cassander fought
for control of parts of Alexander's empire and won most of Macedon and Greece.
He murdered Alexander's mother, widow, and son to secure his position.

Cassandra A legendary Greek prophetess, daughter of King Priam of Troy.
After she had refused to submit to Apollo's advances, he condemned her
prophecies to eternal disbelief. When Troy fell she was taken by Agamemnon,
with whom she was later murdered.

Cassatt, Mary (1844–1926) US painter. She worked chiefly in Paris, where
she exhibited with the impressionists (1879–81, 1886) the only American to do

so. Although she was influenced by her friend *Degas she developed a distinctly American style. Typical of her work are mother-and-child scenes.

cassava A shrubby flowering plant, *Manihot esculentus* (or *M. utilissimus*), also known as manioc, native to tropical America. Many varieties of this species—divided into two groups, sweet and bitter cassavas—are cultivated in the tropics for their edible starchy tuberous roots. These can be processed into tapioca, ground to produce manioc or cassava meal (Brazilian arrowroot), used as animal fodder, or cooked and eaten as a vegetable. Family: *Euphorbiaceae* (spurge family).

cassette A plastic case containing a length of magnetic audio or video recording tape wound onto two spools. Cassettes are easy to use but can hold only relatively short tapes, their length being limited by the minimum thickness of tape that can be used without breakage. Commercial cassettes are two-track, i.e. can be used to record in both directions.

cassia The aromatic bark of a Chinese tree, *Cinnamomum cassia*, used as a substitute for cinnamon. The dried unripe fruits (cassia buds) are also used as a spice. Family: *Lauraceae*.

MARY CASSATT Morning Toilet, *painted in 1886.*

Cassia A genus of trees, shrubs, and herbs (500–600 species) of tropical and warm regions of Asia, Africa, and America. The laxative drug senna is extracted from the dried leaves and pods (fruits) of many cultivated species. The fruit of *C. fistula* (Cassia pods) is also used as a laxative. Some species are grown as ornamentals. Family: *Leguminosae.*

Cassini's division. *See* Saturn.

Cassino 41 29N 13 50E A town in central Italy, in Lazio. It was a key position during World War II and the town and Benedictine monastery (Monte Cassino) were destroyed in the fighting of 1944.

Cassiodorus, Flavius Magnus Aurelius (c. 490–c. 583 AD) Christian writer, born in S Italy, who helped to preserve classical learning. After serving in the government of the Ostrogothic king Theodoric I, Cassiodorus retired to found a monastery at Vivarium in Calabria (550); his most famous work, the *Institutiones*, was a guide to the education of monks.

Cassiopeia A conspicuous constellation in the N sky, lying partly in the Milky Way. The five brightest stars form a W-shape. It contains the remnants of two recent *supernovae—**Tycho's star** and the intense radio source **Cassiopeia A.**

cassiopeium. *See* lutetium.

Cassirer, Ernst (1874–1945) German philosopher and historian. He taught in Hamburg (1919–34) until Nazism forced him into exile in the US. Interested in people's formation of concepts, he added mythical, historical, and practical categories, based on analysis of language, to *Kant's scientific ones, seeing these as complementary views of one reality. His works include *Substance and Function* (1910) and *Philosophy of Symbolic Forms* (1923).

cassiterite The only commercial ore of tin, consisting of stannic oxide. It is found in association with acid igneous rocks and as alluvial deposits. It is brown or black.

Cassius Longinus, Gaius (d. 42 BC) Roman general. Having shown competence in eastern campaigns, Cassius supported *Pompey until Pompey's defeat by Julius Caesar at *Pharsalus. He was then pardoned by Caesar but joined the conspiracy to assassinate him in 44. Outlawed, Cassius committed suicide after defeat in the battle of *Philippi.

Cassivelaunus King of the Catuvellauni, who organized, with some success, resistance to Caesar's invasion of SE Britain in 54 BC. Only after his stronghold was captured did Cassivelaunus agree to peace terms.

cassowary A large flightless bird belonging to a family (*Casuariidae*; 3 species) occurring in rain forests of Australia and New Guinea. The largest cassowary (*Casuarius casuarius*) is 60 in (150 cm) tall and has a black plumage, two red throat wattles, and a blue head with a protective bony helmet. Cassowaries have long powerful legs, each having a long sharp claw, and feed on seeds and berries. Order: *Casuariiformes*.

Castagno, Andrea del (Andrea di Bartolo de Simone; c. 1421–57) Italian *Renaissance painter, who was born near Castagno but settled in Florence. His major frescoes depict the *Last Supper* and the *Passion* (Sta Apollonia, Florence). Later works, showing the influence of *Donatello, include the equestrian portrait of *Niccolò da Tolentino* (Duomo, Florence).

castanets A percussion instrument used in Spain and Italy, consisting of two small cup-shaped pieces of wood (usually chestnut) attached to the finger and thumb of each hand. These are clapped together and dancers often accompany themselves with them. In the symphony orchestra the characteristic sound is produced by two wooden cups attached to a handle and shaken. □musical instruments.

Castel Gandolfo (Latin name: Alba Longa) 41 45N 12 39E A village in central Italy, in Lazio on the shore of Lake Albano. The summer residence of the pope is situated here.

Castellammare di Stabia 38 01N 12 52E A seaport and resort in Italy, in Campania on the Bay of Naples. It was the site of the Roman resort of Stabiae, which was destroyed by the eruption of Vesuvius in 79 AD. Industries include marine engineering and textiles. Population: 68,629.

Castellón de la Plana 39 59N 0 03W A city in E Spain. Its industries include textiles and paper and it exports oranges and almonds through its port, El Gráo. Population (1991): 133,180.

Castelo Branco, Camilo (1825–95) Portuguese novelist. An illegitimate child with little formal education, he led an adventurous life that is reflected in his many popular novels and stories. His best-known work, *Amor de Perdição* (1862), was written while he was in prison for adultery. Suffering from blindness, he committed suicide.

castes The elements of a system of social stratification in which social boundaries are very definite. A pure caste system consists of a hierarchy of hereditary endogamous occupational groups, in which positions are fixed and mobility from one caste to another is prevented by ritual systems. The classical Hindu caste system (Sanskrit word: varna) of India provides the cardinal example. Traditionally there are four main caste divisions: brahmins (priests), ksatriyas (warriors), vaisyas (merchants), and sundras (serfs). Outside these groups are the "outcastes" or "untouchables." Each stratum is elaborately subdivided; the 1901 census identified 2378 main castes, some of which had several hundred subcastes. Vigorous attempts have been made to abolish the system, especially by Mahatma Gandhi, but despite legislation (1947) abolishing "untouchability" and prohibiting discrimination on the basis of caste, prejudice remains strong.

Castiglione, Baldassare (1478–1529) Italian courtier and writer. A member of an aristocratic family, he was born near Mantua and in 1503 entered the service of the Duke of Urbino, whose court was one of the most distinguished in Renaissance Italy. He performed important diplomatic missions for the Duke; he was later Mantuan ambassador in Rome and after 1524 in the service of Pope Clement VII as papal nuncio in Spain. His literary reputation rests on *Il Cortegiano* (1528), prose dialogues, set in the court of Urbino, which describe the qualities of the ideal courtier. The work was translated into English as *The Courtier* by Sir Thomas Hoby (1530–66) in 1561 and exercised a great influence on such writers as Surrey, Wyatt, and Sidney.

Castile A former kingdom in central Spain. Originally a district at the foot of the Cantabrian Mountains, Castile expanded to the Duero River in the 9th and 10th centuries, becoming a united county. In 1035 it became a kingdom and in 1230 was united with the kingdom of *León, a union dominated by Castile. In 1479 Spain was virtually united following the marriage of *Isabella of Castile to *Ferdinand of Aragon and Castile became the political, administrative, cultural, and linguistic center of Spain. Today, opposition to Castilian dominance persists.

Castilho, Antonio Feliciano de (1800–75) Portuguese poet. Blind from childhood, he achieved literary distinction after publishing several volumes of romantic poetry, notably *A Noite de Castelo* (1836). After 1840 he worked mainly on translations, and his advocacy of neoclassical doctrines provoked fierce controversy.

casting metals The process of shaping molten metals in a mold. In casting individual items a sand mold is often used. A solid pattern of the shape, made of wood, plastic, or metal, is placed in a molding box packed tightly with sand bonded with oil or clay. The pattern is then carefully removed leaving a shaped cavity into which the molten metal is poured and allowed to solidify. If the casting is to be repeated, permanent metal molds called dies are used. **Die casting** is faster and can make more complex shapes than foundry sand casting. **Centrifugal casting**, spinning the molten material at a high speed so that the centrifugal force flings it outward into a surrounding mold, is used for pipes and similar shapes.

cast iron A form of impure iron containing between 2.5% and 4.5% of carbon by weight. The high carbon content makes it relatively hard and brittle and it tends to crack under tension. Cast iron is made by casting *pig iron and adjusting its composition to improve the strength. It is used for complicated shapes.

castle A fortified defensive building. Its name deriving from Latin *castellum*, a small fortified place, the castle underwent many changes in its history to counteract the development of increasingly powerful weapons. In the early Middle Ages a castle consisted of a simple building on a mound of earth surrounded by a wooden fence (the motte and bailey castle), a design later copied in stone. The simplest stone castle, such as the White Tower in London, is called a keep or donjon. Later designs became more complicated, involving extensive outworks of battlemented towers and walls (curtain walls), for example Caernarfon Castle in Wales. As they could not be built to withstand cannon fire, castles lost their military usefulness; some, such as Windsor Castle, were converted into large houses.

Castle Hill Rising (1804) An uprising in New South Wales (Australia) led by Irish convicts against the government. The rebels seized the convict station at Parramatta but were defeated by government troops, who killed 15 convicts. Nine rebels were tried and hanged.

Castlereagh, Robert Stewart, Viscount (1769–1822) British statesman, born in Ireland; foreign secretary (1812–22). A member of the Irish Parliament (1780), he became Viscount Castlereagh in 1796. Appointed chief secretary for Ireland in 1798, he resigned in 1801, when George III rejected the Catholic Emancipation bill. He was secretary for war (1807–09), and as foreign secretary he played an important role at the Congress of *Vienna (1814–15).

Castner process The production of sodium cyanide from molten sodium, charcoal, and ammonia. Sodamide and sodium cyanamide are by-products. The extremely poisonous sodium cyanide finds use in the extraction of gold and silver, in hardening steel, and in dye manufacture. Named for Hamilton Young Castner (1859–99).

Castor A white star, apparent magnitude 1.56 and 46 light years distant, that is the second brightest star in the constellation Gemini. It is a *multiple star. Castor and *Pollux are named for the twins of classical mythology.

Castor and Pollux Twin heroes of classical mythology, also known as the Dioscuri. Pollux was immortal, the son of *Zeus and *Leda; Castor was mortal, the son of Tyndareus and Leda. When Castor died, Pollux successfully petitioned Zeus to allow them to remain unseparated. They were transformed into the Gemini constellation and were the patrons of mariners.

castor oil A pale yellow viscous oil extracted from the seeds of the *castor-oil plant. It is used as a laxative and is also a raw material for the manufacture of resins, plastics, and lubricants.

castor-oil plant A flowering plant, *Ricinus communis*, up to 40 ft (12 m) high, native to tropical Africa and Asia. It is cultivated widely in the tropics for its seeds, from which castor oil is extracted, and in temperate regions as an ornamental shrub with attractive fanlike leaves (ornamental forms are seldom taller than 7 ft [2 m]). Family: *Euphorbiaceae* (spurge family).

494

CASTLE

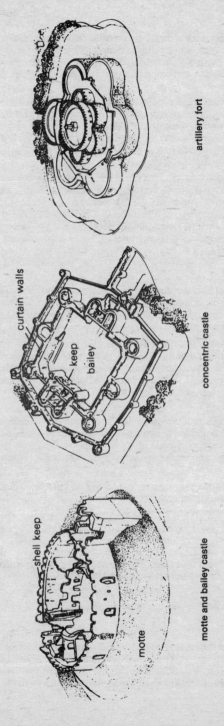

shell keep

motte

motte and bailey castle

curtain walls

keep
bailey

concentric castle

artillery fort

CASTLE *The early medieval motte and bailey plan gave way to the massive fortifications of the 14th and 15th centuries, which were in turn superseded by the artillery fort with its low walls and sweeping lines of fire.*

castration Removal of the testes (orchidectomy) or ovaries (oophorectomy). In medicine, castration may be performed in cases of cancer of the testes: it always produces sterility but—unless done before puberty—need not cause impotence. Testicular castration is widely used in livestock management to increase meat production or docility.

castrato A eunuch singer, fashionable in Italian opera and in church choirs during the 17th and 18th centuries. Castration before puberty ensured that the soprano (or sometimes alto) voice quality remained in adulthood. Among the most technically brilliant of the castrati was Giuseppe Farinelli (1705–1782). Composers of Italian opera, such as Handel, frequently wrote the leading male role in the soprano range for a eunuch.

Castres 43 36N 2 14E A city in S France, in the Tarn department. A Huguenot stronghold in the 16th century, it has a major machine-tool industry. Population: 47,527.

Castries 14 01N 60 59W The chief city and main port of St Lucia, in the Windward Islands. Founded by the French in 1650, it has a fine harbor. Population (1990): 11,147.

Castro (Ruz), Fidel (1926–   ) Cuban statesman. The son of a wealthy sugar planter, Castro became an opponent of the dictator Fulgencio *Batista. On July 26, 1953, he led an unsuccessful attack on the Moncada barracks and was imprisoned until 1955. In 1956 he invaded Cuba from Mexico with a small armed band and after a long guerrilla war he defeated government troops. He entered Havana on Jan 1, 1959. Castro established a socialist government, which the US long attempted to subvert. As a result, Cuba became heavily dependent on the Soviet Union until the end of the 1980s. *See also* Bay of Pigs.

Castrop-Rauxel 51 33N 07 18E A city in NW Germany, in North Rhine-Westphalia in the *Ruhr. Its industries include coal mining and chemicals. Population: 83,100.

Casuarina A genus of shrubs and trees (about 45 species) native to Australia, tropical SE Asia, Malaysia, Polynesia, the Mascarene Islands, and Pacific islands. The young branches, which are slender, green, and drooping, function as leaves (the true leaves are reduced to scales). The she oak (*C. equisetifolia*), up to 145 ft (45 m) tall, is widely cultivated in warm regions for its very hard reddish-brown wood (beefwood or ironwood) and as an ornamental. Family: *Casuarinaceae*.

cat A carnivorous mammal belonging to the family *Felidae* (36 species). Most cats have sheathed claws and sharp canine teeth to kill their prey, which consists of mammals, birds, and fish. Their acute vision (especially in poor light), sense of smell, and hearing are adaptations for hunting stealthily, often at night. With no natural enemies, the kittens (or cubs) are born blind and toothless and learn hunting techniques through play.

The wide range of different breeds of domestic cat (*Felis catus*), including *Persian, *Siamese, and *Abyssinian, are thought to have been developed from the African wildcat, or cafer cat (*F. lybica*) and possibly the European *wildcat. Wild species range in size from the *tiger to the tiny South African black-footed cat (*F. nigripes*), which is smaller than the average domestic cat.

catabolism. *See* metabolism.

catacombs Subterranean cemeteries, especially those containing early Christian graves. The earliest and biggest catacombs are in Rome, particularly those of St Calixtus and St Sebastian along the *Appian Way. Most catacombs consist of narrow passages into the walls of which the burial niches were cut. With the acceptance of Christianity they fell into disuse, although some remained as centers of pilgrimage.

Catalan A *Romance language spoken by about five million people in Catalonia and the Balearic Islands in Spain, Andorra, and the Roussillon region of France. It is closely related to Spanish and to the Occitan language of France. It was the official language of Aragon in the 12th century and has a literature dating from this period.

FIDEL CASTRO *The Cuban leader exhorts the UN General Assembly to give more aid to the developing countries.*

Catalaunian Plains, Battle of the (451 AD) The battle on the Catalaunian Plains, probably near modern Châlons-sur-Marne in Champagne (E France), in which the Huns under *Attila were defeated by a combined force of Romans and Visigoths under *Aetius and Theodoric I.

catalepsy A condition associated with certain abnormal mental states, including schizophrenia and hysteria, in which the patient, usually female, remains motionless, often with the limbs in fixed positions, for a variable length of time.

Catalhüyük A Neolithic site SE of Konya (S Turkey), discovered in 1958. It was a settlement of cattle breeders and agriculturalists, dating from the late 7th and early 6th millenniums BC. Houses built to a standard pattern and luxury goods, such as obsidian mirrors, suggest advanced social organization. Notable finds include numerous shrines with frescoes or plasterwork decorations depicting animals.

Catalonia (Spanish name: Cataluña; Catalan name: Catalunya) A mainly mountainous region of NE Spain, on the Mediterranean Sea. Agriculture is important, the main crops being cereals, olives, and grapes. It is the most highly industrialized region in Spain, being well provided with hydroelectric power from the Ebro River (and its tributaries). Tourism is important, especially on the coast. *History*: united with Aragon in 1137 and Castile in 1497, Catalonia has nevertheless maintained a strong separatist tradition. In 1932 an autonomous government was established and this lasted throughout the Civil War (1936–39), in which Catalonia played a prominent role on the Republican side. A center of opposition throughout the Franco regime, the Catalan government was restored provisionally in 1977. Area: 12,329 sq mi (31,932 sq km). Population (1991): 5,959,929. Capital: Barcelona.

Catalpa A genus of trees (11 species) native to E Asia, North America, and the West Indies. They were widely grown as ornamentals for their attractive heart-shaped leaves, 5–12 in (12–30 cm) long, and trumpet-shaped flowers, which are white with yellow and purple markings. The fruit is a long pod. The genus includes the Indian bean tree (*C. bignonioides*), up to 49 ft (15 m) high, which yields a durable timber. Famiy: *Bignoniaceae*.

catalysis The acceleration of a *chemical reaction by a substance (catalyst) that is not itself consumed in the reaction. Virtually every reaction must overcome an energy barrier as the molecules of the reactants rearrange to form the products. The catalyst allows the reaction to proceed via a different lower-energy pathway. Since the reverse reaction is also accelerated, catalysis does not shift the chemical equilibrium, merely speeds its attainment. Catalysis may be homogeneous (all substances in the same phase), as the catalysis of carbon-monoxide combustion by steam; or heterogeneous (at an interface) as in the *Haber-Bosch process. Catalysis by a reaction product is called autocatalysis. Catalysis is used extensively in industrial chemical processes. In living organisms, *enzymes are catalysts for biochemical reactions.

catalytic cracking A chemical process used in *oil refining. Crude oil, which contains large molecules, is decomposed by heat and pressure in the presence of a catalyst, usually a clay-type substance containing alumina and silica. Without a catalyst the same process, known as thermal cracking, needs a pressure of between 20 and 40 atmospheres and a temperature of 332°F (540°C). Catalytic cracking is carried out at between 2 and 3 atmospheres at a slightly lower temperature.

catamaran A modern sailing vessel with two identical hulls, rigidly fastened parallel to one another, and, usually, a single mast with a triangular mainsail and jib. Becuase of their buoyancy, the hulls of a catamaran offer very little resistance to the water, making it extremely fast. The modern catamaran is modeled on a native canoe-like vessel of the SW Pacific, which in some forms was basically a raft with a sail. *See also* trimaran.

Catania 37 31N 15 06E A port in Italy, in E Sicily near Mount Etna. Destroyed by an earthquake in 1693, it was rebuilt in a baroque style. The university was founded in 1434. Its industries include sulfur refining. Population (1991 est): 364,000.

Catanzaro 38 54N 16 36E A market city in S Italy, the capital of Calabria. Citrus fruit is grown in the area. Population (1991 est): 104,000.

cataract (geography). *See* waterfall.

cataract (ophthalmology) Opacities in the lens of the eye resulting in blurred vision and caused by the deposition of small crystals or changes in the composition of the lens substance. The former condition increases with age; such cataracts are a common cause of blindness in the elderly. Certain diseases, such as poorly controlled diabetes mellitus, can also lead to cataracts. Cataracts are usually treated by surgical removal of the lens and the use of appropriate glasses. In some cases a plastic lens may be implanted to replace the one removed.

catarrh Inflammation of the mucous membranes lining the nose, nasal sinuses, throat, or air passages, causing the production of thick phlegm. Catarrh is commonly due to viral infections, particularly the common cold, and hay fever.

catastrophe theory A theory of dynamic systems using methods of *topology. Originally, catastrophe theory was developed by the French mathematician René Thom (1923–   ), in 1972, as a theory of biological differentiation, in which gradual growth stimulates and is stimulated by "catastrophic" large-scale changes. It has since been applied to other fields, including optics, engineering, sociology, economics, and linguistics. The theory is based on analogy with topological form. For instance, if a system depends on three factors, a particular state of the system can be represented by a point in three-dimensional space and possible states are represented by a region (or shape). The behavior of the system is investigated by considering the topological classification of these representations; in particular the theory shows how discontinuous catastrophic changes can occur. In engineering, a stucture may be stable under a certain range of conditions and collapse if other conditions are applied.

catastrophism A formerly held theory according to which geological changes have occurred as a result of sudden short-lived catastrophes. Such events do occur (e.g. floods), but they have temporary and local effects. *Compare* uniformitarianism.

Catawba American Indian tribe, Siouan-speaking, found in US in present-day North Carolina and South Carolina. Potters and basketweavers, they allied with the colonials and helped fight off other Indians, especially the *Cherokee and *Iroquois.

catchment area The area from which a river is fed with water; it is usually bounded by a *watershed or divide.

catechism A form of instruction in the essentials of Christian doctrine. Catechisms were originally for the instruction of converts preparing for *baptism, frequently taking the form of a set of responses. With the spread of infant baptism, from the 6th century their functions became the basic education of children in the faith, often as preparation for *confirmation. After the Reformation, printed forms of catechisms were also used as an expression of particular churches' beliefs.

catechol (pyrocatechol *or* 1,2 dihydroxy-benzene; $C_6H_4(OH)_2$) A colorless crystalline *aromatic compound used as a developer in photography. *See also* catecholamines.

catecholamines Amine derivatives of the chemical compound *catechol. They include the biologically important compounds *adrenaline, *noradrenaline, and dopamine, which act as neurotransmitters and hormones.

catechu A vegetable extract containing *tannin and used in tanning and dyeing. Black catechu is obtained mainly from the wood of trees. Pale catechu (gambier; terra japonica) is produced from leaves and is used in medicine as an astringent. Extract from betel or areca nuts is also called catechu.

categorical imperative The fundamental moral law in *Kant's ethical theory: an act is moral only if the principle on which it is justified is universally applicable.

catenary The curve obtained by suspending a string between two points. If the middle of the string, the lowest point, is at height a above a reference level, then the height y, at distance x along the string from the middle, is given by: $y = \frac{1}{2}a$ $(e^{x/a} + e^{-x/a})$

caterpillar The larva of a butterfly or moth. Soft-bodied and wingless, all caterpillars have a head and 13 body segments with three pairs of true thoracic legs and five pairs of abdominal prolegs, which aid in locomotion. The mouthparts are variously adapted for chewing leaves or feeding on sap. Some species are serious crop pests. Caterpillars exhibit a wide variety of camouflaging or warning coloration and patterning. Some produce irritating or poisonous secretions. *See also* butterflies and moths.

catfish A *bony fish of the order *Siluriformes* (about 2500 species), with a stout scaleless body, 2–180 in (4–450 cm) long, a broad flat head, and long whisker-like barbels. Freshwater catfish (family *Ictaluridae*), sometimes called bullheads, occur worldwide; marine catfish (family *Ariidae*) inhabit tropical and coastal waters and are generally bottom-dwelling scavengers used as food, game, and aquarium fish. *See also* candiru; wels.

catgut The tough cord made from the intestines of the sheep or sometimes the ox and the horse (but not the cat). It is used for stringing tennis rackets, violin strings, and for surgical stitching.

Cathari (*or* Cathars) A heretical sect in medieval Europe. It spread from Bulgaria, where its adherents were called Bogomils, to W Europe in the 11th century. From the mid-12th century the Cathari flourished in S France (*see* Albigenses) and in Italy until they were wiped out in the 14th century by the Inquisition. Their doctrine, influenced by *Gnosticism and *Manichaeism, taught that the material world was irredeemably evil but that man's soul was good and could secure his reunion with God. They were skeptical about much biblical doctrine, holding, for instance, that Christ was only an angel. They were divided into two classes, the perfect and the believers. The perfect lived in celibacy, marriage being regarded, with all other fleshly indulgences, as evil. The believers could join the perfect immediately before death by receiving the Cathari's chief rite, a laying on of hands, called the *consolamentum*.

Cathay The medieval European name for China, derived from Khitan, the name of a Mongol people who invaded N China in the 10th century. It was introduced to Europe by such early travelers as Marco Polo. China is still called Khitan by the Russians.

cathedral The principal church of an ecclesiastical area (diocese), governed by a bishop or an archbishop. The name comes from Latin *cathedra*, bishop's seat. Generally larger and more magnificent than other churches, cathedrals, such as *St Peter's Basilica, Rome, *St Paul's Cathedral, London, and *Notre-Dame de Paris, contain some of their country's finest works of art.

Cather, Willa (1873–1947) US author. She wrote about the pioneers and their lives on the Nebraska frontier, where she had lived during her formative years, and the Southwest, which she had visited. As a young woman she worked on *The Home Monthly* and taught school before becoming editor (1908–12) of *McClure's Magazine*. Her works include *O Pioneers!* (1913), *My Antonia* (1918), *One of Ours* (1922), for which she won a Pulitzer Prize, *A Lost Lady* (1923), *The Professor's House* (1927), *Death Comes for the Archbishop* (1927), and *Shadows on the Rock* (1931).

Catherine I (1684–1727) The second wife, from 1712, of Peter the Great and Empress of Russia (1725–27). Of Lithuanian peasant origin, Catherine was captured in 1702 in the Great Northern War and became Peter's mistress. After Peter's death in 1725, his adviser Prince A. D. Menshikov (1672–1729), supported by the palace guards, secured the throne for Catherine.

Catherine (II) the Great (1729–96) Empress of Russia (1762–96), who gained the throne in a coup in which her unpopular husband, Emperor Peter III

(1728–62; reigned 1762), was murdered. Catherine's reign was noted for the expansion of Russian territory largely as a result of her successful wars against the Turks (1768–72, 1787–92) and the partition of Poland (1772, 1793, 1795). Influenced by the ideas of the Enlightenment, she professed an interest in reform but abandoned her scheme to emancipate the serfs in the face of opposition from their masters, whose privileges she ultimately reinforced. Of the series of lovers for whom Catherine achieved notoriety, only *Potemkin exerted a durable influence on government.

Catherine de' Medici (1519–89) Regent of France (1560–63) during the minority of her second son, Charles IX, and virtual ruler until his death (1574). The daughter of Lorenzo de' Medici, Duke of Urbino, she married Henry II of France in 1533. Intent on upholding royal authority during the *Wars of Religion, she initially advocated tolerance for the *Huguenots but later supported the Catholic party. She was largely responsible for the *St Bartholomew's Day Massacre. Catherine's influence waned during the reign of her third son *Henry III.

Catherine of Aragon (1485–1536) The first wife (1509–33) of *Henry VIII of England and the mother of Mary I. Failing to bear him a son, she was divorced by Henry, who argued that their marriage was invalid because Catherine was the widow of his brother Arthur. The pope's refusal to accept their divorce provoked the English *Reformation.

Catherine of Braganza (1638–1705) The wife (from 1662) of Charles II of England. A Portuguese princess and a devout Roman Catholic, her unpopularity was intensified by her failure to produce an heir to the throne.

Catherine of Genoa, St (1447–1510) Italian mystic. From a noble family, she married at the age of 16 but underwent a religious conversion 10 years later and devoted herself to caring for the sick. She had a number of mystical experiences, which are recounted in *Vita e dottrina* (1551), a book that is perhaps not all her own work in its present form. Feast day: Sept 15.

Catherine of Siena, St (Caterina Benincasa; 1347–80) Italian nun and mystic. Devout from the earliest age, she joined the Dominican Tertiary Order at 16 and devoted herself to caring for the sick and poor and to contemplation. In 1376 she undertook a journey to Avignon to persuade Pope Gregory IX to return to Rome. She was reported to have received the stigmata on her body in 1375. Her letters and a work on mysticism, the *Dialogue*, are extant. Feast day: April 30.

catheter A tube inserted into a hollow organ of the body in order to drain or introduce fluids. A urinary catheter is inserted into the bladder through the urethra to relieve obstruction (commonly caused by enlargement of the prostate gland in elderly men) to the flow of urine. Cardiac catheters are used to measure blood pressure in the heart; similar catheters are used to inject radio-opaque substances into blood vessels for X-ray examination.

cathode The negative electrode of an electrolytic cell, valve, etc. It is the electrode by which the electrons enter the system. *Compare* anode.

cathode-ray oscilloscope (CRO) An instrument that displays electrical quantities on the screen of a *cathode-ray tube. It can be used to show the variation of a signal strength with time or with another electrical quantity. The CRO is used extensively in electronics laboratories and in other scientific work.

cathode rays A stream of electrons emitted by a *cathode, when a voltage is applied between a cathode and an *anode either in an evacuated glass tube or one containing gas at low pressure. The electron beam can be focused onto a fluorescent screen to produce a visual display. This effect is used in the *cathode-ray tube used in television receivers, radar screens, and oscilloscopes.

cathode-ray tube (CRT) A vacuum tube that converts electrical signals into visible form by projecting a beam of electrons onto a fluorescent screen. It is an essential component of the television receiver and the *cathode-ray oscilloscope (CRO). The electron beam is produced by an electron gun, and deflected horizontally and vertically by an arrangement of plates and magnets, which move it back and forth across the screen and focus it by creating an *electromagnetic field, the strength of which varies according to input signals. In a television tube the beam intensity varies to form the light and dark regions of the picture.

Catholic emancipation A campaign in Britain and Ireland to secure full civil and political rights for Roman Catholics. Since the Reformation, Catholics had been subject to a number of restrictions concerning property ownership, inheritance, and government employment and could not sit in Parliament. In the late 18th century several relief acts were passed but parliamentary representation was still denied until the Catholic Emancipation Act of 1829 restored most rights.

Catiline (Lucius Sergius Catilina; d. 62 BC) Roman politician, who plotted to seize power in 62. Thwarted by Cicero, Catiline fled to a rebel force in Etruria and his fellow conspirators were executed. He was defeated and killed in battle.

Catlin, George (1796–1872) Pennsylvania artist and author. He is famous for his painted and written studies of the American Indians, among whom he lived (1832–40). His best-known book is *Manners, Customs, and Conditions of North American Indians* (1841).

GEORGE CATLIN *A painting by the artist depicting himself (left) in the lodge of a Mandan Indian chief. Catlin made a number of drawings and paintings of this people in 1832.*

catmint A perennial flowering plant, *Nepeta cataria*, native to chalky regions of temperate Europe. The branching stem grows to a height of 16–40 in (40–100 cm) and bears toothed heart-shaped leaves and small white flowers spotted with purple. The plant has a strong minty scent, attractive to cats. Family: *Labiatae*.

Cato Street Conspiracy (1820) A conspiracy against the British government led by Arthur Thistlewood (1770–1820). A fanatical idealist, Thistlewood and four others planned to murder all the ministers of the cabinet as a prelude to insurrection. Their attempt was foiled and the leaders, arrested in Cato Street, London, were hanged.

Cato the Elder (Marcus Porcius C.; 234–149 BC) Roman statesman, who wrote the first history of Rome. A moral and political conservative, Cato as censor (184) legislated against luxury and sponsored improvements in public works. His embassy to Carthage (153) led him to fear the resurgence of Rome's old enemy; "Carthage must be destroyed" was his repeated cry until the third *Punic War was declared (149). His simple writing style was influential and he is the first important Latin prose author.

Cato the Younger (Marcus Porcius C.; 95–46 BC) Roman politician; the great-grandson of Cato the Elder and an opponent of Julius Caesar. Caesar created the first *Triumvirate (60) to neutralize Cato's opposition to his dictatorial ambitions. Forced to support Pompey in the civil war in an attempt to save the Republic, Cato escaped after Pompey's death to Utica, in Africa. There, on hearing of Caesar's victory at *Thapsus, he committed suicide after ensuring the evacuation of his supporters.

Catskill Mountains A mountain range in the N Appalachian Mountains of New York. Consisting of forested steep-sided mountains, it rises to 4204 ft (1261 m) at Slide Mountain. The area supplies water to New York City and is a popular vacation and recreation area for New Yorkers. The mountains are associated with the fictional character Rip Van Winkle, created by Washington Irving.

cat's-tail. *See* reedmace.

Catt, Carrie Lane Chapman (1859–1947) US reformer. She was a leader in the woman's suffrage movement and was, in great part, responsible for the ratification of the 19th Amendment in 1920. She headed the National American Woman Suffrage Association (1915–47), reorganizing it into the League of Women Voters after 1920. She was also deeply interested in peace and disarmament movements, Prohibition organizations, and the United Nations, and she helped found the Daughters of the American Revolution (DAR).

cattle *Ruminant mammals belonging to the genus *Bos* (7 species), also called oxen, native to Eurasia and Africa. Modern domestic cattle (*B. taurus*), which are probably descended from such ancestors as the *auroch, vary in body shape, size, and color according to breed but are generally 35–44 in (90–110 cm) high at the shoulder and weigh 882–1984 lb (400–900 kg). *Zebus and *gayals are similarly now found only in the domestic state. Cattle are used for milk and meat production and for draft purposes (*see* livestock farming). Family: *Bovidae. See also* banteng; gaur; yak.

Cattleya A genus of tropical American epiphytic *orchids (about 65 species), grown commercially for ornament and the florist trade. They have large pseudobulbs, one or two leaves, and clusters of 1–30 large brightly colored flowers. *C. labiata* has been crossed with other orchid genera to produce many showy hybrids.

Catton, (Charles) Bruce (1899–1978) US historian, especially of the Civil War. Editor of *American Heritage* magazine from 1954, he wrote about the Civil War from the participants' point of view. His works earned him a Pulitzer Prize twice, for *A Stillness at Appomattox* (1953) and *The American Heritage Picture History of the Civil War* (1960). Other works include *Mr. Lincoln's Army* (1951), *Glory Road* (1952), *This Hallowed Ground* (1956), *Grant Moves South* (1960), and *The Terrible Swift Sword* (1963).

Catullus, Valerius (c. 84–c. 54 BC) Roman poet. Born in Verona, he became the leading member of a group of young innovative poets in Rome; 116 poems survive, of which the most famous are the 25 lyrics addressed to a married woman named Lesbia, recording in passionate language the shifting moods of love from ecstasy to despair. The other poems include elegies and vicious satirical attacks on Julius Caesar and other politicians.

Caucasian languages. *See* Northeast Caucasian; Northwest Caucasian; South Caucasian.

Caucasoid A race or group of races and peoples originally inhabiting Europe, North Africa, and the Near East. In modern times Caucasoids have spread to North and South America, Australia, New Zealand, parts of Africa, and elsewhere. They are characterized by skin pigmentation ranging from very pale to dark brown, straight to curly hair, narrow high-bridged noses, plentiful body hair, and a high frequency of Rh-negative blood type.

Caucasus Mountains (Russian name: Kavkaz) Two mountain ranges in Russia, Georgia, Armenia, Azerbaijan, and Turkey extending NW–SE between the Black Sea and the Caspian Sea and separated by the Kura River: the **Great Caucasus**, some 621 mi (1000 km) long, to the N and the **Little Caucasus**, about half that length, along the Turkish border. Their highest point is Mount *Elbrus. *See also* Ciscaucasia; Transcaucasia.

Cauchy, Augustin Louis, Baron (1789–1857) French mathematician, who pioneered the study of functions of *complex numbers. He also derived a mathematical basis for the luminiferous ether. An outspoken and extreme conservative, Cauchy went into exile in Italy in 1830 on the accession of King Louis Philippe.

cauliflower A variety of wild *cabbage, *Brassica oleracea* var. *botrytis*, cultivated as a vegetable. The short stem bears a round white heart, up to 9.8 in (25 cm) in diameter, of tightly compressed flower buds surrounded by green leaves. *See also* Brassica.

Cauvery River (*or* Kaveri R.) A river in S India. Rising in the Western Ghats, it flows mainly ENE to the Bay of Bengal. It has a wide delta, the principal channel being the Coleroon, and it irrigates the area by way of a system of canals. It is sacred to the Hindus. Length: 470 mi (756 km).

Cavafy, Constantine (C. Kavafis; 1863–1933) Greek poet. He lived nearly all his life in Alexandria, where he worked as a civil servant. Many of his poems are ironic treatments of subjects from the ancient Hellenistic world; he also wrote erotic homosexual love poems. He spoke and read English and had a strong influence on E. M. *Forster and Lawrence *Durrell.

Cavalcanti, Guido (c. 1255–1300) Italian poet. A friend of Dante, he wrote about 50 poems on themes of love and emotional suffering. He died of a disease contracted while exiled from Florence for his political activities.

Cavalier poets A group of English poets connected with the court of Charles I (1625–49). They included Richard *Lovelace, Robert *Herrick, Thomas Carew, Edmund Waller, and Sir John *Suckling. Their love lyrics and poems about war and honor were characterized by a sophisticated elegance appropriate to their positions as courtiers and gentlemen.

Cavaliers The royalist party during the English *Civil War. After the *Restoration of the monarchy (1660) the name was kept by the court party and was given to the parliament that sat from 1661 to 1679. The cavaliers were distinguished by their elaborate dress, with lace ruffles, feathers, and velvet, in contrast to the sober attire of the *Roundheads.

Cavalli Francesco (1602–76) Italian composer of opera and church music. A pupil of Monteverdi in Venice, he wrote over 40 dramatic works based on legends of gods and heroes.

Cavallini, Pietro (c. 1250–c. 1330) Roman fresco painter and mosaicist. He was the first to abandon the stylizations of *Byzantine art and his chief works are the mosaics of the *Life of the Virgin* for Sta Maria in Trastevere and the frescoes in Sta Cecilia.

cavalry A force of mounted soldiers. Employed throughout the ancient world for its speed and mobility, the invention of stirrups (c. 400 AD) increased its usefulness by enabling heavily armored lancers and swordsmen to fight on horseback. The introduction of *small arms in the 15th century shifted the emphasis in warfare to infantry and the use of *machine guns from the late 19th century rendered the role of cavalry in battle suicidal. Modern armored units have adopted the name and role of cavalry.

Cavan (Irish name: Cabhán) A county in the NE Republic of Ireland, in Ulster. It is generally hilly, drained chiefly by the River Erne, with lakes and *drumlins. Although largely infertile, agriculture is the mainstay of the economy producing oats, potatoes, and dairy products. Some small industries exist in the towns. Area: 730 sq mi (1890 sq km). Population (1991): 52,756. County town: Cavan.

cave fish One of several cave-dwelling *teleost fishes, especially members of the family *Amblyopsidae*, found in fresh water in dark limestone caves of North America. They have translucent colorless elongated bodies, about 4 in (10 cm) long, reduced nonfunctional eyes, and numerous sensory papillae covering the body to compensate for blindness.

Cavell, Edith (1865–1915) British nurse. From 1907 she worked at a training institute for nurses in Brussels. She was executed by the Germans in 1915 for helping Allied soldiers to escape from German-occupied Belgium.

Cavendish, Henry (1731–1810) British physicist. He discovered hydrogen and investigated its properties. He also identified the gases in the atmosphere and showed that water is a compound. The first to measure accurately the universal gravitational constant, he used it to calculate the mass of the earth.

caves Underground hollows, usually opening directly onto the ground surface or connected with it by a passage. In limestone regions, where most caves occur, many constitute part of a system of natural underground drainage and are connected by subterranean streams. These caves are excavated by the slow solution of limestone by slightly acidic rain water percolating through its joints. The other main type of cave is that eroded from the base of a cliff by the sea. Such caves are located at some point of weakness in an otherwise resistant rock, such as a fault plane or bed of softer material

caviar A delicacy, eaten as an hors d'oeuvre, which consists of sturgeon's roe, salted and freed from all fat. It is a Russian specialty. The roe of the beluga is considered the best, although caviar is also obtained from other types of sturgeon. Real caviar is extremely expensive, but a substitute made from lumpfish roe is relatively inexpensive.

Cavite 14 30N 120 54E A city in the N Philippines, in SW Luzon on Manila Bay. Formerly a center of opposition to Spanish and US rule, it was long the site of a major US naval base.

Cavour, Camillo Benso di, Count (1810–61) Italian statesman; the architect of Italian unification (*see* Risorgimento). Committed to liberal politics from boyhood, he helped to found the organ *Il risorgimento* in 1847. In 1852 he formed his first government under *Victor Emmanuel II of Sardinia-Piedmont. Cavour accepted an alliance with France and Britain during the Crimean War and negotiated a further alliance with France at Plombières in 1859 to oust Austria from Italy. He resigned when France came to terms with Austria but became prime minister again in 1860, negotiating the union of Sardinia-Piedmont with Parma, Modena, Tuscany, and the Romagna, and by 1861 had achieved the establishment of a united Italy.

cavy A small South American *rodent belonging to the genus *Cavia* (6 species); the ancestor of the domestic guinea pig. Cavies are mainly nocturnal and live in groups in scrub and grassland, digging burrows and feeding on vegetation and seeds. The adults generally breed twice a year and the young cavies are independent at three weeks. Family: *Caviidae*.

Cawley, Evonne (*born* E. Goolagong; 1951–) Australian tennis player, who twice became Wimbledon singles champion (1971, 1980) and won the doubles in 1974. She was Australian singles champion (1974–76) and Australian doubles champion in 1971, 1974, and 1975.

Cawnpore. *See* Kanpur.

Caxton, William (c. 1422–91) The first English printer. A cloth merchant, Caxton lived in Bruges from 1446 until 1470, when he moved to Cologne. There he learned the technique of printing and in 1474 set up a press that produced the first printed book in English, *Recuyell of the Historyes of Troye* (1475). On returning to England (1476), he set up a press at Westminster, where he printed a long and varied list, including Chaucer's *Canterbury Tales* (1478) and an encyclopedia that was the first illustrated English book, *The Myrrour of the Worlde* (1481).

EVONNE CAWLEY *In action at Wimbledon, England, in 1971, where she beat Virginia Wade to win the women's championship.*

Cayenne 4 55N 52 18W The capital and main Atlantic port of French Guiana, in the NW of the Île de Cayenne. Founded by the French in 1643, it served as a French penal settlement (1854–1938). Cayenne pepper derives its name from a plant grown in the area. Population (1990): 37,097.

Cayley, Sir George (1773–1857) British engineer and pioneer designer of flying machines. He studied the effects of streamlining, the properties of different shapes of wings, and the basic shape of heavier-than-air aircraft. He tested his theories with models and in 1853 built the first successful manned glider. He also invented the caterpillar tractor.

cayman (*or* caiman) An amphibious reptile occurring in rivers of Central and South America; 4–15 ft (1.2–4.5 m) long, it feeds on fish, birds, and insects. Genera: *Caiman* (2 species), *Melanosuchus* (1 species), *Paleosuchus* (2 species); subfamily: *Alligatorine* (alligators and caimans); order: *Crocodilia* (*see* crocodile).

Cayman Islands A British colony in the Caribbean Sea, consisting of three low-lying coral islands (Grand Cayman, Little Cayman, and Cayman Brac) lying about 200 mi (320 km) NW of Jamaica. The population is mainly of mixed African and European descent. *Economy*: depends mainly on tourism, although favorable tax laws have encouraged banking. The main exports are turtle shell, dried turtle meat, and tropical fish. *History*: discovered in 1503 by Columbus, who named them Las Tortugas because of the abundance of turtles. Formerly attached to Jamaica, they gained some self-government in 1959 and became a separate British colony in 1962. Official language: English. Official currency: Jamaican dollar of 100 cents. Area: 100 sq mi (260 sq km). Population (1987 est): 23,000. Capital and main port: Georgetown.

Cayuga North American Iroquoian-speaking Indian tribe, branch of the Five Nations of the *Iroquois League. Found in central New York, they were cultivators, hunters, and warriors. As part of the Iroquois League they supported and fought with the British against the French and against the colonists in the *American Revolution. Today, the remaining Cayuga live on reservations in New York and Oklahoma.

Ceará. *See* Fortaleza.

Ceauçescu, Nicolae (1918-89) Romanian statesman, noted for his opposition to Soviet interference in Romanian affairs. Ceauçescu's rise in the Party hierarchy began in 1948. In 1965 he became the Party's general secretary and in 1967 Romania's leader as president of the state council; he became the republic's first president in 1974. In 1989 he was overthrown and executed.

Cebu 10 17N 123 56E A port in the central Philippines, in E Cebu. The first Spanish settlement in the Philippines (founded 1565), it has a Roman Catholic cathedral and bishop's palace. Its four universities include the University of San Carlos (1595). An important commercial center, its industries include textiles and food processing. Population (1990 est): 610,000.

Cebu An island in the central Philippines, in the Visayan Islands. Its populous coastal plains are cultivated chiefly with coconuts, corn, sugar cane, and hemp. Coal and copper are mined. Area: 1964 sq mi (5086 sq km). Chief city: Cebu.

Cecil, Robert Gascoyne-Cecil, 1st Viscount (1864–1958) British statesman. Cecil was minister of blockade and then deputy foreign secretary in World War I. He took part in the Paris Peace Conference (1919) and helped draft the charter of the League of Nations; he was awarded the Nobel Peace Prize in 1937.

Cecilia, St (2nd or 3rd century AD) Roman Christian martyr. According to legend, she converted her pagan husband Valerian and his brother Tiburtius, who were martyred before her. Although there is doubt concerning her authenticity, she remains the patron saint of sacred music. Feast day: Nov 22. Emblem: an organ.

cecropia moth A large brown and reddish *Saturniid moth, *Platysamia cecropia.* With a wingspan of 6 in (155 mm), it is the largest North American moth. The caterpillars are green and feed on a variety of trees.

cedar A conifer of the genus *Cedrus* (4 species), native to the Mediterranean region and the Himalayas and widely planted for ornament and timber. Cedars usually grow to a height of 130 ft (40 m). Their stiff needle-like leaves grow in tufts of 10–40 on short spurs and their cones are erect and barrel shaped, 2–6 in (5–14 cm) long. The best-known species are the *deodar; the Atlas cedar (*C. atlantica*), from the Atlas mountains; and the cedar of Lebanon (*C. libani*), of the E Mediterranean. Family: *Pinaceae.*

A number of unrelated trees are also known as cedars (*see* incense cedar; Japanese cedar; pencil cedar), and conifers of the genus *Thuja* (*see* arbor vitae) are sometimes called cedars.

Cedar Rapids 41 59N 91 39W A city in E central Iowa. Its industries include cereals and agricultural machinery. Population (1990): 108,751.

celandine Either of two unrelated perennial herbaceous plants. **Greater celandine** (*Chelidonium majus*) is found in cool temperate and subarctic regions throughout Europe and Asia. The brittle branching stems, 12–35 in (30–90 cm) long, bear deeply lobed leaves and bright-yellow flowers. The fruit is a narrow capsule, 1–2 in (3–5 cm) long. Family: *Papaveraceae.*

Lesser celandine (*Ranunculus ficaria*), sometimes known as pilewort, is native to Europe. The branching stems, 2–10 in (5–25 cm) long, bear long-stalked leaves and bright-yellow flowers, which fade to white. The roots form numerous tubers. Family: *Ranunculaceae.*

Celaya 20 32N 100 48W A city in central Mexico. An agricultural trading center, it contains several churches by the noted Mexican architect Francisco Eduardo de Tresguerras (1763–1833). Population (1980): 141,675.

Celebes. *See* Sulawesi.

celeriac A variety of cultivated *celery, *Apium graveolens* var. *rapaceum,* also known as turnip-rooted or knob celery, grown for its globular edible root. The root, up to 6 in (15 cm) in diameter, has a celery-like flavor.

celery The cultivated form of wild celery, or smallage (*Apium graveolens*), a biennial herb native to grassy coastal areas from Europe to India and Africa. Many varieties of cultivated celery have been developed for their edible leafstalks (up to 12 in [30 cm] in length), which may be pink, yellow, or green. Traditionally, the green varieties are blanched to tenderize the tissues. The wild plant has an erect grooved stem, 12–24 in (30–60 cm) long, bearing whorls of clusters of small greenish-white flowers. Family: *Umbelliferae.*

celesta A small keyboard instrument the quiet bell-like tone of which is produced by hammers striking steel plates hung over wooden resonators. Invented about 1880, it was used by Tchaikovsky in his ballet *Casse-Noisette.*

celestial mechanics The study of the motions of celestial bodies subject to mutual gravitational interaction through the application of the laws of *gravitation and of *mechanics.

celestial sphere The imaginary sphere, of immense size, at the center of which lies the earth and on the inner surface of which can be projected the stars and other celestial bodies. The directions of these bodies, as seen from earth, are measured in terms of their angular distances from certain points and circles on the celestial sphere. These circles include the *ecliptic, the observer's horizon, and the **celestial equator,** where the earth's equatorial plane meets the celestial sphere. The reference points include the *equinoxes, the *zenith, and the **celestial poles,** where the earth's axis meets the celestial sphere. The earth's daily rotation causes an apparent and opposite rotation of the celestial sphere.

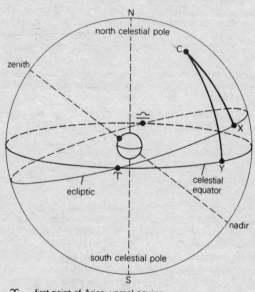

♈	first point of Aries; vernal equinox
♎	first point of Libra; autumnal equinox
C	celestial object
♈Y	right ascension of C (in hours counterclockwise from ♈)
♈X	celestial longitude of C (in degrees counterclockwise from ♈)
YC	declination of C
XC	celestial latitude of C

CELESTIAL SPHERE

celiac disease A disease in which the small intestine is abnormally sensitive to gliadin (a component of the protein *gluten, found in wheat). It results in abnormalities in the cells of the intestine, which cannot digest or absorb food. The symptoms include diarrhea, stunted growth, and general malaise; the condition is treated by a gluten-free diet.

Céline, Louis Ferdinand (L. F. Destouches; 1884–1961) French novelist. The unrelieved cynicism of his controversial first book, *Journey to the End of the Night* (1932), was characteristic of all his novels, including *Death on the Instalment Plan* (1936) and *North* (1960). He suffered imprisonment and exile in Denmark for his outspoken anti-Semitic opinions.

cell The basic unit of living matter, which performs the vital processes of producing energy, synthesizing new molecules from raw materials, division, and self-replication. All plants and animals are composed of cells, the average size of which ranges from 0.0004–0.004 in (0.01–0.1 mm); the simplest organisms (bacteria, protozoa, etc.) consist only of a single cell. The fundamental importance of cells was first recognized by *Schleiden and Schwann in 1838–39. A cell consists essentially of a mass of protoplasm bounded by a membrane. All cells except those of bacteria and blue-green algae and mammalian red blood cells possess a *nucleus, containing the genetic material, and cytoplasm, within which are structures (organelles) specialized for different metabolic functions (*see* Golgi apparatus; lysosome; mitochondria; ribosome). The cells of the body that are not involved in reproduction (called the somatic cells) divide by *mitosis to produce daughter cells identical to themselves. The reproductive cells divide by *meiosis to produce gametes, each containing half the number of chromosomes of the somatic cells. The basic difference between plant and animal cells is the presence in the former of a rigid cellulose cell wall and chlorophyll for use in photosynthesis (*see* chloroplast).

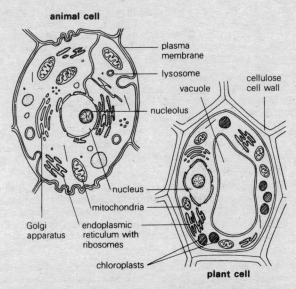

CELL *Plant and animal cells are basically similar but plant cells are supported by cellulose cell walls and contain the green pigment chlorophyll within chloroplasts. Plant cells often also have large fluid-filled vacuoles, which help to control turgidity of the cell.*

Celle 52 37N 10 05E A town in NE Germany, in Lower Saxony. Its former ducal palace (1292) is famed for its theater, used since 1674. Wax and dyes are long established manufactures. The concentration camp of Belsen was nearby. Population (1980): 60,000.

Cellini, Benvenuto (1500–71) Florentine goldsmith and sculptor, famous for his autobiography (1558–62). First published in 1728, it provides a valuable account of his life and times. Cellini worked chiefly as a medalist and craftsman for the papacy in Rome, the Medici in Florence, and Francis I in France. The famous gold saltcellar (Kunsthistorisches Museum, Vienna) was made for Francis. As a sculptor he was largely unfulfilled, although his *Perseus* (Loggia dei Lanzi, Florence) attests to his skills in this medium.

cello (full name: violoncello) A musical instrument of the *violin family, held between the knees and supported at its lower end by an adjustable pin. It has an extensive range above its lowest note (C two octaves below middle C). Its four strings are tuned C, G, D, A. Used to strengthen the bass line in baroque music, it emerged as a solo instrument in the 18th and 19th centuries. In the 20th century its greatest exponent has been Pablo Casals.

celluloid A highly flammable thermoplastic material made from cellulose nitrate and *camphor. It was the first commercially made plastic, introduced over a hundred years ago. Although superseded for many applications by less flammable plastics, there are many specialist uses for which it is still the most suitable material because of its resistance to water, oils, and dilute acids. These include table-tennis balls, mortar-bomb capsules, and film.

cellulose $(C_6H_{10}O_5)_n$ A *carbohydrate that is an important constituent of the cell walls of plants and consists of linked glucose units. Industrially, it is made from wood pulp and is used to manufacture rayon and cellulose-acetate plastics. Cellulose has an important role in the human diet since it—together with other indigestible plant products—constitutes dietary *fiber.

cellulose nitrate (*or* nitrocellulose) A range of compounds made by treating cellulose with a mixture of nitric acid and sulfuric acid. As it is a nitric acid ester the correct name is cellulose nitrate. It is used as an explosive (gun cotton) and rocket propellant.

Celsius scale The official name of the *centigrade temperature scale. It was devised by the Swedish astronomer Anders Celsius (1701–44), who originally designated zero as the boiling point of water and 100° as the freezing point. The scale was later reversed.

Celsus, Aulus Cornelius (1st century AD) Roman scholar, who wrote an encyclopedic work embracing agriculture, law, philosophy, and medicine, of which only the medical section has survived (*De medicina*). Popular during the Renaissance, this work is today of great historical interest, dealing with hygiene, heart attacks, the surgical removal of gallstones, and many other topics common to contemporary medicine.

Celtiberia A region of NE Spain, S of the Ebro River. From the 3rd century BC the area was inhabited by the warlike Celtiberians, who were descendants of the Celtic invaders of Spain and the Iberian natives. The Celtiberians were defeated by the Romans in 195 BC but their capital, Numantia, was not taken until Scipio Aemilianus forced its capitulation in 133 BC.

Celtic art The style of ornamentation developed by ancient tribes in central Europe (*see* Celts). Primitive examples, found in the middle Rhine and Champagne districts, date from around 450 BC: masks and brooches in bronzework with increasingly sophisticated geometric patterns, animal and floral motifs, and, eventually, realistic human-head designs. The most elaborate jewelry, decorated swords, scabbards, and helmets belong to the *La Tène period (c. 350 BC). In Britain, Celtic craftsmanship flourished throughout the Roman occupation, producing work in gold and silver, shields inlaid with enamel, and bronze mirrors. Subsequently, Christian monks adapted traditional designs to adorn religious manuscripts, as in the 9th-century Book of *Kells.

Celtic languages A branch of the Indo-European language family formerly widespread in W Europe. It is divided into two subgroups: Gaulish and Insular Celtic. The Gaulish languages are now extinct, being superseded in early medieval times by *Romance, *Germanic, and other languages. Insular Celtic can be further divided into a Goidelic branch (including *Manx and *Gaelic) and a Brythonic branch (including *Welsh, *Cornish, and *Breton).

Celts A people who occupied a large part of Iron Age Europe. They were known to the Greeks as Keltoi and to the Romans as Gauls. There were numerous Celtic tribes and chiefdoms sharing a culture that can be traced back to the Bronze Age of central Europe (c. 1200 BC). Distinct stages in its development are represented by the *Urnfield and *Hallstatt cultures and it reached its highest level around the 5th century BC, a period represented by the *La Tène culture. The Celtic warrior aristocracy commanded considerable wealth and power. Burials (e.g. at Vix, France) were often rich and elaborate, containing objects of excellent craftsmanship and aesthetic quality. The Druidic priesthood conducted sacrifices and was responsible for the education of young nobles.

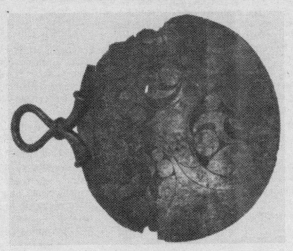

CELTIC ART *A Bronze Age hand mirror decorated with characteristic Celtic patterns.*

cement A powdered mixture of calcium silicates and aluminates. On mixing with water it undergoes complex hydration processes and sets into a hard solid mass. **Portland cement** and similar materials are made by heating limestone with clay and grinding the product. Portland cement was invented by a British stonemason and named for the stone quarried at Portland, Dorset, which it resembles. It is used extensively in *mortars and in *concrete.

cementation The heating of *wrought iron with charcoal powder to form steel. The process was used to make swords and cutting tools before modern methods were developed. It is similar to *case hardening but the iron was often heated for days before quenching.

cementite Iron carbide (Fe_3C), a constituent of *steel and *cast iron. It is a hard brittle white material that combines with ferrite (pure iron) in different ways depending on the type of steel. *See also* pearlite.

Cennini, Cennino (di Drea) (c. 1370–c. 1440) Florentine painter. His paintings have disappeared but he is famous for his *Il libro dell' arte*. Translated as *The Craftsman's Handbook* (1933), it is a valuable source of information about early artistic techniques, particularly *tempera painting.

Cenozoic era (*or* Cainozoic era) The geological era beginning about 65 million years ago and following the *Mesozoic era. It is usually taken to include both the Tertiary and Quaternary periods. During this era the mammals flourished, after the extinction of most of the reptiles dominant in the Mesozoic; the Cenozoic is sometimes known as the age of mammals. Birds and flowering plants also flourished. The *Alpine orogeny took place in the earlier part of this era.

censors Civil magistrates of ancient Rome responsible for the census, public morality, revision of the senatorial roll, and property investment. Two censors were elected every five years. They generally held office for 18 months. The censorship was instituted in about 443 BC and became the most prestigious magistracy until Sulla curtailed its authority in 81. It lasted until 22 BC.

censorship The examination of printed matter, plays, films, broadcasts, etc., and the suppression of any material considered immoral, obscene, or indecent. Censorship is thus the instrument by which religious, political, and moral freedom can be curtailed. It was practiced throughout the ancient world and in the middle ages, but controlling the dissemination of texts and doctrines considered undesirable by the authorities only really became a problem when *printing enabled material to be widely distributed. Now such actions are frequently challenged as unconstitutionally denying freedom of press and speech in contravention of the First Amendment.

The most notorious instance of religious censorship was the Roman Catholic Church's *Index Librorum Prohibitorum*. Instituted in 1564 in reaction to the spread of Protestantism and scientific inquiry, it only ceased publication in 1966.

census A survey ordered by a government to discover certain characteristics of the population, such as its size, occupations, distribution, and trends in fertility, emigration, and immigration. Censuses were taken in ancient China and ancient Rome but the earliest regular census was initiated in the US in 1790. A census is commonly conducted at five- or 10-year intervals. Information about sex, age, race, housing, education, and language spoken may also be gathered to facilitate government policy making.

Census, Bureau of the US agency that collects, tabulates, and publishes a wide variety of statistical data about the nation's people and economy. It takes a census of population and housing every 10 years and five-year censuses of agriculture, trade, manufactures, and transportation; it also compiles current statistics on US foreign trade. It also estimates and projects population and housing. Established in 1902, its headquarters are in Suitland, Md.

centaur In Greek legend, one of a race of wild creatures, half-human and half-horse, living in the mountains of Thessaly and descended from Ixion, King of the Lapiths. They were defeated by the Lapiths in a battle resulting from their characteristically unruly behavior at the wedding of Ixion's son. *See also* Chiron.

Centaurus (Latin: centaur) A large conspicuous constellation in the S sky near Crux. The brightest stars are *Alpha and *Beta Centauri. The constellation contains the huge intense radio source **Centaurus A** and the X-ray binary star **Centaurus X-3**.

centaury An annual or perennial flowering plant belonging to the genus *Centaurium* (or *Erythraea*) (40–50 species), found in most regions except for tropical and S Africa. The common centaury (*C. erythraea*) is widely distributed in temperate regions. Growing to a height of up to 20 in (50 cm), the branching stems bear clusters of small pink flowers. Family: *Gentianaceae*.

Certain plants closely related to *Centaurium* species are also called centaury, e.g. yellow centaury (*Cicendia filiformis*) and Guernsey centaury (*Exaculum pusillum*).

centigrade scale A temperature scale using the freezing point of water as zero and the boiling point of water as 100 degrees. The scale is now officially called the *Celsius scale. Each centigrade (*or* Celsius) degree is equal to one *kelvin.

centipede An *arthropod belonging to the worldwide class *Chilopoda* (about 2800 species). It has long antennae and a slender flattened body of 15–181 segments. The first segment bears a pair of poison claws and nearly all the remaining segments bear a single pair of legs (*compare* millipede). The tropical order *Scolopendrida* contain the largest species, up to 11 in (280 mm) long. Centipedes are found under stones, logs, and leaf litter during the day and at night prey on earthworms, insects, and sometimes small vertebrates. They lay eggs or produce live young.

CENTO. *See* Central Treaty Organization.

Central African Federation. *See* Rhodesia and Nyasaland, Federation of.

Central African Republic (name from 1976 until 1979: Central African Empire) A country in central Africa, consisting mainly of a plateau lying at about 3000 ft (900 m). The dense forests in the S are drained by the Ubangi River, an important channel of communication. Most of the population belongs to the Banda and Baya tribes. *Economy*: chiefly subsistence agriculture, although diamonds have been successfully mined in recent years and there is now a state uranium mine. The main exports are cotton and coffee. *History*: as Ubangi-Shari it was one of the four territories of French Equatorial Africa and from 1958 had internal self-government as a member of the French Community. It became independent in 1960 as the Central African Republic under the presidency of David Dacko. In a military coup in 1965, Jean Bédel *Bokassa came to power. A new constitution was adopted in 1976 in which the country became a parliamentary monarchy known as the Central African Empire, with Bokassa as Emperor Bokassa I. He was ousted following allegations of massacres and forced to flee the country in 1979. Dacko returned to power but was overthrown in a bloodless coup in 1981; he was succeeded by Gen. André Kolingba, who was reelected in 1986. After Bokassa returned to the country in 1986, he was sentenced to death for murder, but his sentence was commuted to life imprisonment in 1988. Official language: French; Sango is the national language. Official currency: CFA (Communauté financière africaine) franc of 100 centimes. Area: 241,250 sq mi (625,000 sq km). Population (1990 est): 2,879,000. Capital: Bangui.

Central America An isthmus of S North America, extending from the Isthmus of Tehuantepec to the NW border of Colombia and comprising an area of 230,000 sq mi (596,000 sq km). It consists of Belize, Costa Rica, El Salvador, Guatemala, Honduras, Nicaragua, and Panama, together with four Mexican states. It is chiefly mountainous with many volcanoes, including Tajumulco, which rises to 13,846 ft (4210 m), and its fertile volcanic regions yield many crops (especially bananas, coffee, and cocoa). The people are mainly of mixed European and Indian origin. Following the overthrow of Spanish colonial rule Costa Rica, El Salvador, Guatemala, Honduras, and Nicaragua formed (1823–38) the **Central American Federation** (*or* United Provinces of Central America). In 1960 Costa Rica, El Salvador, Guatemala, Nicaragua, and Honduras (which withdrew in 1970) formed the **Central American Common Market** to coordinate their economic policies.

central bank A bank that implements a government's *monetary policy, acting as banker to the government and to the commercial banks. Central banks are responsible for holding a country's gold reserves, conducting monetary relations with other countries, and financing the government debt. These objectives sometimes conflict: for example, the bank may wish to depress interest rates to stimulate investment at home, while wishing to raise interest rates to attract money into the country to aid the balance of payments. Most countries have a central bank; in the US it is the *Federal Reserve Bank.

Central Intelligence Agency (CIA) A US government department established in 1947 to coordinate US intelligence operations. In addition to gathering information on the operations and plans of hostile governments, the CIA has also sponsored covert military operations such as the *Bay of Pigs invasion of Cuba in 1961. By law the CIA is not permitted to operate within the US, but its involvement in the *Watergate affair raised considerable concern. In 1976 the Senate Intelligence Committee held extensive hearings on past CIA actions and established strict guidelines for the agency's future operation.

Central Powers The coalition, including Germany, Austria-Hungary, Turkey, and Bulgaria, that opposed the *Allied Powers during *World War I.

Central Treaty Organization (CENTO) A mutual defense alliance between the UK, Iran, Pakistan, and Turkey. It succeeded the *Baghdad Pact. Its objective is military cooperation and the economic development of its Middle Eastern members. Because the UK and the US, which is an associate member, saw CENTO primarily as an anti-Soviet military alliance and neglected the economic development of the organization's Middle Eastern members, Iran, Turkey, and Pakistan founded the Regional Cooperation for Development in 1964. CENTO dissolved in 1979.

center of gravity A fixed point through which the resultant gravitational force on a body always passes no matter what its orientation.

centrifugal force. *See* centripetal force.

centrifuge A device for rotating mixtures of substances at high speed so that the heavier components can be separated from the lighter; the heavier components experience a greater centrifugal force, thus enabling components of different densities (e.g. milk and cream) to separate. The ultracentrifuge is a high-speed device used in the determination of molecular weights and in biochemistry. Large centrifuges are used in physiological research and in training programs to obtain a high *acceleration of free fall (g).

centripetal force A force that acts on a moving body causing it to move in a curved path. An object is constrained to move in a circle by a centripetal force directed toward the center. It has an acceleration toward the center of v^2/r, where v is the object's velocity and r the radius of the circle. The centripetal force is necessary to overcome the object's tendency to move in a straight line and appears to be balanced by an equal **centrifugal force** directed radially outward.

century The ancient Roman unit of a hundred. In the Roman army centuries were the 60 subdivisions, composed of about a hundred infantrymen, of a legion and were commanded by centurions. Centuries were also political divisions of Roman citizens, each of which had a group vote in the assembly of centuries (*see* comitia).

century plant A perennial herbaceous plant, *Agave americana,* native to SW North America. It is stemless but has spiny leaves, 5–6 ft (1.5–1.8 m) long, and after 10–15 years it produces a branched spike of yellow flowers, 25–40 ft (7.5–12 m) tall. After flowering it dies, leaving small plants growing around its base. Century plant is cultivated indoors and outdoors as an ornamental. Family: *Agavaceae.*

ceorl The free peasant (as distinct from the slave) of Anglo-Saxon England. The economic pressures of the Danish invasions and the Norman conquest contributed to the ceorl's declining status and eventual absorption among the unfree *villeins. Thus "churl" has come to mean an uncouth person.

cèpe An edible mushroom, *Boletus edulis.* Common in temperate woodlands from August to November, it has a stout whitish or brown stalk and a hemispherical cap, brown to white in color and 2.5–8 in (6–20 cm) in diameter.

Cephalonia (Modern Greek name: Kefallinía) A Greek island in the E Ionian Sea, the largest of the Ionian group. It is mountainous, rising to 5341 ft (1628 m), but produces crops that include olives and grapes. Area: 360 sq mi (935 sq km).

cephalopod A *mollusk belonging to the class *Cephalopoda* (about 600 species), which includes *octopuses, *squids, and *cuttlefishes. The most advanced of the mollusks, cephalopods are carnivorous and mostly free swimming, with a ring of tentacles around the mouth, well-developed eyes, and shells that are reduced and often absent. They are found in both shallow and deepwater marine habitats. In cephalopods the sexes are usually separate and fertilization is internal, often preceded by courtship behavior.

cephalosporins A group of *antibiotics with a similar action and chemical structure to penicillin. They may be used to treat penicillin-resistant bacterial infections and infections of the urinary tract.

Cepheid variable A highly luminous supergiant star the brightness of which varies very regularly in a period (1–50 days) that depends on the *luminosity of the star. By measuring the period and the average apparent *magnitude of a Cepheid, its distance can be determined. *See also* variable stars.

Cepheus (Latin: whale) A constellation in the N sky near Cassiopeia. The brightest star is the 2nd-magnitude Alderamin. *See also* Cepheid variable.

Ceram (*or* Serang) An Indonesian island in the Moluccas. Mountainous and forested, its exports include copra, dried fish, and birds of paradise. Area: 6622 sq mi (17,150 sq km). Chief town: Wahai.

ceramics Any nonmetallic inorganic material that is made by heat treatment into useful articles. The main categories are heavy articles made of baked clay, such as bricks and tiles, refractories to withstand high temperatures, such as furnace linings, sintered articles, such as abrasives, and domestic products made from earthenware, stoneware, or *porcelain (*see also* pottery). Earthenware is made from clay, which when strongly heated fuses into a hard porous substance. The defect of porosity is overcome by glazing with a vitreous coating of silicate. Chinese examples date from about 3000 BC. Stoneware is made from a more silicaceous clay and fired at a higher temperature than earthenware. It is vitrified, resonant, and almost impervious. Porcelain, developed by the Chinese from stoneware, is vitrified, impervious, resonant, translucent, and white. It need not be glazed but usually is.

Cerberus In Greek legend, the monstrous dog who guarded the entrance to the underworld, usually portrayed as having three heads and a dragon's neck and tail. The final task of *Heracles was to overpower this monster.

cereals Cultivated *grasses selected for their high yields of grain, which constitutes a major item in the diet of man and livestock. *Wheat, *rice, and *corn are the most important cereals, but *barley, *oats, *rye, and *millet are also widely cultivated. Cereals are usually sown annually and, under certain conditions (especially with rice), two or more harvests may be possible in one year. *See also* arable farming.

cerebellum. *See* brain.

cerebral palsy Damage to the developing brain resulting in uncoordinated movements and muscular weakness and paralysis. The brain damage may be caused by injury during birth, insufficient oxygen before birth, or a viral infection of the brain. In some cases intelligence is affected. Treatment includes appropriate physiotherapy to improve movement and special education; speech therapy may also be needed.

cerebrospinal fluid The fluid that surrounds the *brain and *spinal cord. It is produced by special blood vessels inside the cerebrum and is reabsorbed by special bunches of veins. It acts as a shock absorber and support for the central nervous system. A normal adult has 4 oz (130 ml) of clear fluid; samples of it are taken for diagnostic tests for diseases of the nervous system.

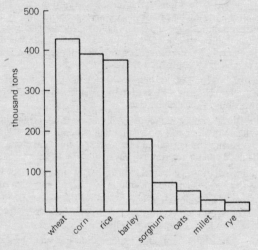

CEREALS *World production of cereals.*

cerebrum. *See* brain.

Ceres (astronomy) The largest *minor planet, 623 mi (1003 km) in diameter, and the first to be discovered (in 1801 by Piazzi). It orbits at between 2.55 and 2.98 astronomical units from the sun, with a period of 4.6 years.

Ceres (mythology). *See* Demeter.

cerium (Ce) The most abundant lanthanide element, discovered in 1803 by Berzelius and others. It occurs naturally in several minerals including monazite, $(Ce,La,Th)PO_4$, and allanite, a complex aluminosilicate. It is used as a catalyst in self-cleaning ovens, in gas mantles, as a polishing agent, and as an oxidant for volumetric analysis. At no 58; at wt 140.12; mp 475°F (799°C); bp 1916°F (3426°C).

Cernauti. *See* Chernovtsy.

Cervantes, Miguel de (1547–1616) Spanish novelist. Son of an unsuccessful surgeon, he was largely self-educated. In 1569 he went to Italy and fought at the battle of Lepanto in 1571. Returning to Spain in 1575, he was captured by pirates and imprisoned in Algiers for five years. After 1580 he held several minor jobs in the civil service while writing a pastoral novel, *La Galatea* (1585), and several plays. *Don Quixote* (Part I, 1605; Part II, 1615), his revolutionary picaresque novel about a self-deluding knight errant and his simple but cunning squire, Sancho Panza, won him fame throughout Europe but little financial reward.

cervix The lower part (neck) of the womb, leading into the vagina (the term is also used for any necklike part). Childbirth is dependent on the effective dilation of the cervix.

Cesenà 44 09N 12 15E A city in N Italy, in Emilia-Romagna on the Savio River. It is the site of the Malatesta library (15th century), which contains many valuable manuscripts. Pope Pius VI and Pope Pius VII were born here.

cesium (Cs) The most reactive and electropositive alkali metal. It was discovered by Bunsen and Kirchhoff in 1860 and occurs naturally in the mica lepidolite and as pollucite, $(Cs,K)AlSi_2O_6.nH_2O$. Cesium reacts explosively with water to give the hydroxide (CsOH) and is used in *cesium clocks and in photoelectric cells. Chief compounds are the nitrate ($CsNO_3$) and chloride (CsCl). At no 55; at wt 132.905; mp 83°F (28.4°C); bp 1275°F (690°C).

cesium clock An *atomic clock that depends on the energy difference between two states of the cesium nucleus in a magnetic field. A nonuniform magnetic field is used to split a beam of cesium atoms into two components. Nuclei in the lower energy state are irradiated by radio-frequency radiation at the difference frequency between the two states, so that some are excited to the higher state. By reanalyzing the mixture, the radio-frequency oscillator can be locked to the difference frequency of 9 192 631 770 hertz with an accuracy of one part in 10^{13}. This extremely accurate clock is now used in the definition of the *second.

České Budějovice (German name: Budweis) 49 00N 14 30E An industrial city situated in W Czech Republic. Founded in 1265, it has an arcaded town square. Manufactures include chemicals, machinery, and pencils. Population (1987 est): 95,500.

Cestoda. *See* tapeworm.

Cetacea An order of carnivorous marine mammals comprising *whales and *dolphins.

cetane number A quality rating for Diesel fuel, similar to the *octane number for petrol. Two reference fuel compounds, cetane and alpha-methylnaphthalene, are given the numbers 100 and 0 respectively. Mixtures of these two have intermediate numbers and other Diesel fuels are compared with them in a standard engine. Most Diesel engines can run on fuel that has a cetane number of 40 or 50.

Cetatea Alba. *See* Belgorod-Dnestrovski.

Cetinje 42 23N 18 55E A city in S central Yugoslavia, in Montenegro. The former capital of the principality of Montenegro, it has a fortified monastery, which was the seat of the Montenegrin prince bishops. Population (1981 est): 20,213.

Cetshwayo (c. 1826–84) King of the Zulus (1873–79), whose kingdom was conquered by the British. Although Cetshwayo inflicted a severe defeat on the British at Isandhlwana (1879) he could not hold out against them and was overwhelmed at Ulundi (1879). Captured, he was allowed to present his case in London and in 1883 was restored to central Zululand.

Ceuta 35 53N 5 19W A Spanish military post and port, forming an enclave in NW Morocco on the Mediterranean coast. It has a fine 15th-century cathedral. Population (1991): 68,288.

Cévennes A mountain range in SE France, constituting the SE edge of the Massif Central and rising to 5755 ft (1754 m).

Ceylon. *See* Sri Lanka.

Cézanne, Paul (1839–1906) French postimpressionist painter, born in Aix-en-Provence, the son of a banker. After studying law for two years, he was encouraged by his childhood friend Emile *Zola to settle in Paris (1861). His crude and often erotic early paintings failed, however, to find favor. In 1872, while working with *Pissarro in Pontoise, he turned to *impressionism, a period represented by *The Suicide's House* (Louvre) but he soon rejected its flickering effects of light and movement in favor of more stability and solidity. His view that nature should be painted in the forms of the cone, cube, and cylinder and his distortion of perspective strongly influenced the development of *cubism. Living mainly in Provence, he painted portraits, e.g. *The Card Players* (Louvre), still lifes, landscapes, especially of Mont St Victoire and L'Éstaque, and a series of *Bathers*.

c.g.s. system A metric system of units based on the centimeter, gram, and second. It includes dynes, ergs, and both electrostatic and electromagnetic units. It has been replaced for scientific purposes by *SI units.

Chablis 47 49N 3 48E A village in central France, in the Yonne department. Chablis is famous for the white wine named for it.

Chabrol, Claude (1930–   ) French film director. He was a leading member of the *New Wave group of French directors in the late 1950s. His films, many of which are influenced by Alfred Hitchcock and use tense murder plots to illuminate bourgeois social relationships, include *Les Biches* (1968), *Le Boucher* (1969), and *Cop au Vin* (1984).

Chaco. *See* Gran Chaco.

Chaco War (1932–35) The war between Bolivia and Paraguay resulting from a long-standing dispute over the vast Gran Chaco region. The dispute, which had arisen in the 19th century, flared up again in the 1920s when new Paraguayan settlements and word of oil deposits in Chaco upset the uneasy truce. Over 100,000 men died in this bloody war. The League of Nations failed to arbitrate a settlement but mediation by Argentina, Brazil, Chile, Peru, and the US led to an armistice. The treaty, signed in 1938, favored the military victor, Paraguay, which received most of the Chaco region.

Chad, Lake A lake in West Africa, between Chad, Niger, Nigeria, and Cameroon. It is shallow and has no outlet; its area varies between 3860–9650 sq mi (10,000–25,000 sq km).

Chad, Republic of (French name: Tchad) A country covering an extensive area in N central Africa, consisting mainly of poor semidesert. The land rises from Lake Chad in the SW to the Tibesti Mountains in the N, reaching heights of about 11,000 ft (3400 m). The majority of the rather sparse population (concentrated in the S) is Sara, a Bantu people; most of the nomadic peoples of the N are Muslims. *Economy*: mainly subsistence agriculture with livestock and fishing. Some oil and other minerals have been found but there is very little industry. The main exports are cotton and meat. *History*: one of the four territories of French Equatorial Africa, it had internal self-government as a member of the French Community from 1958, gaining independence in 1960. Since 1963 there has been considerable rebellion and unrest in the N where the Muslim inhabitants have traditionally opposed the black population of the S. In 1975 Pres. Na-

garta Tombalbaye was assassinated in a military coup and succeeded by Gen.
Félix Malloum. In 1979, following negotiations held in Nigeria, a transitional
government under Pres. Goukouni Oueddei was formed. Conflict between rebel
and government forces continued and in 1982 the capital N'djamena was taken
by rebel forces led by Hissene Habré. In 1983 the civil war was resumed with the
taking of Faya-Largeau by Libyan forces led by Oueddei. Oueddei's support by
Libya's Quaddafi was quickly countered. Allying itself with Habré, the US dis-
patched military and financial aid. Zaire, Nigeria, and eventually France, also lent
support. The crucial dispatch of 1000 French troops and other French military reinforcements succeeded in halting Libyan advances. A cease-fire was reached in
1984, and French and Libyan forces began a mutual withdrawal of troops. Hostilities between French-backed government forces and Libyan-supported rebels
erupted in 1986, but had ended by 1988. Habré was overthrown in 1990 by Gen.
Idriss Déby, who became president. Official language: French. Official currency:
CFA franc of 100 centimes. Area: 495,624 sq mi (1,284,000 sq km). Population
(1992 est): 5,960,000. Capital: N'djamena (formerly Fort Lamy).

Chadwick, Sir James (1891–1974) British physicist, who worked at Cambridge with *Rutherford and went on to discover the *neutron in 1932. By analyzing the radiation emitted by beryllium when bombarded with alpha particles,
Chadwick was able to show that it consisted of neutrons. He was awarded the
Nobel Prize (1935).

Chaeronea, Battles of 1. (338 BC) The battle in which *Philip II of Macedon, and his crack army, defeated Athenian and Theban forces at Chaeronea (on
the Cephisus River in N Boeotia). It forced the Greek city states to acknowledge
Philip's hegemony over Greece and the end of their autonomy. 2. (86 BC) The
battle won by the Roman general *Sulla over *Mithridates VI Eupator of Pontus
at the same spot.

chafer A herbivorous beetle belonging to the family *Scarabaeidae* (*see* scarab
beetle). Chafers cause much damage to trees and crops by eating the foliage and
flowers; the larvae, which live in the soil, attack the roots. Chief genera:
Melolontha (*see* cockchafer), *Cetonia* (rose chafers), and *Phyllopertha* (garden
chafers).

chaffinch A *finch, *Fringilla coelebs,* about 6 in (15 cm) long, that is common in woods and parks in Europe, W Asia, and N Africa. The male chaffinch
has a chestnut back, pinkish breast, grayish-blue crown and nape, and two conspicuous white wing bars. The female has a duller plumage with an olive-green
back. Chaffinches are often migratory and have a lively song.

Chagall, Marc (1887–1985) Russian-born painter and printmaker of Jewish
parentage. After studying in St Petersburg (1907–10) under *Bakst, he visited
Paris (1910). There he painted some of his best-known works, recalling Russian
village life, such as *Me and the Village* (1911; New York). His childlike figures
and objects, distorted in scale and often floating upside down in space, influenced the surrealists. Moving to France (1922), he illustrated Gogol's *Dead
Souls* and La Fontaine's *Fables.* During World War II he lived in the US, where
he designed ballet sets and costumes and subsequently worked on mosaics and
tapestries for the Israeli Knesset building (1966).

Chagas' disease A South American disease caused by infection with a proto-
zoan of the genus *Trypanosoma.* Named for a Brazilian physician, Carlos Chagas
(1879–1934), it is a form of *trypanosomiasis transmitted by bugs. It may result
in serious damage to the heart and brain; there is no effective treatment.

Chagos Islands. *See* British Indian Ocean Territory.

chain 1. A measure of length equal to 66 ft (20 m). **2.** A measuring device used in surveying. A Gunter's chain is 66 ft (20 m) long (consisting of 100 links), whereas an Engineer's chain is 100 ft (30 m) long (also 100 links).

Chain, Sir Ernst Boris (1906–79) British biochemist, born in Germany, who—with Lord *Florey—isolated and purified penicillin and performed the first clinical trials. Coming to England in 1933, Chain worked first at Cambridge under Sir Frederick *Hopkins and then at Oxford with Florey. For their work, Chain, Florey, and Sir Alexander *Fleming, the discoverer of penicillin, were awarded a Nobel Prize (1945).

CHAFFINCH *Although the nest is built by the female, both the male (seen here) and the female care for the young.*

chain mail Body armor made by welding or riveting interlaced iron rings. Lightweight and providing adequate protection, it was popular from c. 1100– c. 1400 AD, when plate, first worn under and then over chain mail, began to replace it. Chain mail garments include coifs, mittens, and stockings, and ultimately covered the entire body. Worn over felt or leather coats, examples from c. 1200 weigh between 30 lb (14 kg) and 50 lb (23 kg).

chain reaction A series of reactions in which the product of each reaction sets off further reactions. In a nuclear chain reaction each nuclear fission is induced by a neutron ejected by a previous fission. For example, the fission of a uranium-235 nucleus produces either two or three neutrons each of which can induce the fission of another uranium-235 nucleus. Chain reactions are used as a source of energy in *nuclear reactors and *nuclear weapons. *See also* critical mass.

chaise A light two- or four-wheeled carriage drawn by one, two, or four horses. A chaise usually had a collapsible hood (calash). "Chaise" could also apply to a *curricle or *phaeton. *Compare* postchaise.

Chaitanya movement A Hindu *Bhakti school, named for its founder, the Bengali brahmin mystic Chaitanya (1485–1533). Through the ecstatic singing of hymns and mantras, devotees express their blissful surrender to *Krishna and Radha, who epitomize the quasi-erotic mutual love of God and the human soul; Chaitanya himself came to be worshiped as an incarnation of these divine lovers. The Sanskrit scriptures of the movement were subsequently evolved by a group of disciples, known as the six *gosvamins*. Most of the present sect leaders are their descendants and bear the same title.

Chakkri The ruling dynasty of Thailand (formerly Siam). Its first king, Phraya Chakkri (1737–1809), styled himself Rama I after his accession in 1782. A capable military commander, he had put an end to the hostilities of the neighboring Burmese by 1792 and then established the new capital of Bangkok. During the reigns of Rama II (1768–1824; reigned 1809–24) and Rama III (d. 1851; reigned 1824–51) Siam's relations with the West improved. Mongkut (posthumously styled Rama IV; 1804–68; reigned 1851–68) and *Chulalongkon (Rama V; reigned 1868–1910) introduced various social and administrative reforms. A revolt against Prajadhipok (Rama VII; 1893–1941; reigned 1925–35) led to the establishment of a constitutional monarchy in 1932; he abdicated in 1935. The present king, Bhumibol Adulyadej (1927–   ), ascended the throne in 1946.

Chalcedon (modern name: Kadiköy) A Megarian colony founded in the 7th century BC on the Asian side of the Bosporus. It was known as the city of the blind because it occupied a less strategic site than the opposite side of the Bosporus on which Byzantium (*see* Istanbul) was built. Absorbed first by Pergamum and later forming part of the Roman province of Asia, Chalcedon eventually became a suburb of Byzantium. It was the site in 451 AD of the Council of Chalcedon, the fourth ecumenical council of the Church. It condemned heresies relating to the dual (human and divine) nature of Christ and reaffirmed the doctrines of the Council of *Nicaea and the first Council of *Constantinople.

chalcedony A cryptocrystalline (submicroscopically grained) sometimes fibrous *silica mineral. The numerous varieties include carnelian (red); agate, onyx, and sardonyx (banded); jasper (red or brown); and chert and flint (opaque gray or black). The last two occur in limestones; others occur mainly in veins and amygdales.

Chalcidice (Modern Greek name: Khalkidhikí) A peninsula in NE Greece. It ends in three promontories, the northernmost of which contains Mount *Athos. There are fertile low-lying areas but it is mostly wooded and mountainous. Area: 1149 sq mi (2945 sq km).

Chalcis (modern name: Khalkís) 38 28N 23 36E The capital of the Greek island of *Eubea, famous as a trading and metalworking center from the 8th to the 1st centuries BC; Aristotle died here in 322 BC. Chalcis established colonies in Italy, Sicily, and the peninsular region named for it, *Chalcidice. It joined Athens against the Persians in 480 BC but the two cities' traditional rivalry was successfully exploited by Philip of Macedon in the 4th century BC. It was partly destroyed in 146 BC by the Romans but was subsequently developed by the

Venetians from the 13th century AD and was incorporated in the kingdom of Greece in 1830. Population (1981 est.): 44,774.

chalcopyrite The principal ore of copper, sometimes called copper pyrites, of composition $CuFeS_2$. It is brassy yellow with a greenish black streak and contains 34.5% copper. It occurs mainly in veins associated with the upper part of an acid igneous intrusion.

Chaldea (*or* Chaldaea) The region of S Babylonia where the new Babylonian empire was established by Nabopolassar (d. 605 BC) in 625 in the last years of the Assyrian empire. At its height under *Nebuchadnezzar II (reigned 604–562), the Chaldean empire, centered on the rebuilt city of Babylon, dominated the Middle East for about 70 years until overthrown by the Achemenians in 539. The Chaldeans' reputation as astronomers survived undiminished until Roman times.

Chaliapin, Feodor Ivanovich (1873–1938) Russian bass. After a penurious youth, he was discovered as a singer and made his debut at La Scala, Milan, in 1901. He became world famous in the title role of Mussorgsky's *Boris Godunov.*

chalk A sedimentary rock that is a pure-white fine-grained variety of *limestone (calcium carbonate). Coccoliths (the calcareous remains of extinct unicellular organisms) are the main constituents of chalk although other invertebrate remains are included. Chalk is very characteristic of the Upper Cretaceous period in W Europe and the Chalk is sometimes used synonymously with the Upper Cretaceous. Nodules of flint are often found in chalk; these are formed from the remains of siliceous organisms, dissolved and redeposited.

Chalmers, Thomas (1780–1847) Scottish preacher and theologian. Ordained in the Church of Scotland in 1803, Chalmers was an influential minister in Glasgow. From 1823 he was a university professor at St Andrew's and then in Edinburgh. He was a leader in the Disruption of 1843, which led to the founding of the Free Church of Scotland.

Challenger Disaster The explosion, shortly after liftoff from Cape Canaveral, Florida, on Jan 26, 1986, of the US space shuttle *Challenger.* All seven crew members, including Christa McAuliffe, the first US school teacher to go into space, were killed. The disaster delayed the US space program until Sept 29, 1988, when a shuttle launch was again made.

chalones A group of substances, found in mammalian tissues, that can inhibit cell division. They are thought to be important in aging processes and in cancer.

Châlons-sur-Marne 48 58N 4 22E A city in NE France, the capital of the Marne department. In 451 AD Attila and the Huns were defeated by the Romans on a nearby plain. The 13th-century cathedral suffered damage in World War II. It is the center of the wine trade of Champagne. Population: 55,709.

chamberlain An officer appointed by a monarch, nobleman, or corporation to carry out ceremonial duties. The chamberlains of medieval England were financial officers and were figures of great political importance in the 12th century.

Chamberlain, Joseph (1836–1914) British politician. He became a Liberal member of Parliament in 1876 and in 1885 presented a program that advocated such radical policies as free education. In 1886 he left the Liberal Party. As leader of the anti-Gladstonian Liberal-Unionists, he supported the Conservatives and became colonial secretary in the Conservative Government (1895–1903). His eldest son **Sir (Joseph) Austen Chamberlain** (1863–1937) became a Liberal-Unionist member of Parliament in 1892. He was chancellor of the exchequer (1919–21) and then foreign secretary (1924–29), when he negotiated the *Locarno Pact and was awarded the Nobel Peace Prize (1925). Joseph's son

(Arthur) Neville Chamberlain (1869–1940) was Conservative prime minister (1937–40), when he advocated a policy of appeasement toward the fascist powers. He recognized Italy's conquest of Ethiopia and kept out of the Spanish Civil War. To avoid a European war he visited Hitler three times in 1938, coming to the *Munich Agreement, which recognized Germany's possession of the Sudetenland. He returned to Britain claiming to have brought "peace for our time" but was forced by Hitler's invasion of Czechoslovakia to abandon appeasement. He declared war after Hitler's attack on Poland but his ineffectiveness led to his resignation in May 1940, when he joined Churchill's war cabinet.

Chamberlain, Owen (1920–) US physicist, who shared the 1959 Nobel Prize with Emilio *Segrè for their discovery of the antiproton (*see* antimatter) in 1955. They created the particle by bombarding a copper target with high-energy protons in the Berkeley *bevatron. During World War II he worked on the development of the atom bomb.

Chamberlain, Wilt (Wilton Norman C.; 1936–) US basketball player. He played for the Harlem Globetrotters (1957) before joining the Philadelphia (later San Francisco) Warriors (1958–65), the Philadelphia 76ers (1965–68), and the Los Angeles Lakers (1968–73). Nicknamed "Wilt the Stilt," he long held the career record for points and was elected to the Basketball Hall of Fame (1978).

chamber music Music written to be played in the intimacy of a room rather than in a large hall, church, or theater. In the baroque period chamber sonatas were distinguished from church sonatas and in the late 18th century Haydn, Mozart, and Beethoven established the piano trio (violin, cello, and piano), the duo sonata (one instrument and piano), and the string quartet (two violins, viola, and cello) as the main chamber music forms. Chamber music has been written for other combinations of players, including the woodwind quintet (oboe, flute, clarinet, horn, and bassoon), the clarinet quintet (clarinet and string quartet), and the piano quintet (piano and string quartet). Haydn, Mozart, Beethoven, Schubert, Brahms, Dvořák, and Britten all wrote important chamber music compositions.

chamber of commerce An organization that protects and promotes the interests of a town's or city's manufacturers and merchants. Chambers of commerce occur in many countries, sometimes government sponsored and sometimes, as in the US, as voluntary organizations. Many are authorized to issue certificates of origin and to certify commercial documents, and some provide an *arbitration service for their members.

chameleon An arboreal lizard belonging to the Old World family *Chamaeleontidae* (84 species) and characterized by its ability to change its skin color; 7–10 in (17–25 cm) long, chameleons have a narrow body, an extensile tongue for capturing insects, and bulging eyes that can move independently. Some species have a helmet-shaped head or conspicuous horns. They may be green, yellow, cream, or dark brown, often with spots, and change color by concentration or dispersion of pigment in skin cells. Genera: *Brookesia, Chamaeleo*. ☐reptile.

chamois An agile hoofed *mammal, *Rupicapra rupicapra,* of mountainous regions in Europe and SW Asia. Chamois grow to about 30 in (75 cm) high at the shoulder and have distinctive narrow upright horns with backward-pointing hooked tips. Their tawny coat becomes darker and longer in winter, when they descend from the high slopes to the forests below. Family: *Bovidae.*

chamomile. *See* camomile.

Chamorro, Violeta Barrios (1929–) President of Nicaragua (1990–). As the widow of a prominent newspaper owner who opposed the dictatorial rule of the Somozas in Nicaragua and was then killed (1978), she became active in the anti-Somoza movement through the family newspaper *La Prensa*. Although she joined the Sandanista government in 1979, she soon resigned because of its Marxist policies and again used the newspaper as an opposition platform. In the 1990 elections she unexpectedly won against the incumbent, Pres. Daniel Ortega. Her programs were directed at reviving the Nicaraguan economy and at exerting greater civilian authority over the military.

CHAMOIS *The hide of this increasingly rare animal was formerly used for chamois leather, which is now made from the skins of sheep and goats.*

Champa An ancient Indochinese kingdom. The Chams were Indonesian in origin but when they established their kingdom on the coastal region of South Vietnam in 192 AD following the collapse of the Chinese Han dynasty their culture became predominantly Indian. Champa's prosperity was greatest between the 6th and 10th centuries, after the demise of Chinese domination and before the Vietnamese kingdom threatened its autonomy. Champa was finally absorbed by Vietnam in the 17th century.

champagne A wine, usually sparkling, produced in the districts around Reims and Epernay, NE France. Champagne is usually made from black (*pinot noir*) and white (*pinot chardonnay*) grapes. After fermentation sugar and yeast are added to the still wine, which, when bottled, undergoes a secondary fermentation, which produces the sparkle. A dosage of sugar syrup determines whether it will be sweet (*sec*) or dry (*brut*) champagne.

Champagne A former province in NE France, now incorporated in the planning region of **Champagne-Ardenne**. Ruled by counts during the Middle Ages, it became important for its trade fairs and at the end of the 17th century began to produce the sparkling *champagne for which it is famous.

Champaigne, Philippe de (1602–74) Painter of portraits and historical and religious scenes, born in Brussels. In 1621 he moved to Paris, where he worked for Marie de' Medici and Richelieu. His association with the Jansenists at Port Royal influenced his later portraits, notably *Ex Voto de 1662* (Louvre), which shows his daughter, a nun, after her recovery from paralysis.

champignon One of several edible mushrooms of the family *Agaricaceae* (*see* agaric). The fairy-ring champignon (*Marasmius oreades*), common on meadows and lawns, has a light-brown cap, 0.8–2 in (2–5 cm) in diameter, and a slender stalk. It often occurs as part of a fairy ring—a ring of mushrooms marking the roughly circular perimeter of the underground body of the fungus.

Champlain, Lake A long narrow lake in North America. It extends S from the Richelieu River in Canada, forming the boundary between Vermont and New York state for much of its length. It is named for Samuel de Champlain. Length: 107 mi (172 km).

Champlain, Samuel de (1567–1635) French explorer. In 1603 he followed in *Cartier's footsteps, exploring the St Lawrence and the coast from a base in Acadia. In 1608 he founded a colony at Quebec—New France—of which he became commandant (1612). When Quebec was captured by the English in 1629 he was taken prisoner. Lake Champlain, which he visited in 1609, is named for him.

champlevé (French: raised field) A technique of decorating metal surfaces with polychrome *enamelwork. The enamel is held in depressions incised in the metal. Fine examples of champlevé survive from Celtic England, medieval Europe, and India.

Champollion, Jean-François (1790–1832) French Egyptologist. After studying *Coptic, he tackled the decipherment of Egyptian *hieroglyphics, building on the intuitions of Thomas *Young about royal names on the *Rosetta Stone. His *Lettre à M. Dacier* (1822) correctly identified and assigned phonetic values to about 40 symbols. These results were confirmed and expanded in the *Précis du système hiéroglyphique* (1824).

chancellor In the UK, the name of various state officials. The chancellor, dating from the 10th century, was the head of the Chancery, the secretarial department of the *Curia Regis (King's Court). By the 12th century he was the monarch's chief minister but his political prominence subsequently declined as his judicial activities developed and since the 17th century the **Lord (High) Chancellor**, as he came to be called, has always been a lawyer. He is appointed by the prime minister, is a member of the cabinet, and speaker of the House of Lords as well as being head of the judiciary. The **chancellor of the exchequer** is the minister responsible for the national economy and the presentation of the annual budget.

Chancellorsville, Battle of (1863) Confederate victory in the Civil War, in N central Virginia. Union forces under Gen. Joseph Hooker and Confederate forces under Generals Robert E. Lee and Stonewall Jackson met at Chancellorsville, near the Rappahannock River. The Union Army of the Potomac hoped to advance to and take Richmond, the Confederate capital. Lee sent Jackson to attack Hooker's advancing rear units, thus forcing the retreat of the Union troops. Casualties numbered in the thousands for both sides, and Jackson died of wounds five days later.

Chancery, Court of In English law, a court that developed in the 15th century as the personal court of the king's chief law officer, the Lord Chancellor (*see* chancellor), in which he dealt with cases for which the *common law could not provide a remedy. It dealt with such matters as partnerships, the administration of estates, and the execution of *trusts.

Chan Chan The capital city of the pre-Inca *Chimú Kingdom, near Trujillo (Peru). Its adobe (mud brick) ruins of temples, residential buildings, cemeteries, and storerooms are divided into nine compounds, covering 14 sq mi (36 sq km). The multiplicity of reservoirs and aqueducts indicate the importance of irrigation in this arid region.

Chandigarh 30 43N 76 47E A Union Territory and city in NW India, on the Haryana-Punjab border. The joint capital of both states, it is a modern city (1953) planned by *Le Corbusier in 30 rectangular sectors for housing, government, and industry. Punjab University was established here in 1947. Area: 44 sq mi (114 sq km). Population (1991): 640,725.

Chandler, Raymond (1888–1959) US novelist. Educated in England, he returned to the US and worked in business before starting to write detective stories in the 1930s. The detective Philip Marlowe features in all his nine novels, which include *The Big Sleep* (1939), *Farewell My Lovely* (1940), and *The Long Goodbye* (1954).

Chandra Gupta I Emperor of India (320-c. 330 AD), who founded the Gupta dynasty. Crowned at Pataliputra, he married the daughter of the king of the neighboring Lichavi clan and established the beginnings of a large empire.

Chandra Gupta II (c. 375–415 AD) Emperor of India (c. 380–c. 415) of the Gupta dynasty; the grandson of *Chandra Gupta I. He extended the imperial boundaries to the Arabian Sea and was a patron of the arts.

Chandragupta Maurya Emperor of India (c. 321–c. 297 BC), who founded the Maurya dynasty (c. 321–185 BC). He ousted the previous Nanda dynasty. According to tradition, he destroyed the garrison left behind by Alexander the Great. He extended his empire over the whole of India. The Greek ambassador and historian Megasthenes left accounts of the splendor of his reign.

Chanel, Coco (Gabrielle C.; 1883–1971) French fashion designer, who revolutionized women's clothes, introducing a note of simplicity and comfort. She opened a fashion house in Paris in 1924, becoming known particularly for her jersey dresses and suits and for her perfumes, including Chanel No 5. She retired in 1939 but began designing again in 1954.

Chang-chia-k'ou. *See* Zhangjiakou.

Chang-chou. *See* Changzhou.

Changchun 43 50N 125 20E A city in NE China, the capital of Jilin province. Jilin University was established here in 1958. Its chief industry is the manufacture of motor vehicles. Population (1990): 1,679,270.

Chang E In Chinese mythology, the moon goddess. She stole the drug of immortality from her consort and fled to the moon, where she lives in the form of a toad.

Chang Jiang. *See* Yangtze River.

Changsha 28 10N 113 00E A port in S China, the capital of Hunan province on the Xiang (*or* Siang) River. It has long been a commercial and cultural center, Hunan University being established here in 1959. Population (1990): 1,113,212.

Changzhou (*or* Chang-chou) 31 45N 119 57E A city in E China, in Jiangsu province on the *Grand Canal. A long-established commercial center for agricultural produce, it has textile and engineering industries. Population (1990): 531,470.

Channel Islands (French name: Îles Normandes) A group of islands in the English Channel, off the coast of NW France. The chief islands comprise *Jersey (the largest), *Guernsey, *Alderney, and *Sark. Since the Norman conquest

(1066) they have been a dependency of the British crown. During World War II they were the only British territory to come under German occupation. Tourism is of major economic importance but the islands are also noted for their early agricultural and horticultural produce, most of which is exported to the UK. This includes flowers, fruit, potatoes, and tomatoes; the Jersey and Guernsey breeds of cattle are world famous. Area: 75 sq mi (194 sq km). Population (1981): 133,000.

Channel tunnel (*or* Chunnel) A tunnel linking Britain with France. First suggested to Napoleon in 1802, digging was actually started by two private companies in each country in 1882 but the project was abandoned in 1883. In 1964 the two governments revived the project, simultaneously considering plans for a Channel bridge. The tunnel was agreed upon and in the early 1970s work again started, to be abandoned on economic grounds in 1974. A successful tunnel was begun in 1986 and opened in 1994.

Channing, William Ellery (1780–1842) US churchman. The pastor (1803–42) of the Federal Street Congregational Church in Boston, he was a founder of Unitarianism. He wrote and delivered his sermon entitled *Unitarian Christianity* in 1819 and is credited with starting the American Unitarian Association in 1825.

cha-no-yu The Japanese tea ceremony. The ceremony originated in China but was practiced by Zen priests in Japan from the 14th century and later by other members of society. Taking place in a room of simple perfection, it is presided over by a tea master. Its object is to achieve a contemplative calm, in which attention is exclusively fixed on the ritual and utensils used. The kettle, tea bowls, bamboo whisk, and serving ladle are chosen for their artistic merit.

CHA-NO-YU *The Japanese tea ceremony requires humility from its participants, who enter the tearoom on their knees.*

chanson de geste A type of epic poem composed in Old French. Versions survive from the early 12th century but the genre is probably at least a century older. Loyalty and valor are typical themes in the *chanson*, many of which relate the real or imaginary deeds of Charlemagne's knights. The most famous is the *Chanson de Roland* about the heroic last stand of some of these knights at Roncesvalles in the Pyrenees (778).

chant The short melodies to which psalms and canticles are sung in the Anglican Church. They may be single (one tune adapted for each verse) or double (alternating tunes for alternating verses). "Triple" or "quadruple" chants are less common. Many are adaptations from Latin plainsong made by John Marbeck (died c. 1585) in his *Booke of Common Praier Noted* (1550).

chanterelle An edible *mushroom, *Cantharellus cibarius,* occurring in temperate woodlands. It is funnel-shaped and yellow with the gills clearly visible and measures 1–4 in (3–10 cm) across the cap. The flesh is regarded as a delicacy if cooked slowly. Family: *Cantharellaceae;* class: *Basidiomycetes.*

Chantilly 49 12N 2 28E A town in France, in the Oise department near the Forest of Chantilly. Once renowned for its lace making, Chantilly is famous for its racecourse and the Grand Château's art collection.

Chao K'uang Yin. *See* Song.

Chao Phraya River The chief river in Thailand, rising in the N and flowing S through Bangkok to a delta on the Gulf of Thailand. Length: 750 mi (1200 km).

Chaos In earliest Greek mythology, the goddess representing the primeval emptiness from which evolved Night, Erebus (darkness), Tartarus (the underworld), and Eros (desire). The concept of a confused and formless mass, out of which the ordered universe was created, dates from the time of Ovid.

chaparral A scrub form of vegetation occurring in S California and NW Mexico. It consists chiefly of sclerophyllous broad-leaved evergreen shrubs and bushes and is closely related to the maquis of lands bordering the Mediterranean. The climate with which this form of vegetation is associated, with mild wet winters and hot dry summers, is sometimes described as the Mediterranean type.

chapbook A small cheap booklet or tract of a few stitched pages in multiples of four. Catering to popular tastes, they related heroic tales, legends, lessons, etc., and were often illustrated with woodcuts. From the 16th century chapmen sold them throughout Europe and subsequently in North America, until they were superseded by magazines in the 19th century.

Chapel Hill 35 55N 79 04W A city in N central North Carolina. Home of the University of North Carolina since 1789, it is mainly a residential town that developed around the university. Population (1990): 38,719.

Chaplin, Charlie (Sir Charles C.; 1889–1975) British film actor. He was recruited by the Keystone Studio while touring the US in 1913. He gained immediate popular and financial success with his portrayals of the Little Tramp, a sensitive but pathetic figure dressed in baggy trousers and a bowler hat, and from 1918 he wrote and directed his own films. These included *The Gold Rush* (1924), *City Lights* (1931), *Modern Times* (1936) and *The Great Dictator* (1940). Accused of having communist sympathies, he left the US in 1952 to live in Switzerland. He was awarded an Oscar in 1973 and was knighted in 1976.

Chapman, George (c. 1560–1634) British poet and dramatist, famous for his translations of Homer's *Iliad* (1598–1611) and *Odyssey* (1616). His epic poem *Euthymiae Raptus* (1609) expresses his complex philosophy. His plays include the comedy *Eastward Ho* (1605), for which he and his collaborators John *Marston and Ben *Jonson were imprisoned, and the tragedy *Bussy d'Ambois* (1604).

CHARLIE CHAPLIN *In a scene from* The Gold Rush *(1924).*

char A food and game fish belonging to the genus *Salvelinus,* related to *trout, especially *S. alpinus,* found in Arctic coastal waters and fresh waters of Europe and North America. Its torpedo-shaped body, about 12 in (30 cm) long, is olive-green to moss-green with yellow spots above and silvery or bright red below.

characin A predatory freshwater fish of the family *Characidae* (about 1000 species), found in tropical Africa and America. Characins have toothed jaws and two dorsal fins. Although they range from 1–61 in (2.5 to 152 cm) long, most species are small and make colorful lively aquarium fish. Order: *Cypriniformes.* *See also* piranha; tetra; tigerfish.

charcoal The form of *carbon that is produced as a black porous residue from the partial burning of wood, bones, etc. It is a very clean smokeless fuel useful, for example, in barbecues and saunas. It is also extensively used in gas filters. *See also* activated charcoal.

Charcot, Jean-Martin (1825–93) French physiologist, noted for his studies of the nervous system. He described various diseases, including **Charcot's joint**—degeneration of the joints associated with disease of the nervous system.

He was a famous teacher—Sigmund *Freud was one of his students—and interested in hypnosis.

chard 1. The blanched leaves of a sucker growth of the globe *artichoke, used as a vegetable. **2.** The edible leaves of a variety of beet, *Beta vulgaris cicla*, also called Swiss chard.

Chardin, Jean-Baptiste-Siméon (1699–1779) French painter of still lifes and domestic interiors in the Dutch tradition of *Vermeer. The writer *Diderot admired the simplicity of his paintings, e.g. *The Housewife* (Louvre) and *The Young Schoolmistress* (National Gallery, London), and his skill at rendering textures. Working in pastel in his later years because of failing eyesight, he produced his celebrated portraits of himself and his wife (both Louvre).

Charente River A river in W central France. Rising in the Haute-Vienne department, it flows mainly W through Angoulême and Cognac to the Bay of Biscay. Length: 225 mi (362 km).

Chari River (*or* Shari R.) A river in N central Africa. Rising in the N Central African Republic, it flows N to Lake Chad, forming part of the Chad-Cameroon border. Length: 1400 mi (2250 km).

chariot 1. A two-wheeled horsedrawn vehicle used for warfare in ancient Asian and European civilizations. Commonly drawn by two horses, a war chariot generally carried two men: the driver and an archer or spearman. **2.** A fashionable small traveling carriage of the 18th and early 19th centuries, drawn by two or four horses.

Charlemagne (c. 742–814) King of the Franks (771–814) and the first postclassical western emperor (800–14). The son of Pepin the Short, he conquered the Saxon tribes (772–81) and became King of Lombardy (773). In 778 he campaigned in NE Spain, where at Roncesvalles his paladin Roland, later to be immortalized as the hero of the *Chanson de Roland,* was killed. In 800, having conquered most of western Christendom, he was crowned emperor of the West by Pope Leo III.

Charlemagne did much to centralize the administration of the empire while maintaining the traditional customs of his conquered territories. His court at Aix-la-Chapelle became a great European center, where Charlemagne, the patron of such scholars as *Alcuin and *Einhard, fostered the cultural revival known as the Carolingian renaissance.

Charleroi 50 25N 4 27E A town in S central Belgium, on the Sambre River. The center of a major coal-producing area, its industries include iron foundries and cutlery. Population (1981 est): 218,944.

Charles (1887–1922) The last emperor of the Dual Monarchy of *Austria-Hungary (1916–18). Charles failed in his attempts to withdraw Austria-Hungary from World War I and following its defeat was exiled. He was formally deposed in 1919.

Charles (Philip Arthur George) (1948–) Prince of Wales and heir-apparent to the throne of the United Kingdom as the eldest son of Elizabeth II. After studying at Trinity College, Cambridge (1967–70), he served in the armed forces before undertaking public duties. In 1981 he married Lady Diana Spencer (1961–). Their first child, Prince William Arthur Philip Louis of Wales was born in 1982; a second son, Henry, was born in 1984. Charles and Diana separated in 1992.

Charles I (1226–85) The first Angevin King of Naples and Sicily, after defeating Manfred (c. 1232–66; reigned 1258–66) at Benevento (1266) and Conradin (1252–68; reigned 1266–68) at Tagliacozzo (1268). Charles' rule gave rise

(1282) to the revolt known as the *Sicilian Vespers and he was driven from his kingdom in 1284.

THE PRINCE AND PRINCESS OF WALES *A wedding portrait of the couple. Their marriage on July 29, 1981, in St. Paul's Cathedral, London, was watched on television by an estimated 750 million people throughout the world.*

Charles I (1600–49) King of England, Scotland, and Ireland (1625–49), succeeding his father James I. Charles's disputes with Parliament led ultimately to the *Civil War and his execution. His first three Parliaments (1625; 1626; 1628–29) were dominated by Puritan members, who distrusted Charles's Roman Catholic queen and his own High Church loyalties. Parliament attempted to make its award of financial grants to the king dependent on his agreement to its demands. Charles resorted to levying taxes without parliamentary consent and ruled without Parliament from 1629 to 1640. His government became increasingly unpopular and his attempt to impose an Anglican prayer book on Presbyterian Scotland led to the *Bishops' Wars (1639–40). The financial demands of the Wars forced Charles to summon Parliament again but the so-called Short Parliament (May Parliament 1640) proved so critical that he soon dissolved it. The *Long Parliament, summoned in November following Charles's defeat by the Scots, demanded far-reaching reforms. In 1642 the Civil War broke out. After his defeat at Naseby (1645), Charles's cause was lost and he surrendered in 1646. He was handed to Parliament (January, 1647), seized by the army (June, 1647), and escaped to the Isle of Wight. Charles was tried at Westminster Hall, found guilty of treason, and beheaded (Jan 30, 1649).

CHARLES I Charles I in Three Positions (c. 1637) *by Van Dyck*.

Charles I (King of France). *See* Charles II (Holy Roman Emperor).

Charles (II) the Bald (823–77) Holy Roman Emperor (875–77) and, as Charles I, King of France (843–77). After the death of his father Louis I, civil war broke out between Charles and his three older brothers. By 843 Charles had procured by the Treaty of Verdun the W Frankish territories, which formed the nucleus of what was to become France.

Charles II (1630–85) King of England, Scotland, and Ireland (1660–85). He fought with his father, Charles I, in the Civil War and, after his father's execution (1649), was crowned by the Scots. Defeated by Cromwell (1651), he was forced into exile. After the fall of the Protectorate (1659), Charles became king after promising a general pardon and liberty of conscience. His advisers were a group of ministers known as the *Cabal. In 1670 he negotiated the Treaty of Dover with Louis XIV, promising to aid France against Holland and, in a secret clause, to declare himself a Roman Catholic, in return for annual French subsidies. His Roman Catholic sympathies became clear with his Declaration of Indulgence (1672). Parliament responded with the Test Act (1673) excluding Dissenters and Roman Catholics from office. Fear of Roman Catholicism exacerbated by the lack of an heir to the throne came to a head with the *Popish Plot (1678). Charles resisted subsequent parliamentary attempts to exclude his brother James from the succession and from 1681 ruled without Parliament. On his deathbed he acknowledged his Roman Catholicism.

Charles II (1661–1700) The last Hapsburg King of Spain (1665–1700). Charles became effective ruler in 1675. His reign saw Portugal regain its independence (1668) and the final eclipse of Spanish power in Europe. Charles's childlessness gave rise on his death to the War of the *Spanish Succession.

Charles II (King of France). *See* Charles III (Holy Roman Emperor).

Charles (III) the Fat (839–88) Holy Roman Emperor (881–87) and, as Charles II, King of France (884–87). Charles was the great-grandson of Charlemagne, whose empire he reunited for the last time after becoming King of Swabia (876), of Italy (879), and of the eastern Franks (882) and western Franks (France; 884).

Charles III (1716–88) King of Spain (1759–88). Charles ascended the Spanish throne after ruling (1734–59) Naples and Sicily. An enlightened despot (*see* Enlightenment), he encouraged efforts to modernize Spain, to develop its economy, and restore its international position. He sided with France in the Seven Years' War, losing Florida until 1783, when he regained it after the American Revolution.

Charles (IV) the Fair (1294–1328) King of France (1322–28). Charles was the brother of *Isabella of France, with whom he conspired against her husband Edward II of England.

Charles IV (1316–78) King of Bohemia (1346–78) and Holy Roman Emperor (1355–78). He made Prague his capital, where he founded (1348) Charles University. In 1356 he issued the Golden Bull, an imperial constitution, which confirmed the status of the seven imperial *electors.

Charles IV (1748–1819) King of Spain (1738–1808), who was dominated by his wife María Luisa (1751–1819) and her favorite Manuel de *Godoy. Military defeat and Godoy's unpopularity led to aristocratic and popular opposition, which caused Charles to abdicate.

Charles (V) the Wise (1337–80) King of France (1364–80) during the Hundred Years' War with England. As regent (1356–60) for his father John II, Charles suppressed the peasants' revolt known as the Jacquerie (1358). Between 1369 and 1375 he regained with the help of Bertrand du *Guesclin most of the territory lost to England by the disastrous Treaty of Brétigny (1360).

Charles V (1500–58) Holy Roman Emperor (1519–56). Charles inherited Burgundy and the Netherlands (1506) from his father Philip of Burgundy (1478–1506); he became King of Spain and Naples (1516) on the death of his maternal grandfather Ferdinand II of Aragon and Holy Roman Emperor on the death of his paternal grandfather Maximilian I. Charles's vast possessions provoked intermittent warfare with *Francis I of France: in 1525, having defeated Francis at Pavia, Charles briefly took the French king prisoner and in 1527, in response to an alliance between France, the papacy, Venice, and Milan, Charles's troops sacked Rome. Their contest for European hegemony ended inconclusively with the Treaty of Crépy (1544). Charles also faced the aggression of the Ottoman Turks, who twice besieged Vienna (1529, 1532), but his commitments elsewhere in the Empire prevented a decisive confrontation and the Turks continued to threaten Christendom.

Charles's reign saw the emergence of the *Reformation and in 1521 he presided over the Diet of Worms, which condemned *Luther. His subsequent attempts to conciliate the Protestants failed and in 1546 Charles took up arms against the Protestant Schmalkaldic League, defeating it at Mühlberg (1547). In 1551, however, two German Protestant rulers allied with Henry II of France and Charles was forced to accept Protestant demands (*see* Augsburg, Peace of). Exhausted by the great and complex problems of his Empire, Charles retired to a Spanish monastery, dividing his possessions between his son, who became *Philip II of Spain, and his brother, Emperor *Ferdinand I.

Charles (VI) the Well-Beloved (1368–1422) King of France (1380–1422).
Charles suffered attacks of insanity from 1392 and the ensuing conflict for the
regency led to civil war between the Armagnacs and the Burgundians. In 1415
Henry V of England invaded France and defeated the French at *Agincourt.
Henry married Charles's daughter Catherine of Valois (1401–37) and was
named as Charles's heir.

Charles VI (1685–1740) Holy Roman Emperor (1711–40), who issued the
Pragmatic Sanction (1713) to secure the succession of his daughter *Maria
Theresa to his Austrian possessions. His claim (1700) to the Spanish throne
gave rise to the War of the *Spanish Succession (1701–14), in which he was un-
successful. In 1716–18 and 1736–39 he fought the Turks; he lost the War of the
Polish Succession (1733–38).

Charles VII (1403–61) King of France (1422–61). He suffered losses to the
invading English and their Burgundian allies until 1429 when, with *Joan of
Arc, he liberated Orleans. By 1453, he had driven the English from all of
France, except Calais. He instituted reforms to strengthen the monarchy but his
last years were troubled by the intrigues of the dauphin. *See also* Hundred
Years' War.

Charles VII (1697–1745) Holy Roman Emperor (1742–45) during the War of
the *Austrian Succession. The Elector of Bavaria (1726–45), Charles joined the
alliance against Maria Theresa when she claimed the Austrian inheritance. He
was elected emperor in opposition to Maria Theresa's husband Francis (subsequently Emperor Francis I).

Charles VIII (1470–98) King of France (1483–98), who unsuccessfully
claimed the throne of Naples. He entered Naples in 1495 but was forced to withdraw in the face of an alliance between Austria, Milan, Venice, and the papacy.

Charles IX (1550–74) King of France (1560–74) during the *Wars of Religion. His mother *Catherine de' Medici dominated his reign and was largely responsible for the *Saint Bartholomew's Day Massacre of Huguenots that
Charles ordered in 1572.

Charles IX (1550–1611) King of Sweden (1607–11). During the absence of
his nephew King Sigismund (1566–1632; reigned 1592–1604), who was also
King of Poland (1587–1632), Charles virtually ruled Sweden, restoring
Lutheranism (1593–99). He defeated Sigismund (1598) to become king.

Charles X Gustavus (1622–60) King of Sweden (1654–60), who attempted
to establish a united northern state. He invaded Poland in 1655 and declared war
on Denmark in 1657, from which he regained lands in S Sweden by the Treaty
of Roskilde (1658). He died during a second campaign against Denmark.

Charles X (1757–1836) King of France (1824–30). Charles lived abroad after
the French revolution, returning at the Bourbon restoration (1815), when he became leader of the ultraroyalist party. His reactionary rule led to his overthrow
(1830) and he fled to England.

Charles XI (1655–97) King of Sweden (1660–97), who reduced the power of
the nobles to establish absolute rule. He was defeated (1675) by the Dutch alliance in the Dutch War of 1672–78 but was victorious (1678) against Denmark,
marrying (1680) the sister of the Danish king. Thereafter he maintained Swedish
neutrality.

Charles XII (1682–1718) King of Sweden (1697–1718) during the Great
*Northern War. In the face of an alliance between Denmark, Poland, and Russia,
Charles invaded Denmark (1699) and attacked Russia, winning a victory on the
Narva (1700). He dethroned the hostile Polish king (1704) and again invaded

Russia (1707), where he suffered defeat and fled to Turkey. He died while invading Norway.

Charles XIV John (King of Sweden). *See* Bernadotte, Jean Baptiste Jules.

Charles, Ray (Ray Charles Robinson; 1932–   ) US singer and pianist. Blind since he was a young boy, he combines gospel, blues, and rock to create a type of soul sound. He rocketed to stardom in the 1950s with his recordings of "I Got a Woman" (1954) and "What'd I Say" (1959).

Charles Albert (1798–1849) King of Sardinia-Piedmont (1831–49) during the Risorgimento (the movement for Italian Unification). Charles Albert introduced many administrative and economic reforms but reluctantly granted representative government to Sardinia in 1848. He joined Milan's revolt against its Austrian government but was defeated at Custoza (1848) and Novara (1849) and abdicated.

Charles Edward Stuart, the Young Pretender (1720–88) The son of the Old Pretender, *James Edward Stuart. Romantically known as Bonnie Prince Charlie, in 1745 he landed in Scotland, rallied his *Jacobite supporters, and marched S to claim the English throne. Lack of support forced his withdrawal again to Scotland. Defeated in battle at Culloden (1746), he escaped to exile in Europe.

Charles Martel (c. 689–741) Mayor of the palace of Austrasia (the eastern Frankish empire). After the death (714) of his father Pepin of Herstal, Charles, an illegitimate son, competed for the succession with Pepin's widow, Plectrude, who was regent for her grandsons. Successful by 719, Charles extended his rule over all the Franks. In 732 near Poitiers, he won a great victory over the invading Muslims.

Charles's law For a gas at constant pressure, its volume is directly proportional to its absolute temperature. The law is not strictly obeyed but is closely approximated in gases above their *critical state. An alternative statement of the law is that gases expand by $\frac{1}{273}$ of their volume at 32°F (0°C) for every 7.8°F (1°C) rise in temperature. Named for Jacques Charles (1746–1823).

Charles the Bold (1433–77) The last Duke of Burgundy (1467–77), who attempted to create a Burgundian kingdom. In 1465 Charles joined a revolt against Louis XI of France, with whom he was repeatedly in conflict until 1477. He extended his territory to the Rhine, conquering Lorraine in 1475. He then invaded Switzerland (1476) but was defeated near Granson and at Morat and died in battle while laying siege to Nancy.

Charleston 38 23N 81 40W The capital of West Virginia. It was the home (1788–95) of Daniel Boone. Industries include chemicals, glass, and paints. Population (1990): 57,287.

Charleston 32 48N 79 58W A city in South Carolina near the Atlantic coast. Founded in 1670, the first military action of the Civil War took place here with the bombardment of Fort Sumter by Confederate troops in 1861. Despite further damage from an earthquake in 1866, many of Charleston's colonial buildings remain, making it a popular tourist center. Its gardens are famous throughout the world. A major port, its manufactures include fertilizer, paper, and steel. Population (1990): 80,414.

Charleston A ballroom dance of the 1920s named for Charleston, S. C. where it had been popular in the early 1900s. It became a national craze following the musical *Runnin' Wild* (1923). Its chief characteristics are $\frac{4}{4}$ time, syncopated rhythms, and twisting toe-in steps.

CHARLESTON *A cartoon view of the 1920s dance craze.*

Charleston, Battles of Two battles of the *American Revolution fought at Charleston, S. C. In the first (1776) the Americans repulsed the British, whose invasion of the South was thus delayed. In the second the Americans surrendered (May 12, 1780) Charleston after a 45-day siege.

charlock An annual herb, *Sinapis arvensis,* also called wild mustard. 12–31 in (30–80 cm) high, with bright-yellow flowers and hairy toothed leaves, it is found throughout Eurasia and N Africa and has been introduced to the Americas, South Africa, Australia, and New Zealand. It is a serious weed, especially of spring-sown crops. Family: *Cruciferae.*

Charlotte 35 03N 80 50W A city in North Carolina. The commercial and industrial center of the Carolina manufacturing belt, its products include textiles, machinery, and chemicals. Population (1990): 395,934.

Charlotte Amalie (name from 1921 until 1936: St Thomas) 18 21N 64 56W The capital of the US Virgin Islands, a port on St Thomas Island. Established by the Danes in 1672, it is now a tourist resort. Population (1980): 11,756.

Charlottenburg 52 31N 13 15E A district of Berlin, Germany, on the Spree River. The 1936 Olympic Games were held here.

Charlottesville 38 02N 78 29W A city in central Virginia. It was the home of Thomas Jefferson, who established the University of Virginia here in 1819. Population (1990): 40,341.

Charlottetown 46 14N 63 09W A city and port in E Canada, the capital of Prince Edward Island. Founded in 1790, it is the province's commercial, industrial, and educational center. Population (1986): 16,000.

charm A property of matter, expressed as a *quantum number, postulated to account for the unusually long lifetime of the psi particle (discovered in 1974). According to this hypothesis a quark (*see* particle physics) exists having the property called charm. The psi particle itself is a meson having zero charm as it consists of a charmed quark and its antiquark. However, there is evidence that some charmed *hadrons exist. Charm is believed to be conserved in *strong interactions and in electromagnetic interactions.

Charon In Greek legend, the ferryman who carried the souls of the dead over the Styx and Acheron Rivers to the underworld. Only the correctly buried dead were taken. A coin placed in the mouth of the corpse was his payment.

Charron, Pierre (1541–1603) French theologian and philosopher. An intimate of *Montaigne, Charron studied law but entered the Church, becoming a fashionable preacher with a court appointment. *Les Trois Vérités* (1594) is a defense of Roman Catholicism. *De la sagesse* (1601), contrastingly skeptical and rationalistic, foreshadows *deism, and offers a moral philosophy divorced from Christian sanctions.

Chartier, Alain (c. 1385–c. 1440) French poet and prose writer. He served as secretary to Charles VI and as foreign emissary for Charles VII. His works include the *Quadrilogue invectif* (1422), a debate on the state of France and a call for national unity, and the poem *La Belle Dame sans merci* (1424).

Chartism A British working-class movement for political reform, centering on William *Lovett's London Working Men's Association (LWMA). Founded in June, 1836, the LWMA drew up a People's Charter (1838) of six points: universal male suffrage, the secret ballot, equal electoral districts, abolition of the property qualifications for members of Parliament, payment of MPs, and annual general elections. The Chartists quickly gained support throughout the country and presented their Charter with 1.2 million signatures to Parliament (1839). It was rejected, as were their two later petitions (1842, 1848). Chartism lost support in the 1840s because of lack of organization, rivalry between its leaders, Lovett and Feargus *O'Connor, and reviving trade and greater prosperity. The movement was spent by the end of the decade.

Chartres 48 27N 1 30E A city in N central France, the capital of the Eure-et-Loire department on the Eure River. The gothic cathedral (begun c. 1194) is famous, especially for its 13th-century stained glass, and there are several other noteworthy churches (particularly St Pierre). Chartres is the principal market town of the Beauce region. Population (1975): 41,251.

Chartreuse, La Grande A *Carthusian monastery in a remote valley in SE France, in the Isère department. The buildings date mainly from the 17th century. The liqueur Chartreuse is made by the monks, the income from it being devoted to maintaining Carthusian monasteries and to several charities.

Charybdis A legendary Greek monster and the whirlpool she formed, traditionally in the Strait of Messina. The dangerous channel between Charybdis and *Scylla was successfully navigated by both Odysseus and the Argonauts.

Chase, Salmon Portland (1808–73) US politician, lawyer, and chief justice of the Supreme Court (1864–73). He spent his early career as a lawyer in Ohio, where he was active in the abolitionist movement. He served as US senator (1849–55; 1860–61), governor of Ohio (1855–59), and secretary of the Treasury (1861–64). As chief justice he presided over the impeachment trial (1868) of Pres. Andrew Johnson, who was acquitted, and he handled a number of landmark cases, such as *Hepburn* v. *Griswold* (1870), in which he held that legal tender was unconstitutional. He sought his party's nomination for president several times but was unsuccessful.

Chase, Samuel (1741–1811) US jurist and lawyer, associate justice of the Supreme Court (1796–1811). He was an active patriot in his native Maryland, serving in the Continental Congresses (1774–78; 1784–85); he was a signer of the Declaration of Independence (1776). In 1804 impeachment proceedings were initiated against him by the Senate for his actions as a Federalist judge; he was acquitted of all charges in 1805.

chat A songbird belonging to the *thrush family. True chats include *stonechats, *whinchats, *wheatears, and *redstarts although the name is also given to certain Australian wrens (family *Muscicapidae*) and to American wood warblers (family *Parulidae*).

chateau A French castle or large country house. In the middle ages it was the fortified stronghold of the local seigneur. By the 16th century, however, defense needs had decreased and chateaus became the lightly fortified country residences of the nobility. Among the most famous are the chateaus of *Blois (1498–1524), *Chambord (1519–40), and d'Azay-le-Rideau (1520) in the Loire Valley. Under Louis XIV chateau building declined with the aristocracy's increasing dependence on the crown for its income and the resultant need to live in Paris.

Chateaubriand, Vicomte de (1768–1848) French writer and diplomat. Son of a minor nobleman, he sailed to America in 1791 but soon returned to fight in the royalist army. He lived in England from 1793 to 1800. On returning to France, he published *Atala* (1801), an unfinished epic based on his experiences with the American Indians, and *Le Génie du Christianisme* (1802). After the restoration of the monarchy in 1814 he served as ambassador and as minister for foreign affairs. He is best known for his *Mémoires d'outre-tombe* (1849–50).

Château-Thierry 49 03N 3 24E A town in N France, in the Aisne department on the Marne River. The site of many battles throughout the centuries, it was the scene of the second battle of the Marne (1918) during *World War I.

Chatham 51 23N 0 32E A city in SE England, in Kent on the Medway estuary. It is a naval base dating from Tudor times, with extensive dockyards. Population (1983): 146,000.

Chatham, 1st Earl of. *See* Pitt the Elder, William.

Chatham Islands 44 00S 176 30W A group of islands in the S Pacific Ocean, comprising part of New Zealand. The main occupation is sheep farming. Area: 372 sq mi (963 sq km). Chief settlement: Waitangi.

Chattahoochee River A river that rises in NE Georgia, flows SW and then S, where it forms the border with Alabama from West Point until its entry into NW Florida. Here it meets the Flint River to form the Apalachicola River. Length: 435 mi (701 km).

Chattanooga 35 02N 85 18W A city in SE Tennessee on the Tennessee River. It was settled in 1815 and was the site of a decisive battle in the US Civil War (1863). It grew rapidly following the provision of cheap hydroelectric power by the Tennessee Valley Authority in the 1930s. Its varied industries include the manufacture of textiles, boilers, nuclear reactors, furniture, and chemicals. Population (1990): 152,466.

Chatterjee, Bankim Chandra (1838–94) Indian novelist. A pioneer of the novel in India, he wrote romances, such as *Anandamath* (1882), the heroes of which are usually champions of Hindu nationalism. Many of his books were first published serially in *Banga Darshan,* the journal he founded in 1872.

Chaucer, Geoffrey (c. 1342–1400) English poet, whose works established the Southern English dialect as the literary language of England. Chaucer made various journeys to Europe as a soldier and diplomat, held positions in the customs service, and received pensions from Richard II and Henry IV. He translated part of the French poem *Le Roman de la rose* into English and his own poems *The Book of the Duchess* and *The Parliament of Fowls* derive from the French tradition of the allegorical dream poem. Chaucer was also influenced by Dante, Petrarch, and Boccaccio; he parodied Dante's *Divine Comedy* in *The House of Fame* and used Boccaccio's poem *Il filostrato* as the basis for *Troilus and Criseyde,* a long poem dealing with the transitoriness of earthly love, human free will, and divine foreknowledge. Chaucer's best-known work is *The Canterbury Tales,* a collection of stories told by a group of pilgrims traveling from

London to Canterbury. The tales range from the tragedy of *The Knight's Tale* to the bawdiness of *The Miller's Tale*. Colorful portraits of each pilgrim are contained in the famous Prologue.

GEOFFREY CHAUCER *An engraving based on an illumination in a manuscript of Chaucer's works.*

chaulmoogra Either of two trees, *Hydnocarpus wightiana* of SW Asia or *Taraktogenos kurzii* of Burma, both of which yield a medicinal oil used in treating leprosy. Family: *Flacourtiaceae*.

Chausson, Ernest (1855–99) French composer. His compositions were influenced by his teacher Franck and by Wagner. His small output includes *Poème de l'amour et de la mer* (for voice and orchestra; 1882–92), *Poème* (for violin and orchestra; 1896), and a symphony (1890). He was killed in a cycling accident.

Chautauqua A system of adult education started in the US by John H. Vincent and Lewis Miller at Lake Chautauqua, N.Y., in 1874. Originally a summer training program for Protestant Sunday school teachers in a rural, peaceful setting, it broadened into general education, with guest lecturers and recreation, followed by home reading and correspondence courses. By 1900 there were adult summer school sessions (called chautauquas) throughout the country; although the system weakened after 1924, due to the rise of advanced media techniques, it is still carried on at Chautauqua, N.Y.

Chavez, Cesar Estrada (1927–93) US labor leader. He worked for the Community Service Organization (1952–62), serving as its director from 1958. In 1962 he founded the United Farm Workers (UFW), which became the AFL-CIO's United Farm Workers Organization Committee in 1966. He led boycotts of grapes, citrus fruits, and lettuce in the late 1960s and 1970s, but disagreements between management and farm laborers continued.

Chebishev, Pafnuti Lvovich (1821–94) Russian mathematician, who made many discoveries in the field of *prime numbers, the most important of which was a method of determining the number of primes below a given number. He also contributed to probability theory and mechanics.

Cheboksary 56 08N 47 12E A port in central Russia, the capital of Chuvash on the Volga River. Its manufactures include electrical equipment and it has a large hydroelectric station. Population (1991 est): 435,000.

Checheno-Ingush Autonomous Republic An administrative division in Russia, in the N Caucasus. The population is 50% Chechen and 10% Ingushe (both Muslim) and 35% Russian. Checheno-Ingush has one of the major Russian oilfields as well as sizable deposits of natural gas and minerals. Its main industries are engineering, chemicals, manufacture of building materials, food canning, and wine and cognac making. The presence of mineral waters has resulted in the development of health resorts. *History*: the Chechens and Ingushes were conquered by Russia in the late 1850s. Each nationality became (1922 and 1924 respectively) a separate autonomous *oblast* (region) before uniting in 1936 to become one autonomous republic. Following collaboration with the Germans in World War II, many Chechens and Ingushes were deported to Central Asia, being returned in 1956. The republic was re-established in 1957. Area: 7350 sq mi (19,300 sq km). Population (1991 est): 1,307,000. Capital: Grozny.

checkers A boardgame for two players that was developed in 12th-century Europe from an ancient Egyptian game. Each player has 12 disk-shaped pieces (usually black for one and white or red for the other), which are placed on the 12 black squares at the opposite ends of a chessboard. The pieces move only on the black squares and black always starts. One piece per turn is moved diagonally forward into a vacant adjacent square. If the next square is occupied by one of the opponent's pieces but the square beyond that is vacant, the playing piece must jump onto the vacant square, removing his opponent's piece from the board. He must make a further jump from there if possible (in the same turn). The 16th-century rule of "huffing" enables a player to remove an opponent's piece that could have jumped but did not. If a piece reaches the opposing back line it becomes a "king" (a second piece is placed on top of it) and it may then move forward or backward. The winner is the player who takes or immobilizes all his opponent's pieces.

cheese A dairy product made from separated milk solids (curd). Curd is made by coagulating milk with rennet or some other enzyme and removing the liquid (whey). It is then salted, pressed into blocks, and left to mature. Cheese is a rich source of protein and calcium. It contains fat but little carbohydrate since most of it is left in the whey. **Hard cheeses,** such as Emmental and Cheddar, are left to mature for some time—years in the case of Italian Parmesan. Cheshire, Port Salut, Edam, and Gouda are **semihard cheeses. Soft cheeses** may be eaten relatively fresh, after one day in the case of fresh cream cheese. Brie, Camembert, and Limburg are surface-ripened soft cheeses. Blue cheese, Stilton, Gorgonzola, and Roquefort are ripened by molds inside the cheese.

cheetah A large *cat, *Acinonyx jubatus,* of Africa and SW Asia, also called hunting leopard. It has a reddish-yellow coat with black spots and grows to about 7 ft (2 m) in length. Cheetahs have nonretractable claws and rough pads and they hunt by running down prey, such as antelope. They are the fastest mammals, sprinting at up to 70 mph (110 kph).

Cheever, John (1912–82) US author. Although his first collections of short stories, *The Way Some People Live* (1943) and *The Enormous Radio* (1953) dealt with urban life, the bulk of his work told of the suburbs with which he was familiar. His short story collections include *The Housebreaker of Shady Hill* (1958), *The World of Apples* (1973), and *The Stories of John Cheever* (1978; Pulitzer Prize). Among his novels are *The Wapshot Chronicle* (1957), *The Wapshot Scandal* (1964), *Bullet Park* (1969), *Falconer* (1977), and *Oh, What a Paradise It Seems* (1982).

Chefoo. *See* Yantai.

CHEKA The first Soviet secret police agency. Founded in 1917, its full name was the Extraordinary Commission to Combat Counterrevolution, Sabotage, and Speculation. It was headed by Feliks Dzerzhinskii (1877–1926) and fought all anti-Bolshevik groups. Owing to its extreme brutality, it came under severe criticism and was reorganized in 1922.

Chekhov, Anton Pavlovich (1860–1904) Russian dramatist and short-story writer. He began writing comic sketches while studying medicine at Moscow University and developed as a more serious writer after graduating in 1884. Suffering from tuberculosis, he bought a farm at Melikhovo in 1892 and, after a hemorrhage in 1897, lived at Yalta in the Crimea. His first play, *The Seagull* (1896), failed at first but succeeded triumphantly when revived in 1898 by Stanislavsky's Moscow Art Theater. His major plays—*Uncle Vanya* (1897), *The Three Sisters* (1901), and *The Cherry Orchard* (1904)—were written for this company, and in 1901 he married one of the actresses, Olga Knipper.

Chekiang. *See* Zhejiang.

chelate An inorganic chemical complex in which a closed ring of atoms is formed including a metallic ion. For example, two molecules of ethylenediamine form two chelate rings with a cupric ion. Chlorophyll (with a central magnesium ion) and hemoglobin (with a central iron ion) are chelates. Chelating agents are used for sequestering unwanted metal ions. For example, they are added to shampoos in order to soften the water used with them by "locking up" calcium and magnesium ions.

Chelmsford 51 44N 0 28E A city in SE England, the administrative center of Essex. It is a market town and manufactures electronic communications equipment, electronic equipment, and bearings. Population (1981): 58,159.

Chelonia An order of reptiles (600 species) comprising the aquatic *turtles and *terrapins and the terrestrial *tortoises, widely distributed in warm and temperate regions. They have a protective shell consisting of an upper carapace and a lower plastron joined together at the sides with openings for the head, tail, and limbs. The neck is long and mobile and can be withdrawn into the shell.

Chelsea porcelain A pioneer soft-paste *porcelain made in the Chelsea district of London between 1743 and 1785. Products included octagonal table wares from Japanese models, copies of Chinese vases and figures, perfume bottles and toilet articles in *Meissen style, and splendid *rococo vases and figures in the Sèvres style.

Cheltenham 51 54N 2 04W A city in SW England, in Gloucestershire. A fashionable spa town in the 18th century, it is famous for its schools (Cheltenham College, a boys' public school, and Cheltenham Ladies' College) and racecourse. Population (1981): 73,229.

Chelyabinsk 55 12N 61 25E A city in Russia. It is one of the country's major industrial centers, whose products include steel and chemicals. Population (1991 est): 1,148,000.

Chelyuskin, Cape 77 44N 103 55E A headland in central Siberia, the most N point of any continent.

chemical bond The force that holds the atoms together in a molecule or the ions together in a crystalline solid. In general, atoms combine to form molecules and ions combine to form crystals in order to increase their stability by sharing or transferring outer electrons in such a way that the stable noble-gas configuration results (*see* atomic theory). In **covalent bonds**, atoms are held together by sharing pairs of electrons in their outer shells. In methane (CH_4), for example, each hydrogen atom forms a bond by sharing its only electron with one of the four electrons in the outer shell of the carbon atom. Each hydrogen atom then has a pair of electrons, giving it the stable two-electron outer shell of helium. The carbon atom, with four pairs of electrons in its outer shell, has the stable eight-electron outer shell of argon. In the **electrovalent** (*or* ionic) **bond** an outer electron is transferred from one atom to another so that ions are formed. The electrostatic force between the ions holds the molecule or crystal together. For example, a molecule of sodium chloride (NaCl) is formed when the single electron in the outer shell of the sodium atom is transferred to the chlorine atom. As the chlorine atom has seven electrons, the additional electron gives it the eight-electron argon stability. **Coordinate** (*or* dative) **bonds** are covalent bonds in which both electrons are donated by the same atom. They thus combine the concepts of sharing and transferring. *See also* hydrogen bonds.

chemical energy Energy released in a usable form by a chemical reaction. In molecules, energy is stored as the potential energy of the electrons. During a reaction, rearrangement of the electrons takes place and excess energy is converted to other forms. The energy is usually transformed into heat, as in combustion, acid-base neutralization, etc., but it can be made available as electrical energy in cells. Occasionally, it gives rise to *luminescence.

chemical engineering The design, maintenance, and operation of equipment used in industrial chemical processes. Chemical engineers study both chemistry and engineering subjects.

chemical reaction A process in which one or more chemical substances change to other substances, either spontaneously or as a result of heat, irradiation, etc. Chemical reaction involves partial or complete transfer of one or more electrons between reacting species and a rearrangement of atoms to form different molecules. For a reaction to occur, reactant atoms (or molecules, ions, etc.) must collide. Most reactions are thus bimolecular (involving collision between two molecules); a few are termolecular (three molecules). Many apparently complicated reactions proceed in a sequence of simple steps. *See also* catalysis.

chemical warfare The use of toxic substances to kill or disable personnel, pollute food or water supplies, or make any other military use of chemicals, for example smoke screens, etc. (explosives are excluded). Toxic substances are generally fired in shells as liquids or solids that form aerosols on explosion. Chlorine, phosgene, and mustard gas were used in World War I but are ineffective against modern protection. They were not used in World War II. Poisons have now been developed to penetrate the skin, circumventing gas masks. Chemical warfare permits great flexibility in the amount and type of injuries inflicted, ranging from the relatively humane *tear gas to the lethal *nerve gases.

chemiluminescence The emission of light without heat in the course of a chemical reaction; often known as cold light. It occurs when the reaction yields product molecules in an excited energy state; light is emitted as the molecules revert to their ground state. Under certain conditions, the oxidation of many organic compounds, including glucose and formaldehyde, results in chemiluminescence. *See also* bioluminescence.

chemin de fe. *See* baccarat.

chemisorption. *See* adsorption.

chemistry The scientific study of matter, especially the changes and interactions it can undergo. Chemistry can be said to have originated with *Aristotle's four-element (earth, air, fire, water) analysis of matter. This totally incorrect view of the substance of the world persisted unchallenged, untested, and unrefuted from the 4th century BC, through some 2000 years of *alchemy, until it was finally demolished by Robert *Boyle in his *Skeptical Chymist* (1661). The modern concept of an element, as a substance incapable of further decomposition, was provided by Boyle, who also correctly distinguished between elements, compounds, and mixtures. The elucidation of the structure of compounds in terms of the elements they contain was developed by such 18th-century chemists as *Cavendish, *Priestley, and *Lavoisier. *Berzelius's law of constant proportions and *Dalton's atomic theory, produced at the beginning of the 19th century, established chemistry on a quantitative basis. However, it was not until the beginning of the 20th century that the work of J. J. Thomson and Rutherford (*see* atomic theory) had established the structure of the atom, enabling the electronic theory of *valence to emerge. This theory made sense of the work of Newlands and *Mendeleyev in ordering the elements into the structure of the *periodic table. **Inorganic chemistry** is concerned with the study of all these elements (except carbon) and their compounds and interactions. **Organic chemistry** is the study of the enormous number of compounds of carbon. It originated with *Wöhler's synthesis of urea in 1828 and developed throughout the 19th century. Organic chemicals fall broadly into two classes: *aliphatic compounds (*see also* alkanes; alkenes; alkynes) and *aromatic compounds. Many industries, including dyeing, explosives, plastics, and pharmaceuticals, depend very largely on organic chemistry. **Physical chemistry** is concerned with the application of physics to a quantitative assessment of the structures and properties of compounds and the laws that control chemical reactions. Electrochemistry and *electrolysis, reaction kinetics, photochemistry, chemical *thermodynamics, and colloid chemistry are some of its main branches.

Chemnitz. *See* Karl-Marx-Stadt.

chemoreception The reception by an organism of chemical stimuli. In man and other air-breathing vertebrates, chemicals ingested in food, etc., are sensed by taste buds on the tongue and walls of the mouth, while airborne chemicals are detected by smell (olfactory) receptors in the lining of the nasal passages (*see also* pheromones). Both smell and taste organs are present in fish but worms and other lower animals have only a general sensitivity to chemicals over the body surface. Chemoreception is used by animals for locating and identifying other organisms, food sources, and scent marks and trails.

chemotherapy The treatment of disease by means of drugs. The term was originally coined by Paul *Ehrlich, for the synthetic chemicals used to treat infectious diseases (e.g. salvarsan for syphilis), but it was later expanded to include antibiotics. Today chemotherapy commonly refers to the chemical treatment of cancer—by means of *cytotoxic and other drugs, which inhibit the action of cancer cells—as distinct from treatment with X-rays (*see* radiotherapy).

Chenab Riber A river in NW India and Pakistan, one of the five rivers of the Punjab. Rising in the Himalayas, it flows SW to join the Sutlej River in Pakistan. Length: 675 mi (1087 km).

Chen-chiang. *See* Jinjiang.

Cheng Ch'eng-kung. *See* Zheng Cheng Gong.

Cheng-chou. *See* Zhengzhou.

Chengde (*or* Ch'eng-te; English name: Jehol) 40 48N 118 06E A city in NE China, in Hebei province. During the 18th and 19th centuries the Qing emperors spent the summers here. It was the capital of the former province of Jehol (1928–56). Population (1984): 326,000.

Chengdu (*or* Ch'eng-tu) 30 37N 104 06E A city in central China, the capital of Sichuan province and the site of its university. An ancient cultural, and now also an industrial, center, it produces textiles, chemicals, and machinery. Population (1987 est): 2,650,000.

Cheng Ho. *See* Zheng He.

Ch'eng-te. *See* Chengde.

Ch'eng-tu. *See* Chengdu.

Chénier, André de (1762–94) French poet, born in Istanbul of Greek-French parentage. He studied in Paris and worked in London before returning to Revolutionary France in 1789. An outspoken political journalist, he was arrested and guillotined. His posthumously published poems, notably the *Iambes* and *Odes,* had a strong influence on later Romantic poets.

Cheops. *See* Khufu.

Chephren. *See* Khafre.

Cher (Cherilyn Sarkisian; 1946–) US singer, entertainer, and actress. She first achieved fame in the 1960s, singing with Sonny Bono, who became her husband, as "Sonny and Cher." A successful early 1970s television variety show followed before the couple divorced. By the early 1980s, Cher was concentrating on a movie career and was acclaimed for her appearances in such films as *Silkwood* (1983), *Mask* (1985), and *Moonstruck* (1987), for which she received the Academy Award as best actress. She also became known as a physical fitness advocate and promoter.

Cher River A river in central France, rising in the Massif Central near Aubusson and flowing NW to join the Loire River near Tours. Length: 220 mi (354 km).

Cherbourg 49 38N 1 37W A seaport in NW France, in Manche department on the Cotentin Peninsula. Cherbourg has civil and military docks and large shipbuilding yards. In the heyday of ocean liners Cherbourg was an important transatlantic port; the cross-channel service to Southampton, England, remains important. Population (1982): 85,500.

Cheremkhovo 53 08N 103 01E A city in SE Russia. A coal mining center, it also refines oil and produces chemicals. Population (1987 est): 106,000.

Cherenkov, Pavel Alekseievich (1904–) Russian physicist, who discovered **Cherenkov radiation** in 1934. This radiation consists of blue-white light emitted by the atoms of a medium through which a high-energy charged particle is passing at a velocity in excess of the velocity of light in that medium. Three years later the effect was explained by *I. M. Frank and Igor Tamm. The three Russian physicists shared the 1958 Nobel Prize for their work.

Cherepovets 59 09N 37 50E A city in Russia on the Volga-Baltic waterway. It is a major transportation center and has a large iron and steel plant. Population (1991 est): 316,000.

Cheribon. *See* Tjirebon.

Cherkassy 49 27N 32 04E A port in Ukraine on the Dnepr River. Once a *Cossack center, it grew rapidly in the 1960s with the growth of its chemical industry. Population (1991 est): 302,000.

Chernenko, Konstantin Ustinovich (1911–85) USSR statesman; president (1984–85). Closely allied with Leonid *Brezhnev, Chernenko was chief of staff of the Presidium (1960–82), in 1977 became a non-voting member of the Politburo, and was granted full membership in it in 1978. Although he was not selected to be Brezhnev's successor in 1982, he assumed the presidency upon the death of Yuri *Andropov in 1984. He served until his own death and was followed by Mikhail *Gorbachev.

Chernigov 51 30N 31 18E A city in Ukraine on the Desna River. It is a railroad junction and its manufactures include tires, pianos, and consumer goods. Population (1991 est): 306,000.

Chernobyl An accident in reactor No. 4 at the Chernobyl nuclear plant near Kiev, Ukraine, during the last week of April 1986, that resulted in more than 250 reported deaths and hundreds of injuries. The spread of radiation, especially across Europe, was detected. The accident prompted a call for stronger nuclear energy safety measures throughout the world.

Chernovtsy (Romanian name: Cernauti) 48 19N 25 52E A city in Ukraine, on the Prut River. It was held by Romania between 1918 and 1940. It is an important rail junction, industrial, cultural, and scientific center. Population (1991 est): 259,000.

chernozem (*or* black earth) A type of soil that is characteristic of the grasslands of the continental interiors. There is a dark surface layer rich in alkaline humus, underlain by calcium carbonate concretions. Chernozems are agriculturally among the richest soils in the world.

Cherokee A North American Indian people speaking an Iroquoian language and formerly inhabiting extensive areas in Georgia, Tennessee, and North Carolina. The Cherokees supported themselves by agriculture and inhabited towns ruled by chiefs who were responsible for the performance of religious and military ceremonies. During the *American Revolution, the Cherokees fought on the side of the British and in 1829, by order of Pres. Andrew *Jackson, they were forced to leave their homelands and resettle in a reservation in Oklahoma. They called this painful and difficult migration the *Trail of Tears. The present Cherokee population is about 75,000, with the majority living in Oklahoma. In 1984 the Cherokees were permitted to reestablish a tribal center in their former homeland.

cherry A tree or shrub of the genus *Prunus,* of N temperate regions, having small rounded juicy fruits surrounding a hard stone containing a seed. Cherry trees produce clusters of white or pinkish flowers in spring, and some varieties are grown only for ornament. Cherries cultivated for their fruits are of two main types—sour and sweet. Sour cherries have been developed from *P. cerasus,* a widespread shrubby tree growing to 23 ft (7 m). Morello—the best variety—has dark-red fruits used in jams and liqueurs. Sweet dessert cherries arose from the gean (*P. avium*), native to Eurasia and N Africa. Found in woods and hedges, it grows to 80 ft (25 m). Fruits of cultivated forms vary from pale yellow to dark red. Hybrids between *P. cerasus* and *P. avium* are used for cooking. *See also* bird cherry.

cherry laurel An evergreen shrub, *Prunus laurocerasus,* 7–20 ft (2–6 m) high, producing spikes of fragrant whitish flowers in spring. A native of SE Europe and SW Asia, it has been introduced and locally naturalized elsewhere in hedges and woodlands. Family: *Rosaceae.*

chert A rock that is a variety of chalcedony, occurring in a stratified form. It consists of minute crystals of silica, of either organic or inorganic origin, found in sedimentary rocks.

cherubim and seraphim Supernatural beings who, according to *Dionysius the Areopagite, are the two highest orders of *angels in the celestial hierarchy. The seraphim are described by Isaiah (Isaiah 6.2–7) as six-winged attendants upon God's throne. The cherubim, who are traditionally depicted as winged heads, appear in the Bible as guardians of the divine presence; for instance, they bar the approaches to the Garden of Eden after the Fall (Genesis 3.24).

Cherubini, Maria Luigi (1760–1842) Italian composer. He spent much of his life in France, becoming director of the Paris Conservatoire in 1822. He was primarily an operatic composer; his *Deux Journées* (1800; English title: *The Water-carrier*) influenced Beethoven. He also wrote two settings of the requiem mass and six string quartets in an original style.

chervil An annual herb, *Anthriscus cerefolium,* 12–20 in (30–50 cm) high, grown for its leaves, used for salads and seasonings. Its white flowers grow in umbrella-like clusters. A native of central, E, and S Europe, it is widely introduced, growing on hedgebanks and waste ground throughout Europe, the Americas, N Africa, and New Zealand. Family: *Umbelliferae.*

Chesapeake Bay The largest inlet on the Atlantic coast, bordering on Virginia and Maryland. Length: approximately 200 mi (320 km).

chess A board game for two players, each of whom controls 16 pieces. The pieces are moved according to strict rules, the object of the game being to force the opponent's king into a position from which it cannot escape. A player attempts to weaken his opponent's position by capturing his pieces. This he does by moving his own pieces onto the squares occupied by his opponent's pieces. Only the kings cannot be captured in this way. After an initial lottery to choose the player who makes the first move, the game becomes one of pure skill with a vast literature devoted to its tactics and strategy. Chess has been variously described as a game, sport, art, science, vocation, and (with advertising) the greatest waste of human ingenuity. To the extent that it simulates war it has been regarded as a psychological sublimation of human aggression, although more lyrical writers have seen it as a source of Indian symbolism and allegory.

Chess pieces dating back to the 2nd century demonstrate the game's antiquity. Well known to 5th-century Hindus, it seems to have reached Europe, via Persia and Arabia, in the 10th century. The rules of the game have hardly changed since the 16th century, although the identities of some of the pieces have.

Since 1922 the rules have been controlled by the Fédération internationale des Échecs (FIDE), which has also organized world championships since 1946. Famous world champions include Emanuel *Lasker (1894–1921), José *Capablanca (1921–27), Alexander *Alekhine, (1927–35; 1937–46), Boris *Spassky (1969–72), Bobby *Fischer (1972–75), Anatoly *Karpov (1975–85), and Gary Kasparov (1985–   ).

chest A large domestic storage box. Chests from ancient Egypt are among the earliest surviving furniture. In Europe they were essential pieces of portable furniture doubling as a bed, table, or seat. The simplest consist of six boards nailed together with one forming a lid, but between the 15th and the 18th centuries they

CHESS

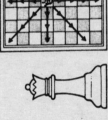

The castle or rook moves any distance vertically or horizontally. Originally represented as a chariot (Arabic: rukh), it is known in many languages as a castle or tower (French: tour).

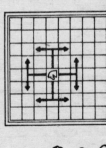

The pawn moves forward one square (or two on its first move). In Arabic it was called a foot-soldier, the English word deriving from the Latin pes, pedis. In some European languages the piece is called a peasant (e.g. German: Bauer).

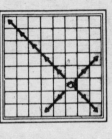

The queen, the most powerful piece, moves any distance in any direction. Originally known as the counsellor, its present name and moves were adopted in the 15th century.

The bishop moves in any direction diagonally. In the Hindu and Arabic games the piece was called an elephant. In the European games the piece has acquired a variety of identities: a bishop in English, a jester (fou) in French, a runner (Läufer) in German, but still an elephant (slon) in Russian.

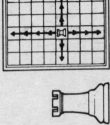

The king, weak and vulnerable, moves only one square at a time (in any direction). The name of the game is a corruption of the Persian word for king–shah.

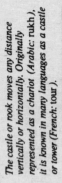
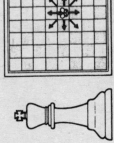

The knight, the only piece to jump over other pieces, moves one square horizontally and two vertically or two horizontally and one vertically. Usually represented by a horse's head, it is sometimes known as the horse (as it was in the Arabic version).

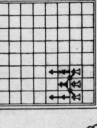

CHESS

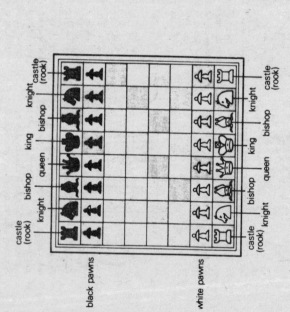

The chessboard ready for play. A white square is always on the player's right. The queen always starts on a square of her own color.

Chess notations. In the algebraic notation each square is referred to by a file letter a–h and a rank number 1–8. In the descriptive notation the files bear the names of the piece on the first rank. The ranks are counted 1–8 away from the player.

BLACK

	a	b	c	d	e	f	g	h	
W8	QR1 QR8	QN1 QN8	QB1 QB8	Q1 Q8	K1 K8	KB1 KB8	KN1 KN8	KR1 KR8	B1
W7	QR2 QR7	QN2 QN7	QB2 QB7	Q2 Q7	K2 K7	KB2 KE7	KN2 KN7	KR2 KR7	B2
W6	QR3 QR6	QN3 QN6	QB3 QB6	Q3 Q6	K3 K6	KB3 KB5	KN3 KN6	KR3 KR6	B3
W5	QR4 QR5	QN4 QN5	QB4 QB5	Q4 Q5	K5 K4	KB4 KB5	KN4 KN5	KR4 KR5	B4
W4	QR5 QR4	QN5 QN4	QB5 QB4	Q5 Q4	K5 K4	KB5 KB4	KN5 KN4	KR5 KR4	B5
W3	QR6 QR3	QN6 QN3	QB6 QB3	Q6 Q3	K6 K3	KB6 KB3	KN6 KN3	KR6 KR3	B6
W2	QR7 QR2	QN7 QN2	QB7 QB2	Q7 Q2	K7 K2	KB7 KB2	KN7 KN2	KR7 KR2	B7
W1	QR8 QR1	QN8 QN1	QB8 QB1	Q8 Q1	K8 K1	KB8 KB1	KN8 KN1	KR8 KR1	B8
	a	b	c	d	e	f	g	h	

WHITE

were elaborated into fine decorative furniture. In Europe specimens were paneled and carved but 16th-century Italian chests (cassoni) might be carved and gilded.

Chester 53 12N 2 54W A city in NW England, the administrative center of Cheshire on the River Dee. It was a Roman fortress (Deva) and a medieval walled city and port (the walls remain intact and there are many half-timbered buildings). The Rows are two-tiered arcades of shops with covered balustrades. Its cathedral dates from the 11th century. Chester is a commercial and railroad center, with clothing and metallurgical industries. Population (1981): 58,436.

chesterfield A kind of settee introduced in 19th-century England. It has a low back curving to form upright armrests and is comfortably upholstered with coil springs.

Chesterfield 53 15N 1 25W A city in N central England, in Derbyshire. Its 14th-century parish church has a famous crooked spire. Chesterfield's industries include engineering, iron founding, chemicals, glass, and pottery. Population (1981): 70,546.

Chesterfield, Philip Dormer Stanhope, 4th Earl of (1694–1773) British statesman, diplomat, and writer. He served as ambassador to The Hague (1728–36), lord lieutenant of Ireland (1745–46), and secretary of state (1746–48). A patron of many authors, he is best remembered for his worldly and sophisticated *Letters to His Son* (1774).

Chesterton, G(ilbert) K(eith) (1874–1936) British essayist, novelist, and poet. His best work was done as literary journalism, although the detective stories featuring a Roman Catholic priest and beginning with *The Innocence of Father Brown* (1911) were also highly successful. He met Hilaire *Belloc in 1900. Their names were often linked as romantic opponents of the socialism of G. B. Shaw and H. G. Wells. Chesterton was converted to Roman Catholicism in 1922, and thereafter most of his work was devoted to religious subjects, for example *St Francis of Assisi* (1923). His published work amounts to more than 100 volumes, among which are the critical studies *Dickens* (1906) and *The Victorian Age in Literature* (1913) and the fictional works *The Napoleon of Notting Hill* (1904), *The Club of Queer Trades* (1905), and *The Man Who Was Thursday* (1908).

chestnut A tree, *Castanea sativa*, also called sweet or Spanish chestnut, bearing large brown edible nuts inside prickly burs. Native to Europe and N Africa and widely introduced, it grows to a height of 98 ft (30 m). The leaves, 4–10 in (10–25 cm) long, are toothed and pointed and the flowers grow in yellow catkins, 4–5 in (10–12 cm) long. The North American chestnut (*C. dentata*)— once one of the largest common trees of E areas—has been largely destroyed by the chestnut blight fungus. Family: *Fagaceae* (beech family). *Compare* horse chestnut.

Chetniks Members of a Yugoslav resistance movement in World War II. They were organized in groups by Gen. Draža *Mihajlović in March 1941, against the German invasion but were chiefly in conflict with the communist Partisans under *Tito. In 1944 the Allies transferred their support from the Chetniks to Tito. After the war the Chetniks were proscribed.

Chevalier, Maurice (1888–1972) French singer and actor. Starting as an entertainer in Parisian revues, he went to Hollywood in the 1930s and starred in many successful musical films. These included *Love Me Tonight* (1932), *Love in the Afternoon* (1957), and *Gigi* (1958).

cheviot A woolen fabric manufactured from the soft, fine, easily spun fleece of Cheviot sheep found in the English-Scottish border country. The cloth is much used as heavy suiting material; *worsted is sometimes added for greater firmness of texture.

Cheviot Hills A range of hills in the UK. They extend along the border between Scotland and England, mainly in Northumberland, reaching 2677 ft (816 m) at The Cheviot.

chevrotain A small hoofed mammal of the family *Tragulidae*. Asiatic chevrotains (genus *Tragulus*; 3–6 species), also called mouse deer, of SE Asia, measure 8–13 in (20–30 cm) at the shoulder and resemble small deer. Their brownish coats have white underparts; some species have white stripes or spots on the body. They are not true deer, lacking antlers and having a three-chambered stomach; males have enlarged upper canine teeth that form tusks. The African water chevrotain (*Hyemoschus aquaticus*) is very similar.

chewing gum A sweetened flavored gum made from *chicle or a synthetic substitute, the milky juice of the sapodilla tree, which is chewed to extract its flavor but not swallowed. It was first patented (1871) in the US.

Cheyenne An Algonquian-speaking North American Indian people of the Great Plains. Originally supporting themselves by agriculture and inhabiting the present state of Minnesota, intertribal wars in the mid-18th century forced abandonment of farming for the nomadic buffalo-hunting culture of the Plains. After a period of wandering, they eventually divided into the Northern Cheyenne and the Southern Cheyenne, who joined the *Arapaho nation in Oklahoma. Both groups shared an elaborate religious ritual, which included the Sun Dance. They were governed by a council of 44 chiefs; an important feature of their social organization was military or warrior societies. With increasing settlement in their territories, they joined other Plains tribes in armed resistance; the Northern Cheyenne joined the *Sioux at the Battle of *Little Big Horn in 1876. The present Northern Cheyenne population, mainly in Montana, is about 2000. The Southern Cheyenne-Arapaho group numbers approximately 3500.

Cheyenne 41 08N 104 50W The capital and largest city of Wyoming. It is an agricultural trading center. Population (1990): 50,008.

Cheyenne River A river that rises in E central Wyoming and flows E into SW South Dakota. Here, at Angostura Dam, it turns NE and meets the Missouri River about Pierre. Length: 527 mi (849 km).

Chiang Kai-shek (*or* Jiang Jie Shi; 1887–1975) Nationalist Chinese soldier and statesman. He took part in the overthrow of the *Qing dynasty in 1911, joined *Sun Yat-sen's *Guomindang (Nationalist People's Party) in 1918, and became commandant of the Whampoa military academy in 1923. After Sun's death (1925), Chiang became leader of the Guomindang and in 1926, in alliance with the communists (*see* United Fronts), launched the Northern Expedition to regain China from the *warlords. The Communist-G coalition ended in 1927 and Chiang, with his capital at Nanjing, fought the communists until Japan invaded China in 1931. Chiang's own army (*see* Xi An incident) forced him to join forces with the communists against their common enemy, Japan (*see* Sino-Japanese Wars), but following Japan's defeat in World War II civil war again broke out in China (1946), ending with Guomindang defeat (1949). Chiang was forced to flee to *Taiwan, where he established the Republic of China. His son **Jiang Jing Guo** (*or* Chiang Ching-kuo; 1910–88), prime minister (1971–78) and president (1978–88) studied in the Soviet Union and married a Russian. On returning to China in 1937, he joined the Guomindang, fleeing with his father to Taiwan in 1949.

Chianti A region of hills in N central Italy, in the Apennines between Florence and Siena. Chianti wine is produced here.

CHIANG KAI-SHEK *At the Cairo Conference (1943) with Roosevelt (center) and Churchill (right). The Allies discussed a joint operation in N Burma.*

chiaroscuro (Italian: light-dark) The overall pattern of light and shade in a picture. Controlled chiaroscuro was an important element of *Renaissance composition, while strong contrasts of light and shade were a main feature of *baroque painting. Chiaroscuro is displayed to supreme effect in the etchings of *Rembrandt and *Whistler.

Chiba 35 38N 140 07E A city and seaport in Japan, in central Honshu on Tokyo Bay. It is the site of an 8th-century Buddhist temple and a university (1949). Industries include steel, paper, and textiles. Population (1991): 829,455.

Chibcha A South American Indian people of the central highlands of Colombia. At the time of the Spanish conquest they were more advanced socially and politically than any people in the area, except the *Inca. Chiefs, treated with great respect, inherited their position matrilineally. Their accession ceremonies, at which the new chief coated his body with gold dust before immersion in a sacred lake, are the probable origin of the *Eldorado legend.

Chicago 41 50N 87 45N A city and major port in Illinois on Lake Michigan. The second largest city in the country, it is the focal point of air, rail, and road routes and the commercial, financial, and industrial center for a large region. Its manufactures include iron and steel, textiles, and chemicals and there are large grain mills and meat-packing plants, although many of the stockyards are now closing as this industry moves further W. The first of its towering skyscrapers was built in 1887 and the Sears Tower (1974) is the world's tallest building, 1454 ft (443 m) high. It has several universities, including the University of Chicago (1892) and Northwestern University (1851); the Chicago Symphony Orchestra enjoys worldwide fame. *History*: founded in 1803 near the site of Fort Dearborn, it became a city in 1837 and expanded rapidly with the construction of the railroads. In 1871 it was almost completely destroyed by a disastrous fire, in which several hundred people were killed. Chicago was subsequently rebuilt in stone and steel. During the Prohibition years (1919–33), Chicago was notorious for its gangster activities, especially those of Al *Capone. Population (1990): 2,783,726.

Chicago River A short river in NE Illinois. It rises at Lake Superior and flows through Chicago where it forks into two branches. The South Branch flows SW as part of the Illinois Waterway and as the Chicago Sanitary and Ship Canal to meet the Des Plaines River. The river serves as boundaries for Chicago's North, West, and South sides. Length: 24 mi (39 km).

Chichén Itzá A Maya city in N Yucatán (Mexico) that was the political and religious center of a wide area under Toltec influence from the late 10th to the 13th centuries. Remains include El Castillo (a pyramidal temple mound), an astronomical observatory, and a cenote (natural well), from which gold, jade, and other sacrificial objects have been recovered.

Chicherin, Georgi Vasilievich (1872–1936) Soviet statesman. Chicherin began his career in the Tsarist ministry of foreign affairs but in 1904, having become a revolutionary, he left Russia and lived in W Europe. In 1918, after the Revolution, he returned to Russia and was entrusted by Lenin with Soviet diplomacy. Chicherin lost his position in 1928, following Stalin's rise to power.

Chichester, Sir Francis (Charles) (1901–72) British yachtsman. He won the first solo transatlantic race (in 40 days) in *Gipsy Moth III* (1960) and in 1966–67, in *Gipsy Moth IV,* was the first to sail around the world singlehandedly: he sailed from Plymouth, England, reaching Sydney, Austrialia, in 107 days, and then back to Plymouth, in 119 days. He was knighted with Sir Francis Drake's sword.

Chickamauga, Battle of (1863) Confederate victory in NW Georgia during the Civil War. The troops of Union Gen. William S. Rosecrans, defending Chattanooga, Tenn. and its valuable railroad facilities, battled the Confederate forces of Gen. Braxton Bragg at Chickamauga for two days. Eventually, Rosecrans's forces were forced to retreat, and the South gained an important victory. Casualties on both sides were high.

chicken. *See* poultry, domestic.

chicken pox A common very infectious viral disease. It is usually contracted in childhood and one attack normally gives an immunity that lasts for life. At the end of the incubation period (about two weeks) the patient develops a fever and an irritating rash. Small raised spots appear on the chest and spread—in the next few days—over the body, face, and limbs. The spots become sore, reddened blisters, which then dry and flake off, usually in less than a week. The patient is infectious until the last blister has flaked off. *See also* shingles.

chick pea An annual plant, *Cicer arietinum,* up to 16 in (40 cm) high, with whitish flowers and edible pealike seeds. It is the chief pulse crop of India, where the cooked seeds are called dhal. Probably native to W Asia, it has long been cultivated in S Europe and is widely introduced, though of little commercial importance, elsewhere. Family: **Leguminosae.*

chickweed A widely distributed annual or overwintering herb, *Stellaria media,* 2–16 in (5–40 cm) high with small star-shaped white flowers. The plant is a common weed and is readily eaten by birds. It was formerly used as a poultice for ulcers and carbuncles. Family: *Caryophyllaceae.*

Chiclayo 6 47S 79 47W A city in N Peru, in the Lambayeque Valley. It is the commercial center for an area producing sugar cane, cotton, and rice. Population (1990 est): 420,000.

chicle A gum formed from the coagulated milky substance obtained from the *sapodilla tree found in Central America. Chicle was formerly used in the manufacture of chewing gum, but it has now been replaced by synthetic substances.

chicory A perennial herb, *Cichorium intybus,* 12–48 in (30–120 cm) high, with bright-blue flowers. The dried ground roots yield chicory, a coffee additive, while the blanched leaves are used in salads. A native of Eurasia and N Africa, it is widely cultivated elsewhere. Family: *Compositae. See also* endive.

Chicoutimi Canadian city in SE Quebec, on the Saguenay River. Part of the Chicoutimi-Jonquière metropolitan area, it was founded (1676) as a trading station and mission. Industries include lumber and wood products, metals, and agricultural products. Population (1991): 62,670.

Chiemsee (*or* Bayrisches Meer) 47 53N 12 25E A lake in S Germany. On one of its islands Louis II of Bavaria built a palace imitating that of Versailles. Area: 33 sq mi (85 sq km).

Chiengmai (*or* Chiang Mai) 18 48N 98 59E A city in NW Thailand, near the Burmese border. The northern commercial and cultural center, it has teak, silver, and silk industries. The university was established in 1964. Population (1989 est): 164,000.

Ch'ien-lung. *See* Qian Long.

chiffchaff A woodland *warbler, *Phylloscopus collybita,* about 4 in (10 cm) long, with a gray-green plumage and whitish underparts. It occurs in Europe and W Asia during the summer and winters in S Europe and Africa. It resembles the willow warbler but can usually be distinguished by its "chiff-chaff" call.

Chifley, Joseph Benedict (1885–1951) Australian statesman; Labor prime minister (1945–49). He introduced welfare reforms and nationalization policies, and encouraged postwar development.

chigger. *See* harvest mite.

chigoe A *flea, *Tunga penetrans,* 0.04 in (1 mm) long, also called jigger or sand flea, that spread to Africa and Asia from South America to become a pest of man. The female burrows beneath the skin, especially on the feet, to form ulcerlike sores that cause intense itching and can become gangrenous. Family: *Pulicidae.*

Chihli, Gulf of (Chinese name: Bohai *or* Po Hai) A large inlet of the Yellow Sea on the coast of NE China.

Chihuahua 28 40N 106 06W A city in N Mexico. Miguel Hidalgo y Costillo, a leader in the Mexican independence movement, was executed here (1811). Its varied industries include smelting, timber, and meat packing and it has a university (1954). Population (1980): 385,603.

Chihuahua A breed of □dog originating from an ancient Mexican breed and developed in the US. Perhaps the world's smallest dog, it has an alert saucy expression. The coat is variable in color and either smooth and glossy or long and soft. Height: about 5 in (13 cm).

Chikamatsu Monzemon (Sugimori Nobumori; 1653–1724) Japanese dramatist. His psychological insight and realistic techniques revolutionized the previously unsophisticated tradition of puppet theater. *The Battles of Coxingo* (1715) and *The Love Suicide at Amijima* (1720) are the best-known examples of his two main types of plays, historical romances and domestic tragedies.

chilblain An itchy red swelling, usually on the fingers or toes, that develops in cold weather. A chilblain may lead to scaling and blistering of the affected part. Prevention, by wearing warm clothing, is the best form of treatment, but drugs that dilate the blood vessels may also be used.

Child, Lydia Maria (Francis) (1802–80) US reformer and writer. Best known for her antislavery stands, she wrote *An Appeal in Favor of That Class of Americans Called Africans* (1833) and was editor of *The National Anti-Slavery Standard* (1841–49). She also advocated women's suffrage. Popular works in-

child abuse 554

clude the novels *Hobomok* (1824), *The Rebels* (1825), and *Philothea* (1836) and the guidebooks *The Frugal Housewife* (1829) and *The Mother's Book* (1831).

child abuse Physical or mental injuries inflicted on babies or young children by adults. It commonly takes the form of facial bruises, cigarette burns, head injuries (often with brain damage), and fractured bones. The parents are often emotionally disturbed or have themselves suffered from childhood abuse. Two-thirds of these children suffer further injury if discharged from the hospital without the support of a social worker and surveillance of a family doctor.

childbirth (*or* labor) The series of events that lead to the birth of a baby. It usually starts spontaneously about 280 days (plus or minus 14 days) after conception but it may be induced by artificial means. The first stage of childbirth may last several hours: it is marked by rupture of the membranes surrounding the fetus and by regular contractions of the womb (uterus). This stage ends when the cervical canal is fully dilated. In the second stage continuing uterine contractions—assisted by conscious pushing by the mother—eases the baby through the cervix and out through the vagina. The *placenta (afterbirth) is delivered in the third stage of labor. The baby is normally born headfirst, although childbirth can occur with the baby in a variety of positions. *See also* Caesarean section; infant mortality.

Children's Crusade (1212) One of the more bizarre episodes of the *Crusades, in which some 50,000 children set out from France and Germany to capture Jerusalem. None reached their destination and few returned home, most being sold into slavery. The enthusiasm aroused by the Children's Crusade encouraged Pope *Innocent III to summon the fifth Crusade.

Chile, Republic of A country in South America, extending in a narrow strip along the W coast of the S half of the continent. There are many islands off the coast, some of which (including *Easter Island) are well out into the Pacific Ocean. Chile also includes half of the island of Tierra del Fuego and has claims to part of Antarctica. The country is dominated by the Andes, which are separated from a lower coastal range by a central valley. The majority of the population is of mixed Spanish and Indian descent. *Economy*: based chiefly on the export of minerals, found principally in the N. Chile is one of the world's largest producers and exporters of copper, while the production of iron ore now exceeds that of nitrates. Coal is also mined in quantity and oil was found in the S in 1945. Production of natural gas is more than enough for domestic needs. The enormous agricultural potential of the country, however, is far from developed, a situation that has been made worse by recent political events. Major land reforms were introduced (1970–73) but much of the land has been returned to its original owners since the fall of the Allende government. The main crops are wheat, sugar beet, potatoes, and maize and there is an expanding wine industry. Fruit and forest production is growing in importance and there are government attempts to promote the dairy industry. *History*: when Magellan, the first European to set eyes on what became Chile, sailed through (1520) the strait named for him, S Chile was occupied by the Araucanian Indians, who continued to control the region until the 19th century. In the N the Atacama Indians had been subjugated in the 15th century by the Incas, who were themselves conquered by the Spaniards in 1532. A Spanish colony was founded at Santiago in 1541 and Chile was attached to the viceroyalty of Peru. It maintained, however, a certain independence and individuality throughout the colonial period, partly because of its inaccessibility. The revolt against Spain began in 1810, when a provisional republic was declared, but victory over the Spaniards was achieved only in 1817 with the military help of the Argentine liberator José de *San Martin. In 1818 the Republic of Chile was established under Bernardo *O'Higgins. Following the ratification of a constitution in 1833 Chile enjoyed political stability and prosperity, becoming the world's leading copper producer. Frontier disputes with Bolivia and Peru culminated in the War of the *Pacific (1879–83), in which Chile, with its superior navy, was victorious, gaining the provinces of Antofagasta from Bolivia and Tarapacà and Arica from Peru. The early 20th century witnessed economic decline, exacerbated by considerable European immigration and resistance from landlords to reform. The enlightened first presidency (1920–25) of Arturo Alessandri Palma (1868–1952) was followed by a military dictatorship and his increasingly right-wing second term (1932–38) led to the election of a socialist Popular Front government. The postwar period saw a return to conservatism and in 1964 Eduardo *Frei, the first Christian Democratic president, was elected. In 1970 Salvador *Allende became the first democratically elected Marxist head of state but was overthrown in 1973 by a military coup led by General *Pinochet. In 1978 Pinochet announced civilian appointments to his cabinet as a step toward the reintroduction of democracy but strong opposition to the regime continued both at home and abroad. The regime's history of repressive measures and human rights violations caused opposition to foment even more fiercely. In a 1988 plebiscite, an overwhelming majority rejected another 8-year term for Pinochet. Free elections took place in December 1989, and in March 1990 Patricio Aylwin, candidate for the Christian Democratic Party, was inaugurated, restoring Chile to civilian rule. In 1992 he proposed constitutional reforms that were opposed by powerful military leaders. Chile is a member of the OAS and LAFTA. Official language: Spanish. Official currency: Chilean peso of 100 centavos. Area: 286,397 sq mi (741,767 sq km). Population (1992 est): 13,500,000. Capital: Santiago. Main port: Valparaiso.

chili A tropical American shrubby plant, *Capsicum frutescens,* also called red pepper, bearing elongated hot-tasting red fruits, 0.8–1.2 in (2–3 cm) long. Sundried for storage, they are used in cooking and are also an essential ingredient of curry powder and tabasco sauce. Family: *Solanaceae.*

Chillán 36 37S 72 10W A city in central Chile, in the Central Valley. It has suffered much damage from earthquakes. Chillán serves an agricultural region producing chiefly grapes, fruit, cereals, and livestock. Population (1992 est): 162,000.

Chiloé Island An island administered by Chile, off the W coast of South America in the Pacific Ocean. The chief export is timber. Area: 3241 sq mi (8394 sq km). Chief town: Ancud.

Chiltern Hills A chalk escarpment in S central England. It extends NE from the Goring Gap in the Thames Valley, reaching 852 ft (255 m) at Coombe Hill. Many of its hills are covered with beech woods.

Chi-lung. *See* Jilong.

chimaera 1. A *cartilaginous fish, also called ghost shark, ratfish, or rabbit fish, belonging to the order *Chimaeriformes* (about 28 species). It has a dark or silvery body, 24–80 in (60–200 cm) long, a slender whiplike tail, a sharp spine in front of the first dorsal fin, and a variously shaped snout. It lives in cold ocean waters, down to 8200 ft (2500 m), and feeds on fish and invertebrates. Subclass: *Holocephali.* □fish. 2. (*or* chimera) An organism that is composed of cells of two genetically different types. Plants with variegated leaves are chimaeras resulting from a mutation in a cell in the growing region (apical meristem). Plant chimaeras can also be produced by *grafting, being known as graft hybrids.

Chimborazo, Mount 1 29S 78 52W An extinct volcano in the Andes, the highest point in Ecuador. Height: 20,681 ft (6267 m).

Chimbote 9 04S 78 34W A port in NW Peru, on the Pacific Ocean. Steel processing and fishmeal production are the chief industries. Population (1990 est): 297,000.

Chimera A legendary Greek fire-breathing monster with a lion's head, a goat's body, and a serpent's tail. After ravaging Lycia she was killed by Bellerophon. The name now applies to any fantastic imaginary creation.

Chimkent 42 16N 69 05E A city in Kazakhstan. It is an important railroad junction and has chemical and textile industries. Population (1987 est): 389,000.

CHIMPANZEE *Probably the most intelligent of nonhuman primates, chimpanzees have great manual dexterity, considerable curiosity, and are capable of simple reasoning.*

chimpanzee An ape, *Pan troglodytes,* of West African forests. Chimpanzees are 40–67 in (100–170 cm) tall when standing erect and live in small groups, mostly on the ground, feeding chiefly on fruit and leaves but occasionally eating meat. They communicate by facial expressions and a repertoire of calls and possess considerable intelligence, often using tools (such as branches). Bonobos are a race of smaller chimpanzees with black faces.

Chimú A South American Indian people who established a large kingdom in Peru during the 14th century AD. Its capital was at *Chan Chan. They were conquered (c. 1470) by the *Incas, whose civilization was based on Chimú achievements in building, road construction, irrigation, and political organization. The Chimú produced elaborate pottery with molded reliefs, fine textiles, and precious metalwork.

Ch'in. *See* Qin.

China, People's Republic of A country in E Asia, covering vast areas of land ranging from the low-lying and densely populated plains of the NE to the high peaks of the Tibetan Plateau in the W, rising well over 16,500 ft (5000 m). In the far NW much of the land is desert or semidesert. China proper falls into three natural regions, formed around the three main rivers: the Yellow River in the N, the Yangtze in the center, and the Xi Jiang in the S. Over 90% of the inhabitants are Han Chinese. *Economy*: mainly dependent upon agriculture, which is constantly threatened by drought and flood. There are, however, schemes to safeguard and increase production by means of irrigation, soil conservation, and fertilization. Agriculture is now socialized through a system of communes, although there are still some very small private holdings. The emphasis is on foodcrops, rice in the S, wheat and millet in the N, as well as livestock, especially pigs. Cotton is grown in the N and tea in the S. The once vast forests have been largely cleared over the centuries but considerable reforestation is now taking place. Coal is extensively mined in all parts of the country and is the major source of power. China has been self-sufficient in oil since 1973 and small amounts of natural gas are also produced. The potential for hydroelectric energy is extensive and there are several projects throughout the country. Iron ore is the most important mineral deposit and China is the main world producer of tungsten ore. Other minerals include antimony, lead, bauxite, and manganese. Traditional small industries continue but there has been considerable development of more modern industries, especially textiles, steel, flour mills, and chemicals. Exports include farm produce, textiles, and minerals. *History*: China is one of the world's oldest civilizations, with a history of organized society going back over nearly four millenniums. The first important recorded dynasty was the Shang in the valley of the Yellow River (18th–12th centuries BC). From the 12th to the 3rd centuries BC the *Zhou spread S and E. Under the *Qin, in the 3rd century BC, a unified empire came into being and the first Great Wall was built. The rule of the *Han dynasty, from the 3rd century BC to the early 3rd century AD, saw spectacular advances in technology and manufacturing but its decline was followed by centuries of struggle between different parts of the empire. With the *Tang dynasty (7th–10th centuries) China was once more reunited and reached the high point of its civilization. It was followed by the *Song (10th–13th centuries), the *Mongol (13th–14th centuries), the *Ming (14th–17th centuries), and the *Qing, which lasted until 1912. From the 16th century Europeans came to China and set up trading posts despite opposition from the Qing. British efforts to open up the country to free trade led to the Opium War in 1839 and to the opening of treaty ports (and also to the cession of Hong Kong). Later other trade concessions were made to several European countries and Chinese opposition to these moves included the Taiping Rebellion (1851–64) and the antiforeign Boxer Rebellion (1899–1900). In 1911 a revolution under the leadership of Sun Yat-sen ousted the Qing and a republic was set up. The 1920s saw the rise of the Guomindang (Nationalist People's Party) under Gen. Chiang Kai-shek and the foundation of the Chinese Communist Party in 1921. In 1926 relations between them broke down and a struggle began that, in effect, continued until after World War II. In the 1930s threats from Japan culminated in open attack and the occupation of parts of the country, which lasted until the end of World War II. This put a temporary halt to internal party struggles, but in 1949 the Guomindang was defeated by the communists and a People's Republic was set up by *Mao Tse-tung.

Chiang Kai-shek retreated to Taiwan, where he set up the Republic of China. During the early years of the communist regime relations with the Soviet Union were close but they later deteriorated, particularly after 1960 when Soviet aid was withdrawn. In 1966 Mao Tse-tung launched the Great Proletarian Cultural Revolution, designed to eradicate "revisionism" and to prevent the rise of a ruling class. From the late 1960s the question of a successor to Mao Tse-tung became an important issue and first *Lin Biao and later *Deng Xiao Ping rose and fell, the latter being dismissed by a "radical" faction of the Politburo, pursuing a policy of constant revolution. Both Mao Tse-tung and the prime minister, Chou En-lai, died in 1976 and were succeeded by the moderate *Hua Guo Feng. Attempts by the "radical" faction (known as the Gang of Four and including Mao's widow Jiang Qing) to gain power were thwarted by the arrest of its members. Deng Xiao Ping was reinstated in 1977; since then he has been a dominant force in government. Hua was succeeded by Zhao Ziyang as prime minister in 1980 and by Hu Yaobang as chairman of the Chinese Communist Party in 1981. In 1982 the post of chairman was abolished and Hu became secretary general. He was forced to resign in 1987 and was replaced by Zhao Ziyang. Student prodemocracy demonstrations increased dramatically in the spring of 1989 and culminated in an army crackdown in Peking's Tienanmen Square. Worldwide outrage at the atrocities committed resulted in the lifting of some restrictions and a change in leadership when Ziyang was succeeded by Jiang Zemin in 1989. Martial law was lifted in 1992. Since 1971 China has had a seat at the UN. Official language: Mandarin Chinese. Official currency: yuan of 10 chiao and 100 fen. Area: 3,704,400 sq mi (9,597,000 sq km). Population (1990 est): 1,130,065,000. Capital: Peking. Main port: Shanghai.

china clay A mineral deposit consisting mainly of kaolin, a hydrous aluminum silicate. Kaolin is produced by weathering or by hydrothermal processes acting on the feldspars in granite. It is used for making high-grade ceramic products and in many industrial processes, including paper making.

chinch bug A *ground bug, *Blissus leukopteris,* that has a black body (up to 0.2 in [5 mm] long), red legs, and white wings. Native to tropical America, it has spread to North America to become a serious pest of cereal crops. The female lays eggs on the roots and stems and the larvae suck the sap.

chinchilla A *rodent belonging to the genus *Chinchilla* (2 species), widely bred for its valuable long soft blue-gray fur. Measuring 12–20 in (30–50 cm) long, wild chinchillas are found high in the Andes, living among rocks and feeding at night on vegetation. They faced extermination before the Chilean government banned hunting and established breeding farms. South American captive chinchillas are mostly short-tailed (*C. brevicaudata*) while in North America the long-tailed species (*C. laniger*) is bred. Family: *Chinchillidae.*

Chinchilla cat A breed of long-haired cat. Chinchillas have a compact body with short legs and a broad head with a snub nose and small tufted ears. The white fur is tipped with black on the back, flanks, head, ears, and tail, giving it a silvery luster. The eyes are emerald or blue-green.

Chinchilla rabbit A breed of domesticated rabbit originating in France in the early 20th century. Although its thick bluish coat does not resemble that of the South American *chinchilla, it has been bred for its pelts.

Chindits The 77th Indian Brigade, organized by Orde *Wingate in 1943 in Burma (now Myanmar) as a "long-range penetration" infantry division. A guerrilla force, the Chindits were so called after the mythological Burmese temple guardian, the *chinthe,* and because they operated beyond the Chindwin River. Initially successful in severing Japanese lines of communication they were later in danger of being encircled and were forced to return to India in small groups.

Chindwin River A river in N Myanmar, flowing S to join the Irrawaddy River near Myingyan. Length: 650 mi (1046 km).

Chinese A language or group of languages of the Sino-Tibetan family spoken widely in E Asia. The many distinct forms or dialects of Chinese, which include Mandarin, Min, Kan, Hakka, Hsiang, Wu, and Cantonese (or Yüeh), are mutually unintelligible. In China there have been attempts recently to standardize the language, using Mandarin as a basis. Chinese is a tonal language, many words, otherwise identical, having quite distinct meanings according to intonation. Words are usually monosyllabic and do not change their form to indicate part of speech. The language is written in logographic characters or symbols of pictorial origin (*see* ideographic writing systems), which enables them to be understood by speakers of any Chinese dialect. There are as many as 40,000 of these of which 10,000 are in common use. Literacy requires knowledge of about 2000 of them. For transliteration purposes, Pinyin (phonetic spelling) is superseding the older Wade-Giles system, which does not attempt as close a phonetic description of the language. Pinyin is used in this book.

Chinese art Early Chinese art (c. 1550–480 BC) consisted of magical, symbolic, and ritualistic objects of jade and bronze. These combine a few symbols to produce evocative nonrepresentational forms. During the Han dynasty (206 BC–220 AD) these forms were succeeded by sculptural art and painting, both influenced by the rise of Buddhism. Funerary ceramic art flourished and produced animal and human forms and copies of everyday artifacts. The Tang dynasty (618–906 AD) continued to make funerary objects, particulary realistic horsemen, warriors, and tomb guardians, but sculptures of Buddhist figures are dominant. The realistic outlook of the period was also reflected in landscape and figure painting.

The ensuing Song dynasty (960–1279 AD) was a golden age, when dreamlike landscape, animal, and bird painting flourished alongside *calligraphy, one of the most ancient and important Chinese arts. Monochrome ceramics of very refined form were made as objects of contemplation. This period saw the end of real creativity, the following Yuan dynasty being one of Mongol-inspired taste with a few exceptions, notably the four masters of the Yuan Dynasty. During the following Ming and Qing periods (14th–20th centuries) ceramic art excelled, the most famous example being the blue and white porcelain. At first it was restorative and of native origin and later innovatory, responding to European influence.

Chinese Exclusion Act (1882) US law limiting immigration of Chinese into the country, the first US law to limit immigration. Large-scale Chinese immigration aroused opposition to them, particularly in the West, and the law banned the immigration of Chinese workers for 10 years. It was subsequently renewed, and eventually immigration quotas were set, a practice that continued into the 1960s.

Chinese lantern plant A hardy ornamental, *Physalis alkekengi,* also called bladder cherry or winter cherry. A native of S and central Europe, it grows to a height of 8–24 in (20–60 cm). The edible fruit is enclosed in a reddish inflated calyx resembling a lantern. Family: **Solanaceae.*

Chinese literature The oldest written records in Chinese date from about 1400 BC. The earliest major literary productions, however, were written mainly between about 200 BC and 200 AD. These were the Confucian classics, nine texts for instruction and discussion by *Confucius and his disciples. They are devoted to poetry, philosophy, history, ceremonies, and codes of protocol and have had a profound effect on Chinese thought and literary style to the present. The earliest is probably the manual of divination, the *I Ching*. The *Shu Jing* (or *Shu Ching*; *Book of Documents*) covers political aspects of Confucian thought: the *Shih Jing* (or *Shih Ching*; *Book of Songs*) contains lyrics some of which are perhaps as early as the 10th century BC. Of the remaining classics, the best known are two books belonging to the historical work *Zuo Zhuan* (or *Tso Chuan*): the *Analects*, a collection of Confucius's sayings and discussions with his disciples, and *The Book of Mencius*. The work of China's first known poet, *Chu Yuan, is a long poem occupying the most prominent place in the *Chuchi* (or *Ch'u Tz'u*), an anthology that, together with the *Book of Songs*, had an enduring effect on verse forms. During the Qin and Han dynasties (221 BC–220 AD), the development of poetry was fostered by the creation in 133 BC of the Yuefu (Music Bureau) for the collection of folksongs. Under Buddhist influences poetry became increasingly individualistic and enjoyed a golden age during the Tang dynasty (618–906 AD). *Li Bo, *Du Fu, and the Buddhist Wang Wei (699–759) were the leading poets, while Han Yu (768–824) pioneered new genres of prose. Musical drama was the major literary genre during the Yuan (Mongol) dynasty (1279–1368), and the novel, originating in printed versions of the tales of professional storytellers, flourished during the Ming dynasty (1368–1644). The two major novels of this period are the *Romance of the Three Kingdoms* and *The Water Margin*, both attributed to Luo Guan-zhong (*or* Luo Kuan-chung; 14th century). These works, dealing with heroic adventures, are skillfully shaped from episodic material and contrast with *The Dream of the Red Chamber* by *Cao Chan (*or* Zao Zhan), which is more realistic and partly autobiographical. The Qing (Manchu) dynasty (1644–1911) was unremarkable for literary work, but western influences were introduced through translations during the 19th century, and in the 20th century there arose a number of writers indebted to western ideas, for example to Romanticism and Symbolism. After the establishment of the republic in 1911, the outstanding poet was Hu Shi (1891–1962) and the leading writer was the satirist Lu Xun. Since the late 1930s literature has been generally subservient to political orthodoxy; although recent official patronage of the arts has encouraged a large number of new writers, no single reputation has become well established outside China.

Chinese water deer A very small *deer, *Hydropotes inermis*, most common along the banks of the Yangtze River in China. Only 20 in (50 cm) high at the shoulder, with a pale-brown coat and short tail, it has no antlers; the male's upper canine teeth are elongated into tusks.

Ch'ing. *See* Qing.

Ch'ing-hai. *See* Qinghai.

Ching-te-chen. *See* Fuliang.

Chinkiang. *See* Jinjiang.

chinoiserie Decorative art and architecture that incorporated Chinese motifs into European fantasy designs and was popular in the late 17th and 18th centuries. The fashion was inspired by importation into Europe of Chinese porcelain, lacquer, etc., in the 17th century. French *rococo artists and architects enthusiastically adopted the style for interiors, furniture, silver, wallpaper, textiles, etc., as did *Meissen designers. Instances of chinoiserie in England include the *willow pattern, combining Chinese elements into a new design.

Chinook A North American Indian people of the NW Pacific coast of the US. The Chinook language is a subdivision of the *Penutian language family. The Chinook supported themselves by salmon fishing and trade, their location along the lower Columbia River being ideally suited for exchanging goods with peoples to the N and S and in the interior. Chinook Jargon, a combination of Chinook, *Nootka, and other Indian languages mixed with English and French words, became the trading language of the entire Pacific coast. The Chinook practiced the *potlatch, and their religion emphasized the quest for a personal guiding spirit by undergoing ordeals of various kinds. They were also known as the Flatheads for their cosmetic custom of intentionally deforming the shape of their children's heads during infancy. The present Chinook population is about 400.

CHINOISERIE *A bedstead in the Chinese style, probably made (c. 1750–55) by Thomas Chippendale.*

chipmunk A *ground squirrel belonging to the genus *Tamias* (18 species), of North America and Asian forests. Chipmunks are 6–12 in (15–30 cm) long and have a black and white striped back and strong feet and claws for digging. They live in burrows and, in the winter, do not hibernate but feed on a store of nuts and dried fruit carried under ground in their large cheek pouches.

Chippendale, Thomas (1718–79) British cabinetmaker, famous for his elegant furniture designs, especially his chairs. His illustrated collection of rococo furniture designs, *The Gentleman and Cabinet Maker's Director* (1754), was the first comprehensive furniture catalogue and was widely influential in England and America, although his later neoclassical styles are considered the finest.

Chippewa

562

Chippewa. *See* Ojibwa.

Chirac, Jacques (1932–   ) French statesman; prime minister (1974–76; 1986–88) under the presidencies of Giscard d'Estaing and François Mitterrand. Differences with Giscard led to Chirac's resignation, after which he reorganized the Gaullist Union des Démocrates pour la République into the Rassemblement pour la République. He became mayor of Paris in 1977. President Mitterrand appointed him prime minister in 1986, but he was replaced in 1988 after an unsuccessful bid for the presidency against Mitterrand.

Chirico, Giorgio de (1888–1978) Italian painter and forerunner of *surrealism, born in Greece. He trained in Munich and was influenced by Nietzsche's philosophy. In Paris (1911–15) he worked on scenes of eerie and deserted Italian squares. At Ferrara (1917) he established with Carlo Carrà (1881–1966) the school of *metaphysical painting, but reverted to a traditional style after 1919.

Chiron In Greek legend, a *centaur, son of Cronos and the sea nymph Philyra. Unlike his fellow centaurs, he was revered for his wisdom and knowledge of medicine. After being accidentally wounded by Heracles he bequeathed his immortality to Prometheus and was transformed into the constellation *Sagittarius.

chiropody The paramedical specialty that deals with the care of feet and the treatment of minor ailments of the feet, such as corns, calluses, and ingrowing toenails.

chiropractic A medical specialty based on the assumption that most diseases originate from disorders of the nervous system, particularly as a result of compression of the nerve roots as they emerge from the spine. A chiropractor attempts to relieve symptoms by manipulating the spine with his hands.

Chiroptera. *See* bat.

chiru An antelope, *Pantholops hodgsoni,* of Tibetan plateaus. About 31 in (80 cm) high at the shoulder, chirus have a dense woolly pinkish-brown coat with white underparts; males have slender black horns up to 28 in (70 cm) long. They live singly or in small groups and excavate shallow depressions for shelter.

Chisholm v. Georgia (1793) A Supreme Court decision that affirmed the right of citizens of one state to sue the government of another state. Alexander Chisholm's heirs, residents of South Carolina, sued the state of Georgia for return of Chisholm's property there, which was confiscated during the American Revolution. The implications of this ruling prompted the passage of the Eleventh Amendment (1798) prohibiting such suits.

Chita 52 03N 113 35E A city in the SE Russian Federation. Founded by the *Cossacks (1653), it is a prosperous city with machine-building, textiles, and food-processing industries. Population (1991 est): 377,000.

chital. *See* axis deer.

chitarrone (Italian: big guitar) A large fretted instrument of the lute family, able to accommodate bass strings of over 5 ft (1.5 m) in length. It was popular for accompanying singing in the early 17th century.

chitin A complex carbohydrate that, in association with proteins, is the principal component of the outer cuticle of insects and other arthropods. Chitin occurs in several other animal groups and is a constituent of the cell walls of fungi.

chiton A primitive *mollusk of the class *Amphineura* (about 600 species), also called sea cradle. Elliptical and measuring up to 12 × 6 in (30 × 15 cm), chitons live on rocky shores, clinging tightly and grazing on encrusted algae. They have eight shell plates with a fleshy girdle and curl up when detached.

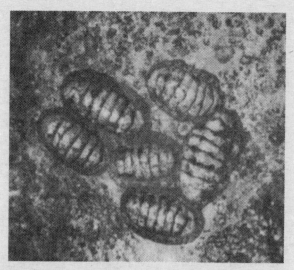

CHITON *Resembling woodlice, these primitive mollusks have a broad muscular foot which enables them to creep over rocky surfaces.*

Chittagong 22 20N 91 48E A city and major port in Bangladesh, on the Indian Ocean. The focal point of road, rail, and air routes, it is the second most important industrial center in the country. Its university was established in 1966. Population (1991): 1,364,000.

chivalry The ideology and code of conduct of the knightly class of medieval Europe. Chivalric behavior depended on the concepts of honor and courtesy and received a notable impetus during the 12th century from the *Crusades and the development of the ideals of *courtly love in such literature as the Arthurian romances. All ties between the chivalric code and military conduct ended with the decline of cavalry and the invention of gunpowder, although elaborate jousts and tournaments kept its memory alive until the 16th century.

chive A small hardy perennial plant, *Allium schoenoprasum,* native to Europe. It has small white elongated bulbs and produces clumps of thin tubular leaves and dense attractive spherical heads of bluish or lilac flowers on long stalks. The leaves are used for seasoning and garnishing foods. Family: *Liliaceae.*

chloral (*or* trichlorethanal; CCl_3CHO) A colorless oily liquid made by treating acetaldehyde with chlorine. It is used in the manufacture of DDT.

chloramphenicol An *antibiotic usually reserved for severe bacterial infections. It is particulary useful in the treatment of typhoid fever and some forms of pneumonia and meningitis. In rare cases chloramphenicol causes serious blood disorders.

chlordiazepoxide. *See* benzodiazepines.

Chlorella A genus of unicellular *green algae found in fresh water or damp soil, some forming symbiotic relationships with fungi to give *lichens. Because they are rich in proteins, carbohydrates, and fats and reproduce rapidly by cell division, their use as a food source for man is now under study.

chlorine (Cl) A greenish poisonous *halogen gas, discovered in 1774 by C. W. Scheele. It is found in nature only in compounds, especially common salt (NaCl), sylvite (KCl), and carnallite ($KMgCl_3.6H_2O$). Chlorine is liberated by the electrolysis of brine. It irritates the respiratory system and was used as a poisonous gas in World War I. Chlorine gas is reactive and combines directly with most elements. Its oxidizing properties make it a useful disinfectant for drinking-water supplies and swimming pools. It is used in the manufacture of *bromine, in bleach (NaOCl), hydrochloric acid (HCl), and carbon tetrachloride (CCl_4). Chlorinated organic chemicals are used in dyes, antiseptics, and insecticides. At no 17; at wt 35.453; mp $-149.8°F$ ($-100.98°C$); bp $-30.3°F$ ($-34.6°C$).

chloroform (*or* trichloromethane; $CHCl_3$) A colorless volatile liquid. It is made by reacting *bleaching powder with acetone, acetaldehyde, or ethanol. Its main use is now in the manufacture of *fluorocarbons but it is also used as a solvent and as an anesthetic.

chlorophyll A green pigment present in organisms capable of *photosynthesis. Higher plants possess chlorophylls *a* and *b*, located in *chloroplasts; chlorophyll *c* is found in some primitive marine plants, and bacteriochlorophyll occurs in photosynthetic bacteria. The chlorophylls absorb red and blue light, trapping light energy for photosynthesis.

chloroplast A structure within a plant cell in which the process of *photosynthesis takes place. It is bounded by a membrane and contains the green pigment *chlorophyll. Chloroplasts vary greatly in shape and number within a cell. The greatest concentration occurs in the palisade mesophyll tissue of the leaves, the main photosynthesizing region.

chloroquine A drug used to prevent and treat malaria. It acts by preventing the digestion of hemoglobin (the red pigment of blood) by the malaria parasite. Chloroquine is also used in the treatment of rheumatoid arthritis and related diseases.

chlorpromazine. *See* phenothiazines.

chocolate. *See* cocoa and chocolate.

Choctaw A North American Indian people formerly inhabiting territories in Mississippi and Alabama. The Choctaw language was a subdivision of the Muskoegan language family. They supported themselves by agriculture, raising corn and beans. The Choctaw practiced an elaborate green corn ceremony to ensure the abundance of their crops. They wore their hair long and practiced head flattening through intentional deformation during infancy. After supporting the French against the English in the 18th century, they were forced to move west in the 1830s, settling in Oklahoma. The present Choctaw population there is approximately 40,000.

Chodowiecki, Daniel Nikolaus (1726–1801) German painter and engraver, who specialized in scenes of middle-class life. A noted book illustrator, he engraved editions of Cervantes' *Don Quixote* and Goldsmith's *Vicar of Wakefield*. His best-known painting is *The Parting of Jean Calas from his Family* (1767; Berlin-Dahlem Museum).

choir 1. A group of trained singers. In the Christian Church the use of a choir was derived from Judaism and traditionally consisted of men and boys only. The choir leads the singing of the congregation as well as singing anthems. The most usual division of parts in a choir is into four: soprano, alto, tenor, and bass (SATB). In secular music the choir is often called a chorus. **2.** The part of the chancel of a church where the choir sits.